EIGHTH EDITION

Experimental Psychology

A Case Approach

M. Kimberly MacLin

University of Northern Iowa

Robert L. Solso

Late, University of Nevada, Reno

PEARSON

Boston   New York   San Francisco
Mexico City   Montreal   Toronto   London   Madrid   Munich   Paris
Hong Kong   Singapore   Tokyo   Cape Town   Sydney

For Bob,
Explorer of the mind and the world
1933–2005

Sponsoring Editor: *Michelle Limoges*
Executive Marketing Manager, Psychology: *Karen Natale*
Production Editor: *Pat Torelli*
Editorial Production Service: *Pine Tree Composition*
Composition Buyer: *Linda Cox*
Manufacturing Buyer: *JoAnne Sweeney*
Electronic Composition: *Pine Tree Composition*
Cover Administrator: *Linda Knowles*

For related titles and support materials, visit our online catalog at www.ablongman.com.

Copyright © 2008, 2002, 1998, 1994 Pearson Education, Inc.

Between the time website information is gathered and then published, it is not unusual for some sites to have closed. Also, the transcription of URLs can result in typographical errors. The publisher would appreciate notification where these errors occur so that they may be corrected in subsequent editions.

Library of Congress Cataloging-in-Publication Data

MacLin, M. Kimberly.
 Experimental psychology : a case approach / M. Kimberly MacLin, Robert L. Solso.—
8th ed.
  p. cm.
 Includes bibliographical references and indexes.
 ISBN-13: 978-0-205-41028-6
 ISBN-10: 0-205-41028-6
 1. Psychology, Experimental. 2. Experimental design. 3. Psychology—Case studies.
I. Solso, Robert L., II. Title.
 BF181.S68 2007
 150.72'4—dc22

                                                              2007016204

Printed in the United States of America

10 9 8 7 6 5 4 3 2 1   11 10 09 08 07

CONTENTS

TO THE INSTRUCTOR

I am so pleased to present this eighth edition of *Experimental Psychology: A Case Approach*. Experimental psychologists have covered a lot of territory during the past century, when psychology became a formal discipline, and the many changes have necessitated changes in books and professional articles. This edition of *Experimental Psychology* reflects the diversity of research areas in psychology and clearly demonstrates how experiments are conducted.

Originally, we wrote this book to identify the basic principles of experimental design as practiced by experimental psychologists. Too often, the teaching of experimental psychology involves lengthy discussions of theoretical statistics, or concentration on a highly specialized area of research. Therefore, after several years of experimenting with how best to present the material for a first course in experimental psychology, we developed a method by which students study actual case examples in psychology and then generalize the ideas from those examples to the principles of experimental design. The approach is "bottom-up," in the vernacular of cognitive psychology, in that we emphasize actual experiments from which principles are derived. Although this approach builds from the basic to the more abstract, it is our intention to give both aspects of experimental psychology due attention. Both examples *and* principles are important in the study of experimental psychology. It is our purpose to teach both.

The pedagogical method in this book uses actual experiments to help the student learn how design principles are applied in research. In this edition of *Experimental Psychology* the student will read, critique, or analyze approximately 75 cases and experiments that exemplify various design principles and problems. In addition to understanding design, the student will become comfortable with the research literature and learn much of the content material of psychology.

Teaching by example has been a traditional means of instruction and is still widely practiced, whether the subject is high-energy physics, carpentry, accounting, computer programming, psychotherapy, creative writing, or cellular biology. But in courses involving experimental design in the psychological sciences, the common practice is to plod through a series of philosophical and theoretical issues that, while important to any scholar's education, are often difficult to relate to the real world of research (especially when you're first learning about it). We believe that teaching by example is essential to the development of critical thought and the practice of research, particularly for students new to psychology, or those on the brink of conducting their own research.

We wrote the book from a tutorial standpoint, as if we were private tutors instructing a student as he or she was reading the material. First, we present a principle or a problem in experimental design. Then we show how the principle or problem has been dealt with in the psychological literature. We provide annotated reviews of actual articles, much as a master teacher might do if he or she sat down with a student and critically read an article with him or her. Based on the comments we have received from students and instructors, this technique is remarkably successful.

Part One of this edition lays out the basic principles of experimental design. The content has been expanded to include current case studies, and reorganized better to mirror the order in which many instructors are already using the text. Although experimental psychology is largely considered a laboratory science, we have expanded discussion of research methods that fall outside the bounds of traditional experimental psychology. As researchers we are called upon to make decisions and justify them every step of the way through the research process. Being able to decide on the best methodology given a particular research question is a skill that students can start to develop as well. Thus, an expanded section on other research methods is included. Comprehensive chapters on the research process have been expanded and updated to include the latest information on electronic databases, planning and doing research (including updated information on institutional review boards), funding research, writing abstracts, preparing posters and attending conferences, writing a professional paper, and publishing manuscripts.

Part Two of the book contains 15 reprinted articles. The scope of the articles in Part Two was carefully selected to sample the major areas of psychology, including industrial psychology, cognitive psychology, social psychology, animal and ethological studies, practical problems, cross-cultural studies, psychotherapy, single-subject designs, educational psychology, behavioral modification, and child psychology, among others. We selected these articles to illustrate the design issues presented in Part One. We have also identified some *special issues* of experimental design that are embodied in some of the articles. These issues include control problems, field-based experiments, subject selection, small *n* experiments, research with animals, clinical research, and social behavior in the laboratory, among others. We have found that by using this format students learn a great deal about the different fields of psychology in addition to learning about the vast diversity of experimental design. Some professors have told us that Part Two of the book is the reason why they select the book for class use, either as the primary text or as a supplementary one. (Curiously, about the same number have told us that they select the book for the contents of the first section!)

Appendixes A and B cover basic statistics, and allow the book to be used in a much wider range of courses in which basic statistics are necessary. The appendixes also allow instructors to demonstrate the computational procedures for a large number of the statistical tests demonstrated in this book. An Instructor's Manual and Test Bank is available that contains test questions, class demonstrations, discussion questions, and lecture strategies.

It is also though with great sadness that I bring this eighth edition to you. My dear friend, mentor, colleague, and co-author Bob Solso passed away in January 2005. Thus, this was the first time we have not undertaken the task of revision together. Bob is and always will be "present" in this book via his tutorial approach and his artful prose.

I would like to acknowledge the assistance of those colleagues and students who have offered critical feedback on the structure and content of this book. I thank the following reviewers of the Seventh Edition: Jeremy Bailenson, University of California, Santa Barbara; Ron Fagan, Pepperdine University, and Barton Poulson, Brigham Young University. Their detailed feedback was very useful in updating this book. Their recommended improvements, as well as our class testing, have strengthened the text considerably. The reviewers to the eighth edition were enormously helpful and I thank them for their time and effort: Bruce Diamond, William Patterson University; Erik Nilsen, Lewis & Clark College; and Lynn Winters, Purchase College, SUNY. Thanks are also due to my students in my research methods course who tirelessly (and with good humor) pointed out inconsistencies, alerted me to sections that could be made more clear and overall were a sounding board for the changes to this edition. Their most vocal request? "We want a glossary!" So with the help of graduate student Abbie Close, a glossary is included in this edition. I'm also grateful to graduate students Amanda Collins, Colin Phelan, and Brad Okdie for their work on market comparisons, updating examples, and overall edits. I also thank the College of Social and Behavioral Sciences and the Department of Psychology at the University of Northern Iowa for providing funding and time for me to complete this revision. Lastly, thanks are due Otto MacLin and Gage MacLin for their patience, understanding, and support during this revision process. Finally, please let me know (really! My email address is below) what you like and what you don't about this book. Comments from instructors and students are enormously helpful in keeping this book up to date and useful to you.

M. Kimberly MacLin
kim.maclin@uni.edu

TO THE STUDENT

Why are we here?! What are you doing in this class? With this book? In this class, using this book, you will learn about *how* we know *what* we know about psychological science. You will learn how to *do* research, as well as hone your reading, thinking, and writing skills. Fundamentally, you will learn about how to find out the answers to the questions you have (or will develop) about human thought and behavior.

This book examines the methods of experimental psychology. A great deal of the book is devoted to controlled psychological experiments and the collection of reliable data based on observations. We use a "case approach," meaning that we illustrate each of the principles of experimental design with an example, or case, drawn from the professional literature in psychology. Study these cases carefully, as they represent excellent examples of skillfully conducted experiments from every major area in psychology—including animal studies, child psychology, social psychology, cognitive psychology, and applied psychology, among others. We also emphasize ethics in experimental research and give some guidelines on how best to develop research ideas, write research papers, and present your research at professional conferences.

You can email me (or find me on Facebook) if you have questions or suggestions about this book. Good luck and let me know how it goes.

Kim MacLin
kim.maclin@uni.edu

PART ONE

Basic Principles in Experimental Psychology

This book is divided into two distinct sections. Part One focuses on the basic principles of experimental psychology, while Part Two analyzes actual experiments drawn from the psychological literature.

The book begins with an introduction to scientific inquiry and methodology in psychology. Each major point is illustrated with an example from the experimental literature. Part One covers the fundamentals of research design as they apply to experimental psychology as well as the ethics of conducting research. A large portion of this material is devoted to the issue of experimental control, which is the means by which experimenters ensure the integrity of a psychological experiment.

Chapter 7 is called "Design Critiques" and offers brief descriptions of experiments that contain at least one conceptual or technical flaw. As you read these critiques, try to discover the error. Practice with these problems can strengthen your own ability to design experiments devoid of error.

Part One also provides you with information on ethical issues, developing research ideas, and the steps in the research process.

Part Two presents actual experiments from the psychological literature. Each experimental case illustrates one or more specific design/experimental issues and, in some cases, is accompanied by detailed analysis. (Several cases are without comment and await your remarks.) You can read these cases as you study the material in Part One to help exemplify the textual material. Upon completion of Part One and Part Two you should be equipped to read, understand, analyze, plan, and carry out research in experimental psychology.

1 An Introduction to Scientific Inquiry

A [person] may be attracted to science for all sorts of reasons. Among them are the desire to be useful, the excitement of exploring new territory, the hope of finding order, and the drive to test established knowledge.

—Thomas S. Kuhn

Is psychology a science? Are *psychology* and *science* incongruent terms? It seems that psychology has lived in the shadow of "real" science for so long that many still believe it is in a prescientific period—a kind of alchemic stage in which everything from the volatile nature of human behavior to the inner workings of the brain and mind is investigated; but could it really be called *science?* Sure! Because science is characterized by its method, not by its subject matter. Science is something you do. Similar to chemistry and biology, psychology has a laboratory tradition, with equipment, experimental techniques, and statistical analyses of data, upon which reliable conclusions are based. The topics of psychology vary greatly, but systematic and experimental inquiry is what separates psychology from philosophy, lay opinion, and arm chair theorizing.

Presently, the experimental investigation of thought and behavior by psychologists follows the basic principles of scientific inquiry prescribed in other fields of science. While the things psychologists study (thought and behavior) distinguish psychology from other scientific fields, the method of inquiry is similar.

The Topics of Experimental Psychology

Experimental psychologists study a wide range of phenomena, such as the physiological components of emotion, eating behaviors of people in fast-food restaurants, poetry learning, the interpersonal relations between people of different status, the predatory behavior of the barn owl, the eye movements of newborn children, personality traits, the etiology of schizophrenia, brain patterns of people solving logic problems, and the attractiveness of average faces. These topics, and many more, are legitimate issues a psychologist could examine using the experimental method.

The lay person frequently ponders these and other topics using speculation, subjective arguments, and personal experiences. These nonscientific interpretations, although sometimes interesting, are frequently unreliable and may lead to invalid conclusions. (Though our own personal experiences often lead us into particular research areas and to particular research questions.) So for example, you've been sort of curious about the best way to approach someone that you are interested in. Can this passing thought be studied experimentally? In fact, it can. Opening conversations have been the focus of research conducted by Kleinke, Meeker, and Staneski (1986), and Cunningham (1988). In one survey Kleinke et al. had research participants rate opening lines such as, "Isn't it cold? Let's make some body heat"; "Are you a student?"; and "I'm sort of shy, but I'd like to get to know you." These lines were conceptualized to represent three different types of social advances: cute-flippant, innocuous, and direct. Overall, respondents agreed that cute-flippant opening lines were the least desirable.

With these normative data, Cunningham (1988) field-tested the opening lines by having researchers approach members of the opposite sex and begin a conversation in a singles bar with different types of social advances. In general, women reacted negatively to the cute-flippant lines and were positive to direct or innocuous opening lines. The reaction of men was ambiguous. Perhaps female-initiated conversation, no matter how innocuous or cute, is perceived by men as positive. The research illustrates that even pick-up lines can be analyzed experimentally.

So yes, it is possible to examine a wide variety of human thought and behavior scientifically, by which we mean that they may be subjected to analysis that follows a prescribed method of investigation in which the conclusions are *reliable* and *valid*. These terms, **reliability** and **validity,** have specialized meaning in psychological science. Reliability refers to the consistency of an experiment, test measurement, or observation. Thus, an experimenter may observe a certain action under specified conditions but, in order for the observation to be reliable, the same or other experimenters must be able to replicate the observation. Validity, on the other hand, is related to the factual accuracy of an observation test, or measurement. If, for example, you develop a test of intelligence and purport such a test will predict success in school, then the degree to which the test accurately predicts such results is called its validity. Validity refers to many types of observations and conclusions in psychological science in addition to tests. The conclusions a scientist makes about his or her observations are based both on the reliability and validity of an experiment; they are both integral to the conduct of good science.

In order to arrive at scientific truth, experimentation and rational analysis—tools of investigation that are less susceptible to subjective interpretation or idiosyncratic bias—are designed to yield reliable and valid conclusions about a wide range of behavior and thoughts. Indeed, the more seemingly bizarre the subject matter, the more rigorous psychologists must be in their application of experimental techniques.

Solso had long been interested in the arts, and as a cognitive psychologist, had interest in the brain and its workings. He was able to use his knowledge and skills as a scientist to scientifically study a topic that interested him: art and artists.

CASE STUDY

Solso (2001) was interested in what brain processes were different among expert artists and nonartists. Using functional Magnetic Resonance Imaging (fMRI), Solso did brain scans of an artist and a nonartist while they sketched geometric forms and photographs of faces. The scans showed that there was in increase in blood flow to the areas of the brain responsible for face processing for both the artist and nonartist. But, while blood flow was elevated for both, the artist did not have as high a level of activation as did the nonartist, indicating that the artist may process face information more efficiently. Additionally, this part of the brain (the right-posterior parietal region) was only activated when the subjects were drawing the faces, not when they were drawing the geometric forms. Furthermore, the artist showed greater activity in the right frontal area of the brain which Solso inferred to mean that the "artist *thinks* portraits more than *sees* them" (Solso, 2001, p. 34).

Science

If students are asked, "What is science?" many answer by giving examples of science: physics, chemistry, biology, and so on. This definition suggests that science is a generic term describing specific subject areas. For example, college students are required to take a number of "science courses," and these courses usually are drawn from physics, chemistry, astronomy, botany, biology, and the like. While some casual support for this definition can be found, it is less than specific and does not appear to be adequate. If you ask why chemistry is a science but history is not, or why physics is a science but music is not, the definition of science becomes more complex and usually confusing. People usually argue that science deals with facts (yet, so does history), or that science deals with theories (so does music), or that it involves laboratory experiments (but what about astronomy or the classification of plants in botany, both of which are usually characterized as sciences and yet frequently do not engage in laboratory experiments?).

The difficulty in finding an adequate definition of science is also shared by scientists and philosophers. Many scientists specify the collection of facts, the use of experimentation as a method of "proof," the use of theories as tentative explanations, and so on as prerequisites for a field to be labeled a science. But other definitions emphasize the ongoing or dynamic nature of science—the search for new "facts" and theories to replace the old, much as some of Einstein's theories replaced those of Newton. James Conant (1951) expressed this quality of science when he defined science as "an interconnected series of concepts and conceptual schemes that have developed as a result of experimentation and observation and are fruitful of further experimentation and observation." We can see this dynamic process when a scientist, through observation and experimentation, attempts to ascertain what is related to what, or what cause is related to what effect. These new facts are put into conceptual schemes. These schemes (usually called theories or models) are tentative; they try to explain the relationship among the information we have on hand. As new information becomes available, that information, and then new conceptual schemes, will arise to replace the old ones.

Modern scientists—be they physicists, geologists, astronomers, anthropologists, or psychologists—approach their specialized fields with a few basic assumptions about the structure of the universe. Common to scientific thought is the assumption that nature is structured by laws that govern its operation. For example, a simple but fundamental law of physics is that objects, such as a lead ball, fall toward the earth if dropped from a high structure, such as the Leaning Tower of Pisa. Furthermore, this observation can be repeated with essentially identical results. Natural laws are reliable and reflect order in the universe.

It is in building upon these assumptions through experimentation and observation that we reach the core of science. For example, we know that the speed at which an object falls can change. An object such as a lead ball falls slowly at first and then accelerates. Through observation, scientists can discover the general "lawful" properties of acceleration, which can lead to general principles or models that incorporate more and more features of the universe in ever-expanding theories. It is this kind of process that demonstrates a clear distinction between nonscientific and scientific thought and between disciplines that can be considered science and those that cannot. Thus, science is something you *do,* not simply a topic.

CASE STUDY

The Greek philosopher Aristotle, writing on the acceleration of falling objects, stated that, based on "logic," heavier bodies should fall at a faster rate than lighter bodies. A boulder would fall to the earth from atop a building faster than a rock because the boulder is heavier. Many people still believe that a large cannonball falls faster than a small lead ball—all other factors that might affect the fall being held constant. The "commonsense logic" seems valid, but science is suspicious of commonsense logic. The scientist Galileo questioned the validity of this logical conclusion and, as all schoolchildren know, decided to observe the relative speed of falling objects. His "laboratory" was the conveniently tilted Leaning Tower of Pisa. (Although any high building would have done just as well, the tower does make a more interesting story and has undoubtedly drawn hordes of tourists to northern Italy over the centuries.)

In retrospect, we can see that the experimental procedure used by Galileo consisted of four stages, which are remarkably consistent with modern scientific inquiry. They are as follows:

1. *Statement of a hypothesis.* Objects of different weight will fall to the earth at the same speed.
2. *Observation.* Measure the relative rates of descent of objects of different weight.
3. *Replicability.* Multiple observations with objects of different weights can be made.
4. *Development of a law (or model).* If the observations confirm a relationship between the weights of objects and the speed with which they fall, a generalized conclusion may be drawn.

Of course, this early experiment had problems, which we call *control problems.* We will discuss these in some detail later, but for now consider a sample of these problems. First, Galileo had to make sure that both objects were dropped at the same time. For example, if he chose to drop them by hand, the tendency might be to drop the larger, heavier object first. Or, if he wanted to support his hypothesis, he may have unconsciously dropped the lighter object first to give it a brief head start. (Even psychological factors enter into scientific observations in physics!) To control for these problems, Galileo may have constructed a box with a trap door to allow both objects to be released at the same time.

Then there was the matter of judging the speed of descent, as measured by which object hit the ground first. Some objective criteria needed to be established so an observer, or observers, could reliably judge the arrival of the objects.

There is another important variable that might affect the rate of descent, and that is the influence of atmospheric conditions, such as air resistance, on the fall of the objects. Observation shows that a feather descends more slowly than a brass ball of the same weight. One means of controlling the variable of air resistance would be to remove all air from the laboratory. But since Galileo's laboratory consisted of the Leaning Tower of Pisa and the space immediately surrounding it, construction of such a vacuum chamber was well beyond the technology of the time. (Subsequent experiments, however, did measure falling objects in a vacuum and such observations confirmed Galileo's observations.)

Since Galileo's time, his simple experiment has been replaced with progressively sophisticated observations that have confirmed that objects, be they feathers or cannonballs, fall at the same rate given a constant force of gravity. The principle upon which this **law** is based is called the principle of equivalence, and

 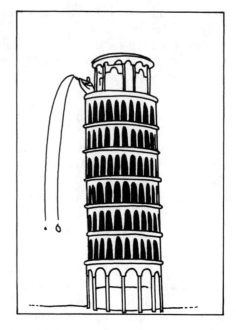

Aristotle: "Logic shows that heavier objects fall to the ground faster than lighter objects."

Galileo: "Experiment shows that all objects of differing weights fall to the ground at the same speed."

FIGURE 1.1 Aristotle's method of rational logic versus Galileo's method of experimentation.

it is considered to be one of the most important laws that govern physical bodies throughout the universe.

The law of gravity and the experiments upon which it is based serve as examples of two levels of scientific inquiry that are critical to science. The first level is basic observation; the second level is the realization that these observations are part of a larger system. Throughout this book, and hopefully throughout your career as an experimental psychologist, you will be cognizant of these two levels. While it may be interesting as a first step to observe that children from upper socioeconomic levels attend college in greater numbers than children from lower socioeconomic levels, the integration of that observation into a larger model of human behavior and society is an important and necessary second step. Without this second step, Galileo's observations would surely be uninteresting to the history of science and, at best, be a tiny footnote about an eccentric Italian who dumped things from the Leaning Tower of Pisa.

Facts, Theories, and Speculation

First, it is important to be clear on some terminology important to understanding research in psychology. Understanding the difference between facts, theories, and speculation is essential to the scientific enterprise, and also to the development of research ideas. **Facts** are things we know are true because we can see, smell, hear, taste, or touch them. They are verifiable in the world by others, through their senses. We can also measure and manipulate facts. **Theories** are possible explanations for why things are the way things are. You can test theories by gathering evidence that will ultimately support or disprove the theory. Some theories may be so "good" that we think of them as fact (like the law of gravity). Others may be still privy to extensive scientific testing and debate (like the ability to clone cells from an organism's own stem cells) and others may have a great deal of data to support them but be socially or politically controversial (like the theory of evolution). **Speculation** is a guess about something that is unknown. Speculation is different from a theory in that it either does not have enough data to support it, or it cannot be tested scientifically. Speculation can be detrimental if it is confused with facts or good (data-supported) theories; but speculation can be very good for science if it is used to spark intellectual curiosity and scientific inquiry. Some important questions do not lend themselves to the tools of scientific inquiry. These questions may be difficult to describe or study, or may not lend themselves to being quantified. Possibly there will be scientific tools in the future that can better tackle these questions. In the meantime, use your curiosity to guide your scientific pursuits.

Psychological Science

You may ask, "Why are psychologists so concerned with developing a science of psychology?" The simple answer is this: Psychologists attempt to understand the **laws of behavior,** and to understand, predict, or control behavior with any precision is a very difficult task. Scientific inquiry seems to offer the best possibility of handling such a task.

Behavioral scientists, including psychologists, go about their work with the same kind of assumptions as did Galileo about the lawful nature of the universe. Only the subject matter and technical equipment, not the scientific method, are different. Psychologists tend to study thought and behavior, not accelerating objects, and while the subject matter and the specialized tools seem to separate these disciplines, the scientific method and the assumption of a lawful universe whose secrets may be revealed through observation and experimentation unites these and all scientists in a common adventure.

George C. Homans (1967) noted that "what makes science [is] its aims, not its results: If it aims at establishing more or less general relationships between properties of nature, when the test of the truth of a relationship lies finally in the data themselves, then the subject is a science" (p. 4).

The scientific inquiry of psychology is based on the same assumption as other scientific fields: There is an underlying reality to behavior and thought that may be revealed through scientific analysis. Our inquiry is based on a further assumption: that the human is basically a system—a very complex system—that may be understood and explained through scientific experimentation and rational analysis of the results of these experiments. While some phenomena may seem beyond the scope of scientific analysis, often they are not! And it is because so often topics are susceptible to such varied interpretation that experimental psychologists must apply scientific methodology with the greatest of precision to their subject matter, be it skin conductivity during periods of stress, eye movements of a dyslexic child, or facial attractiveness.

Laypeople also understand behavior; or, they at least understand it to the extent that they can coexist with other people. They have principles of behavior, such as, "Absence makes the heart grow fonder." But there is also a contradictory principle that says, "Out of sight, out of mind." These contradictions occur because people's interpretations of behavior are highly colored by each person's perspective. Demonstrations at abortion clinics, for example, are called everything from Christian fundamentalism to atheistic radicalism, depending on one's beliefs and attitudes. Psychologists, however, try to avoid this subjectivism by engaging in systematic studies of behavior, formulating hypotheses about behavior, and then testing them in an organized manner. The techniques that psychologists use to test their hypotheses are described as the scientific method.

The Scientific Method

From the earlier discussion it is apparent that an exact definition of science is somewhat elusive. The same problem arises when one attempts to define the **scientific method.** Some authors seem to imply that the scientific method consists of a few simple steps that, if followed, will inevitably lead to amazing and dramatic discoveries about nature (or human nature). But if there is one such method, why does science often progress in such a slow, fumbling, bumbling manner? A well-publicized example is the search for a cure for cancer that has lasted more than half a century. In spite of the use of highly talented researchers and millions of dollars, the progress has been slow. Likewise, the search for the cause of abnormal behavior, such as childhood autism, has also been tortuously slow. Meanwhile, advances in some areas of psychological research have produced brilliant results, some of which have won the accolade of "breakthrough" research. Here we refer to studies of the components of memory, the genetic basis of behavior, the impact on stereotypes on performance, the treatment of dyslexia, and brain imaging breakthroughs, to offer only a brief sample of the considerable list of success stories in modern experimental psychology. Still, the slow pace of progress casts doubt on the idea that the scientific method is simple or infallible.

Our approach to the use of scientific methodology in the study of psychology is established on two principles. The first is that scientific observations are based on sensory experiences. We see, hear, touch, taste, and smell the world we live in. These observations, which are made under certain defined circumstances, or controlled conditions as they are called in experimental psychology, should correspond to the observations made by another scientist under comparable conditions. This feature of replicating the results of an experiment is called reliability of results and is a major requisite of scientific credibility.

However, because our sensory systems are limited in capability as well as scope, many signals outside the range of normal sensitivity remain unnoticed, meaning that those things that are detected take on a disproportionately greater significance. We call this the **tyranny of the senses,** recognizing that it is difficult to consider the importance of some of the real phenomena in the universe that lie outside the range of unassisted human perception.

Consider electromagnetic forces, which are all around us. At one end of the electromagnetic spectrum are cosmic rays, gamma rays, and X-rays, and on the other end are radio waves and television waves. In the middle, between about 380 and 760 nanometers, are waves that are detectable by the human eye. For most of human history, the energy that fell within the visual spectrum was considered to be "reality." The same constricted view of reality applies to all the other senses. Even though we have become aware of the presence of forms of energy that we cannot experience, we continue to emphasize the sensations that we can detect through the ordinary senses.

Some augmentation of the senses has been achieved through the development of technology. Many instruments and techniques in science are designed primarily to make "visible" those things that are "invisible" to the unaided sensory system. These instruments—the microscope, radio telescope, and spectroscope, for example—translate energy outside the normal range of human detection into signals that can be understood by humans. In psychology, many sophisticated instruments have been developed that allow us to see (sometimes literally, with brain imaging techniques) deep within the psyche of a species and reveal secrets of human and animal life that used to be invisible and left to conjecture and speculation. We will encounter many of these techniques in this book, and we remind the reader that if a technique does not yet exist for a topic of interest, there is no prohibition against the invention of one.

The second principle upon which scientific methodology relies is that observations from our senses are organized logically into a structure of knowledge. Frequently in experimental psychology these structures of knowledge are called **models.** Cognitive psychologists may, for example, develop a model of memory based on their observations of two types of memory and the laws that govern their relationship and the storage of information. Models are created from observations, and ultimately may become complete enough to be theories. A major tenet of the scientific method is to subject theories to testing and possible disconfirmation.

Scientific methodology consists of a variety of techniques, approaches, strategies, designs, equipment, and rules of logic. These vary from problem to problem and discipline to discipline. This book gives the student an overview of the experimental techniques used in psychology. In keeping with this overall philosophy, we will now consider a question showing a type of experiment done by psychologists and how it illustrates certain aspects of experimental design.

Experimental Design

Scientific experiments are based on controlled observations. Inferences can then be made about the differences between observations. These inferences can be used to develop theories and to generalize to other similar situations. **Experimental design** refers to the context that the experimenter sets up to observe the contrasts. This requires holding as many conditions constant as possible in the situation, such that anything that varies between groups is predefined and controlled by the experimenter. The manipulated variable is called the **independent variable** and what is being measured is called the **dependent variable.** The controlled situation in which these variables are manipulated and the measured effects comprise the design of the experiment. The simplest design is one in which there is one independent variable.

Let's begin with a "textbook" definition of experimental design in psychology, the design of controlled conditions under which one might make empirical observations of actions, thoughts, or behavior of humans or animals. In practice, observations are made within the context of a testable hypothesis that states the anticipated relationship between the conditions of an experiment and its outcome. To put it simply, you select a group, introduce an element in a controlled environment, and then measure the effects on thought or action. To illustrate the above, suppose you are interested in the likability of a person's face and the size of his or her eye pupils. You might hypothesize that if you see a picture of a person whose eye pupils are dilated you would find that person more likable than another person whose pupils are constricted. (In fact, experimental work on this topic has indicated that such an observation is correct.) In order to test this hypothesis you would want to design an experiment, or a controlled environment under which accurate observations might be made. In this case, you might need an **apparatus,** or specialized equipment, designed for the empirical measurement of thought or behavior. Specific to this experiment, a computer program displaying photographs of people with large and small pupils would be an appropriate apparatus, along with a rating scale in which the research participant could evaluate his or her impression of each face. The experiment might consist of showing a series of faces and asking a number of research participants to give their impressions of the faces along the dimension of the faces' "likability." In an actual experiment, it would be useful to show the same faces with large pupils and the same faces with small pupils to another group of participants in which the size of pupils was reversed. This technique is called *counterbalancing* and will be discussed later. In this instance, counterbalancing would reduce the chance that likability would be related to features other than the size of pupils. This experiment has several features, including the manipulation of events (e.g., the size of pupils) in a controlled environment (e.g., on the computer screen in the laboratory) upon which empirical measurements are made (e.g., participants are asked to judge the likability of faces). All of the necessary features of a psychological experiment are contained in this example.

Applying Assumptions of the Scientific Method to Experimental Psychology

The scientific method, as applied to psychology and other sciences, is based on several assumptions about the nature of the physical and psychological universe. While philosophers of science may debate these assumptions, they form the foundation upon which scientific experiments are based.

Order.   Psychological and physical nature is ordered, not random or haphazard. Furthermore, it is assumed that phenomena are related systematically, and that events follow an orderly sequence that may be observed, described, and predicted. For example, we can see that children crawl before they walk, the sensation of an object precedes its recognition, and hungry animals seek food rewards more aggressively than satiated animals. In the case of sex-linked toy preferences, there appears to be an orderly relationship between the presence of certain hormones (androgens) and a certain behavior (toy selection).

Determinism.   All events have a cause. Determinism is the idea that events are determined by knowable and therefore testable factors. Toy preference in young girls seems to be caused by high levels of a male hormone (although this may not be the universal cause of such behavior). This assumption is called psychological **determinism,** meaning that psychological phenomena (as in the case of the physical world) have antecedents, or preceding circumstances, that cause an event, although in many instances it may be difficult to specify exactly what the cause is. A word of caution is given here regarding psychological determinism: Just because an incident occurs before another event does not *necessarily* mean that it *caused* the second event to occur. Such conclusions are called superstitious causes and are pseudoreasons for explaining psychological thoughts and actions. We define **superstitious causes** of psychological phenomena as "attributing causes to thoughts or actions which are not logically or empirically related to those things." Scientists abhor superstitions—it looks like "voodoo"—and yet, as we shall see, scientists and laypeople frequently fall into the trap of attributing false reasons to psychological phenomena.

To illustrate the above discussion of superstitious thought consider the use of astrology in predicting behavior. All of us know how popular astrological readings and charts are. Virtually every major newspaper throughout the world contains an astrological section. In today's newspaper the horoscope for "Cancer" (the "sign" of one born on June 22) counseled, "Controversial topics are a no–no. An older, more experienced individual makes a brilliant suggestion," and for a friend (a "Capricorn" born on December 25) it portended, "Solitude is preferable to being with someone who is grumpy. A phone call brings unexpected news from a client or lover at a distance." "Magically," both prophecies came true, more or less, but the prediction for one applied to the other person! The Cancer got a phone call from a former lover who lives 3,000 miles away, and the Capricorn got a suggestion on how to keep snow off his pickup truck from an older person. The other recommendations, to avoid controversial topics and grumpy people, are so general and contain little more than "common sense" that they have little meaning. Now, it would be equally scientifically irresponsible to reject the advice of astrologers on the basis of a single example, especially one that is open to misunderstanding and ambiguity. How might an experimental psychologist go about studying the validity of the advice contained in a newspaper's horoscope?

In a class on experimental psychology Solso tried this little experiment. Students were given "their" horoscope three times a week over two weeks and asked to evaluate the validity of the advice. Most students rated the advice as being more accurate than inaccurate. What was not known in advance was that half the class received their "correct" horoscope and half were given horoscopes which did not match their birthdates; in effect, they were given another person's horoscope. Yet, no differences were found in the rated evaluation. A word of caution: Just because no differences were found between the two groups does not mean that there are no differences—just that in this observation none were found. It may be possible to design an experiment that more clearly tests the hypothesis.

To continue with the discussion of the cause-and-effect relations in psychology, let's use schizophrenia as an example. Its cause may be childhood stress, hormonal imbalance, genetic factors, disease, or a combination of factors—perhaps, even, some other factors that have not yet been discovered. The important feature, though, is that schizophrenic behaviors, similar to preference for certain types of toys, nightmares, bed-wetting, intellectual keenness, musical ability, belief in the ideology of the Ku Klux Klan, good grades, "bad" behavior—indeed, all human actions and thoughts—do not spontaneously erupt from nothing. *All human thoughts and actions are caused.*

Finding the cause or causes of our thoughts and actions is frequently a very difficult problem for experimental psychologists, but it is also exhilarating, much as it must have been exciting for Galileo to contemplate the forces of gravity that caused balls of unequal weight to fall to the earth at the same rate. Central to these inquiries is the assumption that behind each thought or action a cause exists. That assumption is basic to the scientific investigation of human thought and behavior.

Empiricism. **Empiricism** is defined as the practice of relying on observation and experimentation, to learn about a particular phenomenon. Empirical research relies on measurements (frequently in the form of numerically expressed measurements), such as evaluating the amount of learning, the strength of a belief, or the number of minutes spent playing with boys' toys. These measurements then are expressed as **data,** which give factual information in numerical form. For example, we measure learning by test scores, beliefs by preference polls, and preference for toys by observing with which toys a child plays.

Not all empirically gathered data are valid. Data can be invalid if they are selectively collected to support a preconceived notion, or if they overlook important aspects of a problem. As for the first case, one can prove almost anything by selecting supporting data and concealing contradictory data for one's theory. Unfortunately, overzealous politicians frequently practice this form of deceit by using polls that support their positions while disregarding data that do not. Such a practice is sometimes called "How to lie with statistics," and while this practice may be helpful in selling candidates, it has no place in scientific psychology.

In the second case, in which relevant information is overlooked, the culprit is ignorance—the scientist is unaware of the many possible causes of behavior and reports only a portion of the available data. Thus, the conclusion may be flawed due to the unintentional disregard of critical information. The cure for this problem is closer attention to the complexity of scientific issues and a broader scope of inquiry.

Parsimony. In general, scientists prefer simple, or parsimonious, explanations of natural phenomena to complex ones. The **law of parsimony** thus posits that simple explanations are preferable to complex ones (and more likely to be correct). You may not realize that when you say 'keep it simple, stupid,' that you are actually encouraging someone to follow the law of parsimony! Parsimonious explanations are based on logic and require fewer observations or logical steps to confirm. You step outside your house and a fallen tree is blocking your driveway. It was a very old tree, part of it was dead, and it had been raining nonstop for three days. So did the old, diseased root structure give way from the muddy earth? Or, did marauding elephants come by in the night and push it over? Which is the most parsimonious explanation?

The assumption of parsimony is important in making generalizations about the broader nature of human behavior because it allows scientists to extrapolate from specific findings to more general statements. In an experiment of hormones and toy preference, the representation of the data is very simple—an antecedent condition for toy preference is the hormone androgen. From this parsimonious statement it may be possible to make judicious generalizations, such as effeminate behavior in men and masculine behavior in women *may* be related to hormone levels. Such a generalization, in order to be validated, needs further empirical research and the collection of appropriate data.

Parsimony also aids us in finding common explanations for research gathered within the same species and even for observations made across species. In the first instance, for example, human vision is similar among all people with normal eyes. When your eye and visual cortex initially process light, the procedure is the same for you as it is for someone from Maryland, Michigan, or Madagascar. Although the interpretation of the things the eye sees varies enormously among humans, the way the eye works in detecting light, converting light energy to neural energy, and passing that information on to the visual cortex is essentially the same for all people. The law of parsimony allows us to make such a generalization without testing each person. In addition, the law also may work across species. For example, data collected on the visual properties of nonhumans, such as rats, chimpanzees, dogs, pigeons, and so on, have some common features with data collected on human vision. For example, at the detailed level of the physiology of the eye, initial processing of visual stimuli is very similar among mammals. Scientists often seek parsimonious explanations for their observations that they may generalize over a wide class of people and species.

C A S E   S T U D Y

The tendency for boys to play with dump trucks, tractors, race cars, and Erector sets, and for girls to play with dolls, doll furnishings, and kitchen equipment, has been known for a very long time. What causes this difference in play between the sexes? How might it be studied and analyzed? What would the results of such a study tell us about gender behavior?

These questions and others were posed by Sheri Berenbaum and Melissa Hines, who work as research psychologists in medical settings. In an article that appeared in *Psychological Science* (Berenbaum & Hines, 1992), entitled "Early Androgens Are Related to Childhood Sex-Typed Toy Preferences," the basis of gender-specific preferences for certain types of toys was examined (This article is analyzed in Chapter 14).

It is well known, not only from the psychological literature but also from common knowledge, that young boys and young girls are encouraged to play with certain toys and are discouraged from playing with others. Boys who play with dolls, for example, soon learn that such behavior may be seen as unacceptable and they may be labeled as "sissies," while girls who eschew kitchen toys for dump trucks may be labeled "tomboys." Although social learning and social pressure surely influence what toys children play with, might other forces be operating, such as hormones and/or genetics? But "common knowledge" is not enough; we must be systematic in our inquiry.

To test this idea, Berenbaum and Hines selected girls who experienced a genetic disorder known as congenital adrenal hyperplasia (CAH), a condition that produces a high volume of the hormone androgen, normally found in large concentrations in boys. (Boys with similar conditions were also reviewed in this study.) The researchers then evaluated the amount of time girls with CAH spent playing with "boys' toys" versus the amount of time with "girls' toys" and "neutral toys." They discovered that girls who had CAH spent more time playing with cars, fire engines, and Lincoln Logs than did girls with similar environmental backgrounds but without CAH. The authors concluded that "early hormone exposure in females has a masculinizing effect on sex-tied toy preferences." Thus, one more part of the determinants of sex-linked behavior was demonstrated.

The Psychological Experiment

We use the term psychological **experiment** to refer to investigations in which at least one variable is manipulated in order to study cause-and-effect relationships. We will emphasize experimental research in which the researcher manipulates some factors (variables), controls others, and ascertains the effects of the manipulated variable on another variable. In some experiments the researcher may not manipulate a variable physically, but can manipulate it through selection, as was the case in the toy selection example. The researchers did not inject androgen into the bloodstream of the girls (although such a procedure might be an even more direct test of the hypothesis, but there may be ethical issues as well, see Chapter 8), but they did select children whom the researchers had good reason to suspect had a high level of androgen in their blood. In this case, the manipulation of one variable was done through selection rather than with the imposition of a factor. It is this search for relationships between specific events and their consequences (cause and effect) that is so characteristic of experimental research.

Development of Hypotheses in Experimental Psychology

One of the most difficult tasks confronting beginning students in experimental psychology is to organize their thoughts and develop a testable hypothesis for a given topic. For many reasons, this is difficult not only for the novice but for the seasoned researcher. A major reason for the difficulty is a lack of knowledge. New research ideas rarely, if ever, erupt spontaneously from an intellectual void. Rather, new ideas and hypotheses usually arise out of a personal experience or interest and then are built on using existing knowledge and past research. Therefore, the best advice on how to develop new thoughts and hypotheses is to immerse yourself in the literature of a branch of psychology that holds some real interest for you. Read, discuss, investigate, and become well versed in the subject matter.

Passive knowledge is not enough, though. As you acquire knowledge about a topic, question the premise, the conclusions, and the technique and relate it to your knowledge of other matters. Just because it is in print does not mean that you cannot (or should not) be a careful and critical consumer of the information. The development of new ideas in psychology, as well as in other disciplines, rests on the acquisition of the fundamental elements of a subject and flexibility in thinking about them, which allows one to combine and recombine the elements of thought in increasingly novel and meaningful patterns.

New ideas are based on old ideas, new inventions on old inventions, and new hypotheses on old hypotheses. Contrary to popular lore and media fiction, scientific advancements often come from small increments of progress, rather than from a single brilliant discovery. Of course, we all aspire to that major scientific breakthrough, and your budding enthusiasm for achieving scientific eminence should not be discouraged. But such profound achievements are rare, and while most research projects fall short of seminal programs, they can nonetheless contribute mightily to the overall growth of scientific knowledge.

To illustrate the point of the accumulation of knowledge, consider an innocent question asked years ago by a son of one of the authors: "Who invented the automobile?" Trying to be instructive, the author told the boy that in about 1886 Karl Benz invented the automobile. "Wow, he must have been a real genius to figure out the engine, the brakes, the spark plugs, the wheels, and how everything worked together!" "Well, there were others, such as Henry Ford, R. E. Olds, and Daimler, and someone else invented the tires; I think it was Firestone. And then there was even the person who invented the wheel. . . ." But then the author experienced a moment of realization. "I think I may have misled you. No one person invented all of the components of the automobile any more than a single person invented the television, the theories of memory, or the symphony. Many people made significant discoveries that led to the invention of the automobile."

The development of knowledge in psychology progresses along similar lines. Given an inquiring and creative mind, knowledge, resources, flexibility, dedication, and a determined heart, many important scientific truths lie waiting to be uncovered by future scientists. Using deductive and inductive reasoning, past discoveries beget future discoveries, past knowledge begets future knowledge, and, indeed, past wisdom may beget future wisdom.

C A S E   S T U D Y

Curiosity about a forwarded email message prompted Keith Rayner and his colleagues to empirically evaluate what for others was just another email to forward on to friends and family. Maybe you remember it. The email claimed an amazing research project at Cambridge University found that "sentences in whcih lettres weer transpsoed (or jubmled up), as in the setnence you are now raeding, were easy to red and that letter position in words was not important to the ability to read successfully"

(Rayner, White, Johnson, & Liversedge, 2006). They found out that Cambridge had actually not conducted such a study, and it did seem that the meaning of the words were easy to read even though jumbled. So they decided to test this idea scientifically. They had college students read sentences where the letters of the words were transposed such that the transposition occurred either in the beginning, middle or end of the word, as well as reading sentences where there were no transpositions. They found that all types of transpositions resulted in slower reading. Specifically, beginning transposition resulted in the slowest reading speed, followed by end transpositions, and then middle transpositions. See! We can find research ideas anywhere!

Other Research Methods

There are many research methods available to the psychological scientist. Some allow researchers to *describe* phenomena (observational studies) and another allows researchers to *explain* phenomena (an experiment). In order to explain phenomena one must be able to determine cause and effect. The only research method that can do that is the experiment. If your research question leads to an experiment, there are decisions that need to be made about what type of experiment you will use. Most of this book will focus on these experimental issues.

But there are many interesting and important psychological issues that do not lend themselves to the experimental paradigm, and we need to investigate these topics with reliable methods. Some of these topics might include the buying habits of steel workers in Pittsburgh, the difference between the number of bipolar personalities in Miami and Seattle, and the trends in fashion over the past century. These topics, and hundreds of others, are interesting, worthwhile, and important to psychologists, and they may be investigated scientifically, studied empirically, and can yield reliable data. The tasks of the researcher are to make decisions and justify them. The first decision is often the type of experiment or study to conduct, given the particular researcher question. First and foremost, your research question drives your method. Therefore, it is important that the student of experimental psychology be familiar with a variety of research methods in order to know when it is (and when it is not) appropriate to use an experimental design.

Observation Methods

Observation methods involve systematic observation and measurement of behavior.

The elements of time and frequency of events are conventional components of observational data. Three different means of quantifying behavior in observational studies are in use. They are the frequency method, duration method, and interval method.

Frequency Method.   The **frequency method** is based on the recording of a specific behavior within a certain time period. Thus, if you were interested in aggressive behavior by children on a playground, you might establish an operational definition (more on this in Chapter 3) of aggressive behavior and record the occurrence of that behavior over a 30-minute time period, for example.

Duration Method.   With the **duration method** you record the length of time that elapses during each episode of a behavior. In the example of aggressive behavior, you might record how long each aggressive behavior lasts.

Interval Method.   The **interval method** is a type of observation in which time is divided into discreet intervals, for example of 3 minutes each. An observer might then note if a specific behavior, such as aggressive behavior, occurs within that time period. Such information can give a clue as to the continuity of behavior, as in the case of a chimpanzee beginning a behavior and continuing it over a series of time intervals.

C A S E   S T U D Y

One of the most engaging and important research projects conducted on primate language and socialization was "Project Washoe" carried out by Allen and Beatrix Gardner at the University of Nevada Reno. Washoe is a chimpanzee who was captured wild and came to live with the Gardners in Reno when she was about 10 months old. They raised her as they would a human child, immersing her into a world where American Sign Language (ASL) was the primary language used (Gardner & Gardner, 1969; Gardner & Gardner, 1989). The Gardners devised a vocabulary test to demonstrate that chimpanzees could communicate in ASL to humans, and in turn, tested not only Washoe, but three other chimps named Tatu, Dar, and Moja. They employed rigorous experimental controls in their procedures and stimuli, as well as using trained, independent observers to determine reliability of the findings. Objects were projected on a screen such that the chimpanzee could see the object, but the human observers could not. The chimpanzee would sign the name of the object to the observers (the observers could not see each other), and name of the sign was recorded. Later, accuracy (both between the chimp's sign and the actual object, and the observers' interpretation of the chimp's sign) could be assessed. They found that between 71%–88% of the time the chimps correctly signed the name for the object (compared to about 6% expected by chance).

The Gardners had communicated with Washoe using ASL about novel information (like when Washoe essentially asked for help to retrieve a toy), but they were able to verify these sorts of field observations in the laboratory using the vocabulary test, and relying on two independent observers, to determine that indeed, the chimps used sign language to tell the human observers things they did not know; in other words they naturally communicated with their human companions using language.

Naturalistic Observations

As suggested by its name, **naturalistic observations** are studies based on observations of subjects in a native setting or "in the field." In general, there is no attempt to manipulate the environment and measure the effect of a specific independent variable, but instead the social milieu and subjects provide the stimuli for actions that are the source of data. In some sense, all humans are naturalistic observers—that is, we all observe others in their natural setting, be it in an airport, a supermarket, a bar, a classroom, or a theater. It needs to be emphasized here, however, that because the subjects are in a natural setting, rather than in a laboratory, the scientific observations are inherently less well defined.

When Charles Darwin planned an expedition to the Galapagos Islands during the early part of the nineteenth century, he did so with the intention of observing the natural life he found there. He did not plan a series of experiments in which factors would be manipulated and their effects measured. Given Darwin's interest and the subject matter, naturalistic observations (i.e., observations made in natural or native settings) led to a theory that has been one of the most influential developments in science. Naturalistic observation involves the systematic recording of perceived information. The setting may be as undefiled by humans as parts of the Galapagos Islands were in Darwin's time, or it may be as "civilized" as the interior of a health club in the heart of Los Angeles. Scrutiny of the minute details of the mating rituals of giant tortoises on the Galapagos Islands or careful examination of the subtle flirting behaviors of patrons of a health club are both examples of naturalistic observations. For a period, naturalistic observations in American psychology seemed as taboo as some of the things observed. Recently, though, they have gained greater popularity and are once again considered an important method of gathering data. Even so, scientists must remember that when making naturalistic observations it is important to make objective and systematic observations so as to guard against distorting information through personal prejudices, feelings, and biases.

Suppose you were interested in a problem that has fascinated people for centuries: nocturnal behavior during a full moon. Legend tells us (experimental psychologists are inherently suspicious of legends) that people are more restless and do strange things when the moon is full; in fact, the word *lunatic* is derived from the same root word as *lunar*. Casual information, which is sometimes a source for hypotheses, suggests that people sleep more poorly, have more dreams, drink more heavily, and carouse more frequently during a full moon than otherwise. Police, hospital personnel, ambulance drivers, and others who deal with emergency conditions attest to the frequency of bizarre behavior during a full moon, and some research has tended to confirm these results. Several years ago an enterprising undergraduate student of ours, who was a night attendant in a mental hospital, collected data on the number of times patients got up during the night, and he looked for a correlation with the phase of the moon. The relationship was positive, but the cause was undetermined. It might have been that lunar light simply provided illumination for patients to make their way to the bathroom without stubbing their toes.

In order to gather reliable data on nocturnal activity and lunar phases, it is important to establish operationally defined criteria for the behavior in question, namely, nocturnal activity. Since the number of times a person uses the toilet during the night may simply be caused by lighting conditions, it is necessary to make more subtle observations to establish nocturnal behavior such as the position of a sleeper, the number of times a person moves during sleep, and the number of dreams one experiences—observations that can then be compared to the phase of the moon. All of these observations must be made as unobtrusively as possible, lest the observer become an unwanted or contaminating stimulus. Furthermore, each factor should be quantified, which may require the use of some sophisticated equipment (although it should be pointed out that many naturalistic observations need no specialized equipment). To record the position of a sleeper, an experimenter might use the number of times a person moves from one position (e.g., face up) to another (e.g., face down) during a night. Activity could be empirically measured (and thus operationally defined) by mounting a bed on four microswitches that would record "jiggles." The frequency of dreams could be measured by attaching tiny electrodes to the sleeper's eyelids to record rapid eye movements (REM), which are associated with dream activity. To quantify these three variables (the dependent variables in the study) the coding sheet in Figure 1.2 is provided.

Note that in the upper right-hand corner of this form spaces are provided to identify the subject, the observer (in case more than one observer collects data), the date, and the MP (moon phase), which should be added later. In a single-blind experiment the subject is not told that the salient experimental variable is the moon phase. In a double-blind experiment both the person collecting the data and the subjects are not informed of the critical independent variables. This double-blind control would guard against both experimenter bias and subject bias.

In this experiment, care must be taken to specify the characteristics of the sample being tested. For example, the activity of elderly single subjects might be less perceptible than that of newly married 18-year-olds, REM measures for subjects who use elevating psychoactive drugs might be higher than for nondrug users, and position activity may be greater among coffee drinkers than among noncoffee drinkers. All of these subject variables need to be considered because they may affect nocturnal activity in profound ways. Thus, the influence of lunar phases on activity (if it really exists) can be obscured by other, extraneous causes.

Many studies in which empirical measurements were made in a naturalistic setting have been done. The next example illustrates one case.

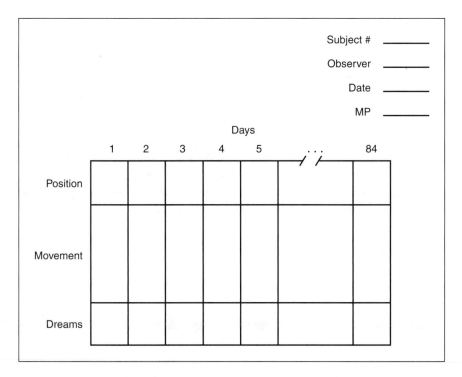

FIGURE 1.2   Data form for sleep activity study.

CASE STUDY

The research scientists Dean, Willis, and Hewitt (1975) were interested in the interpersonal distance between people of unequal status. The hypothesis of their research was based on the assumption that people of lower status stand farther away from people of higher status than they do from people of equal status. A student, for example, may stand a bit farther away from his or her professor than from his or her classmate. The student may stand even farther away from the dean or president of the university. To test this hypothesis Dean et al. unobtrusively measured how far away enlisted men would stand when they approached naval officers. The results of this study showed that the distance between people of different rank increased as the difference in rank increased. Such a study, which tells us something about the dynamics of personal space and perceived status, does not lend itself to traditional experimental methodology but is well suited for naturalistic observation.

Field-based Studies

In yet another example of these types of studies we now illustrate a **field-based study,** that is, a research investigation conducted in a natural setting. The difference between naturalistic observation and field studies is that in naturalistic observation studies, no manipulation or intervention is introduced. In field studies, some element is manipulated by the researchers. A field study was conducted using the "lost-letter technique," which involves the distribution of bogus letters to see if people will mail them to the addressee. The return rate (i.e., the number of lost letters mailed) is measured, for example, for different neighborhoods.

In the following study, Bryson and Hamblin (1988) use the technique to evaluate the return rate of postcards that contained either neutral news or bad news. Note the return rate by type of news and by gender.

Lost-Letter Technique and the MUM Effect
By J. B. Bryson and K. Hamblin

A variant of the lost-letter technique, the lost postcard, was employed to examine attitudes toward informing people of their romantic partner's apparent infidelity. Stamped and addressed postcards were left on the windshields of 180 cars parked near mailboxes, with an accompanying handwritten note reading "Found this by your car—is it yours?"

One-third ($N = 60$) of the cards had a neutral/good news (control) message ("Glad to hear you've worked things out. We're getting along better too. Keep in touch . . ."); 30 of these were addressed to a male, 30 to a female.

The other 120 cards, equally divided by sex, informed the addressee of his (her) girlfriend's (boyfriend's) apparent infidelity, in the following message: Dear Bob (Judy), I hate to be the one to tell you this, but I think I saw your girlfriend Ann (boyfriend Bob) coming out of the TraveLodge off El Cajon Blvd. with another guy (woman) on Thursday. It might not be important, but I didn't know how to tell you in person—Barry (Beth).

Consistent with a MUM effect hypothesis that bad news is not transmitted as often as good news: 35 (58.3%) of the neutral/good news postcards were mailed versus 23 (19.2%) of the bad news postcards ($X^2 = 28.10, p < .001$). There was also a substantial double standard effect caused by sex of the recipient of the bad news postcards: of the 23 cards returned, 19 were addressed to males and only 4 to females ($X^2 = 12.02, p < .01$). Figure 1.3 shows the results.

These findings indicate that, while there is a general unwillingness to transmit bad news (the MUM effect), there is a definite double standard in the willingness to transmit information regarding infidelities—the partner is always the last to know, especially if she is female.

Why should people be less inclined to report a male's infidelities? Two possibilities seem likely: It may be that females' infidelities are less accepted and hence more likely to be reported, or it may be that women are considered less ca-

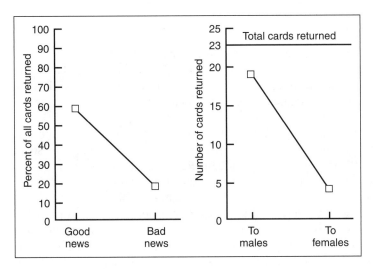

FIGURE 1.3   Percent of good/bad news cards mailed and number of bad news cards mailed to males and females.

pable of dealing with their partner's infidelities and need to be protected from learning of them.

Some field-based studies raise serious ethical questions because they may involve deceit, and the permission of the subject is rarely obtained. Bear this in mind and return to this issue when you read Chapter 3.

Archival Research

As we saw, it is possible to make reliable, empirical observations of behavior even when a specific independent variable is not manipulated. **Archival research** relies on existing records. These records may be in the form of statistics, documents, photos: any information that is already out there that you can gather and quantify (as opposed to creating or collecting yourself).

In general, using observations of archival records as evidence for cause-and-effect behavior is less reliable than are experimental studies in which a specific independent variable is manipulated. For example, one historical trend showed a strong **correlation** between the hardness of asphalt and the number of infant deaths. It is difficult, however, to see how one variable might affect the other, and, in fact, the phenomenon may be due to a third variable or to chance. For these reasons, empirical observations of historical trends must be undertaken with strict adherence to prescribed standards of observation. We now turn to an example of empirical observations of a historical trend.

CASE STUDY

Within the past few years, anorexia and bulimia have become more common, especially among young American women. Why? Might such irregular eating habits be related to the idealized image of "the beautiful woman?" And, if so, might it be possible to investigate the trends in "idealized" images in the common culture?

In a study that investigated these questions, Mazur (1986) traced the history of the changing concepts of feminine beauty and the overadaptation by some women in their effort to conform to idealized forms. This research project posed some very special problems in that the quantification of idealized forms of feminine beauty is not obvious. Some investigators might assert that feminine beauty is something they could recognize but not define operationally. (Such a remark is reminiscent of a statement made by a Supreme Court justice a few years ago about pornography: "I know it when I see it.") Nevertheless, Mazur attempted to quantify some of the attributes of feminine beauty by illustrating some of the physical characteristics of female icons, as demonstrated by Miss America contestants and Playmates from *Playboy* magazine over an extended time period. Some of the data reported in the article is shown in Figure 1.4.

In general, these data suggest that the ideal beauty has grown more slender and taller. While people can do little to affect their height, they can do much to regulate their waist, hips, and bust through dieting. According to Mazur's interpretation of these data, some women have taken dieting to an extreme level, with the result being abnormal eating.

As illustrated, the gathering of information on trends does not conform to the traditional experimental method in which the effect of some variable is measured. Nevertheless, in the previous example the researcher has attempted to study the causes of eating disorders in a scholarly way. A word of caution: Eating dis-

Establish a Base Rate

In observational research that is based on trends, it is important to establish a base rate, or baseline, for the critical variable so that a meaningful contrast can be made. As an example, consider the hypothesis that marital infidelity increases as the sale of alcoholic beverages increases. Correlational research calculated over time may be the first step in establishing a cause-and-effect relationship between these two variables. However, it is important to establish a base rate, or the normal rate of occurrence of marital infidelity as well as liquor sales over time. Since these figures may not be known, it behooves the investigator to collect data on these variables so that meaningful observations can be made.

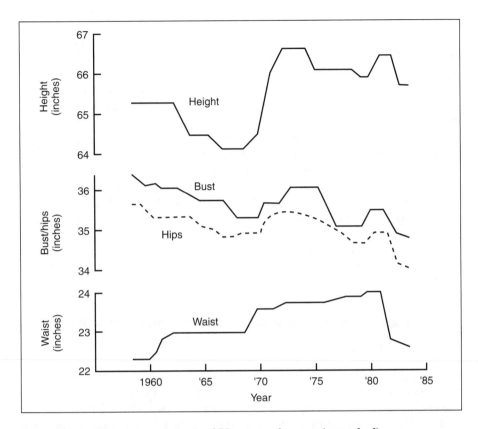

FIGURE 1.4 Body measurements of Playmates, by year (smoothed).

orders, and other psychological phenomena, are likely caused by a multitude of factors, of which idealized body shapes is but one. In order to specify all of the causes of behavior in this case, or in similar cases, additional studies are required—studies that may or may not conform to traditional experimental techniques. The conclusion is that complex behaviors, such as eating aberrations, are likely to be the result of complex causes and that the conscientious investigator is obligated to use a wide range of investigatory techniques in seeking these causes. These techniques may include traditional experimental procedures and nontraditional procedures.

Correlational Studies

The term *studies* rather than *experiments* is used in this section because correlational studies do not involve cause-and-effect relationships (even though they may infer such relationships). **Correlational studies** are studies of the relationship between two variables. They can be valuable if the interpretation of the results of these studies does not go beyond the limited scope of the measure. They can be problematic if we fall prey to an **illusory correlation** where we believe a relationship exists when none does.

An example of a psychological variable that could be examined in a correlational study is intelligence—some people have more and some have less, and a quotient of intelligence can be expressed quantifiably. Running speed is another human variable that can be quantified. A correlational study could be done between these two variables. First, members of a sophomore class at Standard University could run a 50-meter race. Some would run fast, some slow, and quite a lot somewhere in between. The same group then could take a standard intelligence test, the results of which would also vary. Next, the two sets of data (intelligence and running speed) could be correlated by means of a simple statistical test resulting in a **correlation coefficient.** The results would indicate the degree of relationship between the two variables, which in this case would probably be weak but positive (i.e., intelligence and running speed would tend, slightly, to go up and down with each other).

C A S E   S T U D Y

Or consider a correlational study that examined liquor consumption and birthrates in the San Francisco Bay area between 1970 and 1980. Both liquor consumption and birthrates are variables—women practice both activities at varying levels. The study yielded a strong positive correlation between birthrates and the consumption of alcoholic beverages. Did one cause the other? Well, you could make a pretty good case that drinking played a role in more children being born, but then another interpretation could be that the birth of children caused an increased consumption of alcohol. Or it could be that the coincidental data were caused by other factors. Any causal statement based solely on correlational analysis is not possible.

Does intelligence cause running speed (or does running speed cause intelligence), and does drinking lead to more children being born (or vice versa)? While any of these could be true, from a scientific position merely establishing a relationship between two variables *does not mean causality is established.* This point is stressed because lay thinkers often take the co-occurrence of two events as proof of a causal relationship. Many times superstition follows from this thinking, and students can think of many examples of people carrying good luck charms because on one or more occasions they had good luck while carrying such amulets.

Further, correlations do not determine the direction of cause and effect. They merely indicate that a relationship between two variables may occur with a probability greater than one would expect by chance.

CASE STUDY

Jessica Witt and Dennis Proffitt were interested in a curious phenomenon: Athletes often report that when they are doing well in their sport that the size of the target (basketball hoop, golf ball cup, baseball or tennis ball) looks incredibly large. This is in contrast to the perceptual experience of the target looking incredibly small when the players are not doing well. To test this phenomenon, Witt and Proffitt (2005) recruited men and women softball players immediately after their games. They had the players look at a poster with a variety of circles on them, and asked them to indicate the circle they felt best represented the size of a softball. They also collected from the players their "stats" from the game they had just completed (so that the researchers could compute batting averages). So was there a relationship (a correlation) between perceived softball size and batting average? Indeed there was! Those players who had better batting averages in the game they just played reported the ball size as larger than those who had poorer batting averages.

Survey Research Methods

Surveys are useful when you need information from a large number of people. Surveys can be administered by mail, via telephone, mass administration, and in person. Surveys often seem like an "easy" way to collect data. Perceived easiness, though, is no way to choose a research method! Remember, your research question will drive your method. **Survey research,** when done correctly, is as rigorous to plan and conduct as any other type of research method. Surveys must be carefully constructed; samples must be carefully selected; and surveys must be properly administered. Then, survey data must be appropriately analyzed. If you really just want to know what your group of friends think about the next presidential election, designing a survey and administering it to them is fine. However, if you are interested in what college students in general think about the next presidential election, you must be more conscientious about your sampling strategy. Survey samples should be randomly selected if the resulting data are to be used to generalize to the opinions of that larger population. A **sample** is any subset of a population. A **representative sample** is a sample that accurately represents the population. The **population** is the unmeasured, larger group, that the sample comes from, and that you ultimately hope to make generalizations about.

A Final Note

These other research methods can be used alone and thus are termed **nonexperimental** methods. However, they are also often a fundamental part of experiments. You may administer a survey, make observations, and/or consult archival records. The difference here is that these methods are used in an experimental design where variable are manipulated and their effects measured.

2 The Psychological Literature: Reading for Understanding and as a Source of Research Ideas

Science is organized knowledge.

—Herbert Spencer

The scientific literature in psychology has expanded greatly during the last few years. In fact, the number of articles, books, and technical reports exceeds the capacity of any researcher to examine all the sources in his or her own specialty, let alone in all of psychology. Because so much literature is available and because the human mind is limited in its ability to collect and store information, becoming an expert in a particular field in psychology might seem impossible (see Solso, 1987a). Nevertheless, while the task may at first seem difficult, given the guidelines in this chapter it is not impossible.

As you'll see, the psychology literature is organized—and because on-line searching, and storage of information is becoming more prevalent, it is much more thoroughly organized and accessible than ever before. Given several principles that show how this information is organized, you will find it relatively easy to focus your reading of the literature, which is an important step toward developing your own ideas in psychology.

Ideas, Hunches, and the Psychological Literature

Previously, we discussed sources of knowledge. Frankly, finding a truly original idea may appear to be an overwhelming task, especially for new scientists. Unfortunately, no single surefire pathway will inevitably lead to the development of a new idea. But we do have some suggestions that, when combined with an inquiring mind, will enhance the likelihood of an experimental hunch materializing. Those suggestions are as follows:

1. Closely evaluate what your interests are—often ideas come from our own life experiences.
2. Seek out information about psychology from a variety of sources
3. Read the psychological literature selectively and critically.
4. Ask "what if" questions while reading.
5. Evaluate ideas by discussing them with a friend or colleague.
6. Gather some relevant data about the idea.

First, consider the matter of selective reading. Suppose someone is searching for information about experimental psychology. That person could indiscriminately read all the literature available, but that would be impossible, even for the most voracious reader. A far more efficient procedure would be to select a topic of interest—be it perceptual motor processes, thumb sucking by children, language development in chimpanzees, learning mathematics, the use of personality tests in industry, or music and pain—and then find relevant literature on that topic. Fortunately, the current literature in psychology (and other branches of knowledge) is highly organized. All anyone needs to know is the *system* of organization.

Other Sources of Psychological Information

There are several sources for psychology-related information on the Internet that you may find useful in developing ideas and conducting a **literature review.**

Association for Psychological Science	http://www.psychologicalscience.org
American Psychological Association	http://www.apa.org
Psychology Web Resources	http://www.psychwww.com

Several specific journals provide a good source for ideas because they present reviews of various areas in psychology or cutting edge research.

Psychological Science publishes articles from all subfields in psychology, especially those articles that are of general theoretical significance or of broad interest across sub-specialties.

American Psychologist publishes articles on current issues in psychology as well as empirical, theoretical, and practical articles on broad aspects of psychology.

Current Directions in Psychological Science provides a timely source of information spanning the entire spectrum of scientific psychology and its applications, featuring concise, easy-to-read articles.

Psychological Science in the Public Interest. Each issue contains a single analysis of an important issue of public interest related to psychology.

Using the Internet

The Internet is most definitely a huge resource for information on any number of topics. However, you should be cautioned about using Internet search engines (e.g., Google, Alta Vista) and encyclopedia sites (e.g., Wikipedia) to find scientific information. It is not that there aren't worthwhile sites and articles to be found using a search engine: There are. However, as a student just learning about finding and reading research articles, it can be challenging to decipher what information is "good" versus what is junk. Unless otherwise directed by your professor, you should stick with academically oriented databases to find information for research papers and proposals.

Electronic Databases: Indexes, Abstracts, Full Text

In the past, getting a comprehensive review of the literature in any field required going to a library and paging through indexes, reference books, and thousands of journals. It may have even required going to several libraries to find references that were not in one library. This process used to take several days or even several weeks to complete. But with a personal computer, computerized databases, and the Internet, many literature searches can now be completed in under an hour. Electronic libraries provide a wide range of information quickly and conveniently and are often free, though sometimes a fee based on on-line computer time is assessed. Anyone who has access to a computer and Internet access can log on to these systems.

Just like indexes that are in book form, a computerized database is an organized collection of titles, authors, and abstracts (and sometimes the full text) of psychological articles. Using a computer or a terminal and sometimes Internet access, anyone can use the electronic library. After logging on, uncomplicated commands can be used to access information. With these commands the database's contents can be searched at a rate of thousands of items per second.

There are several electronic databases available to the student and researcher. **PsycINFO** (see Figure 2.1) is an electronic database provided by the APA that provides citations with abstracts to the scholarly literature in the psychological, social, behavioral, and health sciences. PsycINFO contains more than 2 million records spanning 1806 to the present. Journal coverage includes material selected from approximately 2,000 periodicals. Chapter and book coverage includes worldwide English-language material published from 1987 to the present; however, there is a substantial number of records covering books published earlier. APA is currently adding approximately 8,100,000 references annually through weekly updates.

PsycINFO, he or she can then access the full articles from the library's holdings and subscription services. PsycINFO offers a comprehensive collection of research abstracts, and all researchers—from the beginner to the expert—should explore the vast references available in this easy to use and time-saving program.

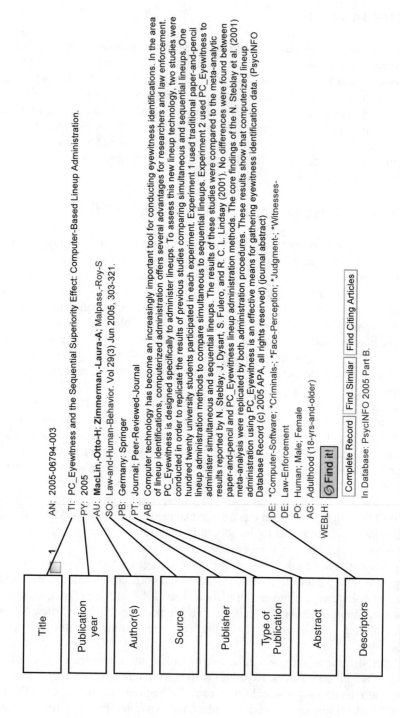

AN: 2005-06794-003

TI: PC_Eyewitness and the Sequential Superiority Effect: Computer-Based Lineup Administration.

PY: 2005

AU: **MacLin,-Otto-H; Zimmerman,-Laura-A;** Malpass,-Roy-S

SO: Law-and-Human-Behavior. Vol 29(3) Jun 2005, 303-321.

PB: Germany: Springer

PT: Journal; Peer-Reviewed-Journal

AB: Computer technology has become an increasingly important tool for conducting eyewitness identifications. In the area of lineup identifications, computerized administration offers several advantages for researchers and law enforcement. PC_Eyewitness is designed specifically to administer lineups. To assess this new lineup technology, two studies were conducted in order to replicate the results of previous studies comparing simultaneous and sequential lineups. One hundred twenty university students participated in each experiment. Experiment 1 used traditional paper-and-pencil lineup administration methods to compare simultaneous to sequential lineups. Experiment 2 used PC_Eyewitness to administer simultaneous and sequential lineups. The results of these studies were compared to the meta-analytic results reported by N. Steblay, J. Dysart, S. Fulero, and R. C. L. Lindsay (2001). No differences were found between paper-and-pencil and PC_Eyewitness lineup administration methods. The core findings of the N. Steblay et al. (2001) meta-analysis were replicated by both administration procedures. These results show that computerized lineup administration using PC_Eyewitness is an effective means for gathering eyewitness identification data. (PsycINFO Database Record (c) 2005 APA, all rights reserved) (journal abstract)

DE: *Computer-Software; *Criminals-; *Face-Perception; *Judgment-; *Witnesses-

DE: Law-Enforcement

PO: Human; Male; Female

AG: Adulthood (18-yrs-and-older)

WEBLH: ⊙Find it!

Complete Record | Find Similar | Find Citing Articles

In Database: PsycINFO 2005 Part B.

FIGURE 2.1 An example of a PsycINFO record.

PsycArticles.   The APA Full-Text Article Database contains the full text of articles from APA journals and Educational Publishing Foundation journals, most from 1985 to the present. The articles are provided in html and pdf format.

High Wire Press.   This database is a division of Stanford University Libraries and hosts a large repository of free, full-text, peer-reviewed content covering 918 journals and over one million articles available on line. It's available at http://highwire .stanford.edu.

Reading and Understanding Psychological Articles

After finding several articles pertinent to an area of interest, how does someone go about digesting the material? Many psychological articles are technical reports that are filled with sometimes complex language, statistics, and graphs, and it takes practice to understand them. To better understand the peculiar language and unfamiliar structure of articles, we suggest two methods. The first is a strategy for reading the article, and the second is an article review form.

1. Become familiar with the consistent structure of articles in psychology.
   - First is the title and affiliation of the author(s).
   - Second is a brief summary or abstract.
   - Third is the body of the paper including a review of previous studies.
   - Fourth is a description of the experiment and the results.
   - Fifth is a discussion of the results.
   - Sixth is the reference list.
   Students should look at an article and try to identify these components.
2. Read with an inquiring mind.
   - The first step is to carefully read the abstract. This will provide you with a framework with which to understand the rest of the article.
   - Next, skim the article to gain an overview of the problem, the design, and the conclusions.
   - Read the article for details.
   - Review the article and identify the most important points.
   - Ask questions when reading. For example, in the first part of an article someone might ask, What is the relationship between past results and the current experiment? Someone could also question the methods, the results, and the conclusions that the investigator reaches.
   - Once you have gone through this process of critical reading, you might find it useful to fill out the form included at the end of this chapter.
3. Develop a strategy for finding and reading relevant articles.
   - One strategy is to start reading general information about a topic and get more specific. You will find the most general information in textbooks. Chapters in books and review articles (like from the *Psychological*

Bulletin, or *Psychological Review*) also provide more general information. All of these sources though, particularly review articles, will have rich reference lists with which to specify your search (see next strategy).

■ Reference lists from a key article are a good source of additional sources. By getting and reading the references cited in an article that you are interested in, you will see how this author(s) built the rationale for his or her study.

■ Read newer articles first and then older ones. If you are using the reference list strategy, you will ultimately be reading new to old and allowing other researchers (the authors of your articles) to do some of the work for you. This way, you'll be reading the work they found to be important for this topic. This shouldn't replace though, your own searching of databases.

A Form for Recording Articles

Comprehending complex experiments in psychology is a teachable skill. In addition to learning the structure of articles and reading with an inquiring mind, psychology students need to organize their notes and thoughts about an article. The form that follows shows one way to organize notes.

After reading an article you should fill out a copy of the form, identifying the topic, the full citation, the problem being investigated and how the researcher(s) did the task, the results and interpretation, and any criticisms you have, including additional research necessary to answer some of the questions raised.

You can keep these brief reviews and refer to them when studying, or even in later classes or graduation school. Even seasoned researchers have found forms like this useful. Those who consistently record their summaries of articles will have a sizable collection of reviews in a short time, and this will inevitably prove useful later when developing research ideas.

A Final Note

In this chapter we have provided you with information on how the psychological literature is organized, how to find research articles, how to read them, and how to use the literature to generate new ideas. Don't dread gathering and reading articles; it is the start of your research enterprise. The next chapter examines some of the basic concepts of experimental design so you can begin to understand experimentation.

Review of Article Form

General Topic _____

APA Style Citation

_____

_____

Topic Details

_____

Hypothesis

_____

_____

Research Method Used

_____

Independent Variable(s)

_____

Dependent Variable(s)

_____

Results

_____

_____

Interpretation

_____

_____

Strengths

_____

_____

Weaknesses

_____

Research ideas

_____

_____

3 Basic Experimental Design in Psychology

*No amount of experimentation can ever prove me right; a
single experiment can prove me wrong.*

—Albert Einstein

The Logic of Experimental Psychology

Experimental psychology is a fairly simple matter; however, as we learned in the
first chapter, the subject matter, analysis of data by statistical means, control measures, theoretical considerations, and implications of research are among the most
complicated matters known to science. Before we can intelligently address some
of these more weighty topics, however, it is important to understand the simple and
exacting methodology used in experimental science. The goal of the scientific
method in general is to understand, describe, and explain.

We begin with an example that illustrates the rudiments of experimental design.

CASE STUDY

Over 200 years ago, the Italian scientist Spallanzani attempted to determine what
part of the male semen fertilized the female egg. On the basis of some earlier
studies, Spallanzani hypothesized that it was the sperm cell. To test this hypothesis, Spallanzani filtered the semen from male dogs to remove the sperm cells, and
then artificially inseminated female dogs with either normal semen or sperm-free
filtrate. The dogs inseminated with the normal fluid became pregnant, whereas
those inseminated with the sperm-free filtrate did not. Thus, Spallanzani demonstrated that it was the sperm that fertilized the egg.

This experiment, although it was conducted in 1785 and was a biological experiment, still illustrates many of the basic principles of experimental design that are presently used in psychology and other sciences. Spallanzani started with a **hypothesis** that was based on previous research. In order to test this hypothesis, he used an artificial insemination technique through which he could *control* the insemination process and *manipulate* the content of the fluid prior to its injection into the dogs. Having this control, he set up a two-group experiment. One group of dogs (the experimental group) was inseminated with the sperm-free filtrate, and the other group (the control group) was inseminated with the normal semen. The two groups were treated alike in all other ways. Since the only difference between the two groups was whether sperm cells were present in the seminal fluid, any difference in the pregnancy rates between the two groups must have been due to this manipulation. It was this type of logic and this type of design that enabled Spallanzani to arrive at his valid conclusion.

As shown in the box below, the basic steps in the experimental process are amazingly simple, and in fact, even more complicated psychological research uses the same simple framework. The principal difference between simple experiments, like the Spallanzani experiment, and complex ones is not in the basic experimental paradigm, but in the inclusion of sometimes complicated factors that need to be properly controlled. The central idea is that experimental design is based on just a few elementary principles. It is wise to keep these basic principles in mind when you study experimental design and plan experiments.

Basic Steps in Experimental Process

Hypothesis → Design Experiment → Perform Experiment →
Make Observations → Conclusion

Operational Definitions

Before a researcher proceeds with an experiment he or she usually has conceptual definitions of variables to be studied—anxiety, intelligence, ego involvement, drive, distributed practice, and reinforcement, for example. But to do credible research, which not only communicates effectively with one's audience but also allows others to replicate one's work, psychologists must operationally define these concepts (words) by specifying precisely how each is manipulated or measured. An **operational definition** is a statement of the operations necessary to produce and measure a concept. In other words, it defines a concept in terms of how it is introduced into the experiment and/or measured. There is considerable variability as to the extent to which variables can be operationally defined in a precise manner that retains the full meaning of the concept. On one hand, variables such as the spacing of practice, as used in the Lorge experiment, or the delay of feedback, as used in More's (1969) experiment later in this chapter, or the presence of congenital adrenal hyperplasia (CAH) in young girls, as indicated in the Berenbaum and Hines experiment, are fairly easy to define operationally. On the other hand, psychologists use abstract concepts such as intelligence, hostility, antisocial behavior, or anxiety, which may be somewhat more difficult to define operationally in a manner that includes the full complexity of the concept and has some empirical basis. What exactly do those terms really mean? Good experimental psychologists insist on the operational definition of terms. Words that describe concepts in psychology need to be tied to objective circumstances. Anxiety is a good example of such a variable. Almost everyone has some idea of what anxiety is. There are several dictionary definitions of anxiety, most of which agree that it is a complex emotional state with apprehension as its most prominent component. In attempting to operationally define this variable, researchers have used pencil-and-paper tests, a Palmar sweat technique, the galvanic skin response, heart rate tests, and eye movement tests. Each of these operational definitions probably measures some part of anxiety, although none of them measures its total complexity. A researcher must choose and develop an operational definition that is suited for the specific research question.

There are generally four methods of operationally defining a concept. You can directly ask the participant questions (through a survey, questionnaire or interview) designed to ascertain whether they possess the factor and to what de-

"And then he raises the issue of how many angels can dance on the head of a pin, and I say you haven't operationalized the question sufficiently—are you talking about classical ballet, jazz, the two-step, country swing. . . ."

Exercise in Operational Definitions

A series of abstract concepts used in psychology follows, and we suggest that you construct operational definitions for each of these concepts.

anxiety	memory	pornography
creativity	learning	insight
aggression	reinforcement	leadership
intelligence	self-esteem	effort
frustration	attitude	death
hunger	punishment	behavior

gree. You can measure some physiological indicator (like blood pressure). You can measure some biological indicator (blood test, hormone levels, etc.). Or you can make empirical observations to detect the presence of the variable under study. Not all factors can be measured in all of these ways. But the point is to recognize that there are many ways to define a concept, and for experimentation purposes, one must be explicit in what definition you are using in the presentation or measurement of the variable that you are interested in.

For example, if we were conducting a study on how the presence of others impacts the effects of alcohol on college students, we would need operationally to define the type, amount, and method of introduction of alcohol into our experiment (with due consideration for ethical issues, see Chapter 8), as well as how the effects of alcohol would be measured. So, we might invite people in groups into the laboratory (some of them in groups of 10, some by themselves), and provide them with 2 ounces of alcohol (per 100 lbs of body weight). We then might be interested in seeing how "drunk" people are, and how they behave. So how will we operationally define "drunk" for our study? How will we know it when we see it? Using our four methods of operational definitions as a guide (asking, physiological, biological, observation) we can come up with many definitions. We could ask the participants how they feel directly. We could do this with one or more verbal questions, we could have them fill out a rating scale, or some questionnaire. If we were to measure "drunk" physiologically, we could have them complete a typical roadside sobriety test, or evaluate their pupil size. If we were to use a biological method, we could measure their blood alcohol content. Finally, if we were to use an observation method, we could have trained observers rate their behaviors using an existing standard for the ratings like Dubowski's Stages of Alcohol Intoxication (though common sense and ethical practice would ensure that we would not be observing participants at the higher end of the scale!) There are many possible ways to operationalize this variable; which one we choose is just one of the many decisions and justifications that need to be made during the research process.

It is absolutely necessary that the variables used in research be operationally defined.

Stages of Alcohol Intoxication

BAC (g/100 ml of Blood or g/210 1 of Breath)	Stage	Clinical Symptoms
0.01–0.05	Subclinical	Behavior nearly normal by ordinary observation
		Mild euphoria, sociability, talkativeness
		Increased self-confidence; decreased inhibitions
0.03–0.12	Euphoria	Diminution of attention, judgment, and control
		Beginning of sensory-motor impairment
		Loss of efficiency in finer performance tests
		Emotional instability; loss of critical judgment
		Impairment of perception, memory and comprehension
		Decreased sensory response; increased reaction time
0.09–0.25	Excitement	Reduced visual acuity; peripheral vision and glare recovery
		Sensory-motor uncoordination; impaired balance
		Drowsiness
		Disorientation, mental confusion; dizziness
		Exaggerated emotional states
		Disturbances of vision and of perception of color, form, motion and dimensions
0.18–0.30	Confusion	Increased pain threshold
		Increased muscular uncoordination; staggering gait; slurred speech
		Apathy, lethargy
		General inertia; approaching loss of motor functions
		Markedly decreased response to stimuli
0.25–0.40	Stupor	Marked muscular uncoordination; inability to stand or walk
		Vomiting; incontinence
		Impaired consciousness; sleep or stupor
		Complete unconsciousness
		Depressed or abolished reflexes
		Subnormal body temperature
0.35–0.50	Coma	Incontinence
		Impairment of circulation and respiration
		Possible death
0.45+	Death	Death from respiratory arrest

Dubowski, 1985.

Independent and Dependent Variables

Psychological research often uses the same logic as did the Spallanzani study. In the simplest case, one factor (variable) is manipulated by the experimenter, who holds all other factors constant.

- The manipulated variable is called the **independent variable (IV).**
- The variable whose reaction is being observed is called the **dependent variable (DV).**[1]

The rudiments of the experimental design used in the Spallanzani experiment are shown below. Usually, one group of subjects receives an independent variable, and another group, which we might call a "control group" does not. Since both groups are treated exactly alike except for the independent variable, then any difference observed in the dependent variable is due in all probability to the change in the independent variable. Through this process, the researcher hopes to ascertain precisely the effects of one variable on another and to build knowledge about cause-and-effect, or functional, relationships in behavior. Some writers have talked about this process in terms of a "theory of control." This label expresses well the idea behind research. An attempt is made to control variables either by manipulation or by holding them constant. Once this control is obtained, the determinants of behavior can more likely be discovered.

With this overview of experimental logic, the following material will illustrate some of the concepts and designs in psychological research.

Stage 1	Stage 2
Semen + Sperm (Control Condition)	Observation (Pregnant)
Semen − Sperm (Experimental Condition)	Observation (Not Pregnant)

It has already been noted that in a simple experiment only one variable is manipulated, and its effects on another variable are observed and measured. The manipulated variable is called the independent variable; the variable being observed is called the dependent variable.

---

[1]It may help you remember these terms if you think of the independent variable as the one experiment is free (or independent) to change or vary; the dependent variable is the result of (or is dependent on) changes in the independent variable.

In experimental psychology, the dependent variable often takes the form of direct answers to an experimenter's questions. These *dependent responses* have been part of experimental psychology for a very long time and continue to be of use today. Meanwhile, there are two types of independent variables used in psychology: The first type occurs when experimenters systematically manipulate a variable, such as when experimenters change the amount of reward given to an animal upon making a correct response. The second type of independent variable is based on the selection of subjects who possess a certain trait or characteristic of interest. We will consider each of these types in turn and see how they can influence a dependent variable.

Experimenter-manipulated Independent Variables

We can illustrate the use of dependent variables and experimenter-manipulated independent variables in a study about police officers' decisions to shoot black and white suspects. The question addressed is: Would there be a bias with officers shooting unarmed black suspects more often than unarmed white suspects? Using a computer simulation, Plant and Peruche (2005) were able to find out, while also clearly demonstrating independent and dependent variables.

CASE STUDY

Ashby Plant and Michelle Peruchen (2005) were interested in the lightning-quick decisions that police officers must make in deciding whether to shoot suspects who appear to pose a threat. Particularly, they wondered whether the race of the suspect impacted these decisions. To study this important question, they recruited police officers and had them participate in a computer simulation where they viewed faces (black or white) coupled with an object (a gun, or a neutral object like a cell phone). They were instructed to "shoot" those faces that were coupled with a gun by pressing the "A" key; and to "not shoot" those faces that had other objects with them by pressing the "L" key. They found that the officers were more likely to shoot black faces that were coupled with a neutral object than white faces that were coupled with a neutral object. In other words, the officers showed a greater tendency to shoot black unarmed suspects compared with white unarmed suspects. Interestingly however, officers only displayed this bias during the first half of the experiment. The authors conclude that with training, officers can learn to overcome this racial bias in decisions to shoot.

In Plant and Peruches' experiment the independent variables were race of face photograph (black or white) and type of object paired with the face (gun or neutral object). The dependent variable was the decision to shoot, operationalized by hitting the "A" key to shoot, or the "L" key to not shoot. In the next experiment, the investigator is interested in whether we give more weight to information we hear first about someone, such as a potential friend, than we do to later information. As you read this example, try to identify the independent and dependent variables.

CASE STUDY

Asch (1952) conducted an experiment to determine whether the first information (primacy information) you hear about another person is more important in forming an impression of that person than later information (recency information). Asch used two groups of subjects. A series of adjectives that were said to describe a certain person were read independently to both groups; however, one group received positive information first and negative information last, while the other group received negative information first and positive information last. The adjectives read to the group receiving positive information first were (in this order):

intelligent	critical
industrious	stubborn
impulsive	envious

The group receiving the negative information first heard the same list but in reverse order. Asch then asked the participants to write down their general impression of the person. The group receiving the positive information first described him as an able person who had certain shortcomings. But the group who received the negative information first described him as a "problem" whose abilities were hampered by serious difficulties. Because the group who received the positive information first tended to have a positive impression of the person, and the group who heard the negative information first tended to have a negative evaluation, the researcher concluded that first impressions are important in forming opinions about a person.

The Experimental Design of the Asch Example

Independent Variable		Dependent Variable
presentation order of adjectives (forward)	→	impression of person
presentation order of adjectives (backward)	→	impression of person

The independent variable in the Asch experiment was the order of presentation of the information—either positive to negative or negative to positive. The dependent variable was the participants' descriptions of the person. All other variables were held constant; for example, both groups received exactly the same adjectives. Because the only difference between the treatment of the groups was the order of presentation, Asch concluded that the different impressions must be due to this manipulation. Thus, Asch was able to demonstrate a "law of primacy" in the formation of impressions.

Experimenter-selected Independent Variables

An experimenter-selected independent variable is usually a **subject variable** such as IQ, authoritarianism, gender, race, presence of male hormone, or some other feature or characteristic that is not easily controllable, or manipulated, and is inherent in the subject. For example, an experimenter may want to ascertain the influence of authoritarianism on concept learning, so he or she can *select* two groups of research participants. One group consists of people who receive high scores on a standard test for authoritarianism and the other group consists of people who receive low scores on the same test. Then both groups can perform the same concept learning task, and the amount or speed of learning is the dependent variable.

Note that the experimenter has not actively manipulated authoritarianism but has selected for it. Some experimental psychologists would view this type of study as being nonexperimental because the independent variable (in this case a subject variable) is selected. Strictly speaking, an experiment in psychology is a piece of research that measures the effects of a *manipulated* independent variable. However, the use of subject variables as legitimate independent variables has proven to be a very useful method in psychological research. From a practical standpoint, some important questions in psychology, such as research on gender, personality types, diagnostic classification, race, age, social status, and other like concepts, can only be addressed through the use of subject variables. We now turn to an example of one such case: Are there gender differences in mathematical ability?

CASE STUDY

A study by Benbow and Stanley (1980) used the subject variable of gender in trying to differentiate mathematical ability between boys and girls. The researchers gathered test scores for 9,927 seventh- and eighth-graders who were matched on (i.e., had equal amounts of) mathematics courses. They then were given the Scholastic Aptitude Test. On the mathematics portion of the test, the boys' average score was significantly higher than the girls' average score. Also, more than 50 percent of the boys scored above 600 (out of a possible 800), while not one of the girls scored above 600. The researchers also reported extreme scores. The highest score for a boy was 190 points higher than the highest score for a girl. As might be expected, the results were controversial, but the researchers stand by their data and suggest that one of the purposes of scientific inquiry is to search for the causes of such data.

There are numerous subject variables that have been used as independent variables. For example, children of wealthy and poor parents have been asked to draw pictures of dimes or quarters in order to examine the relationship between children's economic background and their estimates of the size of money. There are also many experiments that compare the responses of males and females on a variety of tasks. In addition, comparisons have been made between the incidence of lung cancer among people who smoke cigarettes and people who do not. Sometimes such investigations make use of correlational analysis in which, for example, the incidence of lung cancer is compared with cigarette use. But be aware that some critics of this technique point out that the occurrence of two phenomena, for example increased incidence of lung cancer as related to increased use of cigarettes, does not, in and of itself, evince a causal connection between the two, and that in order to establish a cause-and-effect relationship other evidence must be presented. The long-standing battle in the United States over the health hazards associated with cigarette smoking is just one example of the issues that scientists explore using subject variables and correlational research.

Experimental and Control Groups

Whereas in many experiments treatment groups are exposed to different levels of the independent variable, on other occasions an experimental group and a control group are used. Although these experiments can be described using our definition of an independent variable, the concepts are discussed here because they present some unique problems in experimental design.

The **experimental group** is the group that receives the experimental treatment—that is, some manipulation by the experimenter, otherwise known as the independent variable. The **control group** is treated exactly like the experimental group except that the control group does not receive the experimental treatment. The Spallanzani experiment is a good example of this. The group of female dogs receiving the sperm-free filtrate was the experimental group, and the group receiving the normal semen was the control group. In the next example we look at control and experimental groups where the participants are treated differently based on group assignment.

C A S E   S T U D Y

People who are blind are very adept at avoiding obstacles; however, little was known about how they do this. One hypothesis was that blind people developed "facial vision"; that is, they react to air pressure on exposed parts of the skin. A second theory was that avoidance of obstacles comes through the use of auditory cues. Supa, Cotzin, and Dallenbach (1944) set out to test these theories. They had blind people walk around in a large room in which obstacles (screens) had been set up. Two experimental treatments were used. In the first treatment, blind participants wore a felt veil over their face and gloves on their hands (thus eliminating "skin perception"). In the second treatment, blind participants wore earplugs (thus eliminating auditory cues). A third treatment was the control treatment, in which blind participants walked around the room as they would normally. The results indicated that participants in the control group and in the felt-veil group avoided the obstacles every time, but the participants in the earplug group bumped into the obstacles every time. Based on these results, the authors concluded that the adeptness of the blind in avoiding obstacles is due primarily to their use of auditory cues and not to any facial vision.

The previous experiment is an abbreviated version of a series of experiments on the perception of sighted and blind subjects. In this example, it is somewhat difficult to specify an independent variable. The experiment is most easily described as having two treatment groups—one in which facial vision is eliminated and one in which auditory cues are eliminated. The control group is treated the same as the other treatment groups except they do not receive the veil or earplug treatment. The control group provides a baseline to help determine whether the treatments improve or hamper the avoidance of obstacles. The dependent variable in this study—the ability to respond to sensory-deprived cues—was measured by the number of times the subjects walked into the obstacles.

Sometimes more than one control group is needed. For example, in pharmacology a **placebo control group** is frequently used. A placebo group is best described as a group who is made to believe that it is getting a treatment that will improve its performance or cure some symptom, when in fact no treatment is provided. This type of control group is also used in testing the effectiveness of therapy. Consider the following example drawn from the psychological literature.

C A S E   S T U D Y

Paul (1966) conducted an experiment to test the effectiveness of two types of therapy in treating speech phobia. His subjects were students enrolled in public speaking classes at a large university. Paul took 67 students who had serious performance problems in the course and assigned them to one of four conditions. One group of 15 participants received a form of behavior therapy. A second group of 15 participants received an insight therapy. A third group of 15 participants received **placebos** in the form of harmless and ineffective pills, and were told that this would cure them of their problems. A fourth group of 22 participants was informed that they would not be given any treatment and simply answered questionnaires that were also given to the other three groups. All participants had to give one speech before the treatment began and one after the treatment had been completed. The dependent variable was the amount of improvement shown by the participants from the first to the second speech, based on ratings made by four clinical psychologists. The four psychologists were not involved in the treatment the participants received, nor did they know which participants were in which treatment group. The results indicated that 100 percent of the behavior therapy participants improved, 60 percent of the insight therapy participants improved, 73 percent of the placebo participants improved, and 32 percent of the no-treatment control participants improved.

The Paul experiment illustrates the need, in some experiments, for different types of control groups. The interpretation of the results of the experiment would have quite different if Paul had not used a placebo control group. Without it, insight therapy would have appeared effective as a therapy in improving speech-giving difficulties. On the contrary, with the placebo group included in the design it appears that the insight therapy was ineffective as a therapy and may have only acted as a placebo. In fact, the placebo group's performance improved more than the insight therapy group's performance. The experiment also points out the need for a no-treatment control group, as over 30 percent of the subjects in this group improved in spite of the fact that they received no treatment. This can form a baseline to measure the effectiveness of a treatment compared to no treatment at all.

Different types of control groups are used in different areas of research. Researchers who remove a part of the brain of animals and use the animals as an experimental group sometimes use a control group that undergoes all of the surgical procedures except that the brain is left alone. This would control for a factor such as postoperative shock causing the effect found in the experimental group. The point to remember is that the control group must be treated exactly like the experimental group except for the specific experimental treatment.

The Paul experiment also illustrates an important control procedure used to avoid **experimenter bias.** The psychologists who rated the subjects' speaking performances were not the same people who treated the subjects in therapy, nor did they know which subjects were in which experimental group. It is reasonable to assume that therapists might be biased when it comes to evaluating the improvement of their own patients. Furthermore, the four judges might prefer a particular therapy, and if they knew which subjects had received this therapy, they might be prone to see more improvement in these subjects than in subjects in the other experimental conditions. Or perhaps the judges would have assumed that the subjects in the no-treatment control group could not have improved and would therefore rate those people's performances accordingly. Paul controlled for these potential biasing effects by using independent judges and keeping the judges blind as to what experimental group a particular subject belonged.

The term *blind* is used in a special sense in experimental research. **Single blind** usually means that the participants in an experiment are not informed as to which treatment group they are in and might not be informed as to the nature of the experiment. **Double blind** is frequently used in drug research or any research that involves observers who are judging the performance or progress of the participants of an experiment. Both the judges and the participants are kept blind as to the type of experimental treatment that is being used as well as the type of effect that might be expected. The following case study illustrates the influence of experimenter bias in experimental psychology and the serious implications it can have for psychology and other scientific studies.

C A S E   S T U D Y

An obvious demonstration of experimenter bias was shown by Rosenthal and Fode (1963). A group of student experimenters who had some background in experimental psychology was asked to evaluate maze performance with two groups of rats. One group, so the experimenters were told, was selected from a long strain of "maze-bright" rats, while the second group was supposedly selected from a long strain of "maze-dull" rats. The experimenters conducted a study of maze performance and, as expected, the maze-bright rats did significantly better than the maze-dull rats. The odd thing was that the rats were randomly selected from a standard sample of rats—there was no bright or dull distinction. Had the maze-bright rats actually performed better than the maze-dull rats? Probably not, but the experimenters who observed the bright rats expected them to perform better, and this expectation seemed to cloud their observations.

Within-subject Control

Basically, there are two simple types of control used in psychological experiments. In the first type, as illustrated in the previous examples, two or more sets of subjects are treated to different conditions, one of which may serve as a control condition. Contrasts are made between the results of the treatments. This design is called a **between-subject design** (see Chapter 6, Models 1 and 2). We can state the relationship as follows:

Group A	Experimental Condition 1	Measure Effects
Group B	Absence of Experimental Condition 1	Measure Effects

In the second type of design each subject undergoes two or more experimental conditions. The experimenter observes the results obtained after one treatment as contrasted with the results obtained after another treatment or treatments. This type of design is called **within-subject design** (see Chapter 6). We can state the relationship as follows:

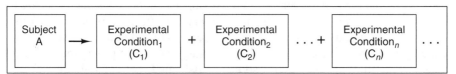

Within-subject designs offer several advantages over between-subject designs. They require fewer subjects, as each subject is treated to several conditions rather than requiring multiple sets of subjects for each experimental condition as in the between-subject design. Also, there is no need to match experimental and control subjects since each subject serves as his or her own control. Finally, from a statistical point of view, the variability (the amount scores vary around an average score) may be less for within-subject experiments than for between subject experiments.

Nevertheless, some real problems may be encountered when using a within-subject design that can render it inappropriate for some experiments. For example, experiments in which one treatment may affect the results of a subsequent treatment are not suited for within-subject designs (unless, of course, that is the focus of the experiment). As an obvious example, consider the ease of learning two computer word-processing programs: Starry Words and Perfect Words. In a typical within-subject design a subject might learn Starry Words and then Perfect Words. The contrast would be between the ease of learning each. However, the experience with Starry Words might make it easier (or harder) to learn Perfect Words. In either case, the experimenter does not know what effects a previous experimental experience might have on the subsequent experience. The results would be spurious.

Computers and Experimental Psychology

Computers now find a place in nearly all experimental laboratories and are sure to play an even more important role in the future. Originally, computers were used in the statistical analysis of data—number crunching. However, psychologists soon discovered that computers were excellent devices for the presentation of stimuli, especially timed stimuli. Software is available that makes the computer one of the most useful and necessary pieces of equipment in the laboratory. In addition, laptops, PDAs (Palm Pilots, Blackberries), and even iPods allow for stimuli presentation and data collection well outside the laboratory.

An additional problem with these designs relates to the **demand charac-teristics** of experimental design, which means that the subject can figure out what the experimenter wants and then either try to supply the desired response or in-tentionally withhold it. This can occur in the within-subject design because a sub-ject experiences several experimental conditions, which may give the subject an idea as to what the experiment is about. He or she can then bias the responses to satisfy (or frustrate) the experimenter. Demand characteristics deserve serious consideration in experimental psychology, especially in studies of social psy-chology, consumer psychology, child psychology, cognitive psychology, and ab-normal psychology. In Chapter 4 some sophisticated means for getting around some of these problems are discussed.

The Two Meanings of Control

The preceding discussion of control groups and single- and double-blind experi-ments points out that there are two uses of the word *control,* and both are impor-tant. In the first, and literal, sense it means the experimenter can make things happen when he or she wants them to happen. This is what was meant by control when it was stated that Spallanzani had control over the insemination process—he could control the contents of the seminal fluid. This kind of manipulation and/or selection of independent variables is a prime example of this type of control. An-other example can be seen when studying how experimenters observe nest build-ing by canaries. Under natural conditions, these birds do small amounts of nest building scattered over rather long periods of time. Hence, in order to study this behavior experimentally, it is necessary to get the birds to build when the exper-imenter is prepared to make his or her observations. Experimenters solve this problem by keeping canaries in cages and giving them the nest material only when the researchers are there to observe. Here the presentation of nest material has been controlled, and precise observations of nest-building behavior can be made.

The second way researchers *control* an experiment is by arranging conditions so that they can attribute the experimental results to the independent variable and not to some other variable. Paul controlled for the judges' biases by keeping the judges blind. The use of control groups is another attempt to ensure that experi-mental results are not due to some other variable. In the Paul experiment the placebo group controls for placebo effects, and the no-treatment group controls for spontaneous remission. This second use of control will be discussed more fully in Chapter 5.

A Final Note

This chapter provided you with the basics of experimental design. Many impor-tant research questions can be answered using these techniques. However, some-times the phenomenon you are interested in is more complex and requires more advanced techniques. These will be introduced in the next chapter.

4 Advanced Design Techniques

Different experiments do different things.

—Abraham Kaplan

Experiments in psychology are done so reliable reports can be made about the psychological life of people and animals. From these reliable reports, or *facts,* theories and models can be constructed. Here it is important to understand a fundamental element of experimental psychology: Psychological experiments are (mostly) designed to show cause-and-effect relationships, for example that food deprivation makes people hungry or conflict causes anxiety. Other valid studies may be purely descriptive, as in the instance of case studies where the method may be observation of people in a "natural" setting. Alas, life is complicated and almost all psychological phenomena have more than a single cause and, to make matters worse, causes have multiple effects on our behavior and thoughts. Therefore, in attempting to show cause-and-effect relationships in science in general, and experimental psychology in particular, researchers have developed sophisticated experimental designs and analyses.

To illustrate by example, your ability to react to highway signs is not only a function of the brightness of the signs (you couldn't see them in total darkness) but also of your ability to understand the meaning of the signs (signs in French or European symbols may be difficult to understand), your state of awareness (if you hadn't slept for 24 hours your reaction time would likely be slower than if you had), your level of drug or alcohol content, your visual acuity, and how fast you might be traveling. In simple, one-factor designs only a single factor is manipulated and other factors are held constant or controlled, but because life is complex—as are the causes of behavior—we will discuss some of the more complex experimental procedures that have been designed to handle these multiple factor situations. In this chapter we will examine experiments in which several factors are manipulated, quasi-experimental designs, and other complex designs.

Factorial Designs

Single-factor experiments (where there is one IV and 1 DV) are important tools in psychology, but it is evident that behavior is rarely a function of a single variable. For example, evidence from developmental psychology indicates that if a child's parents are hostile and excessively controlling, then the child may become withdrawn. On the other hand, if the hostile parental behavior is combined with a tendency to ignore the child and exert no control over his or her behavior, the child tends toward antisocial behaviors. Thus, these two variables—degree of kindness or hostility and degree of control—are both important factors in determining a child's behavior.

In order to determine the influence of two or more independent variables (say, you wanted to include a third variable, heredity) on a dependent variable, researchers employ a **factorial design.** In a factorial design, two or more variables may be manipulated at the same time and their effects on the DV as well as interactions between the IVs on the DV can be assessed. To illustrate the use of a somewhat simple factorial design, we have selected a case from comparative psychology in which the experimenters studied how fast rats run a straight course under varying levels of food deprivation and food reward.

CASE STUDY

Ehrenfreund and Badia (1962) examined the performance of rats under varying food-deprivation and incentive conditions. The apparatus used in the experiment was a 5-foot-long, straight alley with a start box on one end and a goal box on the other end. The dependent measure was the speed at which the rats ran down the alley. Twenty rats were used in this experiment—half were maintained at 95 percent of their ad lib, or free-feeding, weight and the other half were maintained at 85 percent of their ad lib weight. For the purposes of this experiment, the high-deprivation treatment was defined as those rats maintained at 85 percent of their ad lib weight, and the low-deprivation treatment was defined as those rats maintained at 95 percent of their ad lib weight.

Experimenters then put a 45-mg food pellet (low incentive) in the goal box for half of the rats in the high-deprivation treatment, and put a 260-mg food pellet (high incentive) in the goal box for the other half. Using the same incentive treatments with the low-deprivation treatment yielded the four experimental treatments of the experiment:

TABLE 4.1 **Mean Running Time in Seconds for Deprivation and Incentive Groups**

	Deprivation Treatment	
	95% (low)	85% (high)
Incentive treatment		
45 mg (low)	15.15	13.86
260 mg (high)	13.92	10.26

1. high deprivation–high incentive
2. high deprivation–low incentive
3. low deprivation–high incentive
4. low deprivation–low incentive

Using the basic design described by Ehrenfreund and Badia (1962), let's work through this experiment. Assume there were five rats in each of the four conditions. We could measure performance in terms of the speed at which the rats traversed the 5-foot alley. We could record the running speed in seconds for each rat on the last ten trials of the experiment. The mean speed for each rat could then be calculated from the time recorded for the ten trials. Now let's put the mean speed in a table (see Table 4.1) for each of the four treatment groups.

Now by looking at the table we can see that both deprivation and incentive are influential in determining performance. The mean running time for the high-incentive groups is faster than the mean for the low-incentive groups within each deprivation level. Furthermore, both of the means for the high-deprivation groups are faster than the means for the low-deprivation groups.

The preceding example is called a 2 × 2 factorial design. Two levels of one variable (deprivation) are combined factorially with two levels of a second variable (incentive) to yield 2 × 2, or four, separate treatments. Each level of the first variable occurs within each level of the second variable—that is, high and low deprivation are tested both under high- and low-incentive conditions. The design also could be extended to add other independent variables; for example, a 2 × 2 × 3 design would consist of two levels of the first variable, two levels of the second variable, and three levels of the third variable (e.g., type of rat: lab, pet, wild). In this design there would be 12 separate treatments. One of the advantages of the factorial design is that it allows the researcher to ascertain how independent variables combine with one another to determine the values of the dependent variable.

The following case study is a 2 × 2 factorial design applied to attitude formation—a common theme in social psychological research—that illustrates the power of such a design to pick out interactions between variables.

Measuring Attitudes

Social psychologists who measure attitudes toward a variety of topics (e.g., foreign aid, the value of space exploration, abortion, or the death penalty) face several unique problems in their research. Among the most difficult is deciding the way that questions are phrased in a public opinion poll. Take a poll conducted during the 1992 presidential election in which the views about government welfare projects were sampled in one instance the question was phrased: "Would you favor more welfare to the poor?" In a second instance the question was phrased: "Would you favor more assistance to the poor?" In the first case 19 percent of the respondents agreed while in the second case 63 percent agreed.

C A S E   S T U D Y

Several studies have shown that if people are somehow induced to argue in favor of something to which they are opposed, the more they are paid for the task, the more they change their own attitude toward that subject. This result is consistent with a reinforcement explanation—money is a reward, and the more money that is paid for arguing in favor of a position that a person opposes, the more that position is reinforced. On the other hand, several other studies have found the exact opposite effect. These studies support a dissonance theory explanation (Festinger, 1957). This explanation assumes that dissonance (or a state of discomfort) is aroused when a person argues in favor of a position he or she actually opposes. Furthermore, the smaller the amount of money given for doing this task, the greater should be the amount of dissonance, since low sums of money provide inadequate justification for defending something to which a person is opposed. In order to relieve the high level of dissonance, the people must convince themselves that they really are in favor of the argued position. Therefore, more attitude change would occur in the high-dissonance (low-money) condition than in the low-dissonance (high-money) condition.

In an attempt to resolve these conflicting results, Linder, Cooper, and Jones (1967) suggested that the reinforcement hypothesis was applicable when subjects had no choice in arguing for the position they opposed. They further assumed that the dissonance hypothesis was appropriate under conditions in which the subject somehow chose to argue for the opposed position. The logic for their hypothesis was based on the assumption that dissonance can be created only when people choose to do something they oppose, but not when they are forced to do it.

The design used in this experiment was a 2 × 2 factorial design. Subjects were college students who each wrote an essay supporting a speaker-ban law for colleges (a position they were against). The subjects either were told to write the essay (no-choice condition) or were given a choice as to whether or not they would write the essay (free-choice condition). In addition, half of the subjects in each of the two conditions were paid 50 cents for writing the essay, while the other half

TABLE 4.2 **Mean Attitude Change for Choice and Incentive Conditions**

	Incentive	
	50 Cent Incentive	**$2.50 Incentive**
Choice		
No-choice treatment	−0.05	+0.63
Free-choice treatment	+1.25	−0.07

of the subjects were paid $2.50. Thus, the design consisted of the four treatments, and ten subjects were randomly assigned to each treatment. The dependent variable was the amount of change in the subjects' attitudes toward the speaker-ban law. This was measured by having the subjects check the point on a scale that indicated the degree to which they approved of the speaker-ban law. The mean change for the four treatments is given in Table 4.2. These data are also clearly shown in graphic form in Figure 4.1.

Positive scores indicate change toward favoring the speaker-ban law, while negative scores indicate a greater aversion toward the position (a boomerang effect). The results supported the authors' hypothesis. In the no-choice treatment, the $2.50 incentive elicited more attitude change than did the 50 cent incentive. In the free-choice treatment, the opposite result was found.

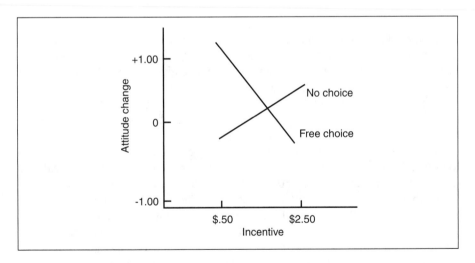

FIGURE 4.1   **Mean attitude change as a function of choice and incentive conditions.**

The appropriate statistical test to analyze the previous results is **analysis of variance.** The actual calculations of this statistic will not be explained here (see Appendix A). However, some of the logic of this test will be described because it gives some insight as to the logic of a factorial design, as well as pointing out how the results are analyzed. The experiment used a 2 × 2 factorial design with two levels of one variable (no choice or free choice) and two levels of a second variable (50 cent incentive or $2.50 incentive). In the analysis of variance, each variable (level of choice and level of incentive) is analyzed separately, and then the interactions between the variables are analyzed. In the previous experiment there were two **factors;** therefore, the analysis of variance will contain (1) an analysis of the main effect of the first variable (choice), (2) an analysis of the main effect of the second variable (incentive), and (3) an analysis of the interaction between the two variables.

One can conceptualize a 2 × 2 analysis in the following form:

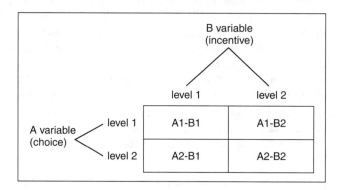

The main effect of the choice variable is analyzed by comparing the mean attitude change of subjects in the no-choice treatment with the mean attitude change of subjects in the free-choice treatment, ignoring the incentive manipulations. The mean of the no-choice treatment is calculated by adding the means for both incentive conditions and dividing by 2 ($-.05 + .63 = .58; .58 \div 2 = .29$). The same process is used in the free-choice treatment with a resulting mean value of .59. These two means are then compared in order to analyze for the main effect of choice. The same process is repeated to analyze the main effect of incentive. The necessary addition and division reveal that the mean attitude change for the 50 cent treatment is .60, and the mean for the $2.50 condition is .28. These two means are then compared to ascertain the main effect of incentive. The next step is to analyze the interaction between the two variables. The test for an interaction effect determines if two variables are independent of each other with respect to their influence on the dependent variable. The variables are dependent if it is demonstrated that one variable affects the dependent variable differently under each of the two levels of the second variable.

Linder et al. (1967) analyzed their results in this manner. Their computations indicated that although the mean attitude did show a change both for the main effect of choice and for the main effect of incentive, these changes were not **statistically significant** (see box), meaning the magnitude of these changes was not greater than would be expected by chance fluctuation in the means. **Chance** is

Statistically Significant

Prior the collection and analysis of data, experimental psychologists commonly anticipate how the data will be analyzed statistically. A researcher often sets **a level of significance,** defined as the statistical point above (or below) which one can infer the operation of nonchance factors. Researchers usually set this level of significance in terms of a probabilistic statement. In many psychological experiments the level may be expressed as "the .05 level" or "the .01 level," which means that the results will occur only .05 (1 in 20) or .01 (1 in 100) times by chance alone. Data that have been statistically analyzed and meet the preestablished criterion (be it .05, .01, or even .001) then are called statistically significant.

It should be pointed out that a result may not be statistically significant but still can be of interest. Often, especially during pilot studies or experiments with few subjects or observations, the results may fail to reach the level of statistical significance but can still suggest that further investigation with perhaps better controls and/or more observations may be worthwhile. At the same time, an experimenter must be cautious not to go on a fishing trip for results by running and fine-tuning an experiment until he or she gets the desired results.

the variation in results that is due to uncontrolled factors, such as guessing, experimental error, and failure to achieve a perfect matching of subjects in each treatment group. Because of a variety of uncontrolled factors, we would expect the means to show some change even if the treatments had no effect. The **interaction** effect, however, was statistically significant in the direction hypothesized by the authors—high incentive facilitated attitude change in the no-choice treatment, but low incentive facilitated attitude change in the free-choice treatment. Thus, the two variables interacted to determine the amount of attitude change.

In many of the examples of statistical tests used in this book the results are interpreted in terms of "statistically significant data": a topic which we now consider.

In another example of a 2 × 2 design, Chi (1978) used two types of subjects and two types of tasks to study the importance of specialized knowledge on memory.

CASE STUDY

In this study, Chi (1978) examined the recall of digits and of chess pieces (A variable) by children and adults (B variable), thus completing the 2 × 2 design. The children were 10-year-olds who were skilled chess players, while the adults were novice chess players. The first task involved looking at chess pieces as they might appear in a normal game and recalling the arrangement after they were removed. In the digit portion of the task, recall was measured using a standard series of digits, such as might appear on an IQ test.

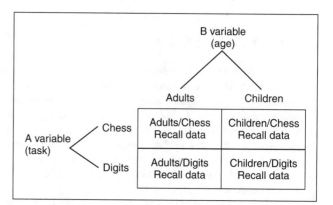

FIGURE 4.2   Design of Chi (1978) experiment examining digit/chess recall by adults and children.

The design can be conceptualized as shown in Figure 4.2.

Figure 4.3 shows a strong interaction. It appears that specialized knowledge, such as chess knowledge, facilitates recall of information in that domain but has little effect on digit memory. Adults who are unsophisticated in chess recall fewer pieces than do children, but perform better on digit recall.

In the text of the study, Chi (1978) presents a statistical analysis that confirms mathematically the results shown in Figure 4.3.

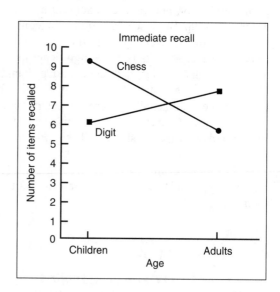

FIGURE 4.3   Children's and adults' recall of chess and digit stimuli.

From Chi (1978). Reprinted by permission.

The 2 × 2 design is the simplest of factorial designs; these designs become increasingly complex as more factors are added, or when several levels of a factor are used. The following example illustrates this point. In it, only two factors are used, but while one factor still has two levels, there are three levels in the other factor. This example was taken from research in social-cognitive neuroscience.

CASE STUDY

Mary Wheeler and Susan Fiske (2005) were interested in how various social goals affect prejudice. They had white participants view photographs of photographs of faces (black and white) while considering a particular social goal (social categorization, social individuation, or simple visual inspection) and providing a response regarding that goal. They did these tasks inside an fMRI scanner so that brain activity in the amygdala could be measured. Previous research has shown that threat responses (potential danger) activates the amygdala. The social categorization goal required that the participants decide whether the face was of a person over 21 years of age. The social individuation goal asked participants to decide whether they thought the person in the photo would like a vegetable (e.g., asparagus, lettuce, radish). The visual inspection task simply had participants indicate whether there was a dot on the face or not, which encourages the participants to think of the face as any other stimuli, and not as a social object as the other two tasks do. For all three types of questions, the participants pressed either a red "no" button in one hand, or a green "yes" button in the other hand. They found that there was no difference in amygdala activity across the different tasks. So the tasks themselves were not causing differences in brain activity. Instead, they found differences in amygdala activity based on what the social goal was when viewing the faces. In particular, they found that a visual task (looking for a dot) caused no difference when looking at a black face, but there was increased amygdala activity during the social categorization task (indicating greater stereotype processing), and decreased activity when engaged in the social individuation task (indicating possibly that focusing on the face as an individual, not as a member of a group, inhibited stereotype responses in the amygdala [see Figure 4.4]).

Based on the symbolic description of factorial studies discussed previously, this procedure has two levels of an A variable (race of face) and four levels of a B variable (social goal). This can be conceptualized as follows:

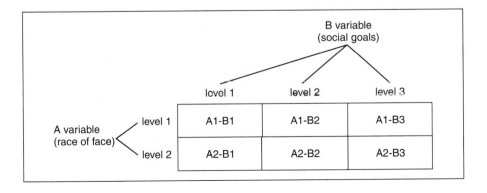

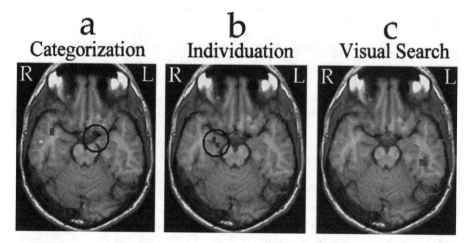

FIGURE 4.4   Researchers using FMRI technology rely on visual images of the scans as well as specialized statistics to determine differences between the experimental groups.

To illustrate a more complex factorial design, consider the color matching experiment by Solso and Short (1979) below that illustrates a 3 × 3 × 2 factorial design.

Complex Factorial Designs

The following case study illustrates several important principles of experimental psychology. The first is the use of a within-subject control. Note that subjects are treated to several conditions in the following experiment and thus serve as their own control. Also, note that measurement of mental processing is introduced in the form of reaction time. The assumption of this measurement is that intellectual processes, such as matching two signals, require time, albeit a very small amount of time. Subtle differences between matching signals can reveal important psychological processes.

CASE STUDY

Psychologists have been interested in the way information is "coded" or recorded in memory after it is perceived. In a series of important experiments done by Posner and his associates (see Posner 1969; Posner, Boies, Eichelman, & Taylor 1969; Posner & Keele, 1968), it was found that participants initially formed visual codes for letters and then formed name codes. Following these experiments, Solso and Short (1979) performed an experiment on color codes. This experiment allows us to introduce several relevant features of contemporary experimental design, including within-subject design, reaction times, tachistoscopic procedures, and visual representation of data.

In the experiment subjects were shown a color square and either an associate to the color, the name of the color, or another color square. The second stimulus appeared either simultaneously with the first color, after 500 msec (½ sec), or after 1,500 msec (1½ sec). Participants were asked to press a reaction-time key as quickly as possible if the two stimuli (the color square and the secondary stimulus) matched. An equal number of nonmatched secondary stimuli were shown to assure that the subjects were really reacting to the matching task. For example, in a given series of trials a subject might see a red square and then 500 msec later the word *blood,* which, being a correct associate, should produce a match response. In a second trial the same subject might see a green square presented simultaneously with the word *green,* which is also a match. In a third trial the same subject might see a blue square followed 1,500 msec later by a green square, which is not a match, and so on. The design could be thought of as a 3 3 × 2 design. The first variable represents the type of relationship being tested: color to associate, color to word, or color to color. The second variable represents the delay between stimuli: 0, 500, or 1,500 msec. The third variable represents either a match (e.g., red–blood) or a mismatch (e.g., red–blue).

The design is a within-subject design. Each subject was treated with each of the experimental variables. The results are shown in Figure 4.5 and indicate that

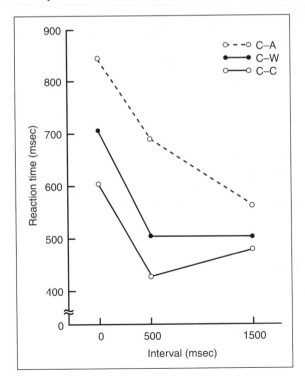

FIGURE 4.5 Reaction times of various match conditions as a function of priming interval: C—A = color to associate; C—W = color to word; and C—C = color to color.

From Solso and Short (1979).

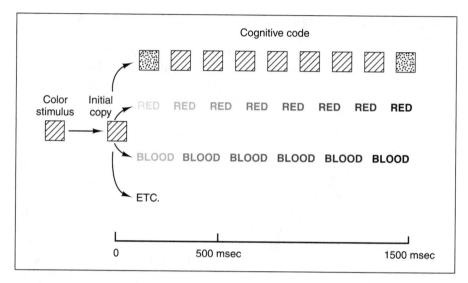

FIGURE 4.6   The development of color codes.

From Solso and Short (1979).

participants initially respond fastest to color–color pairings (e.g., red–red) and slowest to color–association pairings (e.g., red–blood). As the interval between the two stimuli is lengthened to 1,500 msec, however, the reaction time for matching the associate (e.g., blood) decreases significantly, so that the reaction times for all three groups are similar. The authors interpreted the results as a parallel development of codes to colors (see Figure 4.6).

The experiment also introduces the topic of **mental chronometry**—measuring the speed of mental events. This topic has been a favorite tool of many recent cognitive psychologists, but its history can be traced to the nineteenth century. The basic principle involved is that the processing of information requires time, and complex processing requires more time than simple processing.

Reaction-time experiments are usually based on a forced-choice procedure in which the participant is required to make a decision between two (or sometimes more) alternatives. Because reaction-time experiments are highly susceptible to practice effects, participants are normally given a series of warm-up trials to, as some researchers say, "limber up their index fingers." But much more is involved in warm-up, or practice, trials. Familiarization with the apparatus, the experimental environment, the experimenter, the procedure, and the stimuli are all important factors in warm-up and should be considered in all reaction-time experiments, as well as other experiments in which practice effects might be significant.

The experiment also introduces us to a classic piece of equipment: the **tachistoscope,** or T-scope. It was primarily used in experiments that required precision in presenting visual stimuli for brief time periods and accuracy in measuring reaction times. The typical T-scope was an enclosed box that had three channels, or viewing chambers, capable of exposing three different stimuli. The exposure time was controlled by small fluorescent tubes that showed the stimuli when illuminated. Computers have replaced many of the functions of the T-scope.

Quasi-Experimental Designs

The concept of **quasi-experimental design** was introduced by Campbell and Stanley (1966)[1] to overcome some of the problems faced by psychologists who wish to study behavior that occurs in less formally structured environments than a laboratory. Quasi-experimental designs are studies in which the independent variables (the elements whose effects are to be measured) are selected from the natural environment. Sometimes, quasi-experimental designs are termed *ex post facto research,* or "as if" designs, as the collection and analysis of data take place after an event has happened. These designs are similar to naturalistic observations, which were discussed previously. One part of the logic of this design is that had the experimenter been able to introduce an independent variable into a situation, then that variable would have been the same as the variable that was naturally introduced. It is *as if* the experimenter were responsible for the introduction of the experimental variable.

In typical experimental work in psychology, selection of participants is either random or on the basis of certain well-defined characteristics (e.g., sailors between the ages of 19 and 25). The participants are then presented with an experimental variable, frequently in a laboratory setting, which is a controlled environment. The results of the experiment then are often generalized to a larger population or in some way applied to real life (see the discussion of generalization of results at the end of the chapter). Real life occurs naturally, though, and sometimes it is impossible to select participants for an experiment and bring them to a well-controlled laboratory setting for precise recording of data. How could someone study a riot in the laboratory? And if someone could, would the conclusions be generalizable to a real riot? These topics are of interest to experimental and applied psychologists and need to be addressed. Essentially, the problem comes down to the fact that observations based on microcosmic life (as might be observed in the laboratory) may not be valid for macrocosmic life ("real" life).

---

[1]In order to give the reader a sense of the importance of these types of designs in psychology, surveys of graduate departments of psychology have been conducted that have asked which books are most frequently recommended to their graduate students who are preparing for departmental examinations. *Experimental and Quasi-Experimental Designs for Research* by Campbell and Stanley has been one of the most frequently recommended books throughout several surveys. (See Solso [1987b] for details.)

In laboratory work in experimental psychology we are dealing with a highly controlled environment, which has been called a **closed system.** The laboratory has many virtues, and many psychology experiments require this rigid control over stimuli. An **open system** is an environment over which we have little or no control, such as what is called the real world.

We have selected an example of a quasi-experimental design that deals with automobile accidents as related to the severity of traffic laws.

C A S E   S T U D Y

After a record number of automobile fatalities in the state of Connecticut several years ago, harsh action was taken against speeders. Once these measures were introduced, a decline in traffic fatalities was noted. Campbell (1969) made a detailed study of this phenomenon utilizing a quasi-experimental design. The data for Connecticut traffic fatalities are shown in Figure 4.7. In this figure we see a decline in fatalities from 1955 to 1956 after the introduction of harsh treatment of speeders. However, one can correctly argue that many other causes may have entered into this picture (e.g., road conditions may have been improved, better weather may have occurred in 1956 than in 1955, or better driver education may have been available). One might note, however, that the decline in fatalities continued after 1956.

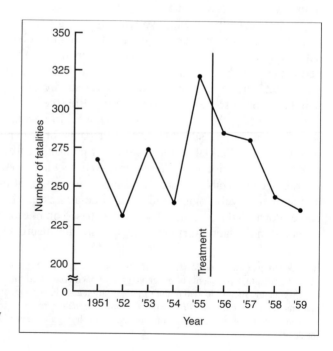

**FIGURE 4.7
Connecticut traffic fatalities, 1951–1959.**

From Campbell (1969). Copyright 1969 by the American Psychological Association. Reprinted by permission.

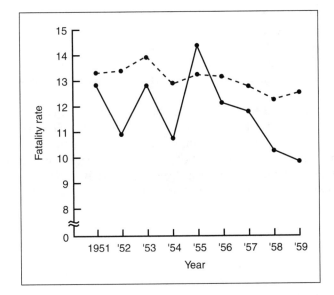

FIGURE 4.8
Connecticut traffic fatality rate (lower line) with the fatality rate of four comparable states.

From Campbell (1969). Copyright 1969 by the American Psychological Association. Reprinted by permission.

Another way to examine the data is to compare the automobile fatality rates among comparable states. Those data are shown in Figure 4.8. In this figure we see that although the fatality rates in these four states fell slightly from 1951 to 1959, the rate of decline for Connecticut was much greater, especially after the 1955 crackdown on speeders. The results, therefore, suggest that the 1955 treatment did have an effect on fatality rates.

In this case, no reasonable laboratory experiment could adequately test the effectiveness of the 1955 crackdown. Yet, the issue is important, and many similar real-world problems need solutions. Given the circumstances, and despite the loss of experimental control in these types of studies, quasi-experimental designs seem to render as close an approximation to valid conclusions as one could expect.

Functional Designs

In factorial designs, as we previously discussed, the usual procedure is to assign several subjects to each experimental treatment. Then the mean (or percent) of the subjects' scores is compared using the appropriate statistical test. While this procedure is common, a different research strategy is frequently used by researchers interested in what they have called "the experimental analysis of behavior." This area of research originated with B. F. Skinner, and people in this field of study are sometimes called "Skinnerians." The design has been called a

functional design because it uses functional definitions of terms and concepts. Developing a functional definition of a concept (e.g., punishment) is accomplished by specifying the relationship between a set of determining conditions and their effects on behavior, both of which can be precisely measured. The requirement that functional definitions be used to some extent leads one to adopt the type of research strategy described here.

Several differences can be noted in contrasting this research strategy with those previously discussed in this book. First, researchers in this area tend to be atheoretical in that they are more concerned with examining variables that control behavior than with testing a theory. Instead of viewing an experiment as a means of theory testing, experimenters systematically explore variables that control behavior with the assumption that theory will emerge inductively from the data.

Small *n* Designs

A second difference is that researchers in this area will sometimes use only one or two subjects, called a **small *n* design,** rather than large groups of subjects in each experimental treatment. These researchers tend to report their data not in the form of means and variances of several treatment groups, but in the form of a typical response curve. This curve is a segment of the subject's behavior that is deemed typical of his or her performance under the particular experimental conditions. Another difference is that a statistical analysis of the data sometimes is not used, but the typical curve (or curves) is presented for visual inspection of the response regularities that are representative of that particular stimulus condition.

A commonly used technique in small *n* studies is an **ABA design** in which a subject's untreated behavior (A) is observed first. This measure is sometimes called **baseline data,** as it serves as a point of departure from which to contrast the effects of experimental treatment. In the second phase the experimental variable is introduced and its effect is measured (B). In the final phase the experimental variable is absent and behavior is observed (A). Schematically, the design appears like this:

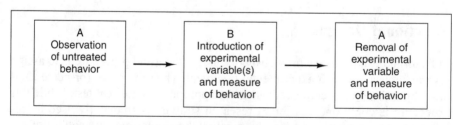

A behavioral therapist may, for example, be interested in treating a patient who overeats. In this case, the dependent variable could simply be the weight of the client. (In more elaborate designs, the dependent variable could involve a range of physiological and psychological measures—metabolic rate, strength, feelings of well-being, absenteeism, and so nn.) Thus, the observation of untreated behavior in the A phase could be the subject's weight before treatment. In the B phase the treatment or independent variable would be introduced, which could be a type of behavioral psychotherapy. Note that in some studies of this sort, two or more independent variables may be used (e.g., the therapist may use positive reinforcement and exerchse). It is critical to understand that the results of studies involving two or more independent variables do not permit unequivocal cause-and-effect conclusions. It is possible, however, to make a valid concluding statement to the effect that treatment by means of conditions 1 and 2 has led to the following results. In the case mentioned, if weight loss occurred, then a statement to the effect that behavioral therapy and exercise led to weight loss would seem justified, but not that behavioral therapy or exercise alone led to the weight loss.

Many of the previous designs are based on an internal validity in which the baseline data for a single subject serves as a control for subsequent observations. If an external control is used, the experiment uses the following setup, sometimes called an **AAA design:**

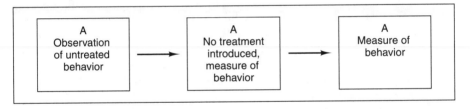

The ABA design can be extended to an ABABA design in which the experimental variable is reintroduced, or to an AB_1AB_2A or $AB_1AB_2AB_3A$ design, in which two or more different experimental variables are used. More elaborate designs are restricted only by the ingenuity of the psychologist.

Researchers performing these types of experiments sometimes use a highly controlled experimental situation. For example, an animal may be placed in a Skinner box—a chamber that typically contains only a bar to be pressed by the animal, a food dispenser, and some signal lights. In this simple situation, numerous independent variables can be manipulated, such as the particular **schedule of reinforcement** under which the food is dispensed. For example, the reinforcement may be dispensed on a fixed-ratio schedule, in which the animal is reinforced with a food pellet after it presses the bar a fixed number of times (e.g., 1 pellet for 1, 16, 47, or 100 presses). In a fixed-interval schedule the animal receives a food pellet for pressing the bar at least once in every fixed time period (e.g., every 30 seconds or every 4 minutes). The dependent variable in these cases is the frequency of the bar-pressing response, usually presented in the form of a cumulative frequency curve. The following example from Ferster and Perrott (1968) illustrates research using a schedule of reinforcement.

C A S E   S T U D Y

The apparatus used in this experiment was a Skinner box. This box was approximately 14 square inches and contained only a small Plexiglas plate and a food magazine on the same wall. The plate and food magazine were connected such that if the plate was pushed, a food pellet would be released from the food magazine. Both the plate and the releaser mechanism were attached to a cumulative recorder that consisted of a pen mounted on a sliding arm. The pen point rested on a strip of paper that passed slowly over a cylinder with the passage of time. If no responses were made by the pigeon the pen point merely left a horizontal line as the paper passed over the cylinder. Each time the pigeon pecked the Plexiglas plate, the pen moved a small step in one direction on the paper and did not return to its original position. When the paper was examined, it was rather easy to see the pigeon's rate of response by noting the rate at which the pen moved upward in a given time period.

The subject used in this experiment was a pigeon that had had previous experience with this apparatus. The pigeon was kept at 80 percent of its free-feeding body weight throughout the experiment, and was placed in the Skinner box for 1 hour per day over a 6-week period. In the box, the pigeon was reinforced for pecking the plate on a fixed-ratio schedule, meaning the pigeon received a food pellet after pecking the plate a fixed number of times. Several fixed-ratio values were used. During the first week, the pigeon received a food pellet after 70 pecks (FR 70); during the second week, a food pellet was received after 185 pecks (FR 185); and during the third week, the food pellet was received after 325 pecks (FR 325). The order was then reversed for the next 3 weeks.

Figure 4.9 shows the performance during each of the three fixed-ratio schedules. Each segment is an excerpt that is typical of the pigeon's daily performance on each schedule. The dots indicate the point at which reinforcement was deliv-

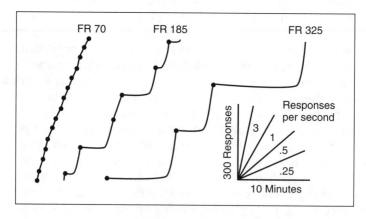

FIGURE 4.9   Rate of responding under three fixed-ratio schedules.

ered. The rate of performance in each segment can be estimated by comparing the overall slope of each segment with the slopes given in the grid in the lower right corner of the figure. The slope of FR 70 indicates that when the pigeon was responding, it pecked approximately three or four times per second. When 70 pecks were required for reinforcement, the bird's pecking was almost continuous, with a very slight pause after each reinforcement. For FR 185 there was a longer pause after each reinforcement; however, when the pigeon began pecking again, it started at a very rapid rate, which it maintained until the next reinforcement. The pause became much longer for FR 325; however, once the pigeon began pecking again, it did so at the same rate that was noted for FR 70 and FR 185. The experiment indicates that the number of pecks necessary for reinforcement does not affect the rate of pecking but does influence the length of pause between the dispensing of a reinforcement and the resumption of pecking.

This example illustrates the design strategy used in this area. A single subject was used to participate in three experimental conditions (i.e., three different fixed-ratio schedules). The data are presented in terms of typical response curves that indicate the regularities of response under the three conditions. No high-level statistics are used. The experimental situation itself is highly controlled, with precise measurement of the reinforcement conditions and the pecking responses.

This same design has been applied to a variety of subjects and experimental situations. The following example is an application of the same strategy in an experiment designed to control abnormal behavior in a chronic schizophrenic.

CASE STUDY

The strength of a response may decrease as a function of continued reinforcement. This phenomenon is called *satiation* and can be easily demonstrated in the laboratory. If an animal is given continuous reinforcement over a long period of time, the animal will stop emitting the reinforced response. Ayllon (1963) used the satiation procedure to control hoarding behavior in a psychiatric patient. The subject was a 47-year-old patient in a mental hospital who collected towels and stored them in her room. Although the nurses repeatedly retrieved the towels, the subject collected more and had an average of 20 in her room on any given day. Ayllon's procedure was, first, to establish a baseline, representing the average number of towels in the subject's room under normal conditions. After a seven-week observation period, a satiation period began. The nurses no longer removed towels from the subject's room; instead they began bringing towels into the room and simply handing them to the patient without comment. During this period the number of towels brought into the room by the nurses increased from 7 per day during the first week to 60 per day during the third week. The satiation period lasted for five

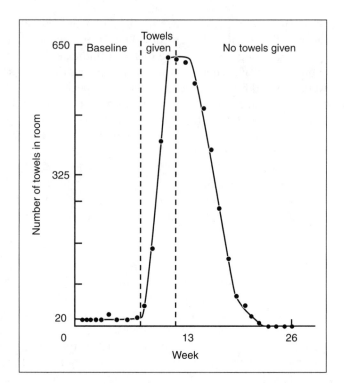

FIGURE 4.10
Number of towels in patient's room prior to, during, and after treatment.

weeks until the subject had accumulated 625 towels and had begun to remove the towels.

Figure 4.10 shows the mean number of towels in the patient's room per week over the life of the experiment. Note that this is not a cumulative record. After the satiation period the subject continued to remove towels from her room until, by week 22, there was an average of 1.5 towels in the room. This average was maintained through week 26. Ayllon (1963) made periodic observations throughout the next year and found that this average continued. The subject never returned to her towel-hoarding behavior, and no other problem behavior replaced it.

___

While the Ayllon (1963) experiment is an interesting demonstration of a "cure" for the hoarding behavior, one should not lose sight of the fact that it is also a nicely controlled experiment using a functional design. Ayllon (1) establishes a baseline for the frequency of a behavior, (2) institutes a well-designed experimental treatment, (3) terminates the experimental treatment, and (4) continues observation of the frequency of the behavior over an extended time period. A single subject is used, and no high-level statistics are used. A point to be emphasized is that sound experimental design is necessary to ascertain the regularity of behavior, whether the subject is a pigeon or a mental patient and whether the behavior is pecking or towel hoarding.

Additional Considerations: Generalization of Results

This chapter has been concerned with the operationalizing of terms and with some of the different types of experimental design used in psychology. While the basic logic of design is rather simple, the design and procedure themselves can become fairly complex, as has already been seen in the case of factorial designs and as will be seen in other types of design in the following chapters.

A point that needs to be considered is that experimenters are always confronted with the question of how far they can generalize the results and conclusions of their experiments. In the Paul (1966) experiment (see p. 40), which showed the superiority of behavior therapy over insight therapy, there are several questions that can be raised concerning the generality of the findings:

1. How far can the results be generalized across "illnesses?" Is behavior therapy superior only for speech phobia or for phobias in general? Does it work only for mild mental problems, including neurosis, or is it superior for all mental problems?
2. How far can the results be generalized across subjects? Are the findings applicable only to college students? Would the same results be found with children or with middle-aged people? Would the same results be found for less intelligent people?
3. Would the same results be found if the therapy time had been longer? Is behavior therapy effective as a quick therapy, while insight therapy needs more time to work?
4. Did improvement generalize to other speaking situations? Was the therapy only effective for speech class situations, for all classroom situations, or for all speaking situations? Was the improvement temporary or permanent? The question of **generalization of results** enters into all research and is not a criticism of an experiment. Rather, it points out the limitations of a single experiment. In a single experiment, the researcher strives for tight control over the variables so that he or she can be certain as to the validity of the results. Control is often achieved by limiting an experiment to a specific behavior, to a specific sample of subjects, to a specific measurement technique, and to a specific time period. While these techniques of control are helpful, perhaps essential, in ensuring the validity of the results, they also raise questions as to whether the results can be generalized. This is why one experiment often leads to several other experiments, and thus makes research an ongoing process with new problems to investigate and new knowledge to acquire.

A Final Note

Now you should have a pretty solid foundation for understanding experimental research and design. The next chapter focuses on how the designs you choose help you, the researcher, control variables in your experiment.

5 Experimental Design and Control

Certain systematic methods of scientific thinking may produce much more rapid progress than others.

—John R. Platt

Controlled Contrasts

Scientific experiments are based on observations of **contrasts,** and from these (commonly) controlled observations, **inferences** are drawn that are designed to generalize to a larger class of phenomena. This principle applies to physics, chemistry, botany, geology, astronomy, and psychology. In some scientific studies contrasts may be more obvious than in others. Take an example from physics: Here, the scientist might be interested in contrasting the effects of the mass of an object. Consider someone's reaction, for example, to hitting a regular tennis ball and hitting one made of lead. The contrast between how well the two balls bounce off (or through!) a tennis racket is pretty obvious. Then, from the study of the contrast, it is possible to make inferences about such general topics as the rate of speed of a regular tennis ball versus a lead one, and the tensile strength of nylon vs. KeVlar strings. Most scientific observations of contrasts are far more subtle, but by this example you can see the main idea. Science is based on observing contrasts. The observations may be in a controlled environment, as in a laboratory, or in nature. These observations form a system of knowledge.

In psychological research, the contrast is commonly between the influence of several levels of an independent variable on a group of subjects, while another group of subjects is observed in the absence of the independent variable. The first group is called an experimental group; the second group is a control group. Comparisons can then be made between all of the groups.

Scientific Inferences

Scientific theories are based on inferences. The arrangement of iron filings changes as a result of an electromagnetic field, much like human behavior and thought changes under a variety of conditions (e.g., drugs, social setting, motivation). Just as the physicist makes inferences about the characteristics of electromagnetic fields, experimental psychologists observe behavior caused by some variable. Psychologists can then sometimes develop models that generalize to a wide class of similar situations and lead to reliable laws about human behavior.

Because the validity of our observations is based on the characteristics of the subjects (as well as on the influence of the independent variable), it is extremely important that the experimental and control groups be as similar as possible. Think, for example, of the erroneous conclusions about electromagnetic fields that would emerge if one scientist used iron filings in the experiment and another scientist used aluminum filings—the observations would be different, not because the laws of electromagnetic flux changed but because different materials were used. And even if observations are valid, if the experiment lacks control, the results may be meaningless or may misdirect future research. These issues are important to the experimental psychologist, and techniques have evolved to safeguard against errors resulting from lack of proper control. We now turn to some of these possible error problems and procedures for their control.

Types of Control

The previous chapters have focused on design strategies. In the examples presented, the experimenter manipulated a particular variable (the independent variable) and observed the effect on the dependent variable. The experimenter controlled the independent variable by determining how much or what kind of variable was presented and, to whom. This is one form of experimental control. It was also emphasized that good design requires that the only variable being manipulated be the independent variable and that all other conditions be held constant for the various treatment groups. **Holding conditions constant** is a second type of experimental control. If the various treatment and control groups are treated exactly alike except for the independent variable, then any differences in the dependent variable must be due to the independent variable. If some other variable is affecting the results, this variable is usually called an **extraneous variable** or a **confounding variable.** The variable is extraneous in that it is an "extra" variable that has entered into the experiment. It is a confounding variable because the experimenter cannot be sure if the results are due to the independent variable or to the extraneous variable or both. Thus, the results are inconclusive, and the experiment must be repeated using a design that eliminates the influence of the extraneous variable.

A variable is extraneous only when it can be assumed to influence the dependent variable. In an experiment studying the perception of visual illusions, for example, variables such as the color of the subject's eyes, height, athletic ability, and knowledge of Swiss mountain cheese probably have no effect on the subject's perception, and the experimenter would be foolish to attempt to control all these individual differences. (Also, these differences tend to balance out when a representative sample of subjects is used in an experiment.) On the other hand, variables such as eyesight and illumination of illusions are likely to affect the results, and these should be controlled.

Whether a variable should be considered extraneous (and therefore in need of control) is largely a function of the dependent variable and will vary from experiment to experiment. Intelligence may be an extraneous variable for someone interested in learning but probably is insignificant in an experiment to determine the threshold of tones of varying frequencies. Knowledge of Swiss mountain cheese probably is unrelated to attitudes toward abortion but may be related to sensory discrimination of dairy products. Of course, anyone can make a case for possible relationships that are improbable (such as a limited level of intelligence being necessary to participate in an experiment on sensory thresholds, or knowledge of cheese being remotely related to abortion views). But don't chase ghosts. There are many important problems to be solved in psychology, and too often novice researchers get bogged down in petty problems.

Good experimental design is characterized by careful attention to the control of *real* extraneous variables and the investigation of *important* topics. Even the most exquisitely crafted experiment cannot save a stupid idea, and a brilliant idea is wasted in an experiment with a serious design problem. Sound judgment combined with knowledge can improve an experimental design so that potential extraneous variables are manageable, thus allowing the experimenter to control only those variables that can be reasonably assumed to influence the dependent variable.

This chapter is primarily concerned with controlling extraneous variables that occur when experimenters manipulate the independent variable. A related problem deals with ensuring that the various treatment groups have the same subject characteristics. This will be discussed in Chapter 6 because a set of specific techniques has evolved to handle this problem.

So far, considerable emphasis has been placed on holding all other conditions constant as a means of controlling for the effects of extraneous variables. Actually, this is only one of two very general techniques of controlling extraneous variables. A second method involves the use of treatment or control groups. All experiments use the first technique of control in that experimenters attempt to manipulate only the independent variable; some experimenters also add treatment or control groups to further control extraneous variables. This latter technique is frequently used when the experimental manipulation may contain an extraneous variable as well as the independent variable. Adding treatment or control groups allows the experimenter to separate, if possible, the effects of the extraneous variable from those of the independent variable.

Holding Conditions Constant

Lorge (1930) conducted an experiment comparing massed and distributed practice. The independent variable was the length of time between practice sessions. This was the only variable that was manipulated. All other variables were held constant: All treatment groups performed the same task; all treatment groups had the same amount of practice; the task was such that it would be difficult for the treatment groups with spaced practice to rehearse between practice sessions; the abilities of the participants in each treatment were equal; and so on. Potentially, all these factors could be extraneous variables. For instance, if one treatment group received more practice than another group, the results could be due to the amount of practice rather than to the spacing of practice. If the different treatment groups had performed different tasks, then the results could be due to a difference in task variables, such as difficulty, rather than being due to the spacing of practice. If the participants in one treatment had better task-related abilities than those in another treatment, then the results could be due to differences in the abilities rather than to the spacing of practice. By ensuring that these variables were the same for all treatment groups, Lorge eliminated them as explanations for his results. This is the logic behind holding all conditions except the independent variable constant.

Subject Variables.   Recall that subject variables are those inherent in the individual subject, and are used as an experimenter-selected independent variable. Subject variables cannot be randomly assigned, so by carefully, and systematically selecting subjects with a particular characteristic, the experimenter is still controlling an independent variable. Holding conditions constant is essential to good experimental design and is easily understood by the beginning psychology student. However, as will be seen in the following examples, even the most competent researchers may unknowingly violate this principle. While it is not possible to construct a checklist of extraneous variables (since they vary from situation to situation), there are some areas in which problems are especially prominent. For example, when the independent variable is a subject variable, there is always a danger that it is related in some systematic manner to another subject variable. If this is true, then any experimental results might be due to the second subject variable, introduced inadvertently, rather than the one the researcher introduced. This problem is called a subject variable–subject variable confound, which is defined as potentially erroneous results which may be attributed to secondary causes based on a confounding or joining of subject variables. You may think (or hypothesize) that you are measuring the effects of subjects but you are in fact measuring a component of the group.

To illustrate this problem, consider a study in which the researcher hypothesized that an authoritarian person would have more difficulty learning complex material than a person who was not authoritarian. This hypothesis was based on the assumption that high-authoritarian people think in a rather simplistic manner and therefore would have difficulty learning complex material. To test this hypothesis, the investigator had high-authoritarian subjects and low-authoritarian subjects learn some complex material. When tested on the material, the low-authoritarian group recalled considerably more than the high-authoritarian group. One criticism that several reviewers leveled against this study was that it is well known that there is an inverse relationship between authoritarianism and intelligence—authoritarian people tend to be less intelligent, and vice versa. Therefore, the fact that the high-authoritarian group learned less could be explained by the fact that they were less intelligent, and authoritarianism may have had nothing to do with the results.

If a subject variable is not being manipulated, then a subject variable–subject variable confound is of little danger. However, the experimenter must be aware of other possible extraneous variables. Some of these problems will be discussed later in this chapter.

Experimental Paradigms

A **paradigm** in experimental psychology is a model or pattern an investigator uses to organize research. In this section, we introduce four experimental paradigms and the methods of control in each, namely:

Model 1.   Between subjects design
Model 2.   Matched subjects design
Model 3.   Within subjects design
Model 4.   Factorial design

Some of these paradigms and controls will be discussed further in later sections.

Here, we will now turn to the four types of design paradigms using a single example:

Suppose that experimenters are interested in how the color of a wine influences how much a person enjoys it. They have developed a device that can change the color of wine without changing its taste. In the test, the natural color of one wine is dark ruby, which can be changed to a deep green. The dependent variable in this experiment is the rating of enjoyment on a 5-point scale; the independent variable is the color of the wine. Since *enjoyment* is not a precise term, it is essential that the experimenters operationally define the term to include the features that are important. For example, one might include taste, bouquet, and color as important features.

The following box shows that even this simple experiment presents some challenging experimental design problems, including the temperature of the wine (should be held constant), the lighting (must not be too dark to see the wine nor too bright), the sequence (tasting one wine first may influence the evaluation of subsequent wines), the experience of the tasters (sophisticated wine buffs may evaluate differently than "chug-a-luggers"), and the ambience (testing should be done individually rather than in groups in which peer pressure may influence one's evaluation). The experiment may be conducted in several ways.

Wine-Tasting Experiment

Independent variable = Color
Dependent variable = Rating (1–5)

:_____	:_____	:_____	:_____	:_____
1	2	3	4	5
Not		Moderately		Very
Enjoyable		Enjoyable		Enjoyable

Potential control problems:

Temperature

Lighting

Sequence

Subject experience

Ambience and peer influence

Model 1: Between-Subjects Design

In one paradigm, called the **between subjects design** or **randomized subjects design** (Model 1), one group is given the artificially colored wine (the experimental group), while another group is given the naturally colored wine (the control group). In this design the subjects in one group are independent from the other group. The sample of subjects for this experiment is defined as 16 university students between the ages of 21 and 30. Although there are no rules governing the size of a sample, in general, 8 participants (or observations) per group for an experiment of this sort would be considered the minimum, and it would be prudent to have twice that number. From this sample, the participants are randomly assigned to either the experimental or the control group. For convenience, we have labeled the subjects S_1, S_2, S_3, ... S_{16}. The arrangement of this procedure might look like the following:

Model 1. Between Subjects Design

Experimental Group (artificially colored wine) DATA		Control Group (naturally colored wine) DATA	
S_1	1	S_9	5
S_2	2	S_{10}	4
S_3	2	S_{11}	3
S_4	1	S_{12}	5
S_5	2	S_{13}	5
S_6	1	S_{14}	4
S_7	1	S_{15}	4
S_8	4	S_{16}	5

Wine-tasting groups: Independent variable–color of wine
Dependent variable–evaluation of quality

In this experiment we have recorded some fictitious data, similar to the data that might be collected in an actual experiment. These data can be further analyzed by means of a t-test. The inspection of raw data is sometimes fascinating in that it lets you know what participants are actually doing, but it lacks mathematical precision. Statistical analysis would indicate that the differences between the groups are statistically significant. While the preconceived notion that green wine is "yucky" is supported by the data, experimental psychologists view these matters with more cautious language. All one can state with scientific certainty is that the differences between the two groups are highly unlikely (i.e., less than 1 in 100) by chance alone. The next step is an inference, albeit a highly probable one, in which an experimenter might conclude that naturally colored ruby wine is preferred over the same wine that has been artificially colored to be green. The reasons for this preference may be cultural, and further inferences are commonly made.

This paradigm is common in psychological experiments, and if the sample is large and representative enough, one might assume that the subject variables that might influence the results (e.g., having a large number of expert wine tasters) will be equally distributed between the two groups on the basis of random distribution.

Model 2: Matched Subjects Design

On the other hand, one may have reason to believe that a subject variable (such as wine-tasting experience) may be so critical to the results that the subjects should be matched on that variable. The assumption is that people who have had experience have developed a level of sensory discrimination that allows them to make critical judgments. Such a design is called a **matched subjects design** or **matched pair design** (Model 2) and might look like this:

Model 2. Matched Subjects Design

Experimental Group (artificially colored wine) DATA		Control Group (naturally colored wine) DATA	
S_{1a}	2	S_{9a}	4
S_{2b}	3	S_{10b}	5
S_{3c}	2	S_{11c}	5
S_{4d}	1	S_{12d}	5
S_{5e}	1	S_{13e}	4
S_{6f}	2	S_{14f}	4
S_{7g}	3	S_{15g}	5
S_{8h}	1	S_{16h}	4

Wine-tasting groups: Independent variable–color of wine
Dependent variable–evaluation of quality
Matching variable–wine-tasting experience

In this example we have labeled the subjects S_1, S_2, ... S_{16} but have added the subscript a, b, ... h to show that S_{1a} and S_{9a} are matched on some basis. In this case we have matched the subjects on wine-tasting experience so that each pair of subjects has about the same level of experience. Furthermore, in this example we may choose to select only people who are expert wine tasters, weeding out the chug-a-luggers. Other experiments may call for matching other attributes, such as sex, age, intelligence, running ability, or training. This design can be powerful, provided that the matching variable is germane to the dependent variable. Also, the independent measure upon which matches are made must be valid. To match people on the basis of wine-tasting experience[1] or intelligence, for example, with an invalid test for these characteristics spoils the basic assumption of this method.

In Appendix A we illustrate the computational procedures used in matched subject designs. This test is sometimes called the **correlated *t*-test** or **dependent *t*-test,** as the two groups are "co-related" or "dependent" in some important dimension. Analysis of the fictitious data indicates the difference between the two groups is highly significant.

Model 3: Within-Subjects Design

A third design, called a **within-subjects design** or **a repeated measures design** (Model 3), is characterized by each subject being exposed to two or more experimental conditions. In our example, each subject would taste both kinds of wine and, as such, would serve as his or her own control.

As shown, S_1 tastes the experimental (colored) wine and the control (natural) wine. By allowing each subject to serve as his or her own control, this design makes it possible to gather more data because two measures rather than one are made for each subject. Reducing the number of subjects in an experiment may be practical with a limited subject sample. However, in conducting a repeated measure design, one problem can arise from the sequence in which the substances are presented. It may be that, when tasting wine, the second taste may seem more enjoyable than the first, not because the taste is better but perhaps because the taster has a slightly rosier outlook on life in general. To safeguard against this, one must create a **balanced sequence.** In this case, balancing the sequence would be achieved by having half the subjects taste the colored wine first, while the other half tasted the natural wine first. We can express this design as shown on page 84.

In this case, S_1 through S_8 would taste and evaluate the control wine first and then the experimental wine, while S_9 through S_{16} would reverse the sequence. Data could also be analyzed by statistical procedures that would identify the

---

[1]We can think of people who have a great deal of wine-drinking experience (i.e., they have consumed copious quantities of wine) but who are not wine connoisseurs!

Model 3. Within Subjects Design

Control Condition (naturally colored wine) DATA		Experimental Condition (artificially colored wine) DATA	
S_1		S_1	
S_2		S_2	
S_3		S_3	
S_4		S_4	
S_5		S_5	
S_6		S_6	
S_7		S_7	
S_8		S_8	

Experimental Condition (artificially colored wine) DATA		Control Condition (naturally colored wine) DATA	
S_9		S_9	
S_{10}		S_{10}	
S_{11}		S_{11}	
S_{12}		S_{12}	
S_{13}		S_{13}	
S_{14}		S_{14}	
S_{15}		S_{15}	
S_{16}		S_{16}	

Wine-tasting groups: Independent variable–color of wine
Dependent variable–evaluation of quality

influence of sequencing. Further elaboration of the design is also possible. One could, for example, have a double or triple repeated design, but the considerations of these designs might be intoxicating.

Model 4: Factorial Design

In the previous models, we have been concerned with the effect of a single independent variable on a dependent variable. Frequently, however, psychologists are interested in studying the effects of several independent variables on a dependent variable. Such factorial designs are very useful in experimental psychology, a fact which has been pointed out in Chapter 4. Although these designs are not specifically constructed to control for subject variables, they are reiterated here to show how these variables may be used in a factorial design. In the present context, suppose that the experimenter chooses wine color and the type of grape used as the two independent variables. In this paradigm, the color of the wine would be either natural or artificial, but, in addition, three types of wines (derived from three different grapes) would be used. For the sake of illustration, a Pinot Noir, a Zinfandel, and a Chardonnay will be used. A simple representation of this type of design can be shown in the following 2×3 matrix (2 columns, 3 rows):

Factorial Design: Within-subjects

		Factor 1 (color)	
		level 1 (natural)	level 2 (artificial)
	level 1 (Pinot Noir)	S_1, S_2, S_3, S_4	S_1, S_2, S_3, S_4
Factor 2 (type of wine)	level 2 (Zinfandel)	S_1, S_2, S_3, S_4	S_1, S_2, S_3, S_4
	level 3 (Chardonnay)	S_1, S_2, S_3, S_4	S_1, S_2, S_3, S_4

In this design, the same subjects are treated to all conditions, as in the repeated measure design. Thus, in Model 4 it is possible to integrate subject control techniques. It must be pointed out, however, that other subject control techniques, such as the independent subject design, may be used in a factorial experiment. This design could be illustrated as shown on the next page.

Factoral Design: Between-subjects

		Factor 1 (color)	
		level 1 (natural)	level 2 (artificial)
	level 1 (Pinot Noir)	S_1, S_2, S_3, S_4	$S_{13}, S_{14}, S_{15}, S_{16}$
Factor 2 (type of wine)	level 2 (Zinfandel)	S_5, S_6, S_7, S_8	$S_{17}, S_{18}, S_{19}, S_{20}$
	level 3 (Chardonnay)	$S_9, S_{10}, S_{11}, S_{12}$	$S_{21}, S_{22}, S_{23}, S_{24}$

Use of Treatment and Control Groups

A control group is defined as a group of subjects similar to an experimental group that is exposed to all the conditions of an investigation except the experimental variable (independent variable). In some cases the control group and the experimental group should be drawn at random from the entire population in order to make generalizations about the results of an experiment.

Some of the techniques used to control extraneous variables have already been briefly examined. Let us consider in more detail the Paul (1966) experiment (see p. 48) on the treatment of speech-giving phobia. The experimenter wanted to compare the effectiveness of two types of therapy. In addition, he had to consider what extraneous variables might vary as the level of a therapy varied. If an extraneous variable varied along with a therapy, then any improvement might be attributed to the extraneous variable rather than to the therapy itself. There are two well-known extraneous variables present when a subject receives some sort of therapy. First, it is well established that some people showing symptoms of a behavior problem will improve over time without receiving any specific treatment. This phenomenon is called **spontaneous remission;** there is a disappearance of symptoms that takes place spontaneously, that is, without any apparent treatment for the problem. In a therapy experiment, the experimenter cannot be sure if the subject's improvement is due to the therapy itself or to spontaneous remission.

Second, it is known that some people who think they are receiving treatment for their problems may show considerable improvement even when, in fact, they are not receiving treatment. This is called the **placebo effect.** The term comes from a Latin word meaning "to please" and was discovered by physicians who would give patients medically inert substances (e.g., sugar water) that resembled an active medication in order to please a patient rather than to provide physical benefit. Interestingly enough, they discovered that some patients improved upon receiving placebo medication, especially those whose illnesses seemed to be psychosomatic. However, it's important to note that placebo effects can occur even when there is a verifiable illness. Since the placebo effect also is assumed to occur in the treatment of psychological problems, any improvement in the therapy groups may have been due to this effect rather than to the therapy itself.[2]

To separate the improvement due to spontaneous remission, to the placebo effect, and to the therapy itself, Paul (1966) used two control groups. Table 5.1 shows the four experimental groups as well as the variables influencing improvement in each of these groups. As indicated in the table, the experimenter can now separate the effects of the various variables on the subjects' improvement. For example, we can subtract the amount of improvement shown in the placebo control group from that in each therapy group. This would give us an indication of the effectiveness of each therapy after we have eliminated the effect of the two extraneous variables.

Researchers will also frequently add treatment groups to an experimental design to ensure that the results are not caused by an extraneous variable. Suppose that in the Asch (1952) study on impression formation (see page 45) Asch had used only a single treatment group, which received the positive adjectives first and the negative adjectives last. With this setup, the subject's evaluation of the person would be generally positive, and this would support the hypothesis of a primacy effect in impression formation. If only this single treatment group were used, several criticisms would arise. One would be that Asch's negative adjectives were not really very negative, and thus the person would have been evaluated positively regardless of the order. Another criticism would be that people tend to evaluate other people positively regardless of what information is given—that is, people look for good traits in others and tend to like others. If this hypothesis is valid, then Asch would have observed a positive evaluation regardless of the order or type of adjectives used. But the experimental design used by Asch eliminated these possible criticisms. One of his treatment groups received a positive-to-negative order of adjective presentation; the second treatment group received a negative-to-positive

TABLE 5.1 **Variables Influencing Improvement in the Four Experimental Groups of the Paul Experiment**

| Experimental Groups | Variables Present Influencing Improvement | | | |
	Therapy	Placebo	Spontaneous Remission	Percent Improvement
1. Behavior therapy	Yes	Yes	Yes	100
2. Insight therapy	Yes	Yes	Yes	60
3. Placebo	No	Yes	Yes	73
4. No treatment	No	No	Yes	32

[2]See "The Placebo Effect" by Brown (1998) in *Scientific American* for an interesting discussion on the healing effect of placebos.

presentation. The subjects' evaluation of the person was positive in the first treatment and negative in the second treatment; therefore, the previously mentioned criticisms and explanations are not valid. Note also that they are demonstrated to be invalid because Asch used two treatment groups instead of one and obtained negative ratings from subjects.

It is difficult to formulate specific principles about the control of extraneous variables. An experimenter usually begins with some problem to be solved or some hypothesis to be tested. In designing an experiment, the experimenter must keep in mind that any extraneous variables that could explain the results have to be eliminated. Certainly this would involve keeping all conditions except the independent variable constant, but it also may include the use of additional treatment or control groups. The best way for the student to learn what extraneous variables are most common in any specific research area is to read experiments in that area. In this manner the student can become aware of the designs used in that area and the extraneous variables that have to be controlled. Some experiments involving control problems follow. The purpose of presenting these examples is to illustrate some problems that have arisen in the past with the hope that they will aid the student in analyzing designs for control problems in the future.

Control Problem: Sleep Learning

C A S E   S T U D Y

An experiment was conducted to determine if learning could take place during sleep. The material to be learned was the English equivalents of German words, and the subjects were ten college students who reported that they had no knowledge of the German language. Each subject slept in a comfortable bed in a sound-proof, air-conditioned laboratory room. Each subject retired about midnight, and at approximately 1:30 A.M. the experimenter entered the room and asked the subject if he or she was asleep. If there was no response, the experimenter turned on a recording that contained German words and their English equivalents: for example, "*ohne* means without." There were 60 different words on the recording, which was played continuously until 4:30 A.M. If the subject awoke during the night, he or she was to call out to the experimenter, and the recording would be stopped until the subject was asleep again. To test for learning, the 60 German words were played to the subjects in the morning, and after each word the subjects reported what they thought was the English equivalent of the word. The number of German words correctly identified was the dependent measure. The results indicated that the mean number of words correctly identified was nine (out of a possible 60), and the highest number correctly identified by any subject was 20. The experimenters interpreted these results as supporting the hypothesis that learning can occur during sleep.

The experiment has several important implications. At a theoretical level it suggests that during sleep the brain is actively processing information received by the senses. At a practical level it suggests that sleep learning may be an easy and effortless way to learn. It should be a boon to college students who, instead of staying up all night to cram for an exam, could simply turn on a tape recorder and go to sleep.

While these results are quite exciting, and one would like them to be valid, two major criticisms have been leveled against the experiment. The first was the failure to use a control group of subjects who had not been presented the learning material but who were given the recall test. While it is true that all subjects said that they had no knowledge of the German language, they may have been able to guess the meanings of some of the words. For example, the German word *Mann* means "man" in English. Furthermore, some German words are frequently used in English, particularly in old war movies—for example, *Schwein* (pig), *nein* (no), and *ja* (yes). Thus, the apparent effects of sleep learning may actually be due to the subjects' ability to guess some words and knowledge of other words; a control group would have checked for this.

A second criticism dealt with the experimenter's operational definition of sleep. Sleep was defined as what the subject did between 1:30 A.M and 4:30 A.M., unless the subject reported being awake. But it is known that there are various levels of sleep, ranging from drowsiness to very deep sleep. It is also known that at the drowsiness level the subject has partial awareness of external stimuli, but at the level at which sleep technically begins there is little or no awareness of external stimuli. In this experiment there was no way of knowing what material was presented at what level of sleep. Therefore, it could be argued that any learning that occurred may have taken place at a drowsiness level rather than at a true sleep level.

CASE STUDY

Simon and Emmons (1956) designed an experiment to correct for the previously mentioned problems. The materials to be learned consisted of 96 general information questions and their answers. They were presented in question form—for example, "In what kind of store did Ulysses S. Grant work before the war?" The answer was then given: "Before the war, Ulysses S. Grant worked in a hardware store." Two groups of subjects were used: an experimental group, who were given the answers to the questions while sleeping, and a control group, who simply took the learning test without having the answers played. To begin the experiment both groups were given the questions and asked to guess the answers. Those questions that the subjects answered correctly were eliminated from the test. Next, the experimental group was presented with the questions and answers while asleep. During this period, recordings were made of their brain waves using an electroencephalograph (EEG). Because brain activity varies at different stages of sleep, EEG records enable experimenters to determine accurately the depth of sleep. As each answer was presented to the subject, the experimenter recorded the subject's level of sleep. Thus, the experimenter had a record of the level of sleep at which each answer was given.

In the morning, the experimental group was tested on the material that was presented during the night. The multiple-choice test consisted of the question and five answers. The subject was to guess which of the answers was correct. A multiple-choice test was used since it probably is a better measure of sleep learning because the subject only has to recognize the correct answer rather than recall it. The control group also took this test.

After the test scores were received, the experimenters separated the questions for each experimental subject into categories determined by the level of sleep at which the answer was played. The experimenters used eight levels of sleep, which have been condensed into three categories in Table 5.2 where the percentage of correct answers in these categories is shown.

The data indicate that considerable learning took place when the experimental participants were awake, and moderate learning appeared at a drowsy level. But there was no apparent learning when the participants were at a true sleep level. At this level the performance of the experimental group was the same as that of the control group, who had no learning experience. The 23 percent correct for the control group represents what could be expected if the participants guessed.

In looking at the design of this experiment, it is important to note that the experimenters instituted several crucial control procedures to allow for a rather clear-cut test of sleep learning. First, to make sure that what appeared to be information learned during sleep was not actually information that was previously known, the experimenters gave all participants a pretreatment test on the material and eliminated the answers participants already knew. Second, because a certain proportion of the answers on the multiple-choice test could be gotten by guessing, the experimenters used a control group to find out what that percentage would be. Third, the experimenters identified different levels of sleep and noted what answers were presented at each level. This technique made it possible to separate material presented when the participant was awake, in a state of drowsiness, and in a state of true sleep. Using these controls procedures, the results suggest that no learning takes place at a true sleep level.

TABLE 5.2   Percentage of Answers Correct at Three Sleep Levels

	Level of Sleep		
	Awake	Drowsy	Asleep
Experimental group	92	65	23
Control group	24	23	23

Control Problem: Social Deprivation and Social Reinforcement

CASE STUDY

It has been repeatedly demonstrated that for animals who have been deprived of food, the effectiveness of a food pellet as a reinforcer is considerably enhanced. An experiment was conducted to determine if the same results would occur with social deprivation and social reinforcement in children. Subjects were 6-year-olds in an elementary school.

The effectiveness of social reinforcement was measured using a marble game. The game consisted of a box with two holes in it in which the participant was to drop marbles one at a time into one of the two holes. For the first 4 minutes of the game the experimenter watched the child play the game. For the next 10 minutes the experimenter verbally reinforced the child every time he or she put a marble in the hole that was used least in the initial 4-minute period. The verbal reinforcement consisted of the experimenter saying "good" or "fine" every time the child put a marble in that hole. The dependent variable was the amount of increase in placing marbles in the desired hole from the 4-minute to the 10-minute period.

To determine the effects of social deprivation, the participants were assigned randomly to one of three treatments. In the social deprivation treatment, the participants were left alone in a room for 20 minutes prior to playing the game. In the nondeprivation treatment, the participants started playing the game immediately. In the social satiation treatment, the participants spent 20 minutes before the game talking with the experimenter while they were drawing and cutting out pictures.

The results indicated that the children in the deprivation treatment showed a greater increase in putting marbles in the desired hole than did either of the other two treatments. Furthermore, the increase was greater in the nondeprivation treatment than in the satiation treatment. The results were interpreted as supporting the hypothesis that the effectiveness of social reinforcement is influenced by conditions of social satiation or deprivation in a manner similar to that found for food or water deprivation.

The previous experiment has wide theoretical implications, in that it suggests that social drives seem to be subject to the same laws that have been established using the primary appetitive drives, such as hunger. The experiment's authors also have developed a nice experimental situation to test their hypothesis in that the experimental manipulations seem fairly clear cut and the dependent measure is easy to record without ambiguity. However, soon after the experiment was published, criticisms of the experiment began to appear, arguing that the results may have been caused by the failure to control extraneous variables.

One criticism of the experiment pointed out that when the experimenters were manipulating social deprivation, they also manipulated general sensory deprivation. For example, in the deprivation treatment, the child was not only isolated from other people but also had no toys with which to play. In the satiation treatment the child not only interacted with the experimenter but also drew and cut out pictures. Thus, the experimenters manipulated an extraneous variable (general sensory deprivation) along with the social deprivation, and the results of the experiment might have been caused by this extraneous variable. Stevenson and Odom (1962) tested this alternative explanation of the results by comparing three groups of subjects. Before playing the marble game, one group of children was isolated and played with attractive toys for 15 minutes, one group was isolated for 15 minutes without toys, and a third group began playing the marble game immediately. The results indicated no difference in the task performance of the two isolation groups, but both groups had higher levels of performance (i.e., dropped more marbles in the desired hole) than the no-isolation group. Since there was no difference in the task performance of the two isolation groups (both of which were socially deprived, but only one of which was deprived of toys), then the higher performance must have been due to the social deprivation. This supports the original interpretation of the experiment, and the influence of the extraneous variable was apparently very minor.

A second group of researchers raised a different criticism of the experiment. The crucial point of this criticism was that being placed in a strange environment by a strange adult should arouse anxiety in 6-year-olds. The greatest anxiety should occur in the deprivation treatment, in which the subjects were left alone in a strange room for 20 minutes. The next highest level of anxiety should occur in the nondeprivation situation, in which the subjects were led directly to the game situation. The least anxiety should occur in the satiation treatment, because after 20 minutes of friendly conversation with the experimenter, the subject should be somewhat comfortable in the experimenter's presence. Because there is evidence demonstrating that heightened anxiety improves performance on some learning tasks (especially simple learning tasks), the results of the experiment could be explained by the difference in anxiety arousal in the three treatments, leaving no need to postulate some social drive.

To test this hypothesis, Walter and Parke (1964) used a 2×2 factorial design in which they used two levels of isolation (either leaving the child alone for 10 minutes or starting the game immediately) and two levels of anxiety arousal. In the low-anxiety condition, the experimenter treated the subject in a pleasant and friendly manner, and in the high-anxiety condition the experimenter treated the subject in a rather cold and abrupt manner. Using these treatments, (1) no statistically significant difference was found in performance between the two levels of isolation, which is evidence against the social drive interpretation; (2) subjects in the high-anxiety treatment performed better than subjects in the low-anxiety treatment, which supports the anxiety arousal interpretation; and (3) the interaction effect was not statistically significant. Thus, it appears that an extraneous variable (arousal level) may have determined the results of the original experiment, and the social deprivation interpretation may be invalid.

Control Problem: Perceptual Defense

The following experiment suggests that there is a process in the unconscious that determines whether a word is anxiety-provoking and that conscious recognition of such words is prevented or at least delayed. This is the notion of **perceptual defense,** and it has far-reaching implications concerning human behavior.

CASE STUDY

It has long been suggested that the human body has certain mechanisms that protect it from anxiety-provoking stimuli. One such mechanism is called perceptual defense. An experiment was designed to test the perceptual defense hypothesis by presenting to participants neutral and taboo words on a tachistoscope. The experimenter theorized that taboo words are anxiety provoking, and while the participant may recognize them at an unconscious level, a perceptual defense mechanism would delay the participant's recognition of them at a conscious level. Based on this assumption, it was hypothesized that longer exposures would be necessary for the recognition of taboo words than for neutral words.

The subjects were eight male and eight female college students. Each participant was tested individually with both a male and a female experimenter present. Eleven neutral words (e.g., apple, trade) and seven taboo words (e.g., whore, bitch) were presented to each participant in a predetermined order. An ascending threshold method was used to determine the point at which the subject recognized the word. For each word, the shutter was set at a very fast exposure speed (0.01 second), and the exposure was gradually lengthened until the subject verbalized the word correctly. This process was repeated for each of the 18 words.

The mean threshold for the recognition of the neutral words was 0.053 second, and the mean threshold for the recognition of the taboo words was 0.098 second. The difference between the two means was statistically significant. Because it took longer exposures (higher thresholds) for the participants to recognize the taboo words, the experimenter concluded that the perceptual defense hypothesis was supported.

It did not take long for other researchers to criticize the design. Howes and Solomon (1950) raised two methodological points. First, they suggested that the results may have been due to the subjects' reluctance to report a taboo word until they were absolutely positive of the identification of the word. The subjects might have been particularly reluctant to verbalize these words in front of an experimenter of the opposite sex. A second methodological point was that neutral words appear much more frequently in print than do taboo words, and therefore the subjects' quicker recognition of the neutral words may have occurred because they had seen these words more frequently. In a follow-up experiment Howes and Solomon

(1951) demonstrated the validity of a word frequency hypothesis. They obtained a listing of the frequency at which some 30,000 words appear in print. They chose 60 words of varying frequencies (all nontaboo words) and determined the recognition thresholds of each word using a procedure similar to that in the previous example. They found a high negative correlation (approximately −.79) between the frequency at which the word appeared in print and its recognition threshold, that is, the more frequently the word appeared in print, the lower its recognition threshold. While this experiment demonstrates that word frequency is a plausible explanation for the results of the original experiment, it still can be argued that taboo words show a higher threshold even if frequency is controlled.

Postman, Bronson, and Gropper (1952) made a more direct test of the word frequency explanation by determining how frequently some taboo words appeared in print and matching them with neutral words that appeared in print at the same frequency. The list of words was presented to the subjects using a procedure similar to that of the previous example. The results indicated no support for the perceptual defense hypothesis. In fact, it was found that the recognition threshold for the taboo words was significantly lower than for the neutral words. This was probably due to an underestimation of the frequency of the taboo words. Although research in this area continues, it appears that the early experimental support for the perceptual defense phenomenon may have been due to the confounding variable of word frequency.

Control Problem: One-Trial Learning

A special type of control problem is found in cases where learning is based on a single trial (**one-trial learning**). This problem also can be found in similar cases. The following example illustrates the problem.

C A S E   S T U D Y

When children are learning to read the alphabet, they are shown the letters A, B, C, and so on, while the teacher pronounces the letters. This is repeated until the child learns the association between the printed letter and the verbalized sound. There is a controversy among learning theorists as to whether this association is built up gradually (incremental process) or whether it occurs in an all-or-none fashion. The latter school of thought would say that if, after some learning trials, the child cannot verbalize a letter's name after being shown that letter, then no association between the letter and its name has taken place. The former school of thought would argue that some association has taken place, but that it is not yet of sufficient strength to allow the child to give the correct answer.

A rather ingenious experiment was performed to determine which of the previous theories was correct. The participant's task was to learn eight nonsense syllable pairs. Each pair was presented to the participants on a separate card. After a participant had seen all eight pairs, he or she then was shown the first nonsense syllable of each of the pairs and asked to give the second nonsense syllable. For example, the participant might have been shown POZ-LER. In the recall test the participant would be shown only the first syllable, POZ, and would have to supply the second syllable.

Two experimental groups were used. For the first experimental group, the experimenter replaced in each trial every nonsense syllable pair that had not been learned. For example, the participant was shown eight pairs and then given a learning test on these eight. Any pair that was not recalled was dropped, and a new pair was substituted into the list of eight. The eight cards (which then included only learned pairs and new pairs) were shown again to the participant, and another recall test was given. The experimenter again eliminated those pairs that were not recalled and substituted new pairs. This process continued until the participant could recall all eight pairs in a single trial. The second experimental group was treated like the first except that these participants were shown the same eight cards on each trial. Thus, eight pairs were shown, a recall test was given, the same eight pairs were shown, another recall test was given, and so on. This process was repeated until the participant could recall all eight pairs in a single trial.

The experimenter then compared the number of trials it took to learn all eight pairs in each treatment group. The mean number of trials for perfect recall for both groups was exactly the same (8.1). Because pairs learned in the first experimental group were learned in one trial (or else they were thrown out), and because there was no difference in the average number of trials necessary to learn the eight pairs, it was concluded that learning (i.e., associations) occurred in an all-or-none fashion. Stated a little differently, the experimenter argued that a gradual buildup of associations through repetition could have occurred in the second experimental group. If repetition is important in learning, then this second group should have learned the eight pairs faster than the first group, who learned eight pairs on a single trial without any repetition. Because there was no difference between the two groups, it was concluded that repetition is unnecessary for learning.

As might be expected, this experiment caused some excitement, particularly among those who support an incremental view of associative learning (since the experiment suggests that this view of learning is invalid). It was not long after the experiment was published that research criticizing it began to appear. One major criticism was that the more difficult pairs were probably dropped from the first treatment group, and thus the final list in this treatment consisted only of the easier pairs. No pairs were dropped from the second treatment group, and thus the final list learned by these subjects consisted of both easy and difficult pairs. The failure of the experiment to find quicker learning in the second treatment was due, therefore, to the fact that the list learned by this group was more difficult than the final list learned by the first treatment group.

In one test of the item-selection hypothesis, Underwood, Rehula, and Keppel (1962) repeated the previous procedure except that they added a control group that received lists composed of the pairs that subjects in the dropout condition received on their last learning trial. Subjects in this condition were given the same word pairs on each trial. The results indicated that subjects in this condition learned the pairs more rapidly than did subjects given a list containing a random sample of all of the pairs used. Thus, it appears that the subjects in the dropout condition of the original experiment were learning easier pairs, and this may explain the results.

A Final Note

The case studies in this book don't just provide you examples so you can see experimental principles at work. They also provide you an opportunity to apply your knowledge and become better versed in experimental design and how to avoid problems. For each of the control problems described in this chapter, consider the experiment, the initial problem, and the corrected problem, and (1) identify the independent variable, (2) identify the dependent variable, and (3) explain how the design corrected for the initial control problem.

6 Control of Subject Variables

The basic problem in the investigation of subject variables . . . is that whatever differences are observed in behavior may be caused by their confounded variables.
—Kantowitz, Roediger, and Elmes (1988)

Equality of Subjects in Treatment Groups

Psychological experiments focus on the actions of some species of animal. Since psychological research uses subjects (human or otherwise), it is not surprising that psychologists have devoted considerable attention to controlling extraneous variables that are due to characteristics of the subjects. In fact, a set of specific techniques has evolved that is applicable to a wide variety of research situations. This chapter will discuss the essential features of these techniques. However, it is important to note that many personality and social psychologists pay special empirical and theoretical attention to individual differences.

In research, the performance of one treatment group is often compared with that of another group. These groups consist of subjects who differ on a variety of traits that could influence the results. It is important that all treatment groups be approximately equal as to these various traits, so that the experimental results are attributable to the independent variable and not to the fact that subjects in one treatment were different in some trait (e.g., IQ) from subjects in another treatment.

Field studies provide the greatest possibility for results caused by subject differences rather than treatment differences. In any study in which subjects are studied in their natural groups or have volunteered specifically for one treatment or another, an important question is: How do the subjects in the various treatments differ? For example, consider a large manufacturing company that held leadership training courses for lower-level employees. These courses were run on a volunteer basis and took place at night on the employee's own time. In evaluating the effectiveness of this course ten years later, it was found that those people who had taken the course had advanced further in the company than had those who had not taken the course. This was interpreted as supporting the effectiveness of the course, but an alternative explanation could be that the course may have attracted only those people who were highly motivated to advance in the company. Thus, the treatment group may have consisted of highly motivated people, and the control group may have consisted of unmotivated people. The course may have had little effect on advancement in the company; the results may have been due to differences in motivation in the two comparison groups.

This kind of problem can be avoided if the researcher assigns subjects to various treatment groups in a manner that ensures that the subjects are approximately equal in all relevant characteristics. There are four general techniques for accomplishing this. The first technique is **random selection.** Random selection means that each member of the population to which generalizations will be made, has an equal probability of being included in the study. Random selection is an ideal (and essential in some research methods, like survey research), but is often difficult to accomplish in experimental research. How would you react to a phone call saying you had been randomly selected to come to your local university at a particular time to participate in an hour-long experiment? Often researchers rely on convenience samples (psychology undergraduate students are one very important group) or specialized samples (veterans, stroke patients, married couples, etc.). Once access to these samples has been secured, the second technique can be used. The second technique is to randomly assign subjects to the separate treatments. The random assignment allows the experimenter to be fairly certain that the subjects in all treatments are approximately equal as to the subject variables. This design incorporates the features of Model 1 introduced earlier. The third technique is matching subjects on some pertinent variable (Model 2). In this design the experimenter scores each subject on some task or test and then assigns subjects to the various treatment groups so that the groups are equivalent with respect to these scores. The fourth technique is within-subject control (Model 3). In this design each subject participates in all experimental treatments, which ensures that the treatment groups are equal as to the subject variables. Incorporating a balanced sequence uses the same subjects in all treatments, but it also compensates for sequencing effects. Random assignment, subject matching and within-subject control will each be addressed next.

Random Assignment

The most common method of assigning subjects to treatments is random assignment. **Random** means that each subject in a pool of subjects has an equal opportunity (or probability) of being selected. If an experiment consists of two treatment groups, a table of random numbers could be used to assign subjects to treatment conditions, or an experimenter could flip a coin for each subject. By using randomization procedures such as these, the experimenter could be fairly certain that, as a group, subjects in treatment A and subjects in treatment B would be approximately equal.

While this procedure is simple to administer and is consistent with the definition of random assignment, it also presents a serious problem. It is quite possible that the experimenter would end up with an unequal number of subjects in the two treatments. For example, it would be possible to end up with 15 subjects in treatment A and only 5 subjects in treatment B. This would be undesirable because the treatment mean based on the 5 in treatment B would probably be less stable than a mean based on a larger number of subjects. A second consideration is that some of the statistical analyses of results are simplified if an equal number (n) of subjects is used in each treatment group. Ideally, a procedure is needed that allows for some random assignment but also ensures an equal n in each of the treatment groups. Such procedures are commonly used, and although they do not conform with a rigid definition of random assignment, they are usually called random assignment or, perhaps more accurately, unbiased assignment.

In the Linder, Cooper, and Jones (1967) experiment (see p. 65), in which the subjects were given 50 cents or $2.50 for writing an essay, each subject was assigned to a treatment when he or she arrived at the lab booth. Experiments of this type usually take place over periods of weeks or months, and an unbiased selection procedure must take into account the possibility that subjects who report earlier for the experiment may have characteristics different from those of people who report later. For example, subjects who report later may have heard something about the experiment from subjects who reported earlier, or perhaps the more motivated subjects appear earlier. One procedure that takes this into account is **block randomization.** With this procedure an experiment is run in a series of blocks so that all treatments are represented within each block, but their order within each block is somewhat random. For example, in a two-treatment experiment, the experimenter might flip a coin for the first subject who reports to the lab booth. If the coin lands on heads the subject is assigned to treatment A, and if the coin lands on tails the subject is assigned to treatment B. The next subject who reports to the lab booth is assigned to the other treatment. Thus, if heads comes up for the first subject, he or she is assigned to treatment A, and the second subject is assigned to treatment B. This is the first block. Then the coin is flipped for the third subject, and the fourth subject is assigned to the other treatment. This process is repeated until all the subjects have participated in the experiment. With this procedure, the two treatments are equally distributed over the time period in which the experiment is conducted, and within each block there is unbiased assignment.

If more than two treatments are called for in an experiment, block randomization can be used by putting slips of paper representing each treatment into a container and drawing one out as each subject reports for the experiment. For example, if six treatments are used, six slips of paper, each with a letter representing one of the six treatments, are put into a container. As each subject reports for the experiment, one slip of paper is drawn out of the container, and the subject is assigned to the treatment represented by the letter on that slip. The slip does not go back into the container, so the second subject draws from the five remaining slips. This procedure continues until all six slips have been drawn. At that point the slips are put back into the container, and the procedure begins all over again.

These procedures are especially applicable to experiments in which subjects report to the experiment over an extended period of time. But in another type of research, the subjects are available to the experimenter at the same time. For example, in the Paul (1966) experiment comparing the effectiveness of insight and behavior therapy in treating speech-giving phobia, the experimenter had to assign 67 students who exhibited speech phobia to the four experimental conditions (see p. 48). In the experiment on employment opportunity training discussed later in this chapter, there were 60 applicants for the course offered by the center, and the director somehow had to assign half of these applicants to the treatment group and half to the control group. There are several ways of accomplishing an unbiased assignment for this type of problem, but only a few of these will be discussed.

Suppose an experimenter has the names of 60 subjects and wants to assign 15 to each of four treatment groups. One procedure would be to use the slips of paper method. In this case 15 slips marked A would be placed in the container with 15 slips marked B, and so on. The names of the subjects would be listed on a sheet in alphabetical order, so as the experimenter went down the list, he or she would draw a slip of paper (without replacing it) for each name and assign that person to a treatment based on the letter on the slip. This procedure might be simplified by putting the names in random order (e.g., by putting each of the 60 names on a 3'' × 5'' index card and shuffling the cards) and then assigning the first name drawn to treatment A, the second name to treatment B, and so on.

In some experiments the experimenter might not have the names of the subjects before the experiment begins, even though all subjects were reporting to the experiment at the same time. Suppose there are 60 subjects in a large room who must be assigned to four treatments. Probably the simplest way to assign groups would be to start at the front of the room and have the subjects count off by fours. All number ones go into one treatment group, all number twos go into a second group, and so on. This would seem to be an unbiased selection, provided that the subjects are not seated in some systematic manner. Frequently, subjects meet in a large room, and the various treatments are represented by the different test booklets passed out to the subjects. For example, Johnson and Scileppi (1969) wanted to study how someone's attitude would change when presented with plausible and implausible communications. These communications were in the form of written messages that appeared in test booklets along with attitude scales that were to be filled out by the subjects. Groups of 10 to 20 subjects were tested at the same time in classrooms. The procedure used in this experiment was to shuffle the test booklets before passing them out. In this way the experimenters were randomly assigning treatments to subjects rather than vice versa.

Similar procedures allow even rather complex assignment problems to be handled fairly easily. For example, a group problem-solving experiment was conducted in which subjects met in groups of three to solve a particular human relations problem. The independent variable was the type of instructions given to the group. We shall call the two groups treatment A and treatment B. Thus, the problem was not only to randomly assign each three-person group to a treatment (either A or B), but to randomly assign subjects into the three-person groups. To further complicate the assignment problem, one member of each three-person group was to be randomly assigned to be the leader of the group. Sixty subjects reported to a large classroom, and somehow the experimenter had to end up with 10 three-person groups in each of two treatments with a randomly assigned leader in each group. This assignment problem was easily solved by giving each subject a number from 1 to 60 upon entering the room. The experimenter had a deck of sixty $3'' \times 5''$ index cards, each with a number from 1 to 60 written on it. The experimenter then shuffled the cards and drew three from the top of the deck. The subject represented by the first number drawn was designated as the leader of the group, and the subjects represented by the other two numbers were designated as members of the group. The experimenter kept drawing blocks of three cards until all 20 groups were formed. The groups formed by the first 10 blocks of three cards were placed in treatment A, and the groups formed by the second 10 blocks of three cards were put in treatment B. Thus, a rather complicated assignment process was handled very quickly and in a reasonably unbiased manner.

Matching Subjects

Another method of ensuring that all treatment groups are equal in terms of subject characteristics is called *matching*. With this method all subjects are measured on some test or task that is assumed to be highly related to the task used in the actual experiment. The subjects then are assigned to the various treatment groups on the basis of this pretest measure, so that the groups will be approximately equalized with respect to pretest scores. The experimenter can then be assured that all the treatment groups will be equal with respect to one subject characteristic that is believed to be highly related to performance on the actual experimental task.

Before discussing matching techniques, note the assumptions made when using this procedure. First, researchers assume that they know what subject characteristic is highly related to performance on the experimental task. Second, they assume that they can get scores for each subject on this characteristic. There is always a danger that the first assumption is invalid and that the second condition cannot be met either because there is no good measure for the characteristic or because an experimenter cannot get the subjects' scores on that measure.

Pretest tasks or tests can usually be divided into two major types. The first are tasks or tests that are quite different from the experimental task but are assumed to be highly related to the task. For example, it might be assumed that intelligence is highly related to a learning task, so the experimenter might want to match subjects on intelligence. In this case the pretest could be an IQ test, which is quite different from the actual experimental task. The second type of pretest task or test is quite similar (or identical) to the experimental task.

Once experimenters choose the matching variable and test the subjects, there are several ways they can then match them. One technique involves matched pairs. With this technique the experimenter takes two subjects with identical scores on the matching variable and assigns one to treatment A and the other to treatment B. Suppose a two-treatment learning experiment is to be conducted, and it is assumed that IQ is highly related to performance on the learning task. First, IQ scores would be obtained for a large number of subjects. The experimenter then would pick out two people with an IQ of 135 and put one in treatment A and one in treatment B. He or she then would pick out two subjects with an IQ of 130 and put one in A and one in B. This process would be repeated until the experimenter had the desired number of subjects in each treatment group. Another example would be a drug therapy experiment on schizophrenics in which an experimenter might want to match on age. He or she could take two 50-year-old schizophrenics and put one in the drug therapy group and one in the placebo group. Next, he or she would take two 46-year-olds, and so on. In both examples there is a perfect matching of subjects in the two treatments. The same procedure could be used if there were more than two treatments; for example, the experimenter could pick three subjects with an IQ of 135 and assign one to each of the three treatment groups.

A difficulty with this technique is that it may be impossible to find subjects with matching scores. In the example, it may be that only one subject with an IQ of 135 may be found. In such cases, the researcher may choose to match on the basis of similar scores (e.g., a range of 130 to 140). But even this latter technique may prove to be difficult.

More frequently than not, precise matching may not be possible. Suppose that in a rat experiment similar to that of the Lambert and Solomon (1952) experiment the experimenter had eight rats and wanted to use a matched pair technique to assign the rats to two treatments (A and B) based on the length of time it took them to leave the start box on the last acquisition trial. The times of the eight rats (in seconds) were 20.5, 17.2, 10.7, 8.0, 7.2, 6.5, 4.3, and 3.2. It is obvious that precise matching is impossible since no two scores are alike, so the experimenter is forced to use an **ad lib matching** procedure in which he or she attempts to balance the scores. The following grouping of scores seems to be the best matching possible for the eight rats:

Treatment A	Treatment B
20.5	17.2
8.0	10.7
7.2	6.5
3.2	4.3
$\bar{X} = 9.72$	$\bar{X} = 9.67$

The means of both groups are approximately the same, and both groups contain high-, moderate-, and low-scoring rats. Still, this "solution" is not without its problems because data generated from such a technique are difficult to analyze with appropriate statistical techniques.

Another matching technique that may be used is a **random blocks technique.** Suppose that 80 people with schizophrenia were to be assigned to four treatment groups in a drug therapy experiment. The experimenter also wants to match them as to age, since he or she has some evidence that the older the patient, the less favorable will be the response to therapy. Using a random blocks technique, the experimenter could rank the ages of the 80 patients and then take the four oldest patients and randomly assign one to each of the four treatments. The experimenter could then take the four next-oldest patients and randomly assign each of them to one of the four treatments, and so on until all 80 subjects have been assigned. The experimenter is taking blocks of patients of approximately equal age and randomly assigning the patients within each block to a particular treatment.

Matching techniques can be very powerful in eliminating bias due to subject characteristics (1) if the experimenter knows what subject variables are highly related to the experimental task and (2) if he or she can get scores on these variables.

CASE STUDY

Melissa Smith, Elizabeth Franz, Susan Joy and Kirsty Whitehead (2005) were interested in size perception abilities of blind and sighted individuals. After recruiting blind individuals, the researchers matched each blind subject with a sighted subject based on sex, education and age (within 2 years). For the experiment, both sighted and blind participants were blindfolded and were instructed to hold and feel each of 10 objects (e.g., jug of milk, can of soda, loaf of bread, carton of eggs) for 6 seconds using both hands. After having held all of the objects (which were presented in random order for each subject), the experimenter randomly called out the name of each object and then the participant estimated the size of the object using their hands (hands and palms stretched out from bent elbows). This distance was measured using a millimeter tape measure. They found that sighted individuals overestimated the size of the objects. Overall, the blind participants were more accurate in determining the size of objects compared to the sighted participants. They concluded that this was due to the more accurate manual representations that blind people have compared to the less accurate visual memory representations that sighted people rely on.

Within-Subject Control

Another way of ensuring that each treatment group is equal with regard to subject variables is to have all subjects participate in all treatments. In this setup it can be assumed that the treatment groups are equal as to subject variables. This type of design has been called a repeated measure design or a within-subject design. The latter term seems preferable and derives its name, as we have discussed, from the fact that comparisons between treatments are made within the same subject. This type of design was used in an experiment exploring the relationship between the frequency of a tone and the absolute loudness threshold. In this experiment each subject was tested at ten frequency levels (25, 50, etc.). The mean absolute threshold for the four subjects at each frequency level formed the points of the curve. The within-subject design is most frequently used in this type of experiment—experiments in which subjects are required to make numerous judgments to different stimuli on different occasions. These different stimuli can be considered the independent variable.

The within-subject design ensures that subject characteristics are equal in all treatments, but this design brings up a problem with regard to the order in which treatments or stimuli will be presented to the subject. The results might change rather dramatically, depending upon the order, because the subject's judgment of a particular stimulus may be influenced by previous judgments. For example, a subject's judgment of the lightness or heaviness of an object is in part determined by the heaviness of previously judged objects. Thus, in discrimination experiments, subjects may become more accurate or proficient at a task as they make more judgments. This is usually called a **practice effect.** The opposite phenomenon, a **fatigue effect,** can occur if subjects become tired or bored and their proficiency decreases. To control for these effects, several designs are available.

One method is the **Latin-square design.** Suppose 15 subjects are to judge three different stimuli (A, B, and C). Using a Latin-square design, different orders of stimuli presentation will be derived such that (1) each stimulus appears once for each group, and (2) the stimuli appear in different sequences for each group. This is illustrated in Table 6.1.

Five subjects receive the stimuli in the order A, B, C; five receive them in the order B, C, A; and five receive them in the order C, A, B. Note that stimulus A is judged or responded to once in position 1, once in position 2, and once in po-

TABLE 6.1 The Latin-Square Design

	Order of Stimulus Presentation		
	Position 1	Position 2	Position 3
1. Five subjects	A	B	C
2. Five subjects	B	C	A
3. Five subjects	C	A	B

sition 3. The same is true for B and C. The means of the judgments of all 15 subjects to the three stimuli can then be compared. These means are independent of order effects because each stimulus appeared equally in each order position. Should the experimenter be interested in order effects, he or she can examine them by looking at the subjects' judgments of each stimulus as a function of the order.

Another procedure for controlling for order effects is a random blocks design similar to that described earlier in this chapter. Suppose that an experiment is conducted in which each subject is required to make ten judgments on each of seven different stimuli. The seven stimuli would be treated as a block, and the order of presentation within the block would be determined by some randomization procedure. The first block would be presented to the subject, and after the subject responded to them, the seven stimuli would be randomized again. This new order would constitute the second block. This procedure would be repeated eight more times to this subject until he or she had made ten judgments on each of the seven stimuli. The same procedure would be repeated for each subject in the experiment.

The within-subject design often appears to be desirable because the same subjects are used in all treatments, which assures the researcher that treatments are equal as to subject variables. It also appears to be desirable because fewer subjects must be used. However, this design cannot be used in many experiments simply because the treatments themselves negate this possibility. If an experiment were performed to compare rats reared in isolation with rats reared in groups, it is obvious that the same subjects could not be used in both treatments. If a study were performed comparing high-IQ subjects with low-IQ subjects, or comparing one method of teaching French with a second method, it is apparent that independent groups of subjects would have to be used in each treatment. In some experimental problems it may be much easier to use independent groups rather than wield the complicated procedure that may be needed for a within-subject design. The within-subject design seems to be most applicable, as we have mentioned, to research problems in which subjects are required to make judgments on numerous different stimuli on different occasions, and in which these stimuli can be considered the independent variable. Another type of experiment that necessitates a within-subject design is one in which order effects are of major interest. Experimenters concerned with what happens when a subject switches from a high-reward situation to a low-reward situation, for example, would need the same subjects to participate in both conditions.

C A S E   S T U D Y

It is almost common knowledge that reading to young children is a good thing, and encourages later reading and maybe even improves reading skill. Mary Ann Evans and Jean Saint-Aubin (2005) were interested in what a child looked at on the storybook page when being read to by an adult. Did they look at the words? The pictures? Both? Did the location of the text impact where the child looked? They set out to answer these questions by outfitting children with eye tracking equipment and having different stories read to them by an adult. Five children between the ages of 4 and 5 participated in the experiment. They were pretested to ensure that none of them could read the words in the stories. The stories varied in terms of the location of the text. One book had the text at the top of the page, then an illustration and then text at the bottom of the page. Another book had the text always to the left of the illustration. Another book had text in bubbles superimposed on top of the illustration. Each of these three books had colored illustrations. Two more books were used with left-sided text, but with simple, monocolor illustrations. The order in which the books were read to the children was counterbalanced in a Latin square design. A 2 (text vs. illustration) $\times$ 5 (type of book) repeated measures analysis of variance (ANOVA) was conducted. It showed that children spent very little time on the text, regardless of location. The children spent most of their time viewing the illustrations, and spent more time looking at illustrations that were more colorful (compared to the books that had simple line drawings).

Subject Loss (Attrition)

We have discussed steps taken to ensure that subject characteristics in treatment groups are approximately equal. A related problem deals with subject **attrition,** or loss of subjects, in the various treatment groups of an experiment. This problem usually occurs in experiments in which subjects have to participate in more than one session, as subjects coming for the first session may not necessarily appear for the second session. Consider the following hypothetical example:

CASE STUDY

An employment opportunities center offered a four-week course designed to teach young adults the techniques and procedures for finding jobs. Classes were held each day and covered such topics as where to go for a job, what type of job to look for, and how to fill out applications, as well as providing practice in taking psychological tests used for employee selection. Of the 60 young adults who signed up for the course, the director of the center randomly selected 30 to participate in the course and used the other 30 as a control group to test the effectiveness of the course. The people in the control group were simply told that there was no room in the course for them and that they would have to find jobs on their own. The dependent variable was the percentage of subjects in the two groups who had found jobs within a month after the course had ended. Of the 16 people (out of 30) who completed the course, 12 (75%) were employed within a month. Of the 30 control group subjects, 15 (50%) were employed within this period. The director of the center took these results as evidence of the effectiveness of his program.

Before criticizing this study, remember that research of this type is difficult to do well. However, it is important research. Training programs such as these should be evaluated as to their effectiveness—there are many types of programs, including therapy, counseling, remedial reading, leadership training, and so on, that are very popular, but so far there has been little research examining their effectiveness.

The main concern in the example is that the statistics are based on only those 16 subjects who completed the course out of the 30 who started. The real question is: Who were the subjects who dropped out? They could have been less motivated about getting a job, less intelligent and therefore unable to understand the materials in the course, or less emotionally stable and therefore unable to accept the routine of coming to the center every day. Thus, the poor employment prospects may have been weeded out of the treatment group. On the other hand, it is difficult to drop out of a no-treatment control group, so all the poor employment prospects were still in that group. The head of the center might have been comparing a group of good employment prospects (the poor ones had dropped out) with a control group that consisted of both good and poor employment prospects. If this explanation is valid, then the effectiveness of the course is highly questionable.

In reality it is not known if this explanation is valid; however, it seems to be a plausible explanation for the results. Anytime subjects are lost from an experiment, particularly if the loss is greater in one treatment group than another, it is important to find out the characteristics of those subjects who dropped out. One possibility would be to look at the employment rate of those who dropped out. If it is only about 25 percent, then it would seem to support the explanation that the poor employment prospects were weeded out. If it is around 50 percent, then the course would seem to be fairly effective.

The primary danger with subject attrition is that a select subgroup—for example, low-IQ subjects—may drop out of one treatment group but remain in another treatment group. If this occurs, the treatment groups cannot be considered equal as to subject characteristics, and the results obtained may be due to subject differences rather than treatment differences. It is important to have as much relevant information as possible about subjects who drop out in order to ascertain if they are a select subgroup. If this information indicates that the dropouts are just a random sample of the original treatment group, the researcher may feel fairly confident that the results are not due to any particular subject differences. But even if the information indicates that the dropouts are a select subgroup, it may be possible to eliminate that subgroup in the other treatment groups and thus make the groups somewhat comparable.

Researchers can sometimes avoid problems of subject attrition by having subjects participate in only a single session. If subjects are needed for more than one session, a standard procedure is to inform them before the experiment begins that they will be needed for more than one session and ask that they participate only if they can attend a second session. Frequently, a phone call will bring in those who have forgotten. In experiments in which subjects are needed for repeated testing for perhaps ten days or so (as in some perception experiments), it is customary to pay the subjects, but on the condition that they complete the required number of sessions. In animal experiments attrition usually is not a problem since the subjects reside in a laboratory colony and can be used at will. However, there is always a danger of loss of subjects due to sickness or death, particularly if deprivation or stress treatments are used.

CASE STUDY

Phillippe Rushton and Trudy Ann Bons (2005) were interested in the spouse and friendship choices that monozygotic and dizygotic twins made. In particular, they wanted to know if people choose social partners who resemble themselves. The researchers sent questionnaires that were designed to assess demographic, attitudinal and personality factors to pairs of twins, with instructions to fill out one themselves, give one to each of their spouses, and one to each of their same-sex best friends. So for each pair of twins, there would be six questionnaires (twin one, spouse one, best friend one; twin two, spouse two, best friend two). Two strategies were used to deal with the problem of attrition, one methodological and one statistical. Methodologically, a follow-up questionnaire was mailed to those twins who had not responded, but whose co-twin had. This resulted in an increase of 25 percent in participation. Statistically, missing data were replaced with the mode for that item (across all data within sex; in other words, if a female data point was missing for a particular question, that data point was replaced with the modal amount for that question across all females in the study). The results indicated that people choose spouses and best friends who resemble themselves.

If possible, subject attrition problems should be avoided by using one of the techniques described previously. But if a study occurs over a long period of time and attrition problems seem inevitable, it is important to collect information on all subjects, including the dropouts. Ideally, this information should include (1) pretreatment information, which might include data on intelligence, motivation, adjustment, and so on; (2) data on the subjects' progress (for example, learning or performance data) up to the point at which they dropped out; and (3) posttreatment data on all subjects, such as employment rates in the earlier example. With this information, the results of an experiment may be more easily interpreted.

A Final Note

Armed with basic and advanced design techniques, and strategies to control independent, dependent, extraneous and subject variables, you are now ready to critique a series of experiments to test your knowledge.

CHAPTER

7 Design Critiques

Practice makes perfect.
—Periander

Psychological research usually starts with a search of the literature to become familiar with previous studies. The researcher recognizes an issue that needs further investigation, which he or she can then formalize in the form of a hypothesis. The next stage involves designing a valid, practical experiment. After all materials and subjects are lined up, the experimenter can collect and analyze data, and finally, conclusions can be made in the form of a discussion. As simple as the process may appear, there are pitfalls lurking at every stage.

In this section and in other sections to follow we will consider a special type of trap into which many seasoned as well as neophyte researchers fall. It is a trap basically caused by imperfect logic that has been manifest in either faulty design or faulty interpretation. Some students of experimental design identify these problems as requiring alternative explanations, inasmuch as the results may be attributed to causes other than the one identified (see cartoon on page 111). Experience leads us to believe that the more practice students have on these problems, the better they will be in discovering design and/or interpretative problems in their own research. In addition to reading and discovering the flaws in the problems presented here, it is useful for students to make up problems on their own.

On the following pages are a series of experiment briefs, each of which has one or more design problems. The problem occurs between what the experimenter did in the experiment and the conclusion that he or she arrived at on the basis of the results. We previously illustrated the basic principles of experimental design. Now our purpose is to show a series of fictitious studies and let students apply their knowledge of experimental design in a critique of the studies. The briefs are a

110

FIGURE 7.1   Suggest an Alternative Explanation

quick way to expose a variety of problems in a variety of research areas. No expertise or technical knowledge is needed in the research area being explored in the study; the problems can be recognized with a knowledge of the design principles previously discussed in the text.

In criticizing the design of the experiment briefs, students should use only the information given—inferences are not necessary. For example, if the experimenter uses a pencil-and-paper anxiety test, students should assume that the test is valid and reliable unless information to the contrary is given. There is at least one major defect in each brief, and students need to concentrate their criticisms on this major problem. Students also must be specific as to the defect. For example, students should not just say that the experimenter should have used a control group but must point out exactly how this control group would be treated.

The following example illustrates how the briefs should be criticized:

C A S E   S T U D Y

A certain investigator hypothesized that the hippocampus (a part of the brain) is related to complex thinking processes but not to simple thinking processes. He removed the hippocampus from a random sample of 20 rats. He had 10 of these rats learn a very simple maze and had the other ten learn a very difficult and complex maze. The first group learned to run the maze without error within ten tries (or trials). It took the second group at least 30 trials to run the maze without error. Based on these results, he concluded that his hypothesis had been confirmed—rats without a hippocampus have more trouble learning a complex task than they do a simple task.

In general, this experiment conforms to Model 1: The independent subject design, in that model subjects are randomly assigned to only one condition.

In criticizing this design, it appears reasonable to assume that any rat would take more trials to learn a complex maze than it would to learn a simple maze. Thus, the experimental results may have nothing to do with the removal of the hippocampus—rats with the hippocampus might show the same results. In other words, although two independent variables were intended (task difficulty and the presence or absence of the hippocampus), only one independent variable was varied. This criticism would suggest that in redesigning the experiment a 2×2 factorial design should be used: One factor should be the presence or absence of the hippocampus, and the second factor should be the complexity of the maze. The design is diagrammed here:

	Simple Maze	Complex Maze
Hippocampus intact	5 rats	5 rats
Hippocampus removed	5 rats	5 rats

This new design conforms to Model 4: Factorial Design, in which the effect of two independent variables is evaluated. The revised design would allow for a more reasonable test of the experimenter's hypothesis than did the original design. Although the new design might become more complex than the original design, it corrects the original defect. Kuhn has talked about science in terms of puzzle solving. In particular, he says that puzzles "serve to test ingenuity or skill in so-lution." The same can be said for the conduct of science. Turn your problem solv-ing (or should we say puzzle solving?) skills toward the faulty designs presented in this chapter.

The following questions may be helpful to you in evaluating each experiment brief:

1. What is the independent variable? Are there (1) at least two levels of it or (2) an experimental group and a control group? If not, there is a design de-fect. In any experiment, one treatment has to be compared with another.
2. Is the independent variable a subject variable or a manipulated variable?
3. What is the dependent variable? How is it measured?
4. Assuming there are two levels of the independent variable, are all groups treated identically except for the experimental manipulation? If not, there is a confound in the experiment.
5. What type of design was used?

What other questions could be asked?

Experiment Briefs

1. An investigator attempted to ascertain the effects of hunger on aggression in cats. She took ten cats, kept them in individual cages, and put them on a food deprivation schedule such that at the end of two weeks the cats weighed 80 per-cent of their normal body weight. She then put the cats in pairs for 15 minutes and watched to see if aggression or fighting would occur. In all cases, the cats showed the threat posture, and in most cases fighting occurred. The investigator concluded that hunger increases aggression in cats.

2. Psychologists working for food and beverage companies have always played a critical role in product development. In one experiment conducted by a con-sumer psychologist, subject preference for two types of cola was measured. The company had noticed that in one marketplace its brand of cola performed signif-icantly worse than its leading competitor's cola. These data were particularly puz-zling, as on a nationwide basis its cola performed significantly better than its competitor's cola.

The researchers were concerned that some local condition may have con-tributed to the rejection of their cola, so they set out to test this hypothesis. The ex-perimental design was a repeated measure design in which each subject tasted two colas. One cola was marked Q (the competitor's brand) and the other was marked M (their brand). A random sample of citizens between the ages of 14 and 62 were asked to participate in the experiment. All subjects tasted brand Q and then brand M, and then gave their preference. Much to the surprise of the experimenters, the subjects reported an overwhelming preference for brand M. The authors concluded that the sample preferred their company's brand and that advertising must have contributed to the consumption of the competitor's brand in that area. Therefore, they suggested a multimillion-dollar advertising campaign to rectify the situation.

3. An experimenter wished to examine the effects of massed and distributed practice on the learning of nonsense syllables. He used three treatment groups and randomly assigned the subjects to one of the conditions. Group I practiced a list of 20 nonsense syllables for 30 minutes for one day. Group II practiced the same list for 30 minutes per day for two successive days. Group III practiced the same list for 30 minutes per day for three successive days. The experimenter then assessed each group's learning with a free-recall test. The mean recall of the 20 syllables for Group I was 5.2; for Group II, 10.0; and for Group III, 14.6. The means were significantly different from one another at the .01 level of significance, and the experimenter concluded that distributed practice is superior to massed practice.

4. A certain psychologist was looking for the cause of failure among college students. She took a group of former students who had flunked out and a group of students who had received good grades. She gave both groups a self-esteem test and found that the group that flunked out scored lower on the test than did the group that received good grades. She concluded that low self-esteem is one of the causes of college failure and suggested further that a person with low self-esteem probably expects to fail and exhibits defeatist behavior in college, which eventually leads to failure.

5. A psychologist designed a study to determine if people with high blood pressure could learn to control their blood pressure using biofeedback techniques. A device that records blood pressure was attached to each patient. The patient then was given feedback as to his or her blood pressure level by a tone that decreased in loudness as the blood pressure decreased and increased in loudness as blood pressure increased. The patient was told to try to keep the tone as quiet as possible. Five patients with high blood pressure each received ten half-hour sessions using biofeedback. All five lowered their blood pressure level considerably over the ten sessions, and the researcher claimed success for this method.

6. An experiment was designed to test a hypothesis that stated that high-drive subjects would be able to learn a simple task much more quickly than would low-drive subjects. The hypothesis further stated that on a difficult task the opposite result would be found—low-drive subjects would learn the task more quickly. The experimenter's operational definition of *drive* was each subject's score on the Manifest Drive Scale. Twenty people who scored high on the scale (high-drive) and 20 people who scored low on the scale (low-drive) were given a difficult task to learn. The low-drive group learned the task more quickly than did the high-drive group, and the experimenter concluded that the hypothesis was correct.

7. An investigator set out to test the hypothesis that fear of punishment for poor performance has a detrimental rather than a facilitating effect on motor performance. As a measure of performance, the experimenter used a steadiness test in which a subject's task was to insert a stylus into a hole so that the stylus did not touch the sides of the hole (like in the "'Operation" game). Each subject inserted the stylus into 15 different holes. The experimenter manipulated fear by threatening the subjects with electric shock if they performed poorly on the task. The experimenter strapped an electric shock apparatus to the leg of each subject before the subject performed the task but never shocked the subjects, regardless of their performance. Subjects were randomly assigned to one of two conditions: One group was threatened with 50 volts of electricity—a mild-fear condition; and a second group was threatened with 100 volts of electricity—a high-fear condition. Contrary to the hypothesis, the high-fear subjects did not perform worse than the low-fear subjects; in fact, the means for both groups were approximately the same. Based on these results, the experimenter concluded that fear of punishment has little, if any, effect on motor performance.

8. An experimenter took 20 subjects who said they believed in astrology, gave them their horoscopes for the previous day, and asked them how accurate the horoscopes had been in predicting the previous day's occurrences. The subjects indicated their opinion on a 6-point scale that ranged from extremely accurate to extremely inaccurate. All 20 subjects reported their horoscopes as being accurate to some degree. The experimenter concluded that horoscopes are accurate.

9. A 2×3 factorial design was used to evaluate the effect of an experimental drug (Remoh) on the treatment of schizophrenia. Two patient classifications were used: (1) new admissions to a particular mental hospital and (2) patients who had been institutionalized for at least two years at that hospital. Both groups had not been hospitalized previously. Patients received one of three levels of Remoh: 3 grams per day, 6 grams per day, or 9 grams per day. Subjects from each patient group were randomly assigned to one of the three dosage levels. There were 20 patients in each of the six groups. In addition to administering the drug, the experimenters also rated each patient each week on the presence or absence of schizophrenic symptoms. After two months, it was found that very few (10%) of the long-term patients in each group had improved, regardless of dosage level. But approximately half of the new patients had improved in each of the three dosage level groups. The researchers concluded that (1) Remoh is effective only for new arrivals and not for chronic cases, and (2) a dosage of 3 grams per day is sufficient to maximize the effectiveness of the drug.

10. An interesting controversy in clinical psychology is whether psychosis is inherited or is caused by environmental experiences. One environmentalist hypothesized that children who live with psychotic parents would be prone to having the same problem themselves later in life. To test this hypothesis, he took 1,000 psychotic adults and 1,000 normal adults and for each subject looked to see if either or both parents had been psychotic. Less than 1 percent of the normal adults had had psychotic parents, but over 30 percent of the psychotic adults' parents were psychotic. Based on this result, the experimenter concluded that psychosis is not inherited but that childhood experiences with a psychotic parent make a person especially prone to the disorder.

11. A group of investigators suspected that rats trained to run on a wheel against a drag would run significantly faster if fed a 20 percent sucrose solution along with their daily rations. The control was a group of rats who received only the daily rations. One hundred Mayflower rats arrived from Plymouth Rock Animal Breeders (known in the rat-running business as "designer rats") and were divided randomly into two groups. Fifty rats on the normal rations ran on the wheel, followed by the 50 rats being fed the sucrose supplement (the order was determined by flipping a coin). The second group ran faster than the first, thus affirming the hypothesis that rats are energized when under a sugar high. The researchers generalized the results to grade-school children who are fed a diet of junk food high in processed sugar.

12. Recently, an association that represented police in New Jersey complained that the incidence of cancer was unusually high among police officers who used radar guns in tracking the speed of drivers. The association brought suit against the state, claiming that those officers who used these radar guns had an incidence of cancer 18 percent higher than a comparable group of government workers from the state park service who were randomly selected for comparison purposes. The comparison sample and the police officers were matched on educational level, age, gender, and years of service. The sample was large: 283 police officers and 231 park workers. Was the case justified?

13. A recent newspaper article announced, "Candy Cigarettes Influence Kids" and went on to report that children who buy candy cigarettes are much more likely to smoke later on than are children who don't buy them. The survey indicated that seventh-grade students who had purchased candy cigarettes at least twice were far more likely to have tried real cigarettes than were students who had not bought candy cigarettes. The results were so clear that school officials wanted to ban the sale of these candy cigarettes because, they contended, the candy cigarettes cause smoking in young children. The survey also indicated that in families where at least one parent smoked the children were much more likely to buy candy cigarettes and to have tried smoking on several occasions. Was the reaction by the school officials justified?

14. A statistics teacher wanted to compare two methods of teaching introductory statistics. One method relied heavily on teaching the theory behind statistics (the theory method). The other method consisted of teaching the students various statistical tests and explaining when to use each test (the cookbook method). The teacher found that a leading engineering school was using the theory method in all its introductory statistics classes and that a state teacher's college was using the cookbook method in all its classes. At the end of each semester the teacher administered a standardized statistics test to both sets of classes. The results indicated that the classes that received the theory method performed far better than did the classes that received the cookbook method. The teacher concluded that the theory method was the superior method and that it should be adopted by statistics teachers.

15. In an effort to determine the effects of the drug chlorpromazine on the performance of schizophrenics, two clinical investigators randomly selected 20 acute schizophrenics from a mental hospital population. The patients were asked to order several stimuli along some dimension, such as ordering eight stimuli by weight. There were several tasks of this sort. The investigators used a within-subject design in which all subjects first performed the tasks after being injected with a saline solution (placebo) and then performed the tasks again several hours later after being injected with chlorpromazine. The results indicated that fewer errors were made in the chlorpromazine treatment, which suggested to the investigators that the drug facilitates more adequate cognitive functioning in this type of patient.

16. It was hypothesized that sensory deprivation inhibits the intellectual development of animals. To test this hypothesis, an experimenter used two rats, each of which had just given birth to eight pups. One rat and her litter were placed in a large cage with ample space and objects to explore. The second rat's pups were separated from the mother, and each was placed in a separate cage. These cages were quite small, and the only objects they could see or hear were the four walls and the food dispenser. After five months, both groups were tested in a multiple-T maze using food as a reward. Following 20 trials, all of the nondeprived pups were running the maze without error, but the deprived pups were still making several errors. This latter group frequently froze and had to be prodded to move. The experimenter concluded that sensory deprivation inhibits intellectual development such that deprived rats did not have the intellectual ability to learn even a simple maze.

17. During World War II an investigator attempted to examine the hypothesis that punishment is more effective than reward for training people. The task she picked to test this hypothesis was the identification of enemy and friendly airplanes. She had subjects sit in front of what appeared to be a radar screen as the silhouettes of enemy and friendly airplanes were flashed on the screen in very short exposures (1 second). As each silhouette appeared, the subject had to respond by pressing one of two buttons—one button was marked "enemy" and the other was marked "friendly." Each subject participated in the experiment for 2 hours on 5 successive days. On the first day, after each stimulus, the subjects were told if they had been right or wrong in their identification. Starting on the second day, the subjects were randomly assigned to one of two groups. In Group A the subjects were given 10 cents after every correct identification but were not punished for a wrong identification. In Group B each subject received an electric shock after every wrong identification but received nothing for a correct identification. This procedure continued for days three and four. The fifth day was considered the test day, and the subjects followed the same procedure except that no reward, punishment, or information was given to the subject. The number of correct identifications per 100 silhouettes was considered the test of the effectiveness of each training method.

As expected, there was some loss of subjects over the 5-day period; about 5 percent of the Group A subjects and about 35 percent of the Group B subjects had dropped out by the fifth day. The results indicated that on the 100 test trials given to each subject on the fifth day, the mean number of correct identifications for Group A was 80, and the mean for Group B was 92. The difference between the means was statistically significant. The experimenter concluded that the hypothesis had been confirmed and suggested that all training programs be based on punishment.

18. A YMCA official in a small town wanted some evidence to prove that his program was valuable in training future leaders. He went back to the group's membership records and got the names of those boys who were active members in his program 20 years earlier and also got the names of some boys who were not YMCA members. He compared the two groups as to present occupations, salaries, and so on, and found that the YMCA group was doing much better. He concluded that this was due to the influence of his program.

19. A psychologist was interested in developing a test that would predict the success of prospective lawyers. She selected a random sample of lawyers listed in *Who's Who* under the assumption that they would be successful lawyers. She sent the lawyers a questionnaire by mail that contained several hundred questions. She then analyzed the questionnaires and compiled a profile of successful lawyers. The questionnaire was subsequently given to a group of prospective law students, and those students whose scores differed significantly from the successful lawyer profile were advised not to pursue a law career.

20. A psychologist had a theory that as members of a group get to know each other better, the productivity of the group will increase up to a point and then will start to decrease slightly. The decrease ("the honeymoon is over" effect) would be at the point at which group members stopped acting in a highly cooperative manner and started jostling for power. To test this theory the psychologist formed groups of individuals who were strangers and had them perform a series of tasks. There were five tasks that each took 35 minutes to perform, and he gave the groups a 5-minute break between tasks. His results indicated that group productivity increased up to the fifth task, but for the fifth task there was a significant decrease in the group's performance. On the basis of this evidence, he considered his theory supported.

21. A clinical researcher examined whether patient interviews or objective tests are better in the diagnosis of a patient's problems and in determining how long a patient would remain in the hospital. The experiment took place at a large mental hospital. In one group, ten clinical psychology students each interviewed six new patients for 1 to 2 hours. In the other group, 60 patients were given a battery of standardized psychological tests, and the test results were interpreted by three clinical psychologists who had several years of experience in interpreting tests for the hospital. Each psychologist interpreted the test results for 20 patients. Both groups were asked to list each patient's major problems and to assign the patient to a diagnostic category (e.g., process schizophrenic, reactive schizophrenic). They were also asked to predict how long the patient would be in the hospital before improving enough to be released. Results indicated that the interviews were 67 percent accurate in predicting diagnostic categories and 22 percent accurate in predicting length of stay. The tests group was 83 percent accurate in predicting diagnostic categories and 65 percent accurate in predicting length of stay. The experimenter concluded that interviews are of questionable value in both diagnosis and prediction of outcome and should be discontinued.

22. An experimenter wanted to test the hypothesis that males are more creative than females. She also hypothesized that the male superiority in creativity would be heightened under conditions involving ego. The design used was a 2 × 2 factorial design in which one variable was sex and the other variable was high and low ego involvement. She manipulated ego involvement by telling half the subjects that the task was a measure of intelligence and that their scores would be posted on a bulletin board (high ego involvement). She told the other half of the subjects that she wanted to test the reliability of a task she was developing and that they should not put their names on the answer sheets (low ego involvement). Her test of creativity was an "unusual uses" test in which a person is given the name of an object (e.g., hammer) and has to write as many different unusual uses for that object as he or she can in 5 minutes. Twenty-five males and 25 females participated in each of the two ego-involvement conditions. The males were members of a senior ROTC class, and the females came from sorority pledge classes. Two objects were used: (1) an army compass and (2) a monkey wrench. Subjects were given 5 minutes for each object. The results indicated that the mean number of unusual uses for the two objects for males was 4.1 under low ego involvement and 7.6 under high ego involvement. The means for the females were 3.2 under low ego involvement and 2.4 under high ego involvement. Since both the main effects and the interaction effect were statistically significant, the experimenter concluded that her hypotheses were supported.

23. A researcher was asked to conduct a quick survey in three large cities to find out what political issues or problems were important to the voters. The survey results were to be used by a political candidate in developing his campaign. The researcher randomly selected names from the phone books and called as many as she could reach between 9 A.M. and 5 P.M. on Monday and Tuesday. The results were collated and presented to the candidate with the statement that they were a valid representation of the attitudes of the voters in the three cities.

24. A psychologist noticed that following the nuclear disaster at Chernobyl in the Ukraine, there was a palpable increase in the incidence of extramarital sex among those who had been exposed to the radioactive fallout. Some people he interviewed told of orgies and other sometimes bizarre forms of sexual activities following the accident. The psychologist concluded that in radioactive fallout a secret type of love potion might be found. He applied for a grant to test his hypothesis with rats.

25. An experimental psychologist working with a basketball coach decided to test a theory of motor learning knowledge and visual feedback on basketball players and college students. In the experiment, subjects threw darts at a dart board. In one condition, as soon as the subject released the dart the lights were turned off so the subject could not see the consequence of the throw. In the other condition, the lights remained on. All the subjects were then given a long questionnaire that probed their knowledge of kinesthetic feedback mechanisms. The athletes did better than the students on the dart-throwing task in both the feedback and nonfeedback conditions, but they did worse on the written task. All groups did better in the feedback condition than the nonfeedback condition, and the interactions were not significant. The experimenters concluded that motor skill does not improve with greater knowledge of kinesthetic theory but does improve through knowledge of results. Is the conclusion flawed? Why or why not?

A Final Note

Practice *does* make perfect. And you'll find that continuing to critically evaluate the research you read will further hone your skills both in understanding research, and conducting it. The next chapter will help ensure that the research you do conduct is done in an ethical manner.

8 Ethics of Experimental Research

Honesty is the best policy.
—Richard Whately

Throughout the history of American psychology, the issue of research ethics has been a topic of concern and debate. The purpose of experimental research in psychology is to enhance our knowledge of the psychological characteristics of the human species. In order to do this, psychologists often use human and animal subjects in their experiments. Some would argue that in certain instances the development of valid laws of psychology requires that a subject be deceived or in some way physically harmed. This point of view is based on the principle that the pursuit of knowledge must continue unabated. After all, it is possible that the ultimate truths revealed in psychological research may be of great benefit to humankind. But a psychologist is also bound by a code of ethics in which the psychological and physical safety of subjects is rigidly safeguarded.

In many psychological experiments it is possible to advance our understanding of psychological characteristics while clearly protecting the psychological and physical well-being of the subject. An experimenter should always be sensitive to the ethical problems that may arise in experiments, and while following the guidelines that must be adhered to, balance the potential harm with the potential gain.

At times, experimenters have used questionable means to obtain results. Such abuses of human and animal subjects have caused great concern among psychologists and some members of the public. (See Larson, 1982, for a trial of an animal researcher.) Because of these concerns, the Committee on Scientific and Professional Ethics has been formed by the American Psychological Association (APA). Through many years of work, this organization has developed a series of ethical principles.

Each of the principles that concerns psychologists is presented in this chapter. Following the principles, we describe case studies in which the principles are illustrated. Some of these cases represent clear violations of the principles, while others do not. These cases are presented for analysis and possible class discussion. In the original document, published by the American Psychological Association, further examples and comments are provided, which should be consulted when ethical questions are raised.

Ethical Principles of Psychologists and Code of Conduct

The version of the code of conduct presented here was adopted by the American Psychological Association in 2003. The code covers conduct in teaching, research, and practice. We present here verbatim, the preamble, general principles, and those aspects of the code that directly relate to research. The full code can be viewed at http://www.apa.org/ethics/code2002.html. Additional information on animal research can be found by reviewing documents prepared by the APA Committee on Animal Research and Ethics (CARE) at http://www.apa.org/science/anguide.html.

Preamble
Psychologists are committed to increasing scientific and professional knowledge of behavior and people's understanding of themselves and others and to the use of such knowledge to improve the condition of individuals, organizations, and society. Psychologists respect and protect civil and human rights and the central importance of freedom of inquiry and expression in research, teaching, and publication. They strive to help the public in developing informed judgments and choices concerning human behavior. In doing so, they perform many roles, such as researcher, educator, diagnostician, therapist, supervisor, consultant, administrator, social interventionist, and expert witness. This Ethics Code provides a common set of principles and standards upon which psychologists build their professional and scientific work.

This Ethics Code is intended to provide specific standards to cover most situations encountered by psychologists. It has as its goals the welfare and protection of the individuals and groups with whom psychologists work and the education of members, students, and the public regarding ethical standards of the discipline.

The development of a dynamic set of ethical standards for psychologists' work-related conduct requires a personal commitment and lifelong effort to act ethically; to encourage ethical behavior by students, supervisees, employees, and colleagues; and to consult with others concerning ethical problems.

General Principles
This section consists of General Principles. General Principles, as opposed to Ethical Standards, are aspirational in nature. Their intent is to guide and inspire psychologists toward the very highest ethical ideals of the profession. General Principles, in contrast to Ethical Standards, do not represent obligations and should not form

the basis for imposing sanctions. Relying upon General Principles for either of these reasons distorts both their meaning and purpose.

Principle A: Beneficence and Nonmaleficence: Psychologists strive to benefit those with whom they work and take care to do no harm. In their professional actions, psychologists seek to safeguard the welfare and rights of those with whom they interact professionally and other affected persons, and the welfare of animal subjects of research. When conflicts occur among psychologists' obligations or concerns, they attempt to resolve these conflicts in a responsible fashion that avoids or minimizes harm. Because psychologists' scientific and professional judgments and actions may affect the lives of others, they are alert to and guard against personal, financial, social, organizational, or political factors that might lead to misuse of their influence. Psychologists strive to be aware of the possible effect of their own physical and mental health on their ability to help those with whom they work.

Principle B: Fidelity and Responsibility: Psychologists establish relationships of trust with those with whom they work. They are aware of their professional and scientific responsibilities to society and to the specific communities in which they work. Psychologists uphold professional standards of conduct, clarify their professional roles and obligations, accept appropriate responsibility for their behavior, and seek to manage conflicts of interest that could lead to exploitation or harm. Psychologists consult with, refer to, or cooperate with other professionals and institutions to the extent needed to serve the best interests of those with whom they work. They are concerned about the ethical compliance of their colleagues' scientific and professional conduct. Psychologists strive to contribute a portion of their professional time for little or no compensation or personal advantage.

Principle C: Integrity: Psychologists seek to promote accuracy, honesty, and truthfulness in the science, teaching, and practice of psychology. In these activities psychologists do not steal, cheat, or engage in fraud, subterfuge, or intentional misrepresentation of fact. Psychologists strive to keep their promises and to avoid unwise or unclear commitments. In situations in which deception may be ethically justifiable to maximize benefits and minimize harm, psychologists have a serious obligation to consider the need for, the possible consequences of, and their responsibility to correct any resulting mistrust or other harmful effects that arise from the use of such techniques.

Principle D: Justice: Psychologists recognize that fairness and justice entitle all persons to access to and benefit from the contributions of psychology and to equal quality in the processes, procedures, and services being conducted by psychologists. Psychologists exercise reasonable judgment and take precautions to ensure that their potential biases, the boundaries of their competence, and the limitations of their expertise do not lead to or condone unjust practices.

Principle E: Respect for People's Rights and Dignity: Psychologists respect the dignity and worth of all people, and the rights of individuals to privacy, confidentiality, and self-determination. Psychologists are aware that special safeguards may be necessary to protect the rights and welfare of persons or communities whose vulnerabilities impair autonomous decision making. Psychologists are aware of and respect cultural, individual, and role differences, including those based on age, gender, gender identity, race, ethnicity, culture, national origin, religion, sexual orientation, disability, language, and socioeconomic status and consider these factors when working with members of such groups. Psychologists try to eliminate the effect on their work of biases based on those factors, and they do not knowingly participate in or condone activities of others based upon such prejudices.

8. Research and Publication

8.01 Institutional Approval: When institutional approval is required, psychologists provide accurate information about their research proposals and obtain approval prior to conducting the research. They conduct the research in accordance with the approved research protocol.

8.02 Informed Consent to Research

a. When obtaining informed consent, psychologists inform participants about (1) the purpose of the research, expected duration, and procedures; (2) their right to decline to participate and to withdraw from the research once participation has begun; (3) the foreseeable consequences of declining or withdrawing; (4) reasonably foreseeable factors that may be expected to influence their willingness to participate such as potential risks, discomfort, or adverse effects; (5) any prospective research benefits; (6) limits of confidentiality; (7) incentives for participation; and (8) whom to contact for questions about the research and research participants' rights. They provide opportunity for the prospective participants to ask questions and receive answers.
b. Psychologists conducting intervention research involving the use of experimental treatments clarify to participants at the outset of the research (1) the experimental nature of the treatment; (2) the services that will or will not be available to the control group(s) if appropriate; (3) the means by which assignment to treatment and control groups will be made; (4) available treatment alternatives if an individual does not wish to participate in the research or wishes to withdraw once a study has begun; and (5) compensation for or monetary costs of participating including, if appropriate, whether reimbursement from the participant or a third-party payor will be sought.

8.03 Informed Consent for Recording Voices and Images in Research: Psychologists obtain informed consent from research participants prior to recording their voices or images for data collection unless (1) the research consists solely of naturalistic observations in public places, and it is not anticipated that the recording will be used in a manner that could cause personal identification or harm, or (2) the research design includes deception, and consent for the use of the recording is obtained during debriefing.

8.04 Client/Patient, Student, and Subordinate Research Participants

a. When psychologists conduct research with clients/patients, students, or subordinates as participants, psychologists take steps to protect the prospective participants from adverse consequences of declining or withdrawing from participation.
b. When research participation is a course requirement or an opportunity for extra credit, the prospective participant is given the choice of equitable alternative activities.

8.05 Dispensing with Informed Consent for Research: Psychologists may dispense with informed consent only (1) where research would not reasonably be assumed to create distress or harm and involves (a) the study of normal educational practices, curricula, or classroom management methods conducted in educational settings; (b) only anonymous questionnaires, naturalistic observations, or archival research for which disclosure of responses would not place participants at risk of criminal or civil liability or damage their financial standing, employability, or reputation, and confidentiality is protected; or (c) the study of factors related to job or organization effectiveness conducted in organizational settings for which there is no risk to participants' employability, and confidentiality is protected or (2) where otherwise permitted by law or federal or institutional regulations.

8.06 Offering Inducements for Research Participation

a. Psychologists make reasonable efforts to avoid offering excessive or inappropriate financial or other inducements for research participation when such inducements are likely to coerce participation.

b. When offering professional services as an inducement for research participation, psychologists clarify the nature of the services, as well as the risks, obligations, and limitations.

8.07 Deception in Research

a. Psychologists do not conduct a study involving deception unless they have determined that the use of deceptive techniques is justified by the study's significant prospective scientific, educational, or applied value and that effective nondeceptive alternative procedures are not feasible.

b. Psychologists do not deceive prospective participants about research that is reasonably expected to cause physical pain or severe emotional distress.

c. Psychologists explain any deception that is an integral feature of the design and conduct of an experiment to participants as early as is feasible, preferably at the conclusion of their participation, but no later than at the conclusion of the data collection, and permit participants to withdraw their data.

8.08 Debriefing

a. Psychologists provide a prompt opportunity for participants to obtain appropriate information about the nature, results, and conclusions of the research, and they take reasonable steps to correct any misconceptions that participants may have of which the psychologists are aware.

b. If scientific or humane values justify delaying or withholding this information, psychologists take reasonable measures to reduce the risk of harm.

c. When psychologists become aware that research procedures have harmed a participant, they take reasonable steps to minimize the harm.

8.09 Humane Care and Use of Animals in Research

a. Psychologists acquire, care for, use, and dispose of animals in compliance with current federal, state, and local laws and regulations, and with professional standards.

b. Psychologists trained in research methods and experienced in the care of laboratory animals supervise all procedures involving animals and are responsible for ensuring appropriate consideration of their comfort, health, and humane treatment.

c. Psychologists ensure that all individuals under their supervision who are using animals have received instruction in research methods and in the care, maintenance, and handling of the species being used, to the extent appropriate to their role.

d. Psychologists make reasonable efforts to minimize the discomfort, infection, illness, and pain of animal subjects.

e. Psychologists use a procedure subjecting animals to pain, stress, or privation only when an alternative procedure is unavailable and the goal is justified by its prospective scientific, educational, or applied value.

f. Psychologists perform surgical procedures under appropriate anesthesia and follow techniques to avoid infection and minimize pain during and after surgery.

g. When it is appropriate that an animal's life be terminated, psychologists proceed rapidly, with an effort to minimize pain and in accordance with accepted procedures.

8.10 Reporting Research Results

a. Psychologists do not fabricate data.

b. If psychologists discover significant errors in their published data, they take reasonable steps to correct such errors in a correction, retraction, erratum, or other appropriate publication means.

8.11 Plagiarism: Psychologists do not present portions of another's work or data as their own, even if the other work or data source is cited occasionally.

8.12 Publication Credit

a. Psychologists take responsibility and credit, including authorship credit, only for work they have actually performed or to which they have substantially contributed.

b. Principal authorship and other publication credits accurately reflect the relative scientific or professional contributions of the individuals involved, regardless of their relative status. Mere possession of an institutional position, such as department chair, does not justify authorship credit. Minor contributions to the research or to the writing for publications are acknowledged appropriately, such as in footnotes or in an introductory statement.

c. Except under exceptional circumstances, a student is listed as principal author on any multiple-authored article that is substantially based on the student's doctoral dissertation. Faculty advisors discuss publication credit with students as early as feasible and throughout the research and publication process as appropriate.

8.13 Duplicate Publication of Data: Psychologists do not publish, as original data, data that have been previously published. This does not preclude republishing data when they are accompanied by proper acknowledgment.

8.14 Sharing Research Data for Verification

a. After research results are published, psychologists do not withhold the data on which their conclusions are based from other competent professionals who seek to verify the substantive claims through reanalysis and who intend to use such data only for that purpose, provided that the confidentiality of the participants can be protected and unless legal rights concerning proprietary data preclude their release. This does not preclude psychologists from requiring that such individuals or groups be responsible for costs associated with the provision of such information.

b. Psychologists who request data from other psychologists to verify the substantive claims through reanalysis may use shared data only for the declared purpose. Requesting psychologists obtain prior written agreement for all other uses of the data.

8.15 Reviewers: Psychologists who review material submitted for presentation, publication, grant, or research proposal review respect the confidentiality of and the proprietary rights in such information of those who submitted it.

Research with Humans

The use of human subjects in a psychological experiment poses special problems. A psychologist is both a scientist and a member of society. Sometimes, in the zealous pursuit of scientific truths, experimenters may become so wrapped up in their research that they overlook some ethical considerations regarding human participants. This is a grievous mistake and will ultimately reflect poorly on experimenters and psychological research in general.

In the early days of psychological research, few ethical guidelines were available, save the researcher's personal ethical code and the laws of society. In fact, some research conducted during that period would not be allowed by current standards, and as a consequence, some prospective participants today are wary of volunteering for experiments.[1] But some researchers have argued that the standards that have since evolved are too restrictive and forbid the collection of important data. Once again, new ethical standards will likely evolve.

This section presents the principles that govern research using human participants. These guidelines are what are used by **institutional review boards** (IRBs) to determine if subjects (human or animal) are protected, a major consideration when IRBs approve studies. See also the section in Chapter 9 on securing human (or animal) subjects approval from your institution.

Research with Human Participants[2]

The decision to undertake research rests upon a considered judgment by the individual psychologist about how best to contribute to psychological science and human welfare. Having made the decision to conduct research, the psychologist considers alternative directions in which research energies and resources might be invested. On the basis of this consideration, the psychologist carries out the investigation with respect and concern for the dignity and welfare of the people who participate and with cognizance of federal and state regulations and professional standards governing the conduct of research with human participants.

a. In planning a study, the investigator has the responsibility to make a careful evaluation of its ethical acceptability. To the extent that the weighing of scientific and human values suggests a compromise of any principle, the investigator incurs a correspondingly serious obligation to seek ethical advice and to observe stringent safeguards to protect the rights of human participants.

b. Considering whether a participant in a planned study will be a "subject at risk" or a "subject at minimal risk," according to recognized standards, is of primary ethical concern to the investigator.

c. The investigator always retains the responsibility for ensuring ethical practice in research. The investigator is also responsible for the ethical treatment of research

---

[1]See Baumrind (1985) for an insightful discussion of deception in social science research.
[2]From *Ethical Principles in the Conduct of Research with Human Participants* (1990). Washington, DC: American Psychological Association.

participants by collaborators, assistants, students, and employees, all of whom, however, incur similar obligations.

d. Except in minimal-risk research, the investigator establishes a clear and fair agreement with research participants, prior to their participation, that clarifies the obligations and responsibilities of each. The investigator has the obligation to honor all promises and commitments included in that agreement. The investigator informs the participants of all aspects of the research that might reasonably be expected to influence willingness to participate and explains all other aspects of the research about which the participants inquire. Failure to make full disclosure prior to obtaining informed consent requires additional safeguards to protect the welfare and dignity of the research participants. Research with children or with participants who have impairments that would limit understanding and/or communication requires special safeguarding procedures.

e. Methodological requirements of a study may make the use of concealment or deception necessary. Before conducting such a study, the investigator has a special responsibility to (1) determine whether the use of such techniques is justified by the study's prospective scientific, educational, or applied value; (2) determine whether alternative procedures are available that do not use concealment or deception; and (3) ensure that the participants are provided with sufficient explanation as soon as possible.

f. The investigator respects the individual's freedom to decline to participate in or to withdraw from the research at any time. The obligation to protect this freedom requires careful thought and consideration when the investigator is in a position of authority or influence over the participant. Such positions of authority include, but are not limited to, situations in which research participation is required as part of employment or in which the participant is a student, client, or employee of the investigator.

g. The investigator protects the participant from physical and mental discomfort, harm, and danger that may arise from research procedures. If risks of such consequences exist, the investigator informs the participant of that fact. Research procedures likely to cause serious or lasting harm to a participant are not used unless the failure to use these procedures might expose the participant to risk of greater harm or unless the research has great potential benefit and fully informed and voluntary consent is obtained from each participant. The participant should be informed of procedures for contacting the investigator within a reasonable time period following participation stress, potential harm, or related questions or when concerns arise.

h. After the data are collected, the investigator provides the participant with information about the nature of the study and attempts to remove any misconceptions that may have arisen. Where scientific or humane values justify delaying or withholding this information, the investigator incurs a special responsibility to monitor the research and to ensure that there are no damaging consequences for the participant.

i. Where research procedures result in undesirable consequences for the individual participant, the investigator has the responsibility to detect and remove or correct these consequences, including long-term effects.

j. Information obtained about a research participant during the course of an investigation is confidential unless otherwise agreed upon in advance. When the possibility exists that others may obtain access to such information, this possibility, together with the plans for protecting confidentiality, is explained to the participant as part of the procedure for obtaining informed consent.

CASE STUDY

In an experiment reported by Smith, Tyrell, Coyle, and William (1987) in the *British Journal of Psychology,* the effects of experimentally induced colds and influenza on human performance were measured to determine whether minor illnesses "alter the efficiency of human performance." The experiment involved recruiting volunteers who stayed at the Common Cold Unit for ten days. They were housed in groups of two or three and isolated from outside contacts. Following a three-day quarantine period the subjects were inoculated with nose drops containing either the virus or a placebo. An incubation period of 48–72 hours followed. Then each participant was assessed by a clinician who evaluated the severity of the illness. Objective measures included temperature, number of paper tissues used, and the quantity of nasal secretion.

Then, two performance tasks were done. In one the participants were to detect and respond quickly to target items that appeared at irregular intervals (a detection task). The second task tested hand–eye coordination.

The results indicated that influenza impaired performance on the detection task but not in the hand–eye coordination task. Colds generally had the reverse effect.

The procedures used in this experiment were approved by the local ethical committee, and the informed consent of the volunteers was obtained. All participants were screened to exclude pregnant women and people who took sleeping pills, tranquilizers, or antidepressant medicines. The participants also took a medical examination, including a chest X ray, and anyone who failed the examination was excluded. The participants were not paid but received food, accommodation, traveling expenses, and pocket money. Other clinical trials were also conducted.

Students should discuss the ethics of this experiment.

1. Did the experimenters follow acceptable (APA) standards?
2. Were the participants coerced?
3. Was the risk-to-benefit ratio worthwhile? (Keep in mind that other tests were done.)
4. Were there alternative means available to collect the data?
5. Were the participants treated in a way consistent with the APA principles?
6. Ask students if they would volunteer for this experiment.
7. Would they collect the data for this experiment? Why or why not?
8. Discuss this case (or the original article) in class.

Case Studies

In this section we present several research projects, some of which are questionable and others that seem to conform to the principles discussed previously. Try to find the flaws and acceptable standards in these projects.

Case Study 1

An experimenter was interested in the personality traits of subjects who had scored well in a test of ESP. The gist of the experiment was to have participants (receivers) report their impressions of an ESP card that was being viewed by another person (sender). The cards were randomly ordered, and the sender was completely concealed from the receivers. Several receivers scored well, but their personality measures did not differ from the rest of the group. Nevertheless, the experimenter thought he had identified a group of participants that was unusually sensitive to receiving ESP signals, so he conducted four additional experiments with these subjects. On the first three experiments the participants scored significantly better than would be expected by chance alone, but on the fourth experiment the group's performance was no better than would be expected by chance. In reviewing the results, the experimenter decided to report only the first three experiments, attributing the results of the fourth experiment to sender and/or receiver fatigue.

1. What could be considered a procedural problem with this study?
2. What is the ethical problem in this study?

Case Study 2

While working at a major eastern university, an experimental psychologist trained in research design and physiological psychology was approached by a large company that produced a health food cereal. The company asked the psychologist to design an experiment that would demonstrate the effectiveness of a cereal in reducing common ailments (e.g., colds) and absenteeism. The company agreed to pay the researcher a large sum of money if she would design the experiment and lend her name to the conclusion in a subsequent advertising campaign. The psychologist agreed to do so, but stipulated that she would have final approval of the advertising copy. She would not be directly involved in the collection of data but was assured that it would be done according to her exact specifications. Although she had little knowledge or training in nutrition, she felt that her background in experimental design and physiological psychology was sufficient to design a valid experiment.

1. Should the psychologist have accepted this offer?
2. Why or why not?

Case Study 3

In an investigation of higher moral standards, an experimental psychologist was interested in the strength of people's moral convictions. An experiment was designed in which participants were told that a child was in critical need of a drug that could be derived from a fungus found in a particular limestone cave. The fungus grew in abundance in this cave, and only a small portion was needed for treatment. However, the owner of the cave refused to allow anyone to use the fungus. The experimenter found that a large percentage of participants reported that they would trespass to obtain samples of the fungus. In a second part of the experiment, the researcher asked some of the participants to obtain the fungus illegally. In justifying the procedure, he argued that a higher moral principle was served and that the results would have a major impact on the knowledge of civil disobedience.

1. Did the researcher's plan conform to the code?
2. Could this research be modified to achieve the psychologist's aim and yet conform to the ethical principles?

Case Study 4

A research psychologist, working on problems of human memory, developed a superior mnemonic technique. She decided to test the technique by becoming a contestant on a television quiz show. After several successful appearances, she decided to write a book on the technique. Because she was well known after her appearance on the television quiz show, she agreed to have her picture on the cover and in the advertising for the book, along with the statement, "You too, can learn the extraordinary memory technique of Dr. Josephine Brown!"

1. What specific ethical issues are raised by this example?

Case Study 5

At a meeting of lawyers, a social psychologist was asked to present the results of her recent research on the decision-making processes of juries. In one of her studies, she interviewed each member of a jury involved in a celebrated murder trial. In the study, the identity of each member of the jury was carefully concealed, but she did discuss the deliberative processes of subgroups. For example, the jury had among its members seven women, two African Americans, one foreign-born Italian American, an architect, and a truck driver, and the researcher referred to the voting and deliberative patterns of these groups. When questioned about the ethical propriety of revealing the findings, she said the names of the jurors had not been used and the jurors were now public figures whose opinions were no longer private.

1. What ethical concerns are raised here?
2. What are your views?

Case Study 6

A doctoral candidate at a large midwestern university was completing his dissertation on the relationship between mothers' religious attitudes and the bed-wetting tendencies of their children. His sample consisted of 48 white mothers between the ages of 20 and 28 who were members of a specific religious group. Their children were healthy. He had nearly completed his study when four subjects dropped out of the experiment. Because the dissertation was due soon, he decided to recruit subjects from his friends who had children. He was careful to make sure that all new subjects were identical on the designated attributes.

The dissertation was successful and he was awarded a doctoral degree. He is now a valued member of a department of psychology at a large midwestern university.

1. Did the candidate act unethically?
2. Is there any way the candidate could have salvaged his study, without starting over, and without recruiting from his friends? If so, how?

Case Study 7

"One of the best graduate seminars I took was in industrial psychology from good ol' Professor B. J. Smith," a colleague told another professor. "Each member of the seminar was given a very specific hypothetical problem concerning the design of work spaces and its effect on productivity. We did an extensive review of the literature and designed an experiment. We even anticipated the results and analyzed and discussed them. The professor gave us the problems and we did all the work, but it was an excellent learning experience."

Several years later the same two colleagues saw each other at a psychology meeting. "Do you remember the story I told you about good ol' Professor Smith?" one began.

"Yes, I do . . ." the other said. "Something about a good seminar you had with him."

"Well, the old fraud," the first said, seething, "he took our research ideas, put them into practice, and published the results in the latest issue of the *Journal of Important Industrial Research*. See, here is a copy."

The design in the article was similar to the one submitted by the seminar group, and the article even cited the very sources in the introductory material that were contained in the original paper.

1. Did the professor act unethically?
2. What could the students and the professor have done to avoid this uncomfortable situation?

Case Study 8

A social psychology experimenter wanted to use a test instrument called "Study of Basic Attitudes" to see if attitudes are related to scholastic achievement. A group of participants reported to a psychology investigator to complete the attitude scale. But when they arrived the principal investigator was absent. Because the test was simple to administer—in effect, it was self-administering—the experimenter decided to have the secretary administer it. The secretary had no formal background in psychometrics but was briefed in the proper procedures for the administration of the test. Following the collection of data, the psychologist discussed the test and its results with the participants.

1. Is the procedure questionable from an ethical standpoint?

Case Study 9

The identification of criminal offenders by eyewitnesses is considered an important social and psychological issue. To study it, a researcher decided to stage a crime in the presence of eyewitnesses and then ask them for a description of the perpetrator. The experiment was conducted in a fast-food outlet, and all employees carefully rehearsed the staged crime. The crime was committed by an actor who entered the store, displayed an unloaded handgun, and demanded all the money from the cash register. He told the employees not to call the police and, in making his getaway, shouted, "The first one out the door is going to get blown away." Immediately after the thief left, the researcher and his associates entered the store with a questionnaire, which they distributed to the patrons. The questions dealt with the physical appearance of the thief, whether or not the person had a weapon, and what he or she said. Then each patron was presented with a series of photographs and asked to identify the thief.

Each patron was thoroughly debriefed after the questionnaire was completed, and the important social and psychological issues were discussed. An opportunity was provided for further debriefing and counseling, but no subject indicated a need for further intervention.

1. Comment on the experiment from an ethical standpoint.
2. Design an experiment that could have evaluated eyewitness identification, without the level of deception used in this study.

Case Study 10

In a study of the effects of vitamin A on maze-learning ability of rats in a semi-darkened environment, a researcher had reason to believe that enhanced performance would occur under minimum dosages but that at higher dosages performance would decrease. The experimenter selected four levels of vitamin A ingestion. The highest level had been shown by previous research to be toxic to rats, but the researcher argued that to demonstrate the hypothesized results such levels were necessary.

Previous research had also suggested that higher levels of vitamin A interfere with maze performance, but the hypothesis had not been tested empirically. Thus, the results would reveal something new and would have important scientific implications.

The rats were well cared for except for the high level of vitamin A ingestion in one group. Upon collecting the minimum amount of data necessary for analysis, the experiment was terminated and the rats were rapidly and painlessly killed.

1. Did the experimenter follow the ethical guidelines established for animal use in research?
2. What are your views on this study?

As the above guidelines show, it is impossible to cover all the ethical questions that might arise in the course of experimental work in psychology, just as civil laws cannot cover all contingencies of human conduct. However, the guidelines we have presented do provide a general structure that can be applied to a wide range of specific situations. These principles are subject to a degree of interpretation and, as such, may be interpreted differently by different investigators. When planning research that might involve ethical questions, the researcher should seek the opinions of other scholars before interpreting ethical principles. Sometimes there is a fine line between ethical and unethical experimentation, and the advice of others may help determine whether a piece of experimental work is advisable.

A Final Note

Conducting research ethically goes beyond avoiding breaking a list of rules. It means behaving honestly and with integrity at all stages of the research process, as well as treating animals and human subjects with the respect they deserve.

9 The Research Process

*Hofstadter's Law: It always takes longer than you expect,
even when you take into account Hofstadter's Law.*
—Douglas R. Hofstadter

This chapter is about the research process. This process includes finding funding for your research, if necessary, actually doing the research, and the methods for presenting that research, through presentation at a conference and writing a paper for publication. In one sense, these are the most complicated steps in the experimental endeavor, but if an experiment has been designed carefully, these steps follow logically. Figure 9.1 shows the essential stages. It should be noted, however, that these steps are only guidelines. Many times in an actual research program, the researcher must backtrack, start over, reconsider hypotheses, read new literature, go back to the drawing board, redesign the experiment, take a long and thoughtful walk, seek help, abandon pet ideas, think new thoughts, consider the practical aspects of the proposal, and always apply logic, creative thought, and, hopefully, wisdom throughout every part of the process. First, consider the matter of doing research.

Doing Research

Steps Involved

Before beginning an experiment, a researcher should be reasonably familiar with the previous findings in the field. It may be that someone else has done the experiment. However, as was mentioned previously, the vast amount of literature in psychology makes it possible to know what has been done and, more importantly, what needs to be done. The information contained in previous studies may also suggest a new **problem**—a term that means a question proposed for solution.

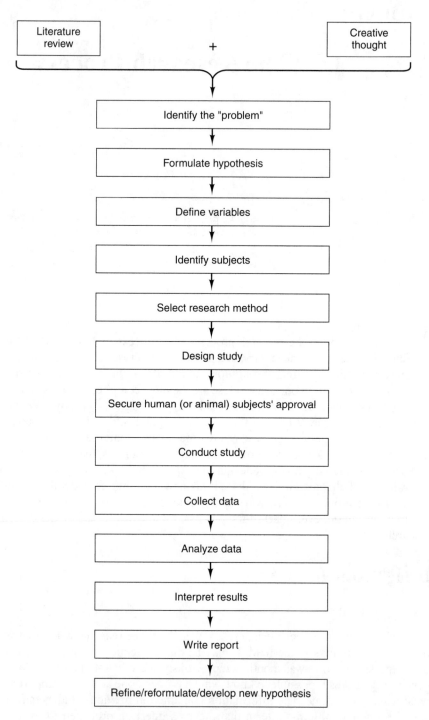

FIGURE 9.1   Steps involved in planning, doing, and reporting research.

Practically, a problem suggests that either the current state of knowledge is lacking in some critical dimension or a gap in knowledge exists. A **hypothesis,** or testable proposition, can be constructed from a problem. After a problem is identified and a hypothesis is developed, a researcher can carefully plan an experiment that will test the hypothesis and solve the problem. In this stage, proper attention should be given to design and control (see previous chapters). Securing human (or animal) subject approval, conducting the experiment, analyzing the data, and writing the research paper round out the research process.

As straightforward as this process may sound—from literature, to problem, to hypothesis, to plan, to experiment, to report—we remind students of Murphy's Law: "Anything that can go wrong will go wrong," and its corollary, "Murphy was an optimist."[1] Be prepared for delays and to have some disappointments; all researchers encounter stumbling blocks. Researchers can, nevertheless, minimize the likelihood of a fiasco through careful planning.

Getting Ideas

Recall from Chapter 2 that many of our research ideas come from our own lives and everyday experiences. Your first glimmer of interest might come from a personal experience. The next step is to review the literature to see what has been done on the topic. When you first encountered Chapter 2, you likely found it useful because you were having to find and read articles for your course. Now, you may be at the point where you are planning your own research. Reviewing Chapter 2 could be helpful at this point. Regardless, now your skills at finding and reading journal articles are much improved. And your goals may have shifted from learning about a topic, to planning a research project. Prior to planning your study, a thorough understanding of the literature, and a critical evaluation of your research idea is essential. Honing your idea into a hypothesis is your next step.

Planning Research Projects That Are Realistic

A key ingredient in planning an experiment that can be completed is the development of a manageable project. If someone is interested in human brain research but has neither the skill nor the equipment necessary, or if someone is interested in the mating behavior of whales in their natural habitat but lives in Nebraska, it is likely that these experiments will never make it out of the researcher's head and into the laboratory.

Numerous credible research projects may involve fancy equipment that is unavailable in many laboratories. If the research is important, though, it may be worthwhile to seek funds through grants or an institution's equipment monies. This process can be very time consuming, and there are no guarantees that your project will be funded. An alternative would be to go to a laboratory (such as a medical school) or setting (such as the ocean) where the project could be done.

---

[1]See also Hofstadter's Law at the beginning of the chapter.

Another practical consideration is the availability of subjects. Nebraska doesn't have any whales. In some areas, it may even be difficult for researchers to find usable rats, college-age subjects, schizophrenics, bed wetters, or third graders. Also, students should be mindful of the ethical considerations involved in working with subjects (see Chapter 8).

Another consideration is whether the proposed research can be done within the time available. In our experience, this component more than any other has caused students (and their professors) the most grief. Experimental projects usually take longer to complete than first anticipated, a fact that can be caused by IRB delays, equipment failure, the necessity to replan an experiment, the failure of participants to show up for an experiment, natural disasters, unreliable coworkers, new discoveries in the field, power failures, spring break, and the like. Good research requires time and dedication, and we know of no prominent researcher who has not devoted a major portion of his or her lifetime to science.

Designing Your Study

Now that you have an idea, and have gone through the initial phases of turning a casual thought into a researchable hypothesis, you need to get to the task of designing your study. Some of your first decisions will be operationalizing all of the concepts and factors in your study (refer to Chapter 3). The content in Chapters 3, 4, 5, and 6 will aid you in designing your study. Keep in mind ethical considerations as well (Chapter 8).

Evaluating Research Resources and Needs

One important step in the research planning process is evaluating what materials, equipment, and other resources you will need. Many research questions are amenable to either "low-tech" or "high-tech" research methods. For example, you could administer a questionnaire using paper and pencil, or you could have it programmed (or program it yourself) on a computer for participants to enter their responses directly. Deciding on which alternative to use depends on your resources, time, energy, and skill level. Some research questions require specialized equipment (an EEG machine, specialized computer software, an eye tracker, etc.). Others rely on more readily available equipment (televisions, VCRs, etc.) or on simple materials (clip boards, pens, paper, etc.). More and more research projects are making use of computers and computer software that allow for direct input of participant responses, capturing of reaction time, and precise presentation of stimuli. Given that computers are, for many, readily accessible and financially feasible, they are becoming "standard" in research practice. Still, a careful evaluation of your equipment needs and available resources is integral to the research planning process.

Funding Research and Applying for Grants

By now, you may realize that there are expenses involved in conducting research. Sometimes, the costs are minimal, and the investigator can bear them. In other instances, the researcher's employer, such as a university, corporation, or research facility, might fund the research. But in many cases, a researcher must find some form of outside funding to support the research efforts, which is the case in many of the research experiments reported in the second section of this book. (Check the first page of these articles for acknowledgement of research support.)

In conjunction with your research supervisor, you should pursue sources of internal funding at your university or college. Many times there are funding opportunities for students and faculty through the department or college. These internal sources of funding usually are in the $100–$500 range, though some schools may have opportunities for larger or smaller requests. In any event, it is always good practice to explore funding opportunities, as they not only help out with the completion of your project but demonstrate to others (e.g., graduate schools, employers) that you are knowledgeable about these opportunities and successful at securing them. These opportunities usually require the submission of a proposal which will be very similar to what is described below (though sometimes not as extensive) for external funding opportunities.

The most common form of external funding is called a *grant* and, although it may be very early in your career to think about these matters, it is important to be exposed to the basic policies and procedures in the application of grant proposals. In addition, understanding the grant proposal process and content may be useful to you as a student because it outlines all the components of the research that are necessary to consider during the planning process, a valuable skill for any researcher.

We see the grant proposal process as involving the following steps:

1. *The generation of a credible research idea and design.* This involves the same type of critical thinking mentioned throughout the book (see especially Chapter 2) and the formation of a tightly controlled research design.
2. *The identification of funding agencies whose interest coincides with the aims of your proposed research plan.* Researchers affiliated with a university, research institute, hospital, or large corporation often have access to grant offices. These offices routinely provide information regarding thousands of granting agencies and can suggest possible matches of organizations that might be interested in providing funding for a project such as yours. If a grant office is not available, the researcher should search the nearest research library, such as one associated with a university, and consult the many directories available that list funding agencies and the types of research they fund.[2] In addition, researchers should consult the Internet sites of major

---

[2]Some directories are *Annual Register of Grant Support, Directory of Research Grants, Grants Register, Foundation Directory,* and *Foundation Grants Index.*

government funders like The National Science Foundation (www.nsf.gov) and the National Institutes of Health and its subsidiary programs (www.nih .gov).

It may be necessary to rework the research plan you developed in the first stage to conform to the requirements of the funding agency. Here we offer a word of advice: If the purpose of the research is valid, in your view, it may be better to seek a funding agency that has requirements you more closely match than to bend your intention too much to meet the needs of the agency. On the other hand, if you are interested in doing someone else's research, which may be an altogether worthy venture (many times these are called "contracts"), then you may choose to design your experiment to meet the advertised need of the agency.

3. *Obtaining and completing grant proposal forms.* After the researcher has collected information about potential granting agencies, he or she should contact the university grant office, or the granting agency itself, and request that particular grant application packet. Also check the websites of these agencies, as many have their forms available on line.

First and foremost, follow directions! As students, this is something you've been told repeatedly. As a researcher, it is essential. Even an excellent proposal will be returned without review if the directions are not followed to the letter.

4. *Submitting the grant proposal and revising, if necessary.* Upon completion of the proposal, it is submitted for review. Some granting agencies still accept hard copy proposals; however, many are requiring electronic submission. Check your university grant office and the funder's website for details.

There are different standards and criteria used by agencies to decide which proposals to fund. Overall, the funding process, while competitive, is not impossible and is increasingly considered to be a central aspect of any researcher's career.

Typical Components of a Proposal

Title Page.   The title page (also called the cover sheet or application form) includes the title of the project, name and address of the applicant organization, name of agency to receive the proposal, inclusive dates of the project, total budget request, signatures of authorized personnel approving submission, and date of submission.

Table of Contents.   Details all sections of the proposal.

Abstract.   The abstract (also called a *Summary* or *Executive Summary*) provides a summary of the proposal with a brief review of the major points covered in the remaining sections.

Introduction.   The introduction (also called *Background*) provides information on the applicant's organization and introduces the structure of the proposal.

Problem Statement.   The problem statement (also called the *Statement of Needs* or *Questions to be Addressed*) provides a clear and precise statement of the problem to be addressed as well as the need for a solution. It should establish the significance, relevance, timeliness, generalizability, and benefits of the project.

Goals.   The goals section (also called *General Objectives* or *Solutions*) is a general statement, describing in qualitative terms the ultimate end to be achieved.

Objectives.   This section (also called *Measurable Objectives, Expected Outcomes,* or *Hypotheses*) provides a specific indication of the proposed outcomes of the project stated as objectives, hypotheses, and/or questions.

Methodology.   The methodology section (also called *Activities, Operating Plans, Action Plan, Strategies,* or *Procedures*) describes how the objectives will be met or the hypotheses or questions tested. It usually includes information about the design, population and sample, data and instrumentation, analysis, and time schedule.

Dissemination.   The dissemination section (also called *Transferability, Distribution of Results, Utilization Plan,* or *Replicability*) summarizes how the final product and findings will be shared with others. Also, it details the reports that will be given to the funding agency.

Facilities and Equipment.   This section (also called *Resources*) describes the facilities and equipment required and how these will be provided.

Personnel.   This section provides information on who will work on the project, their roles, backgrounds, and credentials. It includes vitae of key project personnel. It details new staff: how many, what type, and how they will be selected. It includes a description of the project's administrative organization and identifies individuals who will serve as consultants, describes their backgrounds, and justifies their use.

Budget.   This section details the costs of the project. It is usually divided into categories such as personnel, supplies and materials, travel, data processing, facilities or equipment, and indirect costs or administrative services.

Appendixes.   This section includes relevant materials too lengthy to include in the text; vitae for key personnel; letters of endorsement; documentary material such as maps, graphs, charts, bibliographies; and so on. Carefully read the funder's instructions, because the appendixes are not to be used to circumvent the page limitations of the proposal.

Securing Institutional Review Board (IRB) Approval

Before you start collecting data, you will need to secure human (or animal) subjects' approval from the Institutional Review Board (IRB) at your university. As a student, this will need to be done in conjunction with a professor (see Chapter 8 for additional ethical guidelines as they relate to the treatment of research subjects).

An institutional review board (IRB) is a committee, required by federal regulation, which reviews all research protocols involving human participants and animal subjects. IRBs are designed to support the advancement of research through the careful application of federal regulations, state laws, and university policy. The IRB is formally designated to review, approve the initiation of, and conduct periodic review of all research involving human participants and animal subjects. The primary purpose of this review is to assure the protection of the rights and welfare of human participants and animal subjects. Some universities have separate committees for human and animal research.

An IRB is responsible for protecting the rights of subjects engaged in research. This is achieved through a careful review of the proposed study, including:

- The scientific design
- Methodology
- Study procedures
- Subject population
- Recruitment procedures
- Consent processes

Through this review an IRB seeks to balance the risks to the subjects against the scientific knowledge to be gained and the potential benefits to society.

To ensure that researchers understand the federal regulations, policy requires that all principal investigators and key research personnel complete an on-line tutorial that provides information and training in subject protection. The primary means of gaining certification is through the completion of a training module offered via the web by the National Institutes of Health. You can complete the training yourself by going to: http://cme.cancer.gov/clinicaltrials/learning/humanparticipant-protections.asp.

You will need to complete the appropriate forms, provide a research proposal, and include your **informed consent** document (see box for sample). Contact your university's IRB office for guidelines and forms.

Planning a Research Program

Throughout the years that we have done research with students and collaborators, we have found it useful to follow a prescribed form in planning and thinking about experimental research. A sample research proposal form follows. It includes the working title of the research, the experimenters, the topic, the problem, and the sig-

Human Participants Review Informed Consent

Project Title: (*As it appears on the IRB application*)

Name of Investigator(s): _____

Invitation to Participate: You must provide a formal invitation to take part in the research project. *For example:* "You are invited to participate in a research project conducted through the University of XXX. The University requires that you give your signed agreement to participate in this project. The following information is provided to help you make an informed decision about whether or not to participate."

Nature and Purpose: State clearly and accurately what the study is designed to discover or establish.

Explanation of Procedures: Describe all procedures to be followed, including their purpose(s), duration, frequency, use of any audio or video recording, what will happen to the data/information at the end of the study. Include enough detail that the participant has a reasonable idea of what he/she will be doing and what they will be asked about. State any anticipated circumstances where the participant's participation may end without regard to the participant's consent.

Discomfort and Risks: Describe any physical, psychological, social, legal, and/or economic risk(s) or cost(s) resulting from the project. If there are no more than minimal risks—discomfort, burden, inconvenience—this should be so stated. This may be stated in one of several ways: Risks to participation are minimal. Risks to participation are similar to those experienced in day-to-day life. There are no foreseeable risks to participation.

Benefits and Compensation: Describe any direct benefit(s) that may result from the study. Benefits would include improved physical or mental health (e.g., from treatment), improved skills, etc. Compensation is distinct from benefit and would include cash, gifts, or academic credit provided for the person's time or travel expenses. If the individual participant will receive no direct benefit, this should be stated. If applicable, describe how voluntary or involuntary withdrawal or termination affects benefits. Note that compensation should be equivalent across participant groups and cannot be used to coerce participation. That is, if compensation for time is provided, then a portion of the compensation must be provided (prorated) even if the person terminates their involvement prior to completing the study.

Confidentiality: State the way the participant's confidentiality will be maintained: persons or organizations to whom information from the study will be furnished, nature of the information furnished, purpose of the disclosure. *For*

(continued)

example: "Information obtained during this study which could identify you will be kept confidential. The summarized findings with no identifying information may be published in an academic journal or presented at a scholarly conference".

Right to Refuse or Withdraw: Provide information about the voluntary nature of participation and the ability of the participant to stop at any time without penalty. *For example:* "Your participation is completely voluntary. You are free to withdraw from participation at any time or to choose not to participate at all, and by doing so, you will not be penalized or lose benefits to which you are otherwise entitled."

Questions: Participants should be able to seek additional information about the project. *For example:* "If you have questions about the study or desire information in the future regarding your participation, you can contact (*investigator*) at (xxx) xxx-xxxx or (if appropriate) the project investigator's faculty advisor _____ at the Department of _____, (xxx) xxx-xxxx. You can also contact the office of the Human Participants Coordinator, at (xxx) xxx-xxxx, for answers to questions about rights of research participants and the participant review process."

Agreement: Include the following statement:

I am fully aware of the nature and extent of my participation in this project as stated above and the possible risks arising from it. I hereby agree to participate in this project. I acknowledge that I have received a copy of this consent statement. I am 18 years of age or older.

_____   _____
(Signature of participant)   (Date)

_____   _____
(Printed name of participant)

_____   _____
(Signature of investigator)   (Date)

_____   _____
(Signature of instructor/advisor)   (Date)

[NOTE THAT ONE COPY OF THE ENTIRE CONSENT DOCUMENT (NOT JUST THE AGREEMENT STATEMENT) MUST BE RETURNED TO THE PI AND ANOTHER PROVIDED TO THE PARTICIPANT. SIGNED CONSENT FORMS MUST BE MAINTAINED FOR INSPECTION FOR AT LEAST 3 YEARS.]

nificance. Brief spaces follow for previous research, theory, design, and results, and a section is included for a brief description of the experimental paradigm and the analysis of data. Then, space for a list of the materials needed, including subjects, is provided. Finally, an abbreviated timetable and list of the responsibilities of the researchers ends the form. This is a very important part of research planning. In order to avoid hassles with collaborators, it is important to spell out in detail the responsibilities of each member of a research team. The collaborators can then discuss who will be listed as an author, the order of authorship, who will be mentioned in footnotes, and who will receive no acknowledgment. If two or more authors contribute equally to a project, order of authorship is sometimes determined by flipping a coin, or by alphabetical order. Sometimes contributors to an ongoing program will alternate the order of names on papers. The matter should be not one of ego but of attributing credit for the research in direct proportion to the actual contribution made by each member of the team. This form is an outline that can be expanded, and is a useful tool for the planning of research.

In practice, you should keep detailed records of your experiments, regardless of what stage of development they are in. Some projects may not get beyond the brainstorming phase, others may need more subjects run, and others may have incomplete analyses. It is important to keep all of your documentation so that projects can be completed and/or expanded. Some people find it very helpful to keep a research journal. In this journal you can jot down ideas that come to you while reading articles, after classes, or during any other time or activity that prompts good research ideas.

Performing a Pilot Experiment

Even if a research project is methodically planned to the most minute detail, it is still important to run at least one test trial, or **pilot experiment,** in order to become thoroughly acquainted with the technique and procedure. It also may be necessary to modify the methodology and adjust equipment. In a pilot experiment, you may also make use of research participants who act as judges in evaluating or developing your stimuli. In addition, it is also useful to solicit feedback from your pilot experiment research participants to ensure that instructions are understood and that the methodology that you have laid out is clearly understood and followed by the participants. This is particularly important in studies involving deception (you want to make sure that the participants "bought" the cover story) or when there are many tasks or steps for the participant to complete. You will find that your discussions with your pilot experiment participants will be an invaluable source of information to improve your study—prior to running it.

Conducting Your Experiment

Conducting your experiment requires securing a location (laboratory, auditorium, classroom, computer lab) and recruiting your subjects. Conducting experiments can be stressful. You must be organized! The pilot experiment helps you make sure you are not forgetting anything (from clip boards to passwords) and gives you practice in conducting the study. Remember, you are a potential source of bias in the experiment. So you want your experimental procedures and your own instructions and mannerisms well practiced and as similar as possible across all experimental sessions. Mistakes will happen, and it is important to document them. Your results are only as good as the research process itself. You (or your research supervisor) might be quite upset if something goes wrong. However, it is absolutely critical to document the error and let others know what occurred. Never try to hide a mistake in the collection of data. Better to have to redo a portion of the experiment, than to have the results be compromised due to an error that went unnoticed (or untold). This is part of your integrity as a researcher. Make sure also to always treat your subjects with respect and in accordance to ethical guidelines (see Chapter 8) and common sense.

Analyzing Your Data

The next step is to enter your data into a statistical software package (if it is not automatically recorded in your experiment process) like SPSS or SAS. Universities will have this software available on student-access computers, and/or your research supervisor will grant you access via his or her computers. For the student with an eye toward graduate school, a student version of one of the software packages might be a good investment.

Next comes analysis. Descriptive statistics provide a summary picture of patterns in the data. They are used to describe. Inferential statistics are procedures that allow researchers to determine whether the obtained results support their hypotheses or can be attributed to chance variation. Inferential statistics take measurements from samples and allow you to reach conclusions about larger, unmeasured populations. Depending on what point you are at in your training, you may be expected to do this yourself, you may have help, or it may be something your research supervisor does. In any case, this is the point where you "find out" the answers to your research questions. For some students, the idea of statistics and data analysis is boring, or even scary. No need to be bored or afraid. Statistics are the numbers that tell a story, that provide us with the answers we have been working so hard to find. For many researchers, the analysis phase is the most exciting. See Appendix A and B for more information on statistics in research.

Writing a Research Paper

The final stage of experimentation is the preparation of a research paper; after all, results that are not reported to the scientific community are of little use. After a researcher has formulated a problem (usually after reading the literature in the field), developed and conducted an experiment, and analyzed the data, then he or she faces the problem of how best to communicate the findings to others.

A research paper tells a story. And even the most complex paper follows the same general guidelines you may have learned in high school when writing a

Research Proposal

WORKING TITLE OF RESEARCH _____   EXPERIMENTER(S) _____

_____   _____

_____   _____

_____   DATE _____

TOPIC _____

_____

_____

PROBLEM _____

_____

_____

SIGNIFICANCE _____

_____

_____

PREVIOUS RESEARCH
   THEORY _____

_____

_____

   DESIGN _____

_____

_____

   RESULTS _____

_____

_____

EXPERIMENTAL PARADIGM _____

_____

_____

ANALYSIS OF DATA _____

_____

_____

MATERIALS _____

_____

_____

TIMETABLE AND RESPONSIBILITIES
PREPARATION OF MATERIALS

	PREPARATION OF MATERIALS _____	BY _____
PHASE 1	LITERATURE SEARCH _____	BY _____
	PILOT (DRY RUN) _____	BY _____
	RUN EXPERIMENT _____	BY _____
PHASE 2	ANALYSIS OF DATA _____	BY _____
	WRITE PAPER _____	BY _____
PHASE 3	SUBMIT FOR PUBLICATION _____	BY _____

© R. Solso

five-paragraph essay. You need to have an opening paragraph (or section) that identifies the issue for the reader, some body paragraphs to support your premise, and a closing paragraph to tie it all together. Now research papers tend to be a lot longer than five paragraphs, but they follow the same logic. For many, starting to write is the hardest thing. Some prewriting activities should be to reread your sources and notes, and organize your notes. Writing an outline, where each heading ultimately becomes a paragraph or section, is one way to develop your story and start writing. Another strategy that can help with the writing process is to know and understand the conventions of writing scientific papers. The sections required for a scientific paper guide your writing process.

Nearly all psychological journals use the style found in the APA's *Publication Manual* (2001), therefore the serious researcher should obtain a copy of this guide. The style of the journal articles discussed in this section is consistent with this manual. The APA *Publication Manual* provides guidance and information on (1) content and organization of a manuscript, (2) expression of ideas, (3) using **unbiased language,** (4) APA editorial style, (5) manuscript presentation and a sample paper, (6) manuscript acceptance and production, (7) journals program of the APA, and (8) a very helpful manuscript checklist.

Good scientific writing takes practice. It is unlikely that anyone's first attempt at writing a scientific paper will be acceptable, so we encourage students to revise and rewrite their material frequently. Even experienced writers must constantly revise and rewrite their material. Unlike your schoolwork, for which you might write one and only one draft of a term paper, turn it in, get a grade, and never look at it again, scientific writing thrives on revision! Some guidelines follow that should help in preparing a scientific paper, but we still emphasize the importance of practice, and the benefit of having colleagues review your work, prior to submission.

Writing Style

A good resource for information on scientific writing is Robert Sternberg's *The Psychology Companion: A Guide to Scientific Writing for Students and Researchers* (2003). In a clear and easy-to-read fashion, Sternberg outlines the essentials of scientific writing. He notes that, contrary to what some believe, good scientific writing is creative! It should inform and persuade; what you say *is* as important as how you say it. Furthermore, he reminds us that the writing process itself is integral to the thought process. Often, it is not until we see something in writing (and struggled even to get that down) that we achieve a clarity in our thinking on a particular subject. Sternberg also advises that it is important to commit to a point of view and to present all the facts—not just the facts that support your view.

Another goal of scientific writing is to communicate ideas clearly. To do this, the APA *Publication Manual,* 5 (4th ed.) makes a few suggestions.

To achieve clarity, good writing must be precise in its words, free of ambiguity in its presentation of ideas, economical in expression, smooth in flow, and considerate of its readers. A successful writer invites readers to read, encourages them to continue, and makes their task agreeable by leading them from thought to thought in a manner that evolves from clear thinking and logical development.

A component of good scientific writing is the selection of words that convey precise meaning. Ambiguous words should be avoided. In casual conversation it may be acceptable to use such expressions as "for the most part," "very few," "I would estimate," "an intelligence test was used," or "animals were deprived," but in scientific writing the author must use words and phrases that can be operationally defined. For example, "very few" leaves the reader mystified as to how many, and "an intelligence test was used" does not specify which intelligence test was utilized.

In addition, ideas should be developed logically. This is particularly important when introducing the research and discussing the results, but it is also important when describing the scientific method. To illustrate this, consider the literature review section of a research paper, which is normally the first major section. The purpose of this part of the paper is to introduce the reader to previous research on the subject so that the research question being addressed is placed in a meaningful context. It is impossible and distracting to recount all related research, so the writer must select the most pertinent studies and present them in such a way that the reader can understand the development of previous experiments and/or theories. (Part Two of this book contains many excellent examples of how other authors have logically developed reviews of literature.)

Careful attention should also be given to grammar and paragraph development as well as to the elimination of awkward word sequences. Sentences should be technically correct, but just as important, they must state clearly the intended meaning.

A common error is to incorporate too many thoughts in a single paragraph. A paragraph should have a controlling idea that is supported by every sentence in the paragraph. A number of paragraphs should be organized around a major principle. If the topic is "the auditory feedback in bats in a dark room" or "children's dreams and bed-wetting" or "the influence of green and blue packaging on the sales of laundry detergent," all components of the several paragraphs should revolve around that theme.

Effective Communication

Effective communication is accomplished when one expresses thoughts clearly. It is based, first, on clear thinking, and second, on the skill to represent those thoughts with words. Both clear thinking and skillful writing can be improved with practice and feedback (from a professor, a colleague, or yourself). Clear thinking and writing are as essential in experimental psychology as designing an experiment correctly. As an example of muddied writing (and perhaps muddied thinking), we ran across the following paragraph written by a prominent economist:

> Looking ahead, Mr. Litless believes the potential may exist for moderate- to short-term interest rates to decline an additional 50–75 basis points while long-term rates maintain a relatively steady itinerary. In equity markets, he predicts that corporate productivity gains will continue to be a very positive factor that will translate into better-than-anticipated gains in corporate profits.

Huh? We think this means "Short-term interest rates may decline while long-term interest rates may stay the same. This will result in corporations being more productive and making more money." As an exercise in obfuscation, write a paragraph about psychology in a muddled fashion and then have a colleague or friend decipher it for you.

Guidelines to Reduce Bias in Language

The APA is committed to scientific writing that avoids perpetuating demeaning attitudes or biased assumptions about individuals and groups. Below are some of the guidelines the APA has developed for researchers to follow to ensure that your writing is accurate and unbiased.[3]

- *Guideline 1: Describe at the appropriate level of specificity.* Precision is a necessity in scientific writing; when you refer to a person or persons, choose words that are accurate, clear, and free from bias. The appropriate degree of specificity depends on the research question and the present state of knowledge in the field of study.
- *Guideline 2: Be sensitive to labels.* Respect people's preferences; call people what they prefer to be called (Maggio, 1991). Accept that preferences will change with time and that individuals within groups often disagree about the designations they prefer (see Raspberry, 1989). Make an effort to determine what is appropriate for your situation; you may need to ask your participants which designations they prefer, particularly when preferred designations are being debated within groups.
- *Guideline 3: Acknowledge participation.* Write about the people in your study in a way that acknowledges their participation. Replace the impersonal term *subjects* with a more descriptive term when possible and appropriate—*participants, individuals, college students, children* or *respondents,* for example.
  - *Gender.* Avoid ambiguity in sex identity or sex role by choosing nouns, pronouns, and adjectives that specifically describe your participants. Sexist bias can occur when pronouns are used carelessly, as when the mas-

[3]Portions taken from the *Publication Manual* of the APA (2001). pp. 62–69. Students should review the manual for examples of each of these guidelines. This book is to be used in conjunction with the "Publication Manual of the American Psychological Association (5th Edition)."

culine pronoun *he* is used to refer to both sexes, or when the masculine or feminine pronoun is used exclusively to define roles by sex (e.g., "the nurse . . . she"). The use of *man* as a generic noun or as an ending for an occupational title (e.g., policeman) can be ambiguous and may imply incorrectly that all persons in the group are male. Be clear about whether you mean one sex or both sexes. Replacing *he* with *he or she* or *she or he* should be done sparingly because the repetition can become tiresome. Combination forms such as *he/she* or *(s)he* are awkward and distracting. Alternating between *he* and *she* also may be distracting and is not ideal; doing so implies that *he* or *she* can in fact be generic, which is not the case. Use of either pronoun unavoidably suggests that specific gender to the reader.

- *Sexual orientation. Sexual orientation* is not the same as *sexual preference.* In keeping with Guideline 2, *sexual orientation* currently is the preferred term and is to be used unless the implication of choice is intentional. The terms lesbians and gay men are preferable to homosexual when referring to specific groups.

- *Racial and ethnic identity.* Preferences for terms referring to racial and ethnic groups change often. One reason for this is simply personal preference; preferred designations are as varied as the people they name. Another reason is that over time, designations can become dated and sometimes negative (see Raspberry, 1989). Authors are reminded of the two basic guidelines of specificity and sensitivity. In keeping with Guideline 2, authors are encouraged to ask their participants about preferred designations and are expected to avoid terms perceived as negative. For example, some people of African ancestry prefer Black and others prefer African American; both terms currently are acceptable. In keeping with Guideline 1, precision is important in the description of your sample; in general, use the more specific rather than the less specific term.

- *Disabilities.* The guiding principle for "nonhandicapping" language is to maintain the integrity of individuals as human beings. Avoid language that equates persons with their condition (e.g., neurotics, the disabled); that has superfluous, negative overtones (e.g., stroke victim); or that is regarded as a slur (e.g., cripple). Use *disability* to refer to an attribute of a person and *handicap* to refer to the source of limitations, which may include attitudinal, legal, and architectural barriers as well as the disability itself (e.g., steps and curbs handicap people who require the use of a ramp). Challenged and special are often considered euphemistic and should be used only if the people in your study prefer those terms (Boston, 1992). As a general rule, "person with _____," "person living with _____," and "person who has _____" are neutral and preferred forms of description.

- *Age.* Age should be defined in the description of participants in the Method section. Be specific in providing age ranges; avoid open-ended definitions such as "under 18" or "over 65" (Schaie, 1993). "Boy" and "girl" are correct terms for referring to people of high school age and younger. Young man and young woman and male adolescent and female adolescent may be used as appropriate. For persons 18 and older (or of college age and older), use men and women. Elderly is not acceptable as a noun and is considered perjorative by some as an adjective. Older person is preferred.

The *Publication Manual* provides more information regarding unbiased language than is presented here, along with very informative examples. You are encouraged to consult this section in the *Manual* before you write.

Parts of a Manuscript

As the previous discussions suggest, the author has great freedom in choosing a writing *style* but has much less freedom in the overall *structure* of the report. The structure ensures that critical questions are answered throughout your paper. In the introduction section the questions of *why* and *what* need to be answered. In the method section *who* and *how* are answered. In the results section what was found is answered. And in the discussion section *who cares* is answered. The structure that has evolved in psychology follows a tightly prescribed model, which follows. (This model is discussed further in Part Two.)

> Title page
> Abstract
> Introduction
> Method
> Results
> Discussion
> References
> Appendix
> Author Note

Consider each of these topics:

1. *Title page.* The page includes the title, the author(s) name(s) and institutional affiliation(s), and a running head. The title should be a concise statement of the main topic and should identify the actual variables or theoretical issues under investigation and the relationships between them; for example, The Effects of _____ on _____. The title is followed by the author(s) name(s) and institutional affiliation (their university or college). The title page also has on it a running head for publication. The running head is an abbreviated title that allows readers of the published article to readily see that the page they are on is part of the same article. See the sample manuscript for the location of this heading on the manuscript page.

2. *Abstract.* Here the author should summarize the article. The abstract should not exceed 120 words. The researcher should identify the problem, method, and results. The abstract should interest and inform. Remember, this is what people are reading when they search the literature. A well-prepared abstract can be the most important paragraph in your article.

3. *Introduction.* In a paragraph or two you should answer the following questions: (1) Why is the topic/problem important? (2) How do the hypothesis and design relate to the problem? (3) What are the theoretical implications of the study? (4) How does it relate to previous work in the area? (5) What theoretical propositions are tested? (6) How were they derived? This may seem a lot to convey in just one or two paragraphs. However, the first one or two paragraphs of your introduction just lay the groundwork for the remainder of the introduction where you will more completely develop the background and state the purpose and rationale of your work. The overall length of the introduction varies based on the outlet of publication (or the requirements of your professor). Some journals publish quite brief reports, and others more lengthy articles. See the Guidelines for Authors for the journal you are interested for more information. This section is not labeled (you do not type *introduction* at the beginning of it).

4. *Method.* The method section describes the experimental design in sufficient detail to allow replication of the experiment. There are usually four part to this description: (1) the participants/subjects; (2) the stimuli and/or materials; (3) and the procedure. Additional subheadings for *stimuli* or *design* may be warranted given the complexity of your study. The method section is like a recipe; all of the ingredients and steps must be clearly presented, otherwise the experiment (much like a fabulous cheesecake) can not be replicated.

■ *Participants/subjects.* You need to appropriately identify the research subjects. This is critical for assessing the results and for replicating the study. When humans are the subjects, information on their number, how they were recruited, selected and assigned as well as any compensation given to them is important to include. Also report demographic characteristics such as sex, age, and race/ethnicity. If there are other demographic variables specific to your study, they should be reported as well. If animals are your subjects then report the genus, species, and strain number, and the name and location of the supplier. The number of animals and their sex, age, weight and physiological condition should also be included. If their treatment and handling is integral to your study, that information should be noted as well (see box).

■ *Apparatus/materials/stimuli.* This section describes the apparatus, materials and/or stimuli used in the experiment. Standard equipment like furniture, stopwatches, etc., can be mentioned without detail. Specialized equipment should be identified by supplier and model number. Custom equipment should be described completely and you may include a photograph or drawing. Instead of, or in addition to, the apparatus section, you may need a materials section. It is here where you completely describe any measures

Subjects or Participants?

The most recent version of the APA *Publication Manual* directs researchers to refer to human subjects as participants. This change is to acknowledge the voluntary, agentic nature of the people who participate in our experiments. However, some (see Roediger, 2004; Martin, 2004) have also noted the cumbersome nature of using the term *participants* instead of *subjects,* and the grammatical machinations that are ultimately required (e.g., participants participated is a bit awkward). The term subjects has been useful to psychological science for over 100 years, and you'll note its use in this book, particularly when discussing studies that were done prior to this relatively new convention of referring to subjects as participants. We encourage you always to use unbiased language and to describe appropriately the entities (be they human or animal) who you use in your research. This provides scientifically accurate and replicable information to your reader. Whether you choose to refer to the humans in your research as participants or subjects, is ultimately an individual decision of the researcher (one of the many you'll need to make!).

(questionnaires, scales, surveys, etc.) you will be using. Provide some sample questions and exactly in what format the participants respond. Provide citations if they have been developed by others and include reliability information if possible. If you are presenting stimuli to your research subjects, they should be completely described either in this section (in conjunction with *apparatus* or *materials* as appropriate), or if complex, in a new section title *Stimuli.*

- *Design.* Not every manuscript needs a design section, as many design issues can be clearly explained in the *Procedure* section. However, if your study is complex, a section called *Design* should be added here to completely describe the variables and experimental paradigm.
- *Procedure.* It is in this section where you provide the step-by-step information on the execution of the research. Instructions to human participants, formation of groups and manipulations of independent variables are to be completely described. Randomization, counterbalancing, and other control features must be described as well. The procedure section should read such that you can follow what the experimenter and research subject actually did during the study. If design details become too cumbersome to explain in this fashion, you may want a *Design* section (see above).

5. *Results.* In this section, all relevant data generated by the experiment and the analysis of these data should be reported. All relevant data should be presented or referred to in the text, but some data may best be presented in tables and graphs. Descriptive statistics, which summarize the data, should be presented. In addition, inferential statistics, which report the degree to which your results could be due to chance, should be clearly and appropriately presented. It is not necessary to report information on data entry or the statistical package used. (See Reporting Data below for more information.)

6. *Discussion.* The purpose of this section is to evaluate and interpret the implications of your results. This includes pointing out any reservations about the results, noting similarities or differences between your results and previous findings, suggesting future research, and noting the implications of the results to theory and/or practice in the specific research area. Overall, your goal is to examine, interpret, and qualify your results, and ultimately to draw inferences from them. You may also discuss why the problem is important, how the findings relate to phenomena that are more or less complex than the one under study, and, finally, what (if any) real-life phenomena the findings relate.

7. *References.* All citations in the article should be noted in this section, and every reference must be cited in the text. The general format is as follows: author's name, publication year, article title, journal title, volume, and pages. (For specific examples, see the APA *Publication Manual* or the reference section of this book.)

8. *Appendix.* An appendix is useful for detailed information that may not fit within the flow of the paper itself. A detailed description of equipment, a laboratory floor plan, or an unpublished questionnaire might all be appropriate for an appendix. It may be that at the time of publication an editor may ask you to remove the content due to space considerations (and instead say something in the Materials section like "The questionnaire is available by request from the first author.")

9. *Author Note.* In the author note you identify the departmental and university affiliation of each author, identify any sources of financial support, acknowledge others' contributions or personal assistance, and tell the reader who (which of the authors) to contact for additional information about the study.

Reporting Data

Experimental results can be reported verbally ("The racially prejudiced participants saw more instances of aggression in the environment"), statistically ("The probability of obtaining these data by chance is less than 1 in 100, or $p < .01$"), or graphically. In this book, only a modicum of statistical analyses is discussed,[4] not because they are unimportant—they are—but because in this text we emphasize research design in psychology. Other books deal with statistics in great detail.

Quantifying Observations

In almost every psychological experiment researchers collect numerical data, which can be conceptualized in two categories: descriptive data and inferential data. Conveniently, these two types of data correspond to the two major types of experimental investigation: observational studies and experimental studies.

---

[4]See Appendix A for a discussion of the appropriate use of statistics in psychological research, as well as descriptions of the mathematical procedures used in some of the statistical tests covered in this book.

Observational studies, as discussed earlier, include naturalistic observations, statistical studies, and correlational studies. An example of naturalistic observation might be recording the frequency of high-pitched sounds made by a male blue-winged warbler before and after the mating season. Statistical studies often consist of numerical descriptions of a sample of subjects, such as voters, from which generalizations are drawn. Correlational studies are designed to determine the relationship between two or more variables, such as grades in college and grades in high school, blood pressure and income, creativity and IQ, and so on. In general, the purpose of observational studies is to give an accurate description of a naturally occurring phenomenon. Results of these studies are frequently reported in terms of **descriptive statistics,** which are mathematical techniques used to characterize subjects that are observed. Experimenters may, for example, choose to characterize the intelligence of the sophomore class at the University of Michigan. Those data (IQ test results, for instance) could be summarized in terms of a **mean** score and a deviation score or in the form of a graph. (In psychological journal articles both statistical data and graphical data are reported in order to present the results of a study clearly.)

Experimental studies involve the manipulation of one or more variables, the effect of which is then measured statistically. In both experimental and observational studies, though, an additional type of statistical application might be applied. These are called **inferential statistics,** mathematical techniques in which a sample of information is gathered and generalizations are made based on that sample. One could, for example, study the effect of an advertising campaign for a strawberry-flavored breakfast cereal on people in northeastern Ohio with the aim of generalizing the results to a larger population, such as the entire country.

Statistics.   The testing of hypotheses with **statistical tests** is an important part of modern experimental psychology. A wide range of these problems has already arisen in previous sections and will appear again in the second part of this text. Determining which statistical test to apply to a certain type of data is a major theme in statistics courses, and, with fundamental knowledge of the tests and their assumptions, anyone can properly apply the correct test to the correct situation. Once these decisions have been made, the task is made even easier today with the many computer packages that will calculate a great variety of statistical tests in seconds (SPSS, SAS, for example). These packages allow you to calculate equations, such as those for F, t, and X^2, (chi square; sounds like kai square) and other, more complex statistics, without knowing the mathematical steps involved. Data in, data out! However, the responsibility is still with the researcher to "run" the appropriate types of statistical tests, given the type of data you have (see Appendix A).

Bar Graphs or Histograms.   Data can also be represented graphically. Two such methods are the **bar graph** and histogram. Both are particularly vivid figures that allow the reader to form a quick impression of the results of an experiment.

Typically, the manipulated element (cause) is depicted on the horizontal plane (called the **abscissa**), while the consequence (effect) is shown on the vertical axis (called the **ordinate**).

A **histogram** is constructed from a frequency table. The intervals are shown on the *X*-axis and the frequency in each interval is represented by the height of a rectangle located above the interval. The data for histograms are quantitative and continuous; thus the bars of the histogram are shown as touching one another. A bar graph on the other hand is used for representing qualitative, categorical data and the bars do not touch.

CASE STUDY

An example of a bar graph is shown in an experiment (Figure 9.2) by Diamond and Carey (1986). They were interested in recognition memory for faces, and wanted to explore further the phenomenon that recognition is hindered if the face is presented in an inverted position. As an added twist, they evaluated recognition memory for dogs' faces, as well. The participants were experts (breeders, handlers, or American Kennel Club judges) and novices. They were presented with both human faces and dog faces. The histogram shows that memory for dog faces is as vulnerable to inversion as is human face recognition. It also shows that novices may simply not have sufficient experience with dog faces to be affected by the inversion effect. In other words, their lack of experience allows them to focus on

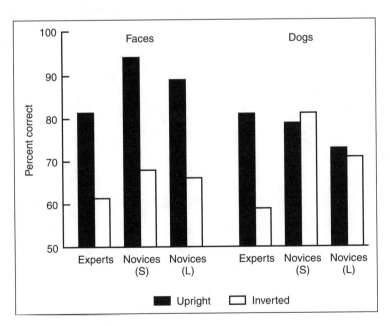

FIGURE 9.2   **A bar graph showing the performance of experts and novices on recognizing human and dog faces presented upright and inverted. Novices (S) were given a small set size in dogs, whereas novices (L) were given the same large set size as were experts.**

other characteristics of the dog's face, and thus they are able to recognize the dog's face even when it is inverted.

Figures and Functions.   A figure can also illustrate the relationship between two or more variables. For example, a curve can be drawn any time an experimenter has values for a dependent variable and for several levels of some other variable (usually the independent variable). Plotting curves allows the researcher to see the relationships between two variables. For example, the shapes of learning curves can be compared to determine more precisely the effects of certain types of reinforcement on conditioning.

   At a more sophisticated level, figures can be used to derive a mathematical equation that describes the relationship between two variables. This mathematical equation, called a **function,** is simply a shorthand method of describing the relationship, so that once the function is derived, all one has to do is substitute the value for one variable to find the value of the second variable. When plotting a curve it is customary to place the dependent variable on the vertical axis (ordinate) and the independent variable on the horizontal axis (abscissa), with increasing values as one moves away from the point at which the two axes intersect. This procedure was followed in plotting the curve in the example (see Figure 9.3 within the case study). The resulting curve clearly illustrates the relationship between the two variables.

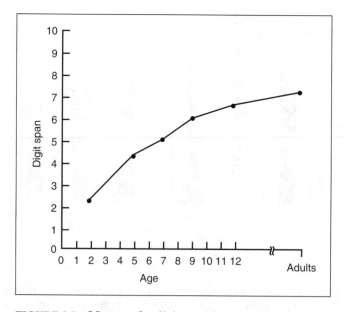

FIGURE 9.3   Memory for digits as a function of age.

From Dempster (1981).

C A S E   S T U D Y

A task that is commonly used in memory research is memory for digits—the digit span test. Digit span tests require subjects to repeat a series of numbers that have been presented. If the experimenter reads 4-8-3-6-9, the subject's task is to repeat the numbers 4-8-3-6-9.

An intriguing question in memory research is whether memory span for digits increases as a function of age, and if so, how that relationship might appear.

In a study by Dempster (1981), children of various ages were given a digit span test. The results are shown in Figure 9.3 and indicate that digit span increases as a function of age. Why this occurs is an even more fascinating puzzle. The answer may be found in the ability of older subjects to group information into more meaningful chunks. An older subject may chunk a series into two well-known mathematical progressions (4-8 and 3-6-9), which would reduce the information load substantially. Everyone uses these types of memory tricks, even if it's done subconsciously.

Illustrations.   In addition to the use of statistics, a researcher can use numerous visual forms to present information. In some instances, these graphic forms can be superior to a verbal presentation. Consider the photographs and drawing used in the following case study.

In this case study, the use of a drawing and several photographs helps the reader grasp the technique used while greatly facilitating the reproduction of the experiment.

The researchers found that a visual stimulus, such as a face, could be differentiated by monkeys, which suggested that visual memory in primates can be represented by a visual code.

C A S E   S T U D Y

Sands, Lincoln, and Wright (1982) studied visual memory in the rhesus monkey. Since monkeys are thought not to have verbal labels for objects, they could help answer the question of how visual memory operates. The experimenters constructed the apparatus that is shown in the drawing in Figure 9.4. Next, the experimenters presented their subjects with two photographs at a time. The photographs were presented one above the other (a banana and an apple are illustrated). The monkey was trained to slide a lever to the right or left to indicate whether the objects were the same or different. Reinforcement was delivered by liquid in the bottle. Some of the faces that were used are shown in Figure 9.5.

Next we turn to a more detailed example of how experimental results can be reported in manuscript form.

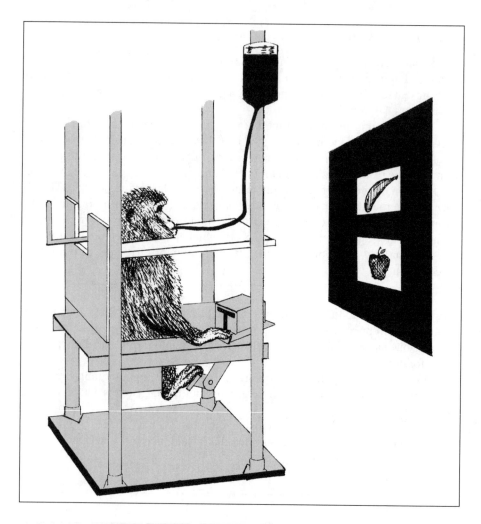

FIGURE 9.4   A rhesus monkey operating an apparatus with a lever in a test of visual memory conducted by Sands, Lincoln, and Wright (1982).

Sample Manuscript

This section contains an actual research article that has been changed slightly from the published version. The article is presented in Figure 9.6 in the form of a manuscript prepared for submission to a professional journal, and it provides a model of good experimental design and demonstrates proper use of APA style. As you read the manuscript, pay close attention to (1) the title, authors, and affiliation, (2) the abstract, (3) the literature review, the problem, and the hypothesis, (4) the method (including subjects, apparatus or materials, and procedure), (5) the

FIGURE 9.5   Some of the faces shown to the rhesus monkeys in Sands, Lincoln, and Wright's study of visual memory (1982).

results (presented both in statistical and graphic forms), (6) the discussion, and (7) the references. We have labeled these sections in the article, but on a submitted manuscript they would not be labeled.

Several features of the paper, written by Loftus and Palmer (1974), are particularly noteworthy. One is the abstract. The authors have done three essential things: They have told the reader something about the methodology, they have reported the basic results, and they have interpreted the results within a theoretical framework.

Also noteworthy is the **literature review,** which is preceded by a series of questions designed to stimulate the reader's interest in the topic. This is not required, but in this experiment it serves an important function. The authors next present several findings of other researchers, and then describe the problem. They go on briefly to describe the method, which is followed by an informal hypothesis. In describing the method, the authors give explicit information about what was done to whom. The results are then presented in verbal, statistical, graphic, and tabular form. The discussion is of particular interest in this manuscript. The authors concisely review the findings and offer two interpretations of the data. Continuing, they discuss the findings and interpretation within the context of previous findings and theories. Their discussion is to the point and does not go be-

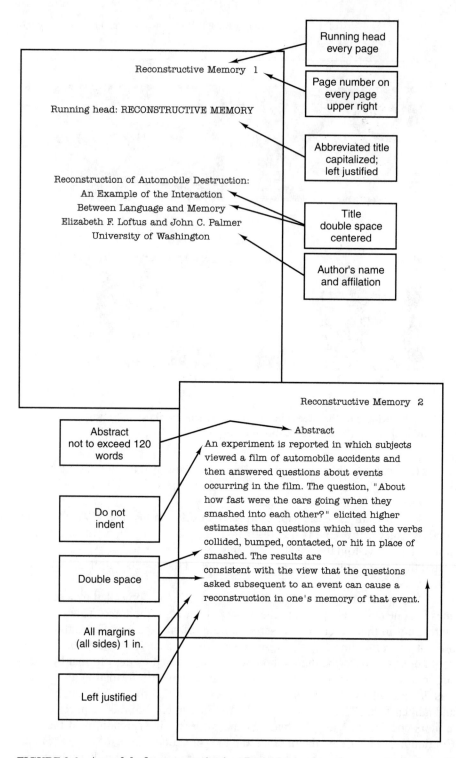

FIGURE 9.6 A model of a manuscript in APA style.

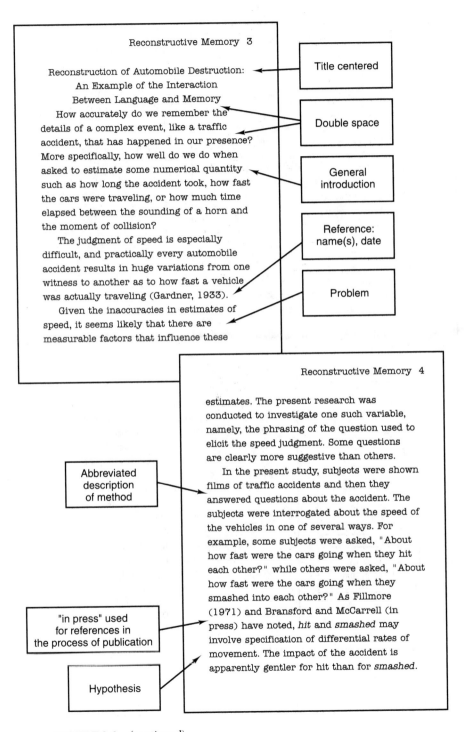

Reconstructive Memory 3

Reconstruction of Automobile Destruction:
An Example of the Interaction
Between Language and Memory

How accurately do we remember the details of a complex event, like a traffic accident, that has happened in our presence? More specifically, how well do we do when asked to estimate some numerical quantity such as how long the accident took, how fast the cars were traveling, or how much time elapsed between the sounding of a horn and the moment of collision?

The judgment of speed is especially difficult, and practically every automobile accident results in huge variations from one witness to another as to how fast a vehicle was actually traveling (Gardner, 1933).

Given the inaccuracies in estimates of speed, it seems likely that there are measurable factors that influence these

| Title centered |
| Double space |
| General introduction |
| Reference: name(s), date |
| Problem |

Reconstructive Memory 4

estimates. The present research was conducted to investigate one such variable, namely, the phrasing of the question used to elicit the speed judgment. Some questions are clearly more suggestive than others.

In the present study, subjects were shown films of traffic accidents and then they answered questions about the accident. The subjects were interrogated about the speed of the vehicles in one of several ways. For example, some subjects were asked, "About how fast were the cars going when they hit each other?" while others were asked, "About how fast were the cars going when they smashed into each other?" As Fillmore (1971) and Bransford and McCarrell (in press) have noted, *hit* and *smashed* may involve specification of differential rates of movement. The impact of the accident is apparently gentler for hit than for *smashed*.

| Abbreviated description of method |
| "in press" used for references in the process of publication |
| Hypothesis |

FIGURE 9.6 *(continued)*

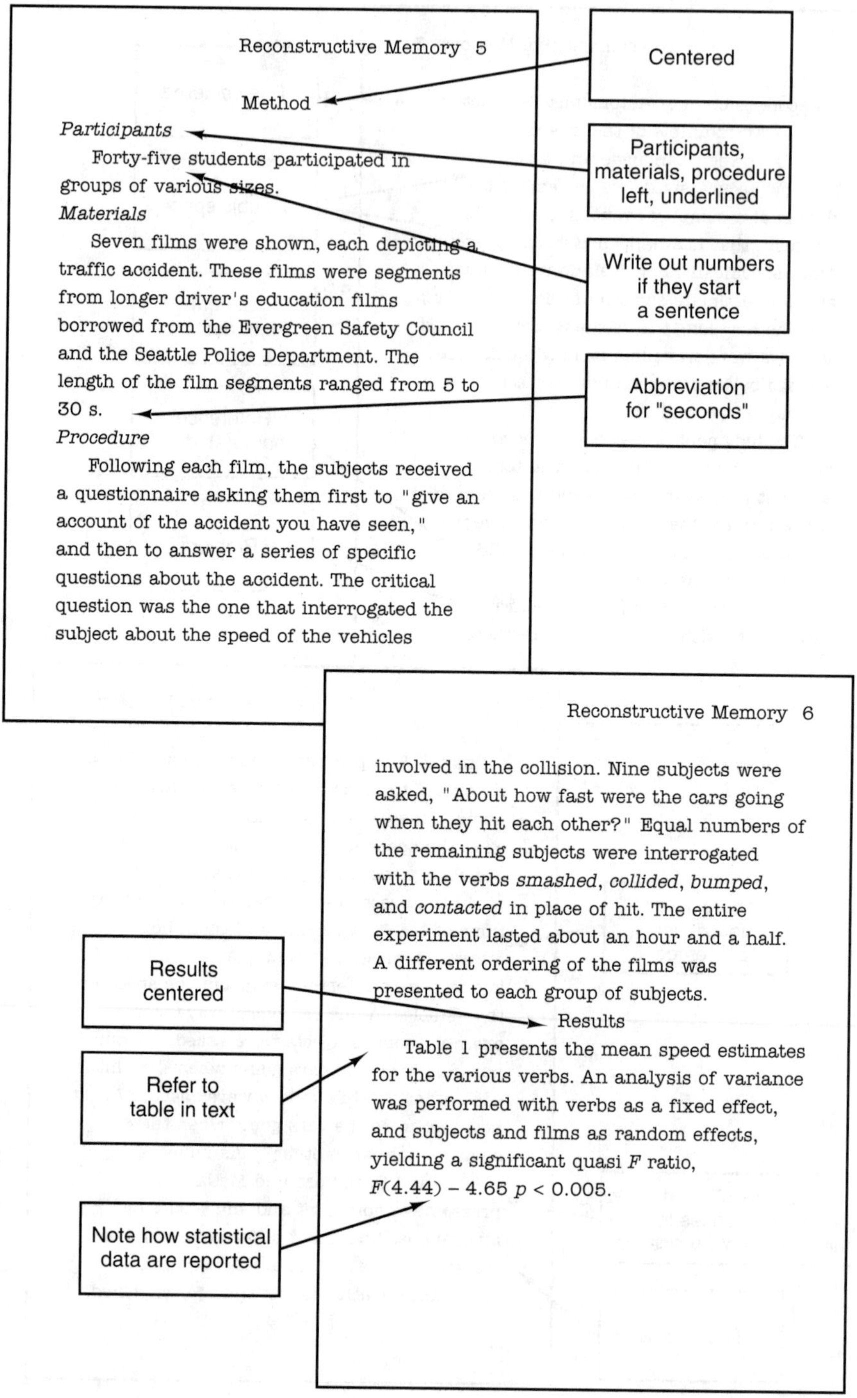

Reconstructive Memory 5

Method

Participants

Forty-five students participated in groups of various sizes.

Materials

Seven films were shown, each depicting a traffic accident. These films were segments from longer driver's education films borrowed from the Evergreen Safety Council and the Seattle Police Department. The length of the film segments ranged from 5 to 30 s.

Procedure

Following each film, the subjects received a questionnaire asking them first to "give an account of the accident you have seen," and then to answer a series of specific questions about the accident. The critical question was the one that interrogated the subject about the speed of the vehicles

Reconstructive Memory 6

involved in the collision. Nine subjects were asked, "About how fast were the cars going when they hit each other?" Equal numbers of the remaining subjects were interrogated with the verbs *smashed*, *collided*, *bumped*, and *contacted* in place of hit. The entire experiment lasted about an hour and a half. A different ordering of the films was presented to each group of subjects.

Results

Table 1 presents the mean speed estimates for the various verbs. An analysis of variance was performed with verbs as a fixed effect, and subjects and films as random effects, yielding a significant quasi F ratio, $F(4.44) - 4.65$ $p < 0.005$.

Centered
Participants, materials, procedure left, underlined
Write out numbers if they start a sentence
Abbreviation for "seconds"
Results centered
Refer to table in text
Note how statistical data are reported

FIGURE 9.6 *(continued)*

Reconstructive Memory 7

The speed estimates for the various verbs are shown in Figure 1. Four of the seven films were staged crashes; the original purpose of these films was to illustrate what can happen to human beings when cars collide at various speeds. One collision took place at 20 mph. one at 30, and two at 40. The mean estimates of speed for these four films were: 37.7, 36.2, 39.7, and 36.1, respectively.

Discussion

The results of this experiment indicate that the form of a question (in this case changes in a single word) can markedly and systematically affect a witness's answer to that question. The actual speed of vehicles controlled little variance in subject reporting, while the phrasing of the question controlled considerable variance.

Centered

Reconstructive Memory 8

Two interpretations of this finding are possible. First, it is possible that the differential speed estimates result merely from response-bias factors. A subject is uncertain whether to say 30 mph or 40 mph, for example, and the verb smashed biases his response toward the higher estimate. A second interpretation is that the question form causes a change in the subject's memory representation of the accident. The verb smashed may change a subject's memory such that he "sees" the accident as being more severe than it actually was. If this is the case, we might expect subjects to "remember" other details that did not actually occur but are commensurate with an accident occurring at higher speeds.

Interpretation of data

FIGURE 9.6 *(continued)*

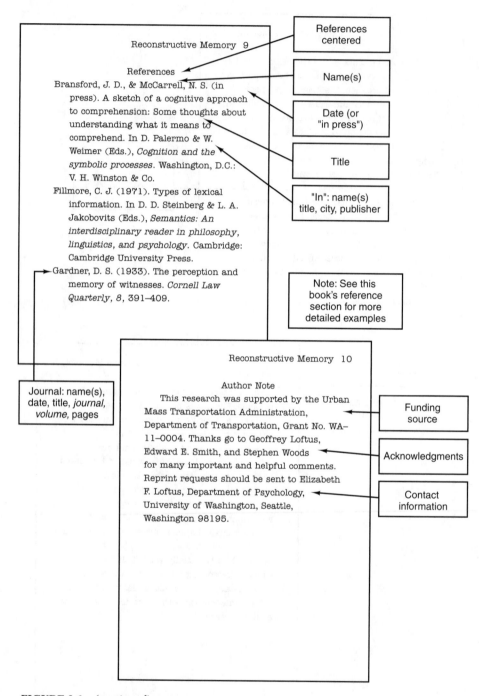

FIGURE 9.6   *(continued)*

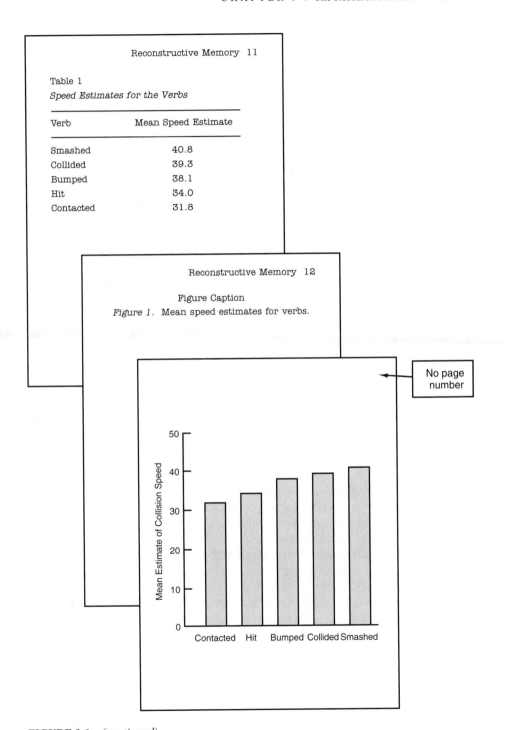

FIGURE 9.6   *(continued)*

yond the results. The final section contains the references; students can use this section as a model when listing references in their own writings.

This experiment clearly portrays many of the essential features of design and style. When students write their own experiments either for class work or for submission to a professional journal, they may want to refer to this manuscript as a model.

Submitting Your Manuscript

After a manuscript has been written, the author submits it to a professional journal for review and possible publication. Selecting the appropriate journal for a manuscript can be difficult, especially for the beginning researcher. In general, researchers prefer to publish their work in accepted, well-known, respected journals. Of course, the difference between "good" and "bad" publications is a matter of interpretation. Journals devoted to empirical studies that are published by the American Psychological Association (e.g., *Journal of Personality and Social Psychology, Journal of Experimental Psychology,* which has four separate editions, *Child Development, Journal of Personality & Social Psychology, Developmental Psychology, Journal of Comparative Psychology,* and others) are well regarded and widely read. The American Psychological Society publishes several high-quality journals, including *Psychological Science* and *Current Directions in Psychological Science.* Also, numerous groups publish periodicals that include important research articles, including the Psychonomic Society (e.g., *Memory & Cognition Perception & Psychophysics, Bulletin of the Psychonomic Society*) and the British Psychological Society (e.g., *British Journal of Psychology, Quarterly Journal of Experimental Psychology*). Many other journals also publish works (e.g., *American Journal of Psychology, Cognitive Psychology, Neuropsychology, Brain and Cognition, Cortex, Journal of Speech & Hearing Research, Science, Journal of Experimental Analysis of Behavior, Journal of Memory & Language,* and so on).

This list is by no means inclusive. Many other high-level publications deal with selected topics in experimental psychology. It is the responsibility of researchers to find the most appropriate journals for their manuscripts. One clue is to find out where researchers working on similar problems are publishing their work. This can be determined by reading and reviewing the literature. Many times a common theme (or several themes) pervade a journal.

Once an article goes to a journal, the review process may take up to a year, although many editors attempt to reach a decision on a manuscript within three months. An outline of the editorial process used by the APA is shown in Figure 9.7 on page 169.

Poster Sessions at Professional Meetings

An increasingly popular forum for presenting current research is in poster sessions at professional meetings. Here, both seasoned researchers and students display their research on large, freestanding boards in a format that allows them to inter-

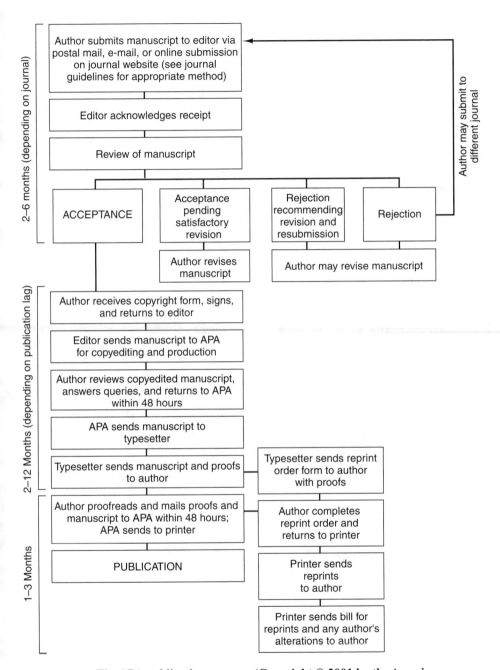

FIGURE 9.7   The APA publication process. (Copyright © 2001 by the American Psychological Association. Reprinted with permission.)

act directly with their audience. Typically, after one has conducted a research project, he or she will perform the necessary statistical tests, write the report, and submit an abstract to a professional organization (see box). If accepted, the researcher will then display the poster at the meeting. Most organizations, including the American Psychological Association, the Association for Psychological Science, Psychonomic Science, and regional associations such as the Eastern Psychological Association, the Midwestern Psychological Association, the Rocky Mountain Psychological Association, and the Western Psychological Association, and specialized organisations like the American Psychology-Law Society and the Association for Behavior Analysts, have poster sessions at their annual meetings and encourage student participation.

Before a paper is accepted for a **poster presentation,** an **abstract** is reviewed by a panel of experts in the field. The standards for accepting a poster are far less rigorous than the standards for accepting a full research paper in a typical psychological journal. Reviewers normally have only an abstract of the paper and therefore do not evaluate in detail the method and results. As such, a researcher can present posters that (1) show only a part of the research findings, (2) reach a tentative conclusion, or (3) invite criticism from others.

It is important to present your poster in a professional, interesting, and clear manner. Todd Heatherton of the Society for Personality and Social Psychology notes in his recommended poster guidelines and specifications that "a poster should be complete and self-supporting so that different viewers may read at their leisure. The author should only need to supplement or discuss particular points raised during inquiry. Remember that several people with varying degrees of interest and experience may be viewing your poster at once. Therefore, make your points as complete and brief as possible." The Western Psychological Association provides some useful guidelines for poster preparation. (1) Construct the poster to include the title, the author(s), affiliations, and a description of the research that highlights the major elements that are covered in the abstract of your work.

Writing an Abstract

An abstract is a concise summary of your project and is usually around 300–1000 words (check the conference submission guidelines for the appropriate length). The abstract should include a clear and specific title; a brief introduction to the topic; a statement of the study's objectives; a clear presentation of the methods; a summary of the results and a statement of the conclusions. Some conferences allow for the submission of abstracts where the outcome is not yet known (because you are still conducting your study, but will have it done by the time of the conference). However, others do not, so carefully read the submission information (sometimes called "the call for papers") to make sure.

(2) Minimize detail and try to use simple, jargon-free statements. (3) Remember that pictures, tables, and figures are amenable to a poster display. (4) If you can, use color in your visuals. (5) Make sure that your lettering is neatly done and is large enough to be read from a distance, that is, do not simply pin up a set of typed pages—reserve these for your handout. (6) Consider using a flow chart or some other method of providing the viewer with a guide to inspecting your display. (7) Above all, don't overwhelm the viewer with excessive amounts of information; rather, construct a poster display that enhances conversation. (8) Be ready to pin up and take down your poster at the specified times. (9) Be sure to bring thumbtacks with you. (10) You should have copies of a printed version of your poster with the details of the research available for distribution, and/or a sign-up sheet on which interested people can request the paper.

You do not have to spend a lot of money to create an effective and professional poster. Do not simply pin up manuscript pages using standard 12-point font! This shows a lack of effort on your part and, more importantly, does not highlight your research effectively. All of your text should be large (at least

Poster session at a professional meeting.

26 point font). Colored construction paper or poster board can offset white 8½ × 11 inch manuscript pages to create a pleasing, but inexpensive poster. Preprinted stationery, banners, school colors, and school decals can all add to the style of your poster (just remember to keep it professional). Alternatively, you can construct your poster in very small font, on a single sheet of paper, and have it enlarged at any major copying or printing store ($6–$15, in black and white). Hotel business centers are expensive. It is to your benefit (both in terms of your nerves and your pocketbook!) to have your poster and handouts prepared prior to arriving at the conference. The bottom line is to present your research in a format that will catch people's interest and be easy to read and memorable.

You will typically be assigned a 4 foot high by 8 foot wide bulletin board. However, you should check your preconference materials to get exact specifications and any special requirements specific to that conference. A grid format arranged in columns is effective. This prevents viewers from having to cross back and forth in front of each other to read your poster. Your poster session will typically be about 2 hours long. You are required to be present at your poster during that time period. Remember, this is a time to meet people and show off your research, so it is to your benefit to be present at your poster. Some conferences have an additional viewing period in which your poster is on display longer than the actual poster session (either before, after, or both).

The idea of a poster session is to provide a venue for new research. The audience mills around the displayed work, reads the contents, and asks questions or makes comments to the researcher. It is usually a lively venue for the exchange of ideas. In light of this opportunity to meet and interact with many people interested in your research, it is important to be alert, prepared, and friendly. You can visit with your own friends, lab mates, and colleagues any time. Many interested people will not approach you to ask questions if you are obviously engaged in friendly, non–poster-related conversation with others. Make eye contact with people and offer to give them a "tour" of your poster or to answer any questions they may have. One important note: Dress professionally. If you have any doubt as to what this means, talk to a trusted friend, advisor, or professor prior to attending the conference. Our last piece of advice? Have fun! Relax and enjoy the opportunity to discuss with others the research that you have worked so hard to complete.

A Final Note

At this point, you have completed the technical part of this book. Next, you will read several actual research articles to further test and expand your knowledge of experimental design.

PART TWO

Analysis of Experiments

Part Two of this book deals with actual experiments that have been carefully selected from the psychological literature to demonstrate a variety of topics and experimental techniques.

After conducting an experiment, the psychologist's next obligation is to report the results to the scientific community. In practice, this means preparing a research paper for a journal. Thus, the ability to write such papers and read them with understanding is one of the most important demands facing the research psychologist.

Because journal space is limited and there are so many other demands on a scientist's time, clarity, and conciseness are crucial in the presentation of research results. At the same time, these articles are aimed at other scientists, particularly those working in the same problem area, making a knowledge of that area's research history and its methodologies a prerequisite. This can make journal articles difficult going, both for students and for psychologists who have different research specialties.

In Part Two some of the articles are presented in edited form; others are presented in their entirety. All of the articles present the information you need to apply your knowledge of experimental design. Most articles are accompanied by an analysis. By repeated exposure to and careful analysis of such papers, the student can begin to feel comfortable reading research reports and may develop an understanding of the principles of experimental design in psychology. Some articles are not accompanied by an analysis; they are to be analyzed by you.

The analyses that are provided correspond to the appropriate section of the article. The original article is in a shaded gray box; the analyses is below it. Many of the experiments in this section were selected because they provide an example which we have titled a Special Issue. These issues are set apart from the main text in our analysis of the article. Each of the issues listed below is addressed in at least one article. There is no right way to read an article, but some suggestions follow that might help you to understand research reports better.

Special Issues	Chapter
1. Control Problems	"Cola Tasting"—Chapter 10
2. Field-based Studies	"Territoriality in Parking Lots"—Chapter 11
3. Selection of Subjects as a Source of Independent Variables and "Politically Incorrect" Findings	"Hormones and Toy Preferences"—Chapter 14
4. The Use of Animals in Psychological Research	"Maternal Behavior"—Chapter 15
5. Small n Designs	"Creative Porpoise"—Chapter 17
6. Single Subject Design in Clinical Studies	"Therapy for Anger"—Chapter 19
7. Multiple Experiments and Studying Complex Social Behavior in the Laboratory	"Alcohol and Condoms"—Chapter 21
8. Subject Variables	"Karate Techniques"—Chapter 22

First, read the title and try to establish the general category within psychology that the study is investigating. Consider an article such as "Two-Phase Model for Human Classical Conditioning" (Prokasy & Harsanyi, *Journal of Experimental Psychology,* 1968, *78,* 359–368). Most people have had some experience with classical conditioning or at least know something about the famous Pavlovian studies with dogs. From the title you could infer that these authors have apparently studied learning by using a conditioning method, and that they have developed some model to describe their results. In addition to simply reading the title, it may help to try to raise concrete questions about the problem and procedures. In this example, you might ask, How did the authors condition the humans—with a bell and meat powder? What are two possible phases of classical conditioning?

It may also help to know that most journal articles contain an abstract at the beginning of the paper where the major findings and the method used are briefly described. A careful reading of this, coupled with an inquiring mind, will facilitate an understanding of the paper.

Then, a reading of the entire paper is suggested. You should carefully read each section: the literature review, the hypothesis, methods, results, and the discussion sections. Pay close attention to the methods section; apply what you've learned about experimental design to your analysis and understanding of what the researcher has done. You may also want to return to the abstract to reestablish a point of view, but the critical aspect of scientific reading is a probing inquiry. When reviewing and reading, *question!*

In reading an article, it may also help to ask some of the following questions, plus many more that would be determined, in part, by the responses to the questions.

1. What is this research all about?
2. What is the general problem?
3. What are the results of others?
4. What is the hypothesis?
5. What materials does the author use?
6. How does the author operationally define his or her variables?
7. What controls does he or she use?
8. How does he or she analyze the data?
9. How does he or she interpret the data?
10. What are the strengths of this article?
11. What are the weaknesses of this article?
12. What additional work needs to be done?
13. Can the data be interpreted in another way?
14. What have I learned from this article?
15. What new research can now be developed?

You might consider answering these questions for each article you read, not just for the analysis of the four articles in Part Two, but for articles you are assigned for your classes as well. If you are able to answer these questions for articles you read, you will have a very good understanding of the concepts that are presented. You can also use the form provided in Chapter 2 to guide your reading.

Some articles are complex or use technical language that may make them difficult to understand. This problem is common among new students (as well as for some experienced students). If this happens, repeating the process suggested above should help. Sometimes students also find it helpful to review an article for a friend and allow him or her to ask questions.

For convenience, the table that follows summarizes some of the relevant characteristics of the articles in Part Two. We suggest that you look at the table prior to reading each article for an overview of the article.

Abbreviated Title	Psychological Subject Matter	Source of Hypothesis	Setting	Treatment of Subjects	Statistical/ Descriptive Analysis	Subjects	Independent Variable	Dependent Variable
Cola Tasting Chapter 10	Perception	Applied research	Laboratory	Paired comparisons within subjects	χ^2, table, percentages	Humans (college students)	Different colas	Identification of cola
Territoriality in Parking Lots, Chapter 11 (to be analyzed by you)								
Fanning Old Flames Chapter 12	Physiological/ emotions	Hypothesis	Laboratory	Assignment via questionnaire	F, graph	Human (college students)	Thought suppression	Physiological responses (SCL)
Picture Memory Chapter 13	Cognitive/ memory	Hypothesis testing/theory	Laboratory	Random group (2 groups)	Table, percentages, t, z	Humans (college students)	Thematic clue	Memory for pictures
Hormones and Toy Preferences Chapter 14	Child/ physiological	Hypothesis	Hospital	Designated subjects	t, graph	Children	Hormone level	Toy preference
Maternal Behavior Chapter 15	Comparative motivation	Hypothesis testing/theory	Laboratory	Random group (4 groups)	F, Mann–Whitney, Duncan's range test, graphic	Rats	Injection of blood	Maternal behavior
Children's Reasoning, Chapter 16 (to be analyzed by you)								

Creative Porpoise Chapter 17	Creative learning	Hypothesis testing/theory (demonstration)	Laboratory/ seminatural setting	Single subject	Graphic, correlation	Porpoises	Reinforcement	Novel behavior
Perspective Shifting Chapter 18	Cognitive	Hypothesis testing	Laboratory	Random group	F, table	Humans (college students)	Role type	Recall
Therapy for Anger Chapter 19	Clinical	Clinical experience	Clinical	Single subject	Figures, correlation	Hospitalized patients	Therapy	Anger control/ reduction
Prosocial Behavior, Chapter 20 (to be analyzed by you)								
Alcohol and Condoms Chapter 21	Social	Hypothesis	Correlational, laboratory, field/4 experiments	Assigned groups and subject variables	Chi square, Cronbach's alpha, F	Humans (college students)	Sober vs. intoxicated	Intentions to engage in sexual intercourse
Karate Techniques Chapter 22	Memory	Hypothesis testing	Laboratory	Subject variables (2 groups)	Correlation, graphic, means	Humans (karate students)	Experts and novices	Recall and frequency estimation
Disputes in Japan, Chapter 23 (to be analyzed by you)								
False Confessions Chapter 24	Social psychology & law	Hypothesis testing/applied	Laboratory	Random group	Chi square, F, table	Humans (college students)	Vulnerability, false incriminating evidence	Social influence

10 Cola Tasting

Introduction

The first experiment in Part Two by Thumin (1962) deals with the identification of cola beverages and presents some interesting design problems. As you read this experiment, ask yourself what variables, both experimental and cultural, may influence a person's preference for one cola drink over another. The purposes of including this experiment are (1) to introduce you to some of the issues involved when controlling variables in a psychological study and (2) to heighten your awareness of how complex the relationships are between a real-world stimulus (cola drink) and the psychological evaluation of the stimulus.

Special Issues

CONTROL PROBLEMS

There are two types of control. The first is when the experimenter makes something occur and the second is when the experimenter prevents something from occurring (extraneous variables). Pay attention to the extraneous variables that were controlled in this experiment.

Relations between Pairs

One cola may be easy to identify when presented with a second cola, but difficult to distinguish from a third. For example, Coke may be easy to identify when it is paired with Royal Crown, but difficult to identify when it is paired with Pepsi. To avoid such problems, each cola was paired with the other colas an equal number of times. Another problem is that within each pair presentation, the first cola may be easier to identify than the second, or vice versa. To eliminate this problem, each cola could have been presented an equal number of times in the first and second position. While Thumin did not systematically control for this, it could easily have been incorporated into the design to strengthen the procedure.

Order Effects

We already know that when subjects make a series of judgments, order effects can appear. Subjects may become more sensitive with practice, or they may become fatigued so that their judgments are not as accurate. In taste experiments it is probable that the subject's judgments will not be as accurate because the previous cola may not have been completely washed out of his or her mouth after each trial, and the residue may distort later judgments. To control for this, Thumin presented the stimulus pairs in random order. This procedure is effective for controlling order effects.

Stimulus Accumulation

Related to the preceding point, the subject washed out his or her mouth with water after each pair of cola tastes. This control procedure attempted to eliminate the confusion of taste from one pair to the next. It is reasonable to assume that a subject could not judge a given pair effectively if the taste of the previous pair was still in his or her mouth. Furthermore, clean cups were used for each presentation to eliminate the possibility of an accumulation of cola in the cups.

Visual Cues

Thumin was testing to see whether or not the subjects could identify the colas by taste. To do this he had to eliminate any other cues that might help the subject identify the cola. One such set of cues are visual cues; for example, Coke may look different from Pepsi. To eliminate visual cues, experimenters should blindfold subjects in experiments of this type.

Temperature

Most people drink colas that are cooled to a temperature of 5°C (46°F). Their experience with tasting cola is limited to this temperature; that is, the taste of Coke is really the taste of Coke at 5°C. To allow for this, Thumin presented all colas at a constant temperature of 5°C.

Guessing

In many judgment experiments, problems arise when subjects guess. Some subjects will guess when they do not know the correct identification, and some subjects will simply say that they do not know. To avoid these problems Thumin told all subjects to guess when they did not know the colas. He was quite explicit about this in his instructions when he pointed out to the subjects that even if they were not sure of the brand, they should tell him what brand they thought it was.

Note also that Thumin has (in a sense) corrected for guessing in his statistical analysis (see footnote to Table 1). There were three choices: One choice was correct and two were incorrect. Thus, the probability of being correct by chance was one out of three. The statistic tested to see if the subjects' identifications were more likely to be correct than would be expected by guessing alone (chance).

Subject Variables

Chapter 6 presented a lengthy discussion of subject variables. Much of this discussion centered around the problem of having people in one experimental treatment who were different as to some individual characteristics from people in another treatment. Thumin avoided this problem by having all subjects participate in all treatments—a *within-subject design.* Thumin controlled for some of the problems of the within-subject design by controlling for order effects. However, another subject variable problem could appear in this experiment. Suppose that only heavy cola drinkers can distinguish between the different brands. Suppose further that the sample of subjects Thumin picked had a small proportion of heavy cola drinkers. Because the sample would contain only a few heavy drinkers (who can make correct identifications), then the majority of light drinkers might make it appear as if the identification of cola beverages is little better than chance. Thumin accounted for this subject variable problem by finding out how much cola each subject drank per week. It is apparent that this subject variable did not influence the data (see Table 2); however, Thumin took this possibility into account and tested to see what effect this subject variable had on the dependent variable.

This discussion of design and control procedures should make it evident to the student that careful planning is needed before an experiment can be executed. It was pointed out previously that control problems vary with each experimental area. The Thumin experiment illustrates some of the considerations that must be taken into account in experimenting with the identification of the taste of substances.

IDENTIFICATION OF COLA BEVERAGES

Frederick J. Thumin
Washington University

An attempt was made to overcome certain methodological inadequacies of earlier studies in determining whether cola beverages can be identified on the basis of taste. Some 79 Ss completed questionnaires on their cola drinking habits and brand preferences, then were tested individually on samples of cola beverages presented under methods of paired comparisons. Significant chi-square values were obtained for Coca-Cola and Pepsi Cola, due to the large number of correct identifications for these brands. Correct identification of Royal Crown, however, did not differ from chance expectancy. No significant relationship was found between ability to identify cola beverages and degree of cola consumption; nor were Ss any better at identifying their "regular" brand than they were other brands.

Earlier studies attempting to determine whether cola beverages can be identified on the basis of taste[1] have, in the main, obtained negative results (Bowles & Pronko, 1948; Pronko & Bowles, 1948; Pronko & Bowles, 1949; Pronko & Herman, 1950; Prothro, 1953). These results may, in part, be attributed to certain methodological difficulties. For example, in the majority of these studies,

a   **the subjects were not informed as to what brands they were attempting to identify. This lack of restriction encouraged guessing behavior, which resulted in the naming of irrelevant beverages (e.g., Dr. Pepper),** as well as relatively frequent mentions of the more heavily advertised brands such as Coca-Cola.

----

[1]In this report, the word "taste" is used in the broad sense—that is, to include gustation, olfaction, and possible tactual qualities as well.

Source: Reprinted by permission from *Journal of Applied Psychology,* 1962, *46* (5), 358–360. Published by the *American Psychological Association.*

Analysis

Literature Review, Statement of Problem, and Hypothesis

The first paragraph attempts briefly to describe the previous research on cola identification and to note the scope of the present research. Although it is not common to define terms in research papers, the author uses an acceptable method to define *taste* in a footnote.

Three methodological factors (**a, b,** and **c**) were not controlled effectively in the previous literature, which may have affected the results. These factors were **(a)**

b Moreover, the subjects were expected to identify the various colas on the basis of past experience, yet apparently **no attempt was made to determine whether the subjects had ever tasted these beverages, or to relate identification to degree of cola consumption.**

c Each of these previous studies used essentially the same method of stimulus presentation; **namely, all beverages were presented simultaneously to the subject,** and only one such presentation was made. This technique, while satisfactory, would appear to be somewhat less sensitive than the method of paired comparisons, which requires the subject to identify each brand a number of times under various experimental conditions.

d Thus, the purpose of the present study was to determine whether methodological inadequacies in the earlier studies may have contributed to the subjects' relative inability to identify brands. The primary modifications in experimental design were as follows: an indication of cola consumption habits was obtained, subjects were told in advance what beverages they were attempting to identify, and the method of paired comparisons was used for presentation of stimuli.

not informing the subjects of the colas to be identified, **(b)** not determining the subjects' experience with cola beverages, and **(c)** presenting the colas simultaneously. The author tentatively identifies the possible biasing (or confounding) result of each of these uncontrolled factors.

In **(d)** a succinct statement is made about the methodological differences between this and previous studies.

In this experiment, *paired comparison* was used. This is a standard technique in which a subject is given two stimuli and asked to judge them. The judgment in this study was a qualitative one; subjects were asked to identify specific colas by taste. (It should be noted that this method of comparison also permits quantitative judgments. For example, in this experiment the subjects could be asked to identify greater or lesser amounts of a certain quality.) A related procedure, which Thumin mentions in **(c)** as the predominant procedure used in cola tasting, is *multiple comparison*. In this method, subjects are asked to make judgments on a variety of different stimuli.

This study does not clearly state a hypothesis to be tested, yet the reader can provide his or her own statement of a hypothesis with the material presented. How would you state the hypothesis?

METHOD

Seventy-nine subjects were employed, all of whom were either college students or college graduates between the ages of 18 and 37 years. The subjects were first asked to fill out a questionnaire on their cola consumption habits and brand preferences. The cola beverages were presented to the subjects individually in an experimental room which was kept dimly lighted to eliminate possible visual cues. Instructions were as follows:

> I would like to have you taste and identify some cola drinks. I will place two cups at a time in front of you—one on your left and one on your right. Taste these two colas in any order you wish; then tell me what brand you think each one is. Be careful not to change the position of the cups while you are tasting them; that is, keep the left cup on the left, and the right cup on the right. Each time you finish with one pair of cups, rinse your mouth well by taking a few swallows of water from the water cup. When you have done this, I will give you the next pair.
>
> There are three colas involved in this study—Coca-Cola, Pepsi Cola, and Royal Crown. Even if you are not sure of the brand in some cases, I still want you to tell me what brand you think it is. The two members of a pair are always different brands; that is, a brand is never compared with itself. Are there any questions?

Using the method of paired comparisons, six pairs of beverages were presented to the subject, one pair at a time. The subjects were exposed to each brand four times for a total of 12 judgments. The order of presentation of stimulus pairs was randomly determined. Stimulus cups contained 2 ounces of the beverages at an approximate temperature of 5° centigrade.

Method

The method section of this report is fairly brief, but it contains the necessary information (including the exact instructions given to the subjects) to allow the study to be replicated **(e)**. However, there are some features of the design that the author does not make explicit.

Type of Design

In this experiment the independent variable is three types of colas, whereas in the audition experiment the independent variable was tones of different frequencies. In the audition experiment the dependent variable was the absolute threshold of the tone, that is, some hypothetical point above which the subject could hear the tone and below which he or she could not hear the tone. In the cola experiment the dependent variable is the correctness of the identification of the cola. In both experiments there were multiple presentations of the same stimulus; in the audition experiment there were six attempts to determine the threshold for each tone, three using the descending method and three using the ascending method. In the

RESULTS

f **The chi-square was used to determine whether ability to identify brands differed significantly from chance expectancy.** As Table 1 shows, the chi-square values for both Coca-Cola and Pepsi Cola were significant at the **0.01**
g **level of confidence,** while that for Royal Crown was not significant. Inspection of the data indicates that the significant divergencies obtained with Coca-Cola and Pepsi Cola are due to the large number of correct identifications of these brands; for example, more than twice the expected number of subjects were able to identify these brands correctly at least three times out of four.

cola experiment the subjects were exposed to each brand four times. By using several presentations of the same stimulus, the experimenter may get a more stable or reliable measure of each subject's judgments. The basic difference in the two experiments is that in the audition experiment the experimenter presented one tone at a time. This was an appropriate method for that problem because the experimenter was asking, "When can you hear the tone?" In the Thumin experiment the problem is identifying the cola: "Which cola is it?" To get an answer to this question, Thumin argues that presenting two stimuli at the same time (paired-comparison method) is more effective than the methods previously used.

Results

The basic findings and the summary of the statistical analysis are the principle parts of the results section.

The χ^2 (chi-square) statistical procedure was used to treat the data **(f)**. This is a relatively simple procedure in which the results are compared with what one would expect by chance alone. *Chance* is defined as the variation in the results that is due to uncontrolled factors, such as guessing, experimental error, failure to mask stimuli perfectly, failure to achieve a perfect matching of subjects or randomization in experiments using different groups of subjects, and so on. In this experiment subjects who had no knowledge of the cola but simply guessed would be correct sometimes. But if the experimental results vary greatly from what would be expected by chance, then some experimental conditions are probably responsible for this difference.

The level of confidence, or "level of significance" **(g)**, is a reflection of the probability that the results would be obtained by chance alone. In this study the author establishes a level of confidence of $p = .01$; that is, the probability that such results would occur by chance alone is 1 in 100. Frequently, the level of confidence is set at .05 (or 5 in 100), but in some research it may be useful to demand lower levels.

TABLE 1   Chi-Square for Observed and Expected Frequencies of Brand Identification

BRAND OF COLA	OBSERVED AND EXPECTED FREQUENCIES	NUMBER OF CORRECT IDENTIFICATIONS				
		0	1	2	3 or 4	χ^2
Coca-Cola	(f_0)	13	23	24	19	14.57**
Pepsi Cola	(f_0)	12	20	26	21	22.14**
Royal Crown	(f_0)	18	28	19	14	4.60*
All brands	$(f_c)^a$	15.6	31.2	23.4	8.8	

Note: For each comparison, $df = 3$.
[a]Expected values were obtained from the expression $N(\frac{1}{3} + \frac{2}{3})^4$. Each sample had one chance in three of being identified correctly, and each brand was presented to the subject four times.
* $p > .05$.
** $p < .01$.

The results presented in Table 2 indicate that ability to identify cola beverages correctly was unrelated to degree of consumption; that is, correct identifications were essentially the same for heavy, medium, and light cola drinkers. Further analysis of the data showed that ability to identify a given brand was also unrelated to whether that brand was considered by the subject to be his or her "regular" brand.

By telling the subjects in advance what brands they were attempting to identify, irrelevant brand naming was eliminated as well as excessive naming of heavily advertised brands. Specifically, Coca-Cola was mentioned 317 times, Pepsi Cola 321 times, and Royal Crown 310 times.

TABLE 2   Chi-Square for Brand Identification as Related to Consumption

Number of Colas Consumed per Week	NUMBER OF CORRECT IDENTIFICATION		
	0–3	4–6	7–12
Heavy (7 or more)	10 (8.5)	14 (12.0)	3 (6.5)
Medium (3–6)	7 (8.2)	9 (11.5)	10 (6.3)
Light (0–2)	8 (8.2)	12 (11.5)	6 (6.3)

Note: Expected values appear in parentheses.
$\chi^2 = 5.44$; $df = 4$; $p < .05$.

DISCUSSION

h | The present study clearly demonstrated that certain brands of cola can be identified on the basis of taste. The significant chi-square values obtained with Coca-Cola and Pepsi Cola were due to the large number of correct identifications for these brands. **The subjects' inability to identify Royal Crown Cola can probably be attributed to a lack of recent experience with this brand. Some 58 percent of the subjects said they had not had a Royal Crown for at least 6 months prior to the experiment.**

i | No relationship was found between ability to identify cola beverages and degree of cola consumption (i.e., number of colas consumed in an average week). Moreover, the subjects were no better at identifying their regular brand than they were at identifying other brands. Thus, it would appear that the subjects needed a certain minimal amount of recent experience with a brand in order to identify it, but beyond this minimal amount, additional experience (i.e., heavier consumption) did not help.

j | Within the framework of this study, **the method of paired comparisons proved to be sufficiently sensitive to detect small but significant abilities to identify cola beverages.** There appeared to be no problem with the development of sensory adaptation as successive pairs of stimuli were presented. Analysis of the data revealed that, as trials progressed, the subjects showed small (though nonsignificant) increases in ability to identify brands.

REFERENCES

Bowles, J. W., Jr., & Pronko, N. H. (1948). Identification of cola beverages: II. A further study. *Journal of Applied Psychology, 32,* 559–564.

Pronko, N. H., & Bowles, J. W., Jr. (1948). Identification of cola beverages: I. First study. *Journal of Applied Psychology, 32,* 304–312.

The author makes a clear summary statement and also provides the reader with two tables that contain the experimental data. Note that two of the obtained x^2 values exceed the .01 level.

Discussion

In the discussion section the author reviews the major findings **(h)** and offers a plausible explanation for the lack of statistically significant findings regarding the Royal Crown condition **(i)**.

Finally, the sensitivity of the paired-comparison technique in detecting abilities to identify colas is mentioned **(j)**.

Pronko, N. H., & Bowles, J. W., Jr. (1949). Identification of cola beverages:
   III. A final study. *Journal of Applied Psychology, 33,* 605–608.
Pronko, N. H., & Herman, D. T. (1950). Identification of cola beverages: IV.
   Postscript. *Journal of Applied Psychology, 34,* 68–69.
Prothro, E. T. (1953). Identification of cola beverages overseas. *Journal of
   Applied Psychology, 37,* 494–495.

Note: The author wishes to express his appreciation to A. Barclay who served as critical reader for earlier drafts of this paper.

Questions

1. In the design of this experiment each cola was paired with the other colas an equal number of times, and the presentation of stimulus pairs was randomly determined. Using a within-subject design, lay out exactly how one sequence of 12 pairs might have been presented to a subject.
2. Why was a dimly lighted room used **(e)**? What effects would a brightly illuminated room have? What effects would a red-illuminated room have? A green-illuminated room? A nonilluminated room? Would these conditions be worthy of research?
3. Why did the subjects rinse their mouths? Should they eat something neutral (e.g., a cracker) between tests? Do you think this is a critical variable?
4. How would you interpret the fact that some subjects could not correctly identify the beverages? What factors could determine a person's preference for one cola over another?
5. Design an experiment to test whether or not subjects can correctly identify whole, skim, and powdered milk.
6. Design an experiment to test whether whole, skim, or powdered milk tastes better.

11 Territoriality in Parking Lots

Introduction

The article may be interesting in that the results may tell you something about your own behavior, but the purpose of including this paper is to demonstrate two special issues: *field-based studies* and *unobtrusive measures*. Pay close attention to these issues as you read the article.

This article is the first of five in Part Two that we have left for you to analyze. We suggest that you follow the format in the previous chapter to write your analysis. Try to identify the essential features of experimental design in this paper.

Special Issues

FIELD-BASED STUDIES

Psychological research can be divided into two categories: laboratory experiments and field experiments. Most research takes place in controlled laboratory settings. The reason psychologists tend to favor a laboratory setting is for methodological control. In the experimental laboratory the researcher can isolate the participant from the noisy world and precisely control the type of stimulation he or she receives. In effect, the experimental laboratory allows the researcher to create a microcosm in which the only factors that are allowed to operate are those that the experimenter wishes to influence the subject; other cues can be either eliminated or brought under experimental control. Paradoxically, in this very strength of laboratory experimentation lies a weakness: the artificial nature of the laboratory setting. By removing the person from his or her natural setting, as is done in laboratory experiments, the participant is deprived of the forces that are necessarily part of his or her normal life, and these forces may help determine the participant's reactions. In technical language, some stimuli that are eliminated or controlled by the laboratory setting may be critical independent variables that significantly affect the dependent variable.

In choosing between a laboratory experiment and a field experiment, one critical question should be answered: Are the desired experimental results significantly related to the social situation? Many types of research problems that are of interest fall into this category. Consider mob behavior. The very presence of other members of a mob undoubtedly influences the behavior of any given individual, and his or her behavior may in turn influence the others. How can an experimenter control for these pressures and other independent variables (e.g., the presence of an inflammatory stimulus, such as a lynched body)? It may be simply impossible to recreate such a complex situation in a laboratory. Therefore, a researcher interested in mob behavior must either isolate some hypothesized factors of the larger issue for laboratory investigation, or turn to the field study. A large number of worthy research projects must be studied in the context within which they occur.

Attributes of Field Experiments

As mentioned above, field experiments generally lack the control of laboratory experiments, but they are not devoid of controls. In many experiments the researcher can specify the nature of the participants, the independent variable, the dependent variable, and many situational stimuli that may influence the results. Before considering some specific issues raised by this article, note that among positive attributes of field techniques is the fact that they can be conducted in the participant's natural setting, with little disturbance of his or her normal behavior. This tends to enhance the credibility (and external validity) of the study. In some forms of field research, the person is unaware that he or she is a participant.

Unobtrusive Measures

When people know they are being observed, they frequently behave differently than when they are not being observed. This generalization is true not only for human participants in a psychological experiment but also in some cases of biological research in which animals are being observed. A partial explanation of this phenomenon is that the experimenter becomes part of the field the influence of which he or she is attempting to measure. By way of analogy, consider the problem of making critical temperature measurements. A thermometer inserted into a substance not only reacts to the temperature of the substance but also to its own temperature. In a similar way, an experimental psychologist is not only an observer of behavior, but also a part of the environment to which the subject reacts.

Because precise control over stimulus variables in field-based experiments is sometimes impossible, their effect on response variables is also sometimes questionable. As you may recall from our previous discussion of scientific theory and methodology, a cardinal principle of experimental research is to identify the precise cause of a specific effect. If the causes of behavior (in experimental terms, the independent variables) are doubtful, then the behavior (the dependent variable) may or may not be related to the cause. The resolution of this profound dilemma is not easy; however, the issue has been reviewed in two influential books: Webb, Campbell, Schwartz, and Sechrest, *Unobtrusive Measures: Nonreactive Research in the Social Sciences* (1966), and Cook and Campbell, *Quasi-Experimentation: Design & Analysis Issues for Field Settings* (1979). In these sources (and others), experimental psychologists grapple with the problem of the intrusion of an observer into the psychological field. To reduce the influence of an observer in a psychological experiment—especially in a field-based experiment—the authors suggest a number of unobtrusive means experimenters can use to collect information. The interested student is referred to these sources for a more complete discussion of the issue.

However, the use of unobtrusive measures in field-based experiments can raise questions of experimental ethics: Is it proper or ethical, for example, to skulk around with a clipboard, collecting data on unsuspecting people? Although questions may be raised about the propriety of some field-based experiments and procedural avenues, it would be erroneous to conclude that such experiments are unethical. We do, however, strongly recommend that in the planning of all experiments, including field experiments, the experimenter consult the APA ethical standards reprinted in Chapter 8.

TERRITORIAL DEFENSE IN PARKING LOTS: RETALIATION AGAINST WAITING DRIVERS

R. Barry Ruback[1]
Department of Sociology
Pennsylvania State University

Daniel Juieng
Georgia State University

Three studies showed that drivers leaving a public parking space are territorial even when such behavior is contrary to their goal of leaving. In Study 1 (observations of 200 departing cars), intruded-upon drivers took longer to leave than nonintruded-upon drivers. In Study 2, an experiment involving 240 drivers in which level of intrusion and status of intruder were manipulated, drivers took longer to leave when another car was present and when the and when the intruder honked. Males left significantly sooner when intruded upon by a higher rather than lower status car, whereas females' departure times did not differ as a function of the status of the car. There was evidence that distraction might explain some of this effect. In Study 3, individuals who had parked at a mall were asked about how they would react to intruders. Compared to what they believed other people would do, respondents said they would leave faster if the car were just waiting for them to leave but they would take longer to leave if the driver in the car honked at them.

Territorial behavior involves marking, occupying, or defending a location in order to indicate presumed rights to the particular place. The value of a territory usually stems from the fact that it contains desirable resources (e.g., game for hunting, grazing, pastures). Most often, territorial responses are based on a cost-benefit analysis: If the perceived cost of resisting an intruder outweighs the benefit of that territory, flight is likely, but if the benefit outweighs the cost, defense is more probable (Barash, 1977; Brown, 1987). For example, although intruded-upon subjects did not typically defend library tables, they usually resisted intrusion when they were at library carrels, which were more valuable as study sites (Taylor & Brooks, 1980).

The cost of defending a territory depends in part on the nature of the intruder. The more aggressive and the more powerful an intruder is, the more costly territorial defense becomes (Barash, 1977). Relatedly, Barash (1973) found that invaded-upon subjects were more apt to leave a territory in a library

---

[1]Correspondence concerning this article should be addressed to Barry Ruback, Department of Sociology, Pennsylvania State University, University Park, PA 16802.
Source: Journal of Applied Social Psychology, 1997, **27,** 9, pp. 821–834.

when the intruder was of high status than of low status. Other studies have shown that high-status confederates were intruded upon less frequently at water fountains than were low-status confederates (Barefoot, Hoople, & Mc-Clay, 1972; Rosenfeld, Giacalone, & Kennedy, 1987). These studies show rational behavior; if intruders or occupants of public territories look formidable, then avoid them.

Public territories are those that almost anyone can occupy for a short period (Altman, 1975). Because public territories are not important to the lives of occupants and because occupants have only minimal rights to public territories, occupants of public territories are likely to retreat when intruded upon (Brown, 1987). For instance, Felipe and Sommer (1966) found that subjects tended to leave the library sooner when a confederate sat in a chair beside them than when the confederate sat in a chair across the table from them. Other investigators have also shown that occupants tend to flee public territories following intrusions (e.g., Barash, 1973; Efran & Cheyne, 1974; Patterson, Mullens, & Romano, 1971).

Sometimes, however, occupants of public territories resist intrusion, that is, occupy the territory longer than if no intrusion occurred. For example, male subjects tended to linger significantly longer in library aisles when intruded upon by a male confederate than when alone in the aisles (Ruback, 1987). And, callers at public pay phones who were intruded upon by someone waiting to use the phone spent significantly more time on the phone than did callers who were not intruded upon (Ruback, Pape, & Doriot, 1989). Importantly, Ruback et al. (1989) also showed that distraction alone could not account for the increased time spent at the pay phones when intrusion occurred, in that a control group (involving confederates using an adjacent phone) did not increase the subjects' time at the phone.

Although a territory is valuable because of the resources it encompasses, particularly if the resources are unique, it can also take on symbolic value, linking ownership with identity, control, and competence (Brown, 1987). Whereas responses to territorial intrusion are likely to be based on a rational cost-benefit analysis if the value of the territory is the primary concern, rational analysis may not be as important if the primary value of the territory is symbolic. Under such conditions, defense may occur even if there is nothing tangible to be protected or gained.

Common experience and anecdotal evidence (e.g., Richman, 1972) suggest that automobiles have a symbolic value that magnifies perceived restrictions. Thus, for example, individuals are likely to be upset if a car stopped in front of them at a red light does not move quickly enough when the light turns green (Doob & Gross, 1968). Similarly, it is likely that much of the territorial behavior observed on streets and highways (e.g., refusing to let someone pass after he or she has signaled a desire to do so) is the product of concerns with identity and control rather than the defense of actual resources.

The present series of studies tested whether or not occupants of a public territory use their temporary ownership to retaliate against intruders. Specifically, we wondered whether occupants would be territorial even when they had completed their task at the location and the territory no longer served any function for them. We tested this hypothesis in a series of three studies of individuals' behavior in parking lots. Resistance to intrusion when leaving a parking space would be counterproductive because the space is no longer needed, and leaving is actually the goal of the departing driver. Territorial resistance in such circumstances would seem unnecessary, detrimental, and even nonrational. However, because automobile drivers may be especially sensitive to perceived attacks on their status and control, they may be willing to be territorial despite the apparent costs.

Study 1

The first study, a naturalistic observational study, examined whether the amount of time drivers take to leave a parking space is related to whether or not another driver is waiting for the parking space. Because a parking space has minimal value to a departing driver, intrusion should facilitate a speedier departure. However, because concerns with identity and control are so tied to driving, it was predicted that intrusion would induce territorial defense. It was also hypothesized that the higher the status of the intruding drivers' cars, the sooner the departing drivers would leave, because it was assumed that high-status intruders would be seen as having more power and would therefore be seen as a greater threat.

Method

Subjects.   Two hundred drivers were observed leaving their parking spaces in front of the main entrance to an Atlanta-area shopping mall. There were 103 females and 97 males. In terms of race, there were 105 Whites, 77 African Americans, and 18 of other groups.

Procedure.   Two researchers stood in front of the main entrance to the mall and observed only those shoppers parked in the 52 spaces along the closest four columns of spaces, excluding handicapped spaces. For each departing shopper in the defined area, the researchers started timing the moment the departing shopper opened the driver's side car door and stopped timing when the car had completely left the parking space. None of the subjects appeared to be aware of being observed. The three drivers who waited in their car for more than 2 min were not included in the data because the researchers assumed those drivers had certain time-consuming tasks to complete before leaving (e.g., waiting for another shopper or looking at a map).

In addition to recording departure times, the researchers also noted when another driver was waiting for the departing driver's parking space. Intrusion was considered to have occurred when, prior to opening their driver's side door, subjects turned their head toward the car of the waiting driver. Furthermore, the researchers recorded the gender and race of the departing drivers and the number of people accompanying the departing drivers. Finally, the researchers noted the model, condition, and approximate age of the departing cars and of any intruding cars. The researchers used this information about the cars to determine the approximate dollar value of the cars from the most recent edition of *VMR Standard Used Car Prices* (Karpatkin, 1993). Based on a subset of 25 cases, interrater reliability on the departure times of the cars was very high, $r(23) = .99$, $p < .001$. The reliability of the estimates of car dollar value was also high, $r(16) = .95$, $p < .001$. There was perfect interrater agreement on gender and race of departing drivers and on when intrusion occurred.

Results

Of the 200 departing drivers observed, 76 (38%) were intruded upon by another driver. The number of people in the cars ranged from 1 to 8 ($M = 1.89$, $SD = 0.97$). The dollar value of 193 departing cars (7 cars were not listed in the book) ranged from $1,000 to $60,000 ($M = \$7,943$, $SD = \$6,333$). The dollar value of 68 intruding cars (8 cars were not listed in the book) ranged from $1,000 to $33,050 ($M = \$8,435$, $SD = \$6,802$). The difference between the value of the departing car and the value of the intruding car ranged from $-\$28,275$ to $+\$16,700$ ($M = -\$438$, $SD = \$7,428$).

The amount of time the departing drivers took to leave (the departure time), ranged from 10.61 s to 113.35 s ($M = 34.76$ s, $SD = 14.97$ s). The departure time was positively correlated with the number of people in the car, $r(198) = .24$, $p < .001$. Male drivers had significantly more passengers in the car with them ($M = 1.10$) than did female drivers ($M = 0.68$), $t(198) = 3.14$, $p < .01$, but male drivers and female drivers did not differ in their departure times. Although African American drivers ($M = 1.00$) had more passengers than did White drivers ($M = 0.65$), $t(180) = 3.00$, $p < .01$, the two groups did not differ significantly in their departure times. The value of the departing cars, the value of the intruding cars, and the difference in value between them were not significantly correlated with the departure time.

Because number of people in the departing car was related to time it took to depart, $r(198) = .24$, $p < .001$, we used this variable as a grouping factor in subsequent analyses. A 2×2 ANOVA of the departure times was conducted using intrusion and number of people in the departing car as grouping variables, with number in the car being dichotomized into (a) only one person in the car or (b) more than one person in the car. Drivers departed sooner when not intruded upon ($M = 32.15$ s) than when intruded upon ($M = 39.03$ s), $F(1, 196) = 10.43$, $p < .001$. And, drivers departed sooner when alone ($M = 30.64$ s) than when with passengers ($M = 37.45$ s), $F(1, 196) = 10.35$, $p < .01$. There was no significant interaction of intrusion and number in the car. A logarithmic transformation of the raw scores (to reduce skewness) showed similar results: a main effect for intrusion, a main effect for number in car, and no interaction.

Discussion

In this observational study, departing drivers took longer to leave their parking spaces when they were intruded upon by another driver than when they were not. Although longer departure times following intrusion may indicate territorial behavior, causality cannot be inferred with this observational study because other factors may be operating. For instance, the presence of the intruding cars may have distracted the departing drivers, causing them to need more time to leave the parking space. A related possibility is that departing drivers took longer to leave when intruded upon because they wanted to be careful to avoid a collision with the intruding car.

Regarding the absence of a relation between status of intruding cars and departure time, it may be that status effects occur only at the extremes. That is, the status of intruding cars may influence departing drivers' times only when intruding cars have either a noticeably low dollar value or a noticeably high one. If this explanation is true, then this observational study would not have found an effect because most intruding cars were of moderate status.

STUDY 2

The second study was conducted to determine whether the findings from the observational study that intruded-upon drivers took longer to leave were due to territorial behavior or to some alternative explanation. In this study, four intrusion conditions were compared to a no-intrusion condition, allowing a test of whether intruded-upon drivers take longer to depart than nonintruded-upon drivers. Further, a distraction condition, in which a confederate drove by the subjects, allowed a test of whether the mere presence of another driver affected departing drivers, independent of whether this other driver was waiting for a parking space. Based on the findings of Study 1, it was hypothesized that intruded-upon departing drivers would take longer to leave than would nonintruded-upon departing drivers.

This study also examined the effects of level of intrusion. In addition to the no-intrusion and distraction conditions, confederates either intruded upon the drivers while honking (high intrusion) or intruded without honking (low intrusion). It was hypothesized that departing drivers would take longer to leave following a greater intrusion because the greater intrusion (honking) creates a greater challenge to the occupants' control over the territory (Brehm, 1966). Therefore, more territorial defense (longer departure times) should be displayed.

Another purpose of the second study was to test the effects of the intruders' status on departing drivers by using a car of either very high value or very low value. Past studies have shown that high-status confederates were intruded upon less frequently at water fountains than were low-status confederates (Barefoot et al., 1972; Rosenfeld et al., 1987). Furthermore, Barash (1973) found that intruded-upon subjects were more apt to leave a territory in a library when the intruder was of high status than of low status, and Doob and Gross (1968) found that drivers were more likely to honk at a car stopped in front of them at a green light when the car was of low rather than high status. Based on this prior research, it was hypothesized that higher status intruders, compared to lower status intruders, would cause departing drivers to leave faster.

Method

Subject.   A total of 240 individuals (120 males, 120 females), drivers who were leaving their parking spaces at a mall, served as subjects in this experimental study. There were 171 Whites, 56 African Americans, and 13 of other races.

Procedure.   The study was conducted during the afternoons and evenings of three Thursdays, three Fridays, and three Saturdays at a mall located in a more affluent part of Atlanta than the mall used in Study 1. Only cars that had been driven into the parking space front bumper first were used in the study.

The status of the intruding cars was manipulated by using cars that varied greatly in value. The low-status car was a 1985 Nissan Maxima station wagon worth about $5,200. The high-status car was a 1994 Infiniti Q45 worth about $57,000 or a 1993 Lexus SC 400 worth about $43,000. The second manipulation was level of intrusion. In the high-intrusion condition, the confederate (one of two males) stopped his car four spaces from and facing in the direction of the departing car. Then, the confederate flashed the turn signal in the direction of the departing car and honked the horn once after the driver sat behind the wheel. In the low-intrusion condition, a confederate simply stopped the car four spaces from and facing in the direction of the departing car.

In addition to this 2 × 2 (Status $$$× Level of Intrusion) design, there were two control conditions. In the first control condition (no intrusion), a researcher observed departing drivers who were not intruded upon by another driver waiting for the space. In the second control condition (distraction), a confederate drove his car past the parking space of the departing car as the driver opened the driver's side car door. Then, the confederate entered the next row of parking spaces. Thus, with the two control conditions, there were six conditions: (a) no intrusion, (b) distraction, (c) high intrusion by a high-status car, (d) high intrusion by a low-status car, (e) low intrusion by a high-status car, and (f) low intrusion by a low-status car. The six conditions were randomized within replicates (i.e., the experiment was conducted in multiple sets of the six conditions, and within each set the six conditions were randomly ordered). There were 40 participants (20 males, 20 females) in each of the six conditions.

The observers started timing when the departing shopper opened the driver's side car door. When the front bumper of the car left the parking space, the researchers noted the elapsed time which, as in Study 1, was the measure of departure time.

In addition to noting departure times, the researchers recorded the gender and race of the departing drivers, the number of people in the departing car, and the type and year of the departing cars. Later, the researchers determined the dollar values of the departing cars by using the *Blue Book Used Car Guide* (Kelley, 1994). To determine the reliability of these measures, two researchers independently recorded all variables for the first 25 cases. The interrater reliability of the measure of departure time was very high, $r(23) = .99, p < .001$. The two researchers' measurements were within 0.50 s 60% of the time, 0.75 s 68% of the time, and 1 s 92% of the time. The interrater reliability for car status was also high, $r(23) = .94, p < .001$. There was perfect interrater agreement on the number of people in the departing car and on the departing drivers' gender and race.

Results

The number of people in the cars ranged from 1 to 5 ($M = 1.52, SD = 0.77$). The dollar value of the departing cars ranged from $1,325 to $48,730 ($M = $10,833, SD = $7,670$). Departure time ranged from 20.79 s to 96.42 s ($M = 34.11$ s, $SD = 16.52$ s).

Correlations among departure time, number of people in the departing car, the value of the departing car, and the difference between the value of the departing car and the value of the intruding car revealed only one significant effect: Departure time was positively correlated with the number of people in the car, $r(238) = .13, p < .05$. In terms of gender, male drivers departed sooner ($M = 31.74$) than did female drivers ($M = 36.43$), $t(238) = 2.21$, $p < .05$. Male drivers ($M = 1.65$) also had more passengers in the car with them than did female drivers ($M = 1.39$), $t(238) = 2.69, p < .01$.

Level of Intrusion.   The first analysis was designed to test whether or not the four levels of intrusion differed significantly. This one-way ANOVA, involving the high intrusion (honking), the low intrusion (no honking), and the two control groups (no intrusion and distraction), indicated a significant difference among the four groups, $F(3, 236) = 13.50, p < .001$. Three orthogonal contrasts were used to compare the means. First, a planned contrast of the means indicated that departure times were significantly longer when another car was present (i.e., distraction, low intrusion, or high intrusion; $M = 34.88$ s) than when there was no other car present ($M = 26.47$ s), $F(1, 236) = 3.13, p < .01$. A second planned contrast comparing the distraction condition to the two intrusion conditions indicated that drivers who were intruded upon ($M = 36.78$ s) did not stay significantly longer than did those who were distracted ($M = 31.09$ s), $F(1, 236) = 2.09$, ns. The third planned contrast indicated that, given that an intruding car was present, departure times were significantly longer when the confederate honked ($M = 42.75$ s) than when he did not ($M = 30.80$ s), $F(1, 236) = 5.20, p < .001$.

Gender and Level of Intrusion.   The initial ANOVA indicated that the presence or absence of an intruding car affected the time it took drivers to leave. In the second set of analyses, which excluded the two control conditions, a 2 2×2 ANOVA of the departure time was performed, in which the grouping variables were level of intrusion (horn or no horn), status of the intruding vehicle, and gender of the departing driver. Because similar results were obtained when number of people in the car was used as a covariate, the results of the ANCOVA are not presented.

The Intrusion $\times$ Status $\times$ Gender ANOVA revealed a significant effect for intrusion. As above, drivers took longer to depart when the confederate in the intruding vehicle honked the horn than when he did not, $F(1, 151) = 16.23, p < .001$. There was no significant main effect for either the status of the intruding vehicle or the gender of the driver. However, there was a significant two-way interaction of status of the intruding vehicle and gender of driver, $F(1, 151) = 7.36, p < .01$. According to a post-hoc Newman–Keuls test, male drivers left significantly sooner when intruded upon by the high-status car ($M = 30.39$ s) than when intruded upon by the low-status car ($M = 39.72$ s), whereas for female drivers there was no difference in departure time as a function of the status of the car ($Ms = 41.06$ s and 36.64 s, for high- and low-status cars, respectively). ANOVA on log-transformed data yielded results similar to those conducted on the raw data.

Discussion

Consistent with the observational study, in this experimental study, departing drivers took longer to leave "their" parking spaces when another driver was present than when no other driver was present. Furthermore, the departing drivers took longer the greater the intrusion (i.e., honking vs. no honking). In other words, departing drivers were territorial about a space they wanted to leave.

In addition, male drivers were more territorial (i.e., took longer) when intruded upon by a driver in a low-status car than by a driver in a high-status car, whereas female drivers did not respond differently as a function of the status of the intruding cars. Males, compared to females, may have responded to the status of the cars because they are more generally attuned to symbols of status. Alternatively, females, like males, may in general respond to indicators of status, but they may not have responded differently to the status of cars in this study because they did not pay attention to or recognize the different values of the intruding cars. The fact that in this study only males responded to the status of the cars may explain why we did not find the interaction of status and intrusion that others have (e.g., Barash, 1973; Doob & Gross, 1968).

The longer departure times of intruded-upon drivers may be taken as a sign of territorial defense. But, these longer times may also be due to drivers' being distracted by the intruding cars and, relatedly, to departing drivers' wanting to avoid colliding with the intruding cars. The fact that there was no difference between the distraction condition and the low intrusion condition suggests that the delay in leaving was due in large part to departing drivers' concern with avoiding the car behind them. However, it should also be noted that the distraction condition may not have been a pure manipulation of distraction, in that even though the distracting car was not waiting for the departing driver, the presence of the distracting car could have primed departing drivers about the value of the space they were about to leave.

Moreover, the finding that the status of the intruding car affected males' departure times would suggest that distraction cannot be the sole explanation, because it would be difficult to understand how the high-status car could be more distracting than the low-status car. It is possible that drivers took 12 s longer to leave after greater than lesser intrusion (honking vs. no honking) because they believed more care was needed to avoid the honking driver, even though in both conditions the car was waiting the same distance away from the experimental subjects. In sum, although distraction accounts for some of the difference, territorial defense seems to be at least part of the explanation for why the departing drivers took longer to leave when intruded upon than when there was no intrusion.

Study 3

A third study was conducted to determine whether people are aware of how an intruding driver affects the amount of time they take to leave "their" parking space. A total of 100 individuals who had parked at a shopping mall (66 females, 34 males; 73 Whites, 26 African Americans, 1 other race) completed a 13-item questionnaire. Respondents ranged in age from 21 to 62 years ($M = 40.9$, $SD = 8.9$). The questionnaire contained three 7-point semantic differential scales (*bad–good, uncomfortable–comfortable, anxious–calm*) that respondents used to rate how they would feel while leaving a parking space under three different conditions: with no one waiting, with one driver waiting, and with a driver waiting who honks the horn. In each of the three conditions, each of the three scales was divided by its standard deviation, the three scale scores were summed, and this total was divided by 3 to form a composite measure, with lower numbers representing more negative ratings. Internal reliabilities for the three composite scores were very high (αs = .95, .96, and .95, respectively). A repeated measures ANOVA with composite scores as the within-subjects factor revealed a significant repeated-measures effect, $F(2, 198) = 146.94$, $p < .001$. Respondents said they would feel significantly more negative when the waiting driver honked ($M = 3.14$) than when the waiting driver did not honk ($M = 5.02$), and significantly more negative when there was a nonhonking waiting driver than when there was no waiting driver ($M = 6.27$).

The questionnaire also contained four items concerning respondents' beliefs about how a driver waiting for their space and a honking driver waiting for their space would affect how long it would take them and others to leave. Respondents made their judgments on 7-point scales, ranging from 1 (*make it shorter*) through 4 (*no effect*) to 7 (*make it longer*). These four items were analyzed by a 2 × 2 within-subjects ANOVA, with the two variables being role (self vs. other people) and level of intrusion (no honking vs. honking). There was a significant effect for role, $F(1, 99) = 8.48$, $p < .001$, with individuals believing that they would take less time to leave ($M = 3.38$) than would others ($M = 3.62$). There was also a significant effect for level of intrusion, $F(1, 99) = 196.22$, $p < .001$, such that respondents said they and others would leave faster if there were a driver waiting ($M = 2.35$) than if the driver honked ($M = 4.64$).

In addition to these two significant main effects, there was a significant Role × Level of Intrusion interaction, $F(1, 99) = 68.28$, $p < .001$. As shown in Table 1, respondents said they would leave a space sooner if another driver were waiting for their space but would take longer to leave if the waiting driver honked. Likewise, respondents believed others would leave sooner (but not as soon as they would) if another driver were waiting for the space. And, respondents believed others would take longer (but not as long as they would) if the waiting driver honked. A post-hoc test indicated that the four means were all significantly different. In other words, respondents saw themselves as more polite than others with regard to a silently waiting driver, but less polite than others with regard to a honking driver.

TABLE 1   Mean Ratings of Own and Others' Behavior Following Low Intrusion (No Honking) or High Intrusion (Honking) When Leaving a Parking Space (Study 3)

	Low Intrusion	High Intrusion
Own behavior	1.87	4.88
Others' behavior	2.83	4.40

Note. These ratings were made on 7-point scales ranging from 1 (*make it shorter*) through 4 (*no effect*) to 7 (*make it longer*). Means not sharing a common superscript are significantly different according to a post-hoc Newman–Keuls test ($p < .05$).

It is interesting to note that respondents in this study recognized their territorial behavior in parking lots under high intrusion (honking) conditions because an earlier study had indicated that people do not recognize their territorial behavior with regard to public telephones (Ruback et al., 1989). One reason for this difference might be that individuals in the United States are aware of the extent to which self-concept and self-esteem are tied to automobile ownership and use. Alternatively, it may be that drivers recognize their territorial behavior only when the intrusion is clearly negative, as it is when the waiting driver honks. What is especially interesting about the survey results is that the respondents believed it is normative to be territorial when a potential new occupant of the territory is highly intrusive.

GENERAL DISCUSSION

The present series of studies is consistent with prior findings that people display territorial defense in public territories (Ruback et al., 1989; Ruback & Snow, 1993, Taylor & Brooks, 1980). Specifically, in both Study 1 and Study 2, departing drivers took longer to leave "their" parking spaces when they were intruded upon by another driver than when they were not. And, consistent with research in libraries (Ruback, 1987), greater levels of intrusion led to greater territoriality.

What is new about the present research is that it suggests people sometimes display territorial behavior merely to keep others from possessing the space even when it no longer has any value to them. Thus, even though they were leaving the parking space, departing drivers took longer when someone else wanted the space than when no one else wanted the space. Past research suggests that territorial defense follows a cost-benefit analysis by which occupants leave a territory if resisting intruders might cost more than the territory is worth (Barash, 1977; Brown, 1987). The present studies are unique in that the defense displayed for these task-specific territories (the parking spaces) is counterproductive from the standpoint of time, because the primary goal of the occupant is to leave the space.

That departing drivers stay longer suggests one or both of two possibilities. First, departing drivers may use a cost–benefit analysis and reassess the value of their space when they see that someone else wants it. Such a reassessment would not be surprising, given research in other contexts indicating that scarcity is linked to higher subjective value (Brock, 1968; Cialdini, 1988). Second, departing drivers may become territorial out of a desire to reassert control against intrusions on them (Brehm, 1966). Because territories can take on a symbolic value, linking ownership with control (Brown, 1987), even occupants of temporary territories may link possession with control. In such circumstances, resistance to intruders may provide a feeling of control, and resistance to greater intrusion (e.g., honking) may provide an even greater sense of control. This notion would be consistent with the idea that passive continued possession of a temporary territory can be a legitimate, nonaggressive response to a perceived threat to status.

Although territoriality and reactance may be confounded in the context of parking lots, the two processes would seem to make different predictions. Presumably, reactance comes into play only when people lose the opportunity to choose. When a car is waiting for a driver to leave, the threat to freedom is relatively minimal; in fact, there may be more perceived freedom, in that drivers can choose to leave faster (as they say they will do), leave slower (as they are likely to do), or not change their behavior at all. When the intruder honks the horn, however, the threat to freedom of action is clear and drivers are likely to want to restore their threatened sense of freedom. Thus, reactance theory would predict slower departures only when the waiting driver honked, whereas an explanation based on territoriality would predict, as we found, slower departures both when the driver was silent and when he honked. Future work might fruitfully address whether reactance and territoriality can be separated, as hypothesized here.

Assuming that territoriality is the cause of this behavior, it would be interesting to investigate factors that reduce or exaggerate this effect. For example, just as group cohesiveness can reverse the bystander effect in emergency situations (Rutkowski, Gruder, & Romer, 1983), familiarity, cohesiveness, and expectations of future interaction (as in a parking lot shared by co-workers) can probably also reverse the observed territoriality in the situation studied here. However, we might expect extreme territorial behavior were a stranger to want to use the group's lot.

REFERENCES

Altman, I. (1975). *The environment and social behavior.* Monterey, CA: Brooks/Cole.

Barash, D. P. (1973). Human etiology: Personal space reiterated. *Environment and Behavior, 5*, 57–63.

Barash, D. P. (1977). *Sociology and behavior.* New York, NY: Elsevier.

Barefoot, J. C., Hoople, H., & McClay, D. (1972). Avoidance of an act which would violate personal space. *Psychonomic Science, 23*, 205–206.

Brehm, J. W. (1966). *A theory of psychological reactance.* New York, NY: Academic.

Brock, T. C. (1968). *Implications of commodity theory for value change.* In A. G. Greenwald, T. C. Brock, & T. M. Ostrom (Eds.), Psychological foundations of attitudes (pp. 243–275). New York, NY: Academic.

Brown, B. (1987). *Territoriality.* In D. Stokols, & I. Altman (Eds.), Handbook of environmental psychology (pp. 505–532). New York, NY: John Wiley & Sons.

Cialdini, R. B. (1988). *Influence: Science and practice* (2nd ed.). Glenview, IL: Scott, Foresman, and Company.

Doob, A. N., & Gross, A. E. (1968). Status of frustrator as an inhibitor of horn-honking responses. *Journal of Social Psychology, 76,* 213–218.

Efran, M. G., & Cheyne, J. A. (1974). Affective concomitants of the invasion of shared space: Behavioral, physiological, and verbal indicators. *Journal of Personalty and Social Psychology, 29,* 219–226.

Felipe, N., & Sommer, R. (1966). Invasions of persnal space. *Social Problems, 14,* 206–214.

Karpatkin, H. R. (1993). *VMR standard used car prices.* Yonkers, NY: Consumers Union.

Kelley, M. (1994). *Blue book used car guide.* Irvine, CA: Kelley Blue Book.

Langer, E. J., Blank, A., & Chanowitz, B. (1978). The mindlessness of ostensibly thoughtful action: The role of "placebic" information in interpersonal interaction. *Journal of Personality and Social Psychology, 36,* 635–642.

Patterson, M. L., Mullens, S., & Romano, J. (1971). Compensatory reactions to spatial markers. *Sociometry, 34,* 114–121.

Richman, J. (1972). The motor car and the territorial aggression thesis: Some aspects of the sociology of the street. *Sociological Review, 20,* 5–27.

Rosenfeld, P., Giacalone, R. A., & Kennedy, J. G. (1987). Of status and suit: Personal space invasions in an administrative setting. *Social Behavior and Personality, 5,* 97–99.

Ruback, R. B. (1987). Deserted (and nondeserted) aisles: Territorial intrusion can produce persistence, not flight. *Social Psychology Quarterly, 50,* 270–276.

Ruback, R. B., Pape, K., & Doriot, P. D. (1989). Waiting for a phone: Intrusion on callers leads to territorial defense. *Social Psychology Quarterly, 52,* 232–241.

Ruback, R. B., & Snow, J. N. (1993). Territoriality and nonconscious racism at water fountains: Intruders and drinkers (Blacks and Whites) are affected by race. *Environment and Behavior, 25,* 250–267.

Rutkowski, G. K., Gruder, C. L., & Romer, D. (1983). Group cohesiveness, social norms, and bystander intervention. *Journal of Personality and Social Psychology, 44,* 545–552.

Taylor, R. B., & Brooks, D. K. (1980). Temporary territories? Responses to intrusions in a public setting. *Population and Environment, 3,* 135–145.

Questions

1. Review the basic problems associated with field-based experiments.
2. What three research methods are exemplified in this article?
3. What are the independent variables in Study 2?
4. Can you think of any alternative explanations for the findings?
5. Would the results have been different if a different type of parking lot had been used (nightclub, postoffice)? Why or why not?

12 Fanning Old Flames

Introduction

The next paper by Gold and Wegner (1991) was a poster presented at an APA meeting. It examines the effect of thoughts for former lovers on a participant's physiological reactivity. It is accompanied by an analysis.

FANNING OLD FLAMES: AROUSING ROMANTIC OBSESSION THROUGH THOUGHT SUPPRESSION

Daniel B. Gold and Daniel M. Wegner
University of Virginia

We examined whether thought suppression intensifies physiological reactivity to thoughts of old flames. We asked subjects to think about an old flame, and found that those who thought about a still-desired relationship showed higher skin conductance levels (SCLs) than those who focused on one no longer desired. Then, the subjects were instructed either not to think about their old flame, or not to think about the Statue of Liberty. In a subsequent second thinking period, subjects who were asked to think of the still-desired relationship and had just suppressed that thought showed elevated SCLs compared to the others. These results suggest that trying not to think about a past relationship may prolong one's emotional responsiveness to thoughts of the relationship.

Ruminations about past loves can be painful and persistent. Hank Williams (1947) captured the reflections of despondent lovers everywhere (as well as those of generations of other songwriters) when he wrote "I can't get you off of my mind, when I try I'm just wasting my time. Lord I've tried and I've tried, and all night long I've cried—but I can't get you off of my mind." Unwanted thoughts about lost loves can be distressing, with thoughts of "old flames" sometimes turning into obsessions that interrupt daily lives and hinder the ability to form new relationships.

Analysis

Literature Review

Gold and Wegner capture the human pathos involved in the painful thought of a lost lover by quoting country and western songwriter Hank Williams: "I can't get you off my mind." And how true that is! Anyone who has left a relationship has recurrent thoughts of the other person and what might have been. But where do these thoughts come from, and is there a physiological component that accompanies them?

a   There are several theories of how these thoughts begin. Martin and Tesser (1989) have argued that unsatisfied desires generally promote ruminations. The goal of a romantic relationship that is unfulfilled results in obsessive thinking about the lost love. It has also been hypothesized that the unwanted thoughts themselves are serving a beneficial purpose. Epstein (1983) believes that ruminations are coping strategies that promote habituation to the stressful situation. In this view, romantic ruminations help the person get over the loss.

b   A different way of viewing ruminations has been proposed by Wegner (e.g., Wegner, 1989; Wegner, Schneider, Carter, & White, 1987; Wegner, Shortt, Blake, & Page, 1990). Ruminations may develop not from unsatisfied desires or from needs to habituate, but rather from the common response people have to unwanted thoughts— **the suppression of the thought. By suppressing an unwanted thought, people may gain some immediate relief from psychological distress.** But at the same time, they prevent themselves from habituating to the bothersome thought. The distress associated with that thought will be novel each time the thought reenters the stream of consciousness.

c   **The continued distress fuels further rumination, which in turn prompts suppression and renews the problem.**

    This study was designed to examine this reasoning by testing whether thought suppression can intensify physiological reactivity to thoughts of an old flame. We asked subjects first to think about an old flame for a period of time, expecting that those who focused on a relationship that was still desired (a hot flame) would show higher skin conductance levels (SCLs) than those who focused on a relationship no longer desired (a cold flame). Then, subjects

d   were instructed either not to think about their old flame, or not to think about the Statue of Liberty. In a second expression period, we invited subjects again to think about their old flame, reasoning that those who had just suppressed the thought of a hot flame would continue to show elevated SCLs. Those suppressing thoughts of the cold flame, in turn, or those who suppressed the irrelevant thought, were expected to show reduced SCL in this second expression period.

    In section (a) several of the past theories of the origin of these thoughts are mentioned, and an alternate hypothesis (b) suggests that suppression of the thought of a lost love may give some immediate relief, but this does little to help the person adjust and may cause further anguish (c). In a poster session, the researcher gets to the point directly. The next paragraph (d) gives a brief but informative synopsis of the research plan.

METHOD

Procedure and Design

University of Virginia undergraduates (38 men and 32 women) were tested individually. Each completed a questionnaire about a "meaningful past relationship," identifying this person by initials. SCL measurement electrodes were explained while the subject was being attached. The subject was then asked to think aloud for tape recording.

e　From an adjacent room, the experimenter prompted subjects by intercom to perform three tasks for ten minutes each. **Two-minute baseline think aloud periods,** during which subjects were instructed to think about anything, began and ended each task session. In the three task sessions, subjects

f　were asked first to express ("... **think of the person**"), then suppress ("... **try NOT to think of the person, however, mention it if you do**"), and then

g　express again their thoughts of the past relationship. **Control subjects in the suppression period were asked to suppress an irrelevant target (the Statue of Liberty) instead of their thoughts of the past relationship.**

Physiological Measurement

The measurement of SCL was accomplished as recommended by Fowles et al. (1981) for finger electrode placement. Ag/AgCl electrodes were adhered to the second phalanges of first and third fingers of the subject's right hand

h　and attached to a J & J Electronics I-330 PC Interface System, which continuously recorded the results. Each suppression or expression period was divided into three 3-minute periods, and the deviation each minute from one minute of baseline directly preceding that period was used for analysis.

Method

Of particular interest in this experiment is the establishment of a baseline task in which subjects were asked to think about anything that came to mind **(e)**. After the baseline measures had been established the subjects were asked to think of a person **(f)** and then were asked not to think of that person **(f)**; the suppression part of the experiment is the independent variable. The control subjects were given the same instructions as the experimental group except that the control group was asked to suppress (presumably) an irrelevant "person" such as the Statue of Liberty during the final stage **(g)**. The design is classic in form and straightforward.

The dependent variable is the measurement of skin conductance level (SCL). The exact procedures for making these measurements are described in **(h)**.

RESULTS

i An initial median split of subjects was made into **hot and cold flame** groups according to their questionnaire responses about their degree of longing for their old flame. The numbers of subjects were hot = 36 (16 in the suppress "old flame" group, 20 in the suppress "Statue of Liberty" group) and cold = 34 (18 suppressing "old flame," 16 suppressing "Statue"). Analyses for each task period used a 2 (Hot vs. Cold Flame) × 2 (Suppression Target: Flame vs.

j Statue of Liberty) × 3 (Time: first, middle or last 10 minutes) ANOVA, with repeated measures on the last variable. No effect for subject gender was found in any of the task periods, therefore subject gender was collapsed in further analyses.

In all three task periods, a significant main effect was found for hot vs. cold flame. Subjects thinking of hot flames significantly differed from those thinking of cold flames in the first expression period, $F(1,66) = 4.05, p < .05$, in the suppression period, $F(1,66) = 7.78, p < .01$, and in the second expression period, $F(1,66) = 5.59, p < .05$, respectively, with the subjects in the hot flame condition becoming more physiologically aroused than those in the

k cold flame condition.

In the second expression period, however, subjects who were in the hot flame condition who had previously suppressed the thought of the past relationship continued to show an increase in physiological responsiveness (see Figure 1). Subjects who suppressed the comparison target showed decreased SCL as time went by, while subjects in the cold flame conditions showed a similar decline in SCL across the expression period. This interaction effect was significant $F(2,132) = 5.91, p < .01$.

Results

Here the researchers recognize the potent impact of an old relationship that one still desires (a "hot flame") and the less acute impact of an old relationship one does not desire (a "cold flame"). Section (**i**) explains the rationale. An overall analysis of variance (ANOVA) was also conducted (**j**).

The results from each group are reviewed in section (**k**). The results of the appropriate statistical analysis are disclosed with the probability values. The data from the second expression period are also presented in Figure 1, which shows that the skin conductance level was lowest for neutral thoughts, was higher for thoughts of a hot old flame, and was highest when the thoughts of the hot old flame were suppressed. Other measures of skin conductance seemed to decline over time.

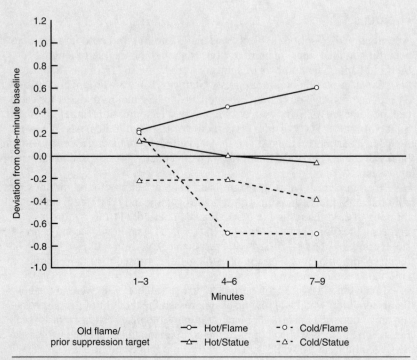

FIGURE 1   **Skin conductance deviation (uS) in second expression period.**

DISCUSSION

These results indicate that the process of suppression may be responsible for extended physiological responsiveness to a lost love. Subjects who were prompted to suppress the thought of their still-desired old flame subsequently showed enhanced SCL on thinking about the flame. Those who were not initially responsive to the old flame—who indicated initially that the flame was "cold," were not prompted to become more responsive by suppression. It seems that suppression may prevent normal habituation to a stimulus that is already exciting, thus making the electrodermal reaction to that stimulus similar to if it was novel each time. **In choosing to suppress emotional thoughts rather than express them** (see Pennebaker, 1988), **people may create the very emotional reactions they seek through suppression to eliminate.** It seems that if people follow Hank Williams' example and try to get a past love off their minds, they may come to suffer the same fate: **"All night long I've cried."**

l

m

n

Discussion

In the final section **(l)** of the poster the authors restate their findings and offer a further explanation that may have important applications **(m)**. Finally, they add poignancy to the paper in **(n)**.

REFERENCES

Epstein, S. (1983). Natural healing processes of the mind: Graded stress inoculation as an inherent coping mechanism. In D. Meichenbaum & M. E. Jaremko (Eds.), *Stress reduction and prevention* (pp. 39–66). New York: Plenum Press.

Fowles, D. C., Christie, M. J., Edelberg, R., Grings, W. W., Lykken, D. T., & Venables, P. H. (1981). Publication recommendations for electrodermal measurements. *Psychophysiology, 18,* 232–239.

Martin, L. L., & Tesser, A. (1989). Toward a motivational and structural theory of ruminative thought. In J. S. Uleman & J. A. Bargh (Eds.), *Unintended thought* (pp. 306–326). New York: Guilford Press.

Pennebaker, J. W. (1988). Confession, inhibition, and disease. In L. Berkowitz (Ed.), *Advances in experimental psychology* (Vol. 22, pp. 211–242). Orlando, FL: Academic Press.

Wegner, D. M. (1989). *White bears and other unwanted thoughts: Suppression, obsession, and the psychology of mental control.* New York: Penguin.

Wegner, D. M., Schneider, D. J., Carter, S. R. III, & White, L. (1987). Paradoxical effects of thought suppression. *Journal of Personality and Social Psychology, 53,* 5–13.

Wegner, D. M., Shortt, J. W., Blake, A. W., & Page, M. S. (1990). The suppression of exciting thoughts. *Journal of Personality and Social Psychology, 58,* 409–418.

Note: Presented at the meeting of the American Psychological Association, August, 1991, San Francisco, CA. This research was supported by National Science Foundation Grant BNS 90-96263. Correspondence should be addressed to Daniel M. Wegner, Department of Psychology, Gilmer Hall, University of Virginia, Charlottesville, VA 22903 (E-mail DMW2M@VIRGINIA.EDU).

Questions

1. What other type of data could have been collected?
2. What follow-up experiments are suggested by these data?
3. Based on this study, suggest how the use of SCL data might be used to distinguish deeply disturbing events from less disturbing events.
4. Some people have been known to "carry a flame" for someone for years. Design a study that could distinguish people who have carried a flame for a long time from people who have just recently broken up.
5. Design an experiment that could measure other emotional factors (e.g., the loss of a loved one).
6. Search the literature for examples of skin conductivity (also called Galvanic Skin Response) and emotional reactions. Prepare a brief report on the use of this technique in gathering experimental data.

13 Picture Memory

Introduction

Of all our perceptual attributes, identification of visual scenes occupies a central position in our cognitive domain. In this experiment, Bower, Karlin, and Dueck (1975) demonstrate that contextual cues greatly facilitate the way we learn and store simple line pictures in memory.

Enhancing memory by "priming" a participant with mnemonic devices has often been used in the study of linguistic material. Consider the following syntactically correct but hard to understand and memorize sentence: *The notes were sour because the seams split.* Nonsense, you might think, but suppose you put this sentence into the context of "bagpipe." Suddenly, you easily understand why the notes were sour, and your ability to memorize that sentence is significantly enhanced. Do we memorize pictures, especially ambiguous pictures, in a similar way? Two well-designed and interesting experiments by Bower et al. indicate that we do.

COMPREHENSION AND MEMORY FOR PICTURES

Gordon H. Bower, Martin B. Karlin, and Alvin Dueck
Stanford University

The thesis advanced is that people remember nonsensical pictures much better if they comprehend what they are about. Two experiments supported this thesis. In the first, nonsensical "droodles" were studied by subjects with or without an accompanying verbal interpretation of the pictures. Free recall was much better for subjects receiving the interpretation during study. Also, a later recognition test showed that subjects receiving the interpretation rate as more similar to the original picture, a distractor, which was close to the prototype of the interpreted category. In Experiment II, subjects studied pairs of nonsensical pictures, with or without a linking interpretation provided. Subjects who heard a phrase identifying and interrelating the pictures of a pair showed greater associative recall and matching than subjects who received no interpretation. The results suggest that memory is aided whenever contextual clues arouse appropriate schemata into which the material to be learned can be fitted.

The following experiments address the question of how people remember pictures. We may begin with the observation that pictures (drawings, diagrams, photographs) comprise a two-dimensional notational system which, like language, has both a "surface structure" (the medium) and a meaningful "deep structure" (the message). Like language, pictures have a terminal vocabulary (of strokes, shadings, etc.), sets of combination rules, often a referential field, and conventional rules for interpreting what a picture is about (see Gombrich, 1960; Goodman, 1968). Pictures, especially "realistic" ones, denote objects or scenes in a manner that parallels the symbolic way that words and sentences do. And just as language appears to be acquired as a

Source: Reprinted by permission from *Memory and Cognition,* 1975, 3, 216–220.

Analysis

Literature Review

In this experiment pictures were conceptualized as a "two-dimensional notational system" with features similar to those of language structure and usage. As such, pictures, like language, are a communicative medium. But the rules that govern pictorial memory and understanding may or may not be similar to the linguistic rules that govern its

perceptual motor skill, so also does it appear that children learn the conventional rules for interpreting the notational symbolism of pictures. These rules guide our construction of what a picture is about—what conceptualizations it expresses or what objects it symbolizes. That we learn to interpret drawings is illustrated clearly by the difficulty novices have acquiring the symbolic system of their profession, such as ballet Labanotation, musical scoring, molecular structure, and the like.

a   We are interested in memory for pictures. **The hypothesis to be tested is that a major determinant of how well a person can remember a picture is whether or not he "understands" it at the time he studies it.** If he comprehends the picture—achieves a compact interpretation of it—then he should remember it much better than if he fails to comprehend it.

This hypothesis was suggested by the work of Bransford and Johnson (1972), Bransford and McCarrell (1974), and Doll and Lapinski (1974) on memory for *linguistic* material. They showed convincingly that a person's ability to recall a sentence depends on whether the sentence causes him to call to mind an appropriate referential situation. For example, consider causal sentences such as: (1) The notes were sour because the seams split; (2) The voyage wasn't delayed because the bottle shattered; (3) The haystack was important because the cloth ripped. Though simple in syntax and word mean-

b   ings, such sentences prove difficult to understand and recall. The mind boggles because a causal connection is asserted to hold between two apparently unrelated events; the subject cannot call to mind an appropriate schemata (known scenario) into which the events can be substituted and thus related causally. But all difficulties dissolve if the subject is provided with a clue as to an appropriate causal schemata: The clue is a simple "thematic prompt" (for the three sentences above, *bagpipe, ship christening, parachutist*). The clue calls to mind a known scenario (see the "frames" theory of Minsky, 1974) into which the events mentioned in the sentence can then be fitted. The sentences then become comprehensible and memorable.

We wish to advance here a parallel argument for the role of comprehen-

c   sion in memory for pictures. **Our experiments will, therefore, expose subjects to pictures which are very difficult to "understand" unless one is given a thematic clue; we then later test memory for pictures that had been shown with or without the clues.** Of course, this means that we are in-

understanding. On an intuitive level, our "understanding" of a picture at the time we see it ought to influence how well we remember that picture. The researchers in this experiment set out to see if that was true, stating their hypothesis in **(a)**.

Their hypothesis was suggested by contemporary research on memory for linguistic material **(b)**. This experiment asks, If memory for pictorial material were similarly primed, would the effect be similar? An abbreviated description of the experimental design is found in **(c)**. Notice how clearly these psychologists set the stage for their experiments. First, they must be convinced that memory is facilitated by presenting a cue that assists understanding. They then illustrate the

vestigating memory for "nonsensical" pictures, one for which subjects usually have no interpretation. But what makes a picture nonsensical or meaningless? There are doubtless several kinds of nonsense, but included would be pictures for which the viewer (1) does not know the conventions for interpretation (e.g., a musical score for a musician who only "plays by ear"), (2) does not know the conceptual denotations of the symbols (e.g., the step sequences corresponding to ballet Labanotation), or (3) knows both of the above but still can achieve no coherent understanding by applying the standard conventions because the picture does not supply enough interpretive clues. Examples of the latter kind, which we shall use in our research, occur with "impoverished" pictures: These are pictures which reduce or eliminate the salient clues or distinctive features of objects which typically guide our selection of their schemata from memory. Such pictures present fragments of hidden figures which may be seen only by suggestion. They appear uninterpretable until a clue retrieves from memory an appropriate conceptual frame which can then be fit onto the line fragments.

A curious side effect results from finally finding a conceptual schema which fits: The tension of "What is it?" dissolves with laughter into "Oh, now I get it!" Many of us became familiar with such visual jokes in the early 1960s with the "droodles" rage in America: A droodle was an uninterpretable drawing that turned out to have a funny interpretation (see Price, 1972). Figure 1 shows two of the examples used in our experiment.

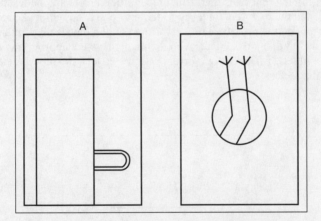

FIGURE 1   **Droodles of Experiment I. Panel A: A midget playing a trombone in a telephone booth. Panel B: An early bird who caught a very strong worm.**

memory technique they use in terms of verbally interpreted "droodles" **(d)**. One droodle we remember from years ago is shown on the next page. It is either a used lollipop or the side view of a postcard.

Experiment I

The first experiment used free recall to assess the effects of comprehension on picture memory. Subjects studied a series of droodles pictures that they were to recall. Some subjects heard the interpretation as they saw each picture; other subjects, the controls, simply viewed the pictures without hearing any interpretive comment. The session ended with subjects drawing copies of those pictures they could recall.

e

A second, minor hypothesis tested was that subjects might distort their memory of the picture in a direction which provided a better fit to the prototype of the category used to interpret the picture upon original viewing. This "assimilation hypothesis" is an old one (see Carmichael, Hogan, & Walter, 1932; Riley, 1963), but the evidence regarding it has been equivocal. To test the hypothesis, we had subjects return after a week for a recognition memory test. Besides the correct picture, the multiple-choice set for each item contained two distractor pictures that were equally similar to the correct picture in terms of a line-overlap measure. One of these distractors exemplified a minor variation on the target which made it look even more like the interpreted prototype than did the original target (call this the "prototype" distractor). The other distractor involved a similarly minor line alteration but was done in such a manner as to violate the fit of the interpretive schema to the picture (call this the physically "similar" distractor). The expectation of the assimilation hypothesis is that, when recognition errors are made, subjects who learned the picture with a suggested interpretation will make relatively more errors on the prototype distractor than on the physically similar distractor. On the other hand, subjects who do not achieve the appropriate interpretation should tend to divide their errors evenly between the prototype and similar distractors.

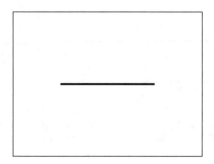

Once you "see" it, your memory for the object is significantly altered. Let's return to the experiments and see how the authors use these simple line drawings to describe empirically how cueing pictures affects memory.

Method

f **The subjects were 18 undergraduates fulfilling a service requirement for their introductory psychology course. They were tested individually, assigned in random order to the "label" or "no-label" condition of the experiment.** All subjects studied a series of 28 simple droodles pictures shown on 3 × 5 in. cards at a rate of one every 10 seconds. As each picture was shown, its appropriate interpretation was given by the experimenter to the subjects in the label group but not to subjects in the no-label group.

g **Following presentation of the list, subjects had 10 minutes to draw all the pictures they could remember in any order they wished.** The recall sheets were 8 × 11 in. papers marked off into a 3 by 3 matrix; the subject was instructed to recall by quickly sketching a recalled picture in one of the nine boxes on his recall sheet and to use as many sheets as necessary to complete his list recall. Before recall commenced, it was emphasized that the subject should aim for sketching the "gist" of the pictures recalled rather than for

Experiment I

From **(c)** we already have a good idea what the experimental design will be. The first experiment's dependent measures were a free-recall task that was given immediately after the presentation of the stimuli and a recognition memory test that was given one week later. Subjects were assigned either to a group that heard an interpretation with each picture or to a group that saw only the ambiguous pictures.

In addition to the general hypothesis, the experimenters were also trying to find support for the assimilation hypothesis **(e)**, which states that subjects distort their memory for a picture to make it more representative of the interpretation than the actual picture itself.

Method.   In the experimental procedure all subjects were shown a series of 28 simple droodles at the rate of one every 10 seconds. However, one group heard the appropriate interpretation after each picture (label group), whereas the other group did not (no-label group). In all other respects the two groups were treated exactly alike. Thus, we have a simple two-group experiment.

The authors note that the 18 subjects were randomly assigned to either the label or the no-label group **(f)**, but they do not report the order in which they presented the 28 pictures to the subjects. However, that really doesn't matter in this experiment because we are not concerned with any possible order effects of the cards (do you know why?). The important point is that the order of presentation was exactly the same in both the label and the no-label groups.

After the participants had seen the 28 cards, they were asked to recall as many of the pictures as they could in a free-recall situation **(g)** where the participants had

providing a lot of artistic detail of each picture. (The pictures could in fact be drawn very simply.) Following completion of the recall task, the subject was dismissed with an appointment to return the next week **"for other experiments."**

Upon returning the next week, subjects received the three-alternative multiple-choice test over 24 of the 28 pictures of the originally learned list (for four of the original pictures, we were unable to think up two similar distractors which met our criteria). The subject received a six-page booklet, with four multiple-choice triplets arranged in rows down each page. He was told that each triplet (row) contained one picture he had seen the week before as well as two closely similar pictures. **He was asked to rank order the three alternatives in each row, placing a 1 beside that test figure he considered most like the one he remembered seeing, a 2 beside the next most similar one, and a 3 beside that picture he considered least similar to the one he remembered.** The test was self-paced. Upon completing the test, the subject was debriefed and dismissed. One subject of the no-label group failed to return for the 1-week test, leaving eight subjects in that group at that point.

Results

Free Recall.   A first noteworthy fact is that we had relatively few problems in scoring for "gist recall" of the sketches. We had anticipated severe problems produced by interfering or confused combinations of several pictures, or at least deletions causing the sketch to be unidentifiable. But subjects tended

to sketch the pictures in any order from memory. Each participant had 10 minutes for this task. Experimenters have to set a time limit on tasks such as these because otherwise the participants could sit for hours trying to recall another droodle. Usually, researchers choose a time limit by "pretesting" the material to find out how long it takes most subjects to recall most of the pictures that they know.

Note that when the participants were dismissed, they were asked to return the next week "for other experiments" **(h)**. If the participants had been told that they were coming back to recall the droodles, they could have practiced during the week. To eliminate these practice effects, the participants were led to believe they were coming back for a different experiment. The use of deception is an ethical concern. It is something that must be carefully considered and justified to the institutional review board (see Chapter 9).

Each participant returned the next week and took a recognition test. Three versions of each droodle were shown to the participant—one was the original droodle, one looked more like the interpretation given to the droodle in the label group (prototype distractor), and one was similar to the original but did not correspond to the interpretation. The participant was asked to rank order the figures **(i)**. We assume the arrangement of the three pictures for each droodle was random across each row. Note that the participants for both groups were treated exactly alike—the instructions and materials were the same for both groups. Also note that

to recall (sketch) the pictures either relatively accurately or not at all. The primary result of interest is that an average of 19.6 pictures out of 28 (70%) were accurately recalled by the label group [standard error of the mean (SEM) = 1.25], whereas only 14.2 pictures (51%) were recalled by the no-label group (SEM = .92). **The means differ reliably in the predicted direction** [$t(16) = 3.43$, p < .01]. Thus, we have clear confirmation that "picture understanding" enhances picture recall.

Recognition Memory.   Despite the closeness of the distractors to the target, recognition of the correct target at the 1-week retention interval was very high. Subjects who received labels during study correctly recognized (gave a 1 rating to) a mean of 22.0 out of the 24 test triplets (92%); subjects receiving no labels during study correctly recognized a mean of 20.1 pictures (84%). With standard errors of .83 and 1.08, respectively, the means do not differ reliably.

Even noting the high levels of recognition accuracy, we may still ask whether the label and no-label subjects react differently to the prototype vs. the physically similar distractor. There are several indications that the label

enough of the experimental procedure is included to allow the replication of the experiment.

Results

In this experiment two groups were tested in the free-recall task. The results are portrayed in Figure 13.1. From these data the authors used the *t* statistic to test for statistical significance and found **(j)** that the two means differed in the predicted direction for the 0.01 level of probability. Therefore, the authors concluded that labeling enhances picture recall.

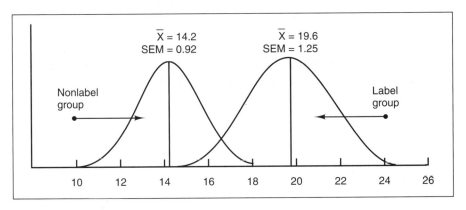

FIGURE 13.1   Number of pictures remembered using free recall (theoretical distribution based on data by Bower, Karlin, & Dueck, 1975).

subjects considered the prototype distractor much closer subjectively to the target. First, considering only cases when the correct picture was not ranked first, the conditional probability that the prototype (rather than the similar distractor) was ranked first was .75 for the label subjects but only .38 for the no-label subjects. However, these conditional probabilities are based on very few observations. A more stable measure of differentiation is provided by the difference in rankings (on similarity to the remembered target) between the prototype distractor and the physically similar distractor. For the label group the mean rank assigned to the prototype was 2.17, whereas that for the similar distractor was 2.76, a difference of .59. In contrast, for the no-label group, the rankings of the two distractors was closer: 2.34 were for the prototype and 2.48 for the similar distractor, a difference of only .14. The difference in rankings is reliably larger for the label group than for the no-label group [$t(15) =$

k   2.79, $p < .02$]. **This result accords with the assimilation hypothesis: Subjects receiving the picture interpretation during study later reported that the distractor which moved in the direction of the interpreted prototype was closer to the target than was the distractor which involved a similarly minimal physical alteration but one which violated the interpretation given to the original target.** In contrast, the no-label subjects showed no comparable differentiation between the two kinds of distractors.

EXPERIMENT II

The initial experiment demonstrated the role of semantic comprehension in facilitating free recall of pictures. Having a meaningful name for a picture

l   may facilitate recall because it provides a memorable summary or cue for later free recall. But an interpretation does more than provide a meaningful mnemonic label for a picture; it also causes unification or knitting together of the disparate parts of the picture into a coherent whole or schema.

m   **The second experiment sets out to test more directly the influence of the unifying coherence of an interpretation upon picture memory. The**

The second part of the experiment involved recognition memory for the pictures after a one-week interval. Both groups recognized the original figures with a high degree of accuracy. The authors also speculate on the nature of the recognition task and the assimilation hypothesis **(k)**.

Experiment II

The first experiment established that a meaningful name helped the recall of a picture. What about more complex learning, as when two ambiguous pictures are paired? Would a label that cleverly tied the two pictures together facilitate the association between them?

The second experiment was designed to answer these questions **(l)**. In **(m)** the experimenters give an abbreviated description of what they are going to do.

subject was asked to study pairs of nonsensical pictures and was later tested by cueing with one member of each pair for recall (in drawing) of the other member of the pair. Again, half the subjects received no interpretation of the pictures, whereas half heard a phrase that made both pictures and their pairing a meaningful sequence. Examples of picture pairs are shown in the three rows of Figure 2. Their interpretations are (from left to right panels in each pair): (1) rear end of a pig disappearing into a fog bank, and his nose coming out the other side of the fog; (2) piles of dirty

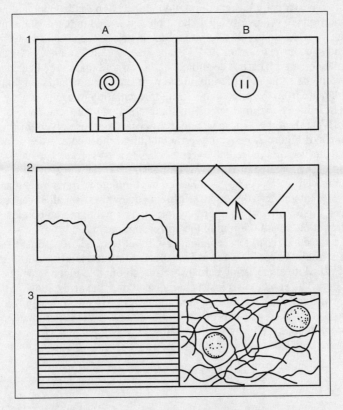

FIGURE 2 Pairs of nonsensical pictures used in Experiment II. See the text for an explanation of their contents.

Such a statement puts the reader "in the ball park" so that he or she can read the technical method section with a clear frame of reference. The hypothesis is stated in **(n)**.

n   clothes, then pouring detergent into the washing machine to wash the clothes; and (3) uncooked spaghetti, then cooked spaghetti and meatballs. **The hypothesis is that subjects hearing such interpretations during study will show much higher associative recall than will subjects who study the pictures without the interpretations.**

Method

The subjects were 16 university students attending summer school. They were recruited by an advertisement and paid $1.50 for their participation. They were tested individually, assigned in random alteration to the label and no-label conditions ($n = 8$ per group). The subject was told to learn 30 picture pairs that were shown to him at a rate of one every 12 sec. The pairs were drawn and shown by means of 3×5 flashcards, one picture on a white card and its mate on a pink card. The subject had been told that in the later recall test he would be shown the picture on the white card and would have to recall (draw) its mate from the pink card. During presentation of each pair, the label subjects heard the experimenter supply an interactive interpretation to bind the picture-pair together. These were descriptions like those given for the three panels of Figure 2. Following presentation of the 30 pairs, the white deck was shuffled and presented as recall cues at a 20-second rate. "Gist" sketching of the recalled pictures was emphasized. If the subject had begun his drawing before 20 sec, he was allowed to complete it; otherwise, the next
o   cue was presented after 20 seconds. **Subjects drew their recall sketches in numbered boxes, nine to a page;** they left blank any numbered box for which they could recall nothing to the corresponding cue.

After the cued recall test (conducted without feedback regarding the cor-
p   rectness of subject's recall), **the subject received an associative matching test.** The 30 white and 30 pink cards were spread out in a random array over the table top. The subject was instructed to scan over the array, looking for the pairs of white and pink pictures he had studied. As pairs were recognized, the two cards were picked up by the subject and handed to the experimenter. The subject continued this pairing until he had selected all pairs he could remember: because they were asked not to guess, many subjects stopped short of

Method

The method in this experiment involved presenting pairs of nonsense pictures. As in the first experiment, half of the subjects also received an interpretation, which in this case linked the pictures conceptually, while half of the subjects received no interpretation. The authors hypothesized that subjects who had the interpretation would have better associative recall of the pairs than subjects who did not receive the interpretation.

The authors supply the pertinent details for this experiment: subjects, independent variables, description of stimulus materials, and procedures of the experiment. The dependent measures were an associative recall test (**o**) and an associative matching test (**p**).

pairing off all members. The subject's associative matching score was simply the number of correct pairs he selected from the array before terminating. (The expected correct pairs obtainable by guessing in an associative matching test is about one, regardless of the number of pairs to be guessed at. (See Feller, 1957, p. 97.) After completing the matching test, the subject was debriefed and dismissed.

Results
Associative Recall.   Again, no problem was encountered in scoring correct gist recall of the cued picture. **Cued recall averaged 21.75 pictures out of 30 (73%) for the label subjects (SEM = 1.78) and 13.13 (44%) for the no-label subjects (SEM = 2.41).** These percentages differ reliably [$t(14) = 2.87$, $p < 02$]. The effect is remarkably consistent over items, too: for 22 items the label subjects recalled more than the no-label subjects, for three items the no-label subjects recalled more, and there were five ties. The 22/25 predominance of items with more recalls by label subjects exceeds chance of 50% ($z = 6.55$, $p < .01$). Thus, the label group is uniformly superior in recall to the no-label group.

Results

In the results section, we see that the influence on memory of labeling ambiguous pictures was statistically tested by means of a *t*-test, which indicated that labeling strongly facilitates associative learning. The average number of correctly recalled items was 21.75 for the label group and 13.13 for the no-label group **(q)**. The hypothetical distribution of scores is shown in Figure 13.2.

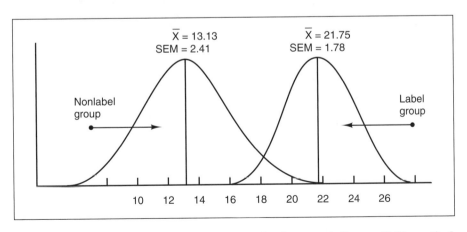

FIGURE 13.2   Number of pictures remembered using associative recall (theoretical distribution based on data by Bower, Karlin, & Dueck, 1975).

r

Associative Matching.   **The number of correct matches (of pairs) averaged 27.50 for the label subjects (SEM = .98) compared to 16.63 for the no-label subjects (SEM = 2.80). These differ reliably** $[t(14) = 3.66, p < .01]$. Moreover, the relative gain in recognition performance above what could be recalled was much larger for the label subjects (70%) than for the no-label subjects (21%). The data show that the label subjects still exhibit superior associative coherence even when all the pictures are available and do not need to be recalled.

DISCUSSION

It has been argued that memory for a picture depends upon the subject achieving a conceptual interpretation of the picture as he views it. The hypothesis is the pictorial analog of that relating sentence recall to comprehension (e.g., Bransford & McCarrell, 1974). The point is intuitively obvious once it has been noticed (as are many other "facts" of psychology), and the

s

experiments above are primarily demonstrational in nature. **Subjects provided with meaningful interpretations of single droodles show superior free recall. Subjects who hear an interpretation identifying and relating two pictures together show greater coherence of the pictures on later association tests.** Although control subjects were probably trying to come up with some sensible interpretation of the pictures, the difficulty of the task precluded much success. Presumably, if we had collected control subjects' attempts at interpretations (recording their "thinking aloud"), those pictures for which they achieved a meaningful interpretation would more likely have been recalled (see, e.g., Montague, 1972). The likelihood of this being the case remains to be checked.

One might question whether the associative coherence found in Experiment II is a result merely of identifying the objects in each picture or whether

t

it depends in addition upon providing the meaningful linking relationship between the two pictures of a pair. For some pairs the linking relation was that the pictures in Figure 2 denoted different parts of the same object (the pig),

The number of correct matches is reported in (**r**).

Discussion

The results of these experiments are succinctly summarized (**s**), and the authors suggest that their results have empirically demonstrated something that may have been suspected about human nature for some time.

The authors are thorough in their discussion and are careful not to come to wild conclusions that are not supported by the data in the experiments. In one instance they worry about the results of Experiment II (**t**) and check their hunch by varying the procedure slightly for a small group of subjects.

different states of an object as it underwent changes (the spaghetti), or different objects associated with a common process (the clothes and washer). We feel these relations are very important for promoting associative coherence of the elements of the pair. To illustrate this point, four further subjects from the same source were tested under the same procedure as Experiment II, except that new pairs were constructed by re-pairing the old pictures in a random manner. As the pair was shown, each picture was separately interpreted (e.g., a pig's tail and detergent pouring into a washing machine). No linking relation other than contiguity was stated for connecting the two contents. These four subjects averaged only 7.75 correct in cued recall (SEM = 1.89) and 8.25 correct in associative matching (SEM = 1.11). If anything, the scores are lower than those for the controls who studied the original pairs without hearing the objects or relation identified. Quite possibly, this "mispairing" list was so difficult because semantically related objects appeared in different pairs, creating intrapair interference. Teasing out the several contributors to this poor learning would be a task for further experimentation. The significant fact we wish to glean from this poor recall of mispaired items is that associative coherence depends heavily upon relating the two identified pictures and relatively little upon identifications per se that do not call to mind a known relationship between the two pictures.

How are our results to be related to previous work on picture memory? Previous work on learning of nonsense figures typically used recognition rather than reproduction measures and have been largely concerned with testing hypotheses of acquired distinctiveness or acquired equivalence of forms induced by learning different or the same arbitrary labels for the forms. Of more direct relevance to our results are those by Ellis (reviewed by Ellis, 1973), who found that the learning of "representative labels" to complex polygons enhanced their later recognition. Of course, the "representative labels" were simply a plausible name or interpretation of the figures. The fact that pairing with a representative label makes the pictures more memorable seems quite consistent with our hypothesis relating picture comprehension to memory. Since "association value" or "codability" has been a common variable in research on pictorial memory, one may ask whether our notion of a "semantic interpretation" of a picture is just a fancy name for an association to it. We think not. We intend "semantic interpretation" to be much more specific than the concept of "picture association" suggests. Associations may occur to many surface features of a picture or to fragments of it, all without improving memory for it. Presumably, picture memory would improve with greater "depth of processing," as does memory for words (Craik, 1973) or

u

In the final paragraph (**u**) Bower et al. fit their newly found information into what we already know about picture memory.

faces (Bower & Karlin, 1974). But this implies comprehending the picture, figuring out what conceptualization it expresses or what object it denotes: It means getting the "message" behind the "medium."

REFERENCES

Bransford, J. D., & Johnson, M. K. (1972). Contextual prerequisites for understanding: Some investigations of comprehension and recall. *Journal of Verbal Learning and Verbal Behavior, 11,* 717–726.

Bransford, J. D., & McCarrell, N. S. (1974). In W. Weimer & D. Palermo (Eds.), *Cognition and the symbolic processes.* Hillside, N.J.: Lawrence Erlbaum Associates.

Bower, G. H., & Karlin, M. B. (1974). Depth of processing pictures of faces and recognition memory. *Journal of Experimental Psychology, 103,* 751–757.

Carmichael, L., Hogan, H. P., & Walter, A. A. (1932). An experimental study of the effect of language on the reproduction of visually perceived form. *Journal of Experimental Psychology, 15,* 73–86.

Craik, F. I. M. (1973). "Levels of analysis" view of memory. In P. Pliner, L. Krames, & T. Alloway (Eds.), *Communication and affect: Language and thought.* New York: Academic Press.

Doll, T. J., & Lapinski, R. H. (1974). Context effects in speeded comprehension and recall of sentences. *Bulletin of the Psychonomic Society, 3,* 342–345.

Ellis, H. C. (1973). Stimulus encoding processes in human learning and memory. In G. H. Bower (Ed.), *The psychology of learning and motivation* (Vol. 7). New York: Academic Press.

Feller, W. (1957). *An introduction to probability theory and its applications.* (Vol. 1, 2nd ed.) New York: Wiley.

Gombrich, E. (1960). *Art and illusion.* New York: Pantheon.

Goodman, N. (1968). *Languages of art* (2nd ed.). Indianapolis, Ind.: Bobbs-Merrill.

Minsky, M. (1974). *Frame systems.* Unpublished manuscript. M.I.T. AI Project.

Montague, W. E. (1972). Elaborative strategies in verbal learning and memory. In G. H. Bower (Ed.), *The psychology of learning and motivation: In research and theory* (Vol. 6, pp. 225–302). New York: Academic Press.

Price, R. (1972). *Droodles.* Los Angeles: Price/Stern/Sloan.

Riley, D. A. (1963). Memory for form. In L. Postman (Ed.), *Psychology in the making.* New York: Knopf.

Note: The authors thank Susan L. Karlin for creating most of the stimulus materials for Experiment II. The research was supported by Grant MH 13905-07 from the National Institute of Mental Health to Gordon H. Bower.

Questions

1. Devise another experiment to test the assimilation hypothesis mentioned in this experiment.
2. Why did the experimenters use two dependent measures in Experiment I: (1) a free-recall test and (2) a recognition test one week later?
3. The authors state that it is intuitively obvious that providing a conceptual interpretation for ambiguous pictures facilitates recall of the pictures. Why, then, must it be experimentally tested?
4. Design an experiment that tests whether groups of musical notes are easier to remember if they are accompanied by a verbal explanation.
5. Describe some practical and creative applications of this study.
6. The authors don't state specifically how they randomly assigned the 18 subjects into two groups (such that there were 9 subjects per group). How would you do it?

CHAPTER

14 Hormones and Toy Preferences

Introduction

"Little boys play with dump trucks and little girls play with dolls." Once in a while, though, the preference for play objects reverses; some girls prefer dump trucks and some boys prefer dolls. At an early age, however, these role reversals are often discouraged—girls may be taunted and called tomboys and boys may be called sissies, and sometimes the expressions are even more explicit and harsh. Sooner or later, however, most young children learn to play with toys normally associated with their own gender. Some psychologists have developed elaborate theories of social learning that suggest that gender role behavior is essentially a result of the socialization process and that genetics and/or hormones are of little consequence in the selection of gender-specific toys. In a striking contrast to these theories, however, Berenbaum and Hines (1992) present experimentally supported evidence that hormones (specifically, androgen levels in young girls) have a pronounced effect on what types of toys girls play with.

Special Issues

SELECTION OF SUBJECTS AS A SOURCE OF INDEPENDENT VARIABLES

In many experiments it is possible to use subject characteristics as an independent variable. This is sometimes a practical route in studies measuring the differences between two or more groups of subjects who may react differently to some test or experience. Perhaps the most commonly used subject variable is gender. In this study by Berenbaum and Hines, the researchers ask the question, "Are sex-typed toy preferences related to androgens?" To answer this they used male and female children who had a particular genetic disorder that caused elevated levels of androgens. Other researchers may choose to study schizophrenics, gays, Mexican-Americans, military people of differing ranks (see Chapter 11), good students, football players, people living in Connecticut, poor people, stutterers, dyslexic readers, and so on. Although some experimental psychologists argue that the selection of a group of subjects who exhibit certain characteristics introduces special types of control problems, many times this technique is the only one available. Furthermore, if used prudently, this technique can yield reliable data that researchers can use to make valid conclusions.

"POLITICALLY INCORRECT" FINDINGS

Some scientific findings may be socially or politically unpopular. However, it is important to remember that ideally, science is conducted with "blinders on." This means that researchers attempt to keep biases out of their experiments. Therefore, findings are a reflection of the experiment itself, and not of the researcher's opinions, or of the opinions of the society at large. Therefore, when reading articles, especially those that come to conclusions that are contrary to your experience or intuition, the appropriate tactic is to evaluate the method critically. Pay attention to the sample that the authors used. Is it appropriate? Were their experimental manipulations effective? Did they control for extraneous variables? Did they analyze their data using the appropriate statistics? Are there alternative explanations that the authors did not consider? Upon examining an article's method, and coming to the conclusion that the method is rigorous and appropriate for the phenomenon or question under study, one should conclude that the results can be trusted.

EARLY ANDROGENS ARE RELATED TO CHILDHOOD SEX-TYPED TOY PREFERENCES

Sheri A. Berenbaum
University of Health Sciences

Melissa Hines
University of California at Los Angeles

Girls with congenital adrenal hyperplasia (CAH) who were exposed to high levels of androgen in the prenatal and early postnatal periods showed increased play with boys' toys and reduced play with girls' toys compared with their unexposed female relatives at ages 3 to 8. Boys with CAH did not differ from their male relatives in play with boys' or girls' toys. These results suggest that early hormone exposure in females has a masculinizing effect on sex-typed toy preferences.

Sex differences in children's toy preferences have been demonstrated repeatedly. Boys prefer construction and transportation toys, whereas girls prefer dolls, doll furnishings, and kitchen supplies (Connor & Serbin, 1977; Liss, 1981). **These preferences appear to be partially learned, through modeling and reinforcement.** For example, children at various stages of development emulate the behavior of same-sex models in preference to opposite-sex ones (Bussey & Bandura, 1984; Huston, 1983). We present evidence that these sex-typed toy preferences are also related to prenatal or neonatal hormones (androgens).

Gonadal hormones play a major role in the development of sex differences in behavior and the brain in a variety of species, including rodents, songbirds, and primates (Arnold & Gorski, 1984; Beatty, 1979; Goy & McEwen, 1980; MacLusky & Naftolin, 1981). **A unique opportunity to**

a

b

c

Source: Reprinted with permission of *Psychological Science,* 1992, 3, 203–206.

Analysis

Literature Review

The authors begin by stating a commonly accepted supposition regarding the etiology of boys' preferences for dump trucks and girls' preferences for dolls: "These preferences appear to be partially learned, through modeling and reinforcement." **(a)** On the other hand, in **(b)** Berenbaum and Hines suggest that hormones also appear to play an important role in sex differences, especially in animals (e.g., rats, birds, and primates). In **(c)** we find that it is possible to study the effect of

study hormonal influences on human sex-typed behavior is provided by the genetic disorder congenital adrenal hyperplasia (CAH). Because of an enzymatic defect, individuals with CAH produce high levels of adrenal androgens beginning *in utero.* Postnatal treatment with corticosteroids (and mineralocorticoids for the 75% who are also salt-losers) normalizes hormone levels (White, New, & Dupont, 1987).

d

If early hormone exposure affects the development of sex-typed behavior in human beings as it does in other species, then CAH girls should show behavior similar to that of normal boys. Previous studies have suggested that CAH females show intense physical energy expenditure, "tomboyism," rough outdoor play, preference for traditionally masculine toys and activities (Ehrhardt & Baker, 1974; Ehrhardt, Epstein, & Money, 1968), and greater spatial ability than their female relatives (Resnick, Berenbaum,

d₁

Gottesman, & Bouchard, 1986). These findings parallel those reported in other samples with prenatal exposure to masculinizing hormones due to maternal ingestion during pregnancy (Ehrhardt & Meyer-Bahlburg, 1979; Hines, 1982), and are especially interesting in light of recent reports of sex differences in human brain structure (Allen, Hines, Shryne, & Gorski, 1989; Hines & Green, 1991; Swaab & Fliers, 1985).

Although prior studies of CAH girls suggest that hormones can influence childhood behavior, methodological limitations encouraged us to pursue this issue. Specifically, in prior studies, (a) behavior was assessed from interviews rather than direct observation; (b) data were collected with knowledge of the patient or control status of the subject; (c) behaviors were usually rated as present or absent, rather than as continuous traits; and (d) masculine and feminine behaviors were often not assessed separately, but instead treated as opposite ends of a single continuum. Therefore, the present study of individuals with CAH focused on objective, quantifiable measures of sex-typed toy preferences, with assessments made by raters blind to the patient or control status of subjects. **We hypothesized that CAH girls would show greater preference for boys' toys than their unaffected female relatives, and reduced preference for girls' toys.** We did not predict effects for CAH boys because androgen treatment has inconsistent effects in male experimental animals (Baum & Schretlen, 1975; Diamond, Llacuna, & Wong, 1973).

e

f

adrenal androgens on behavior by studying children who are born with a congenital disorder called congenital adrenal hyperplasia (CAH). This condition produces high levels of androgens (the male hormone) in patients with the disorder.

In **(d)** a working hypothesis is presented [a formal hypothesis **(f)** is also shown] in which the authors let us know the general scheme of the investigation. In section **(d₁)** the authors provide a literature review, which, in general, supports the idea that CAH leads to male-related behavior.

In section **(e)** the problems are stated, and in section **(f)** Berenbaum and Hines formally state their hypothesis.

METHOD

Subjects

g_1 We recruited 3- to 8-year-old children with CAH from pediatric endocrine clinics at eight hospitals in the Midwest and California and tested 26 girls and 11 boys. Because of the restricted age range studied and family constellations, only 16 patients (43%) had a same-sex control. Therefore, we combined relatives of male and female patients to obtain our control groups.

g_2 The control groups consisted of 15 unaffected female relatives (10 sisters and 5 first cousins) and 18 unaffected male relatives (14 brothers and 4 first cousins). Patients and controls did not differ significantly in birth order or

g_3 age. Mean ages in months were as follows: female patients, 66.54 (range: 36–99); female controls, 61.80 (range: 36–93); male patients, 64.18 (range: 41–101); and male controls, 69.78 (range: 33–99).

Illness Characteristics

Although behavioral changes in CAH girls may be caused by androgen influences on the developing brain, it has been suggested that these changes might instead result from social or illness factors (Quadagno, Briscoe, & Quadagno, 1977; Slipjer, 1984). For example, because androgen levels are high *in utero*, females have masculinized genitalia. Surgical reconstruction is often necessary, although postnatal treatment prevents further virilization. Parents may treat their CAH daughters in a masculine fashion as a response to this masculine appearance at birth. Therefore, we asked parents to complete a questionnaire which included the item "I encourage my child to act as a girl should." The questionnaire was available for 24 CAH and 11 control girls.

We also examined characteristics of the child's disease: age at diagnosis, degree of genital virilization at diagnosis, and salt-losing status. This information was obtained from medical records, available on 25 girls and 10 boys. Medical ratings were made by two research assistants who had no knowledge of the child's behavioral scores. Age at diagnosis and salt-losing status were recorded with perfect reliability. Most patients were diagnosed in the early neonatal period: Median age at diagnosis was 11 days for girls (range: 0 days to 64 months) and 30 days for boys (range: 14 days to 54 months). Degree of virilization was rated on a scale ranging from 0 (normal female) to 6 (normal male), with intermediate values reflecting varying degrees of clitoral enlargement and fusion of the labia (Prader, 1954). Interrater reliability was .82; mean ratings were used. All girls had some degree of genital virilization: The mean Prader score was 3.0 (range: 1–5). One girl had been raised as a boy for the first month.

Method

The method section begins with a description of the subjects used in the study (g_1), the control groups (g_2), and the children's ages (g_3). Note that the researchers used close relatives of the experimental group to form the control groups. Thus, these groups approximated the genetic and environmental features of the experi-

Toy Preference Materials and Procedure

h **Toy preference was measured by the amount of time the child played with toys shown by others to be preferred by girls, by boys, or equally by the sexes (neutral).** The boys' toys included transportation toys (a helicopter, two cars, and a fire engine) and construction toys (blocks and Lincoln Logs). The girls' toys included three dolls, kitchen supplies, a toy telephone, and crayons and paper. Neutral toys, used as a control, included books, two board games, and a jigsaw puzzle. The toys were arranged in a standard order on the floor of the pediatric clinic or the child's home, in an area approximately 8 ft by 10 ft surrounded by screens.

i The child was brought into the play area individually and told to play with the toys however he or she wanted. **The 12-min session was videotaped for later scoring.** The first 10 min of each session were usually scored; the additional 2 min were scored only if sections of the initial 10 min were un-scorable (e.g., if the child attempted interaction with the videotaper). Order of testing the patient and control was random.

j We scored the amount of time the child played with each toy and then summed the time spent in play with the toys in each of the three categories, to produce total scores for play with boys' toys, girls' toys, and neutral toys. **All tapes were rated by the same two raters, who had not tested the children and who were blind to their patient or control status.** Interrater reliability was very high: The median correlation was .99 for individual toys and .99 for total scores. Data reported here represent the mean scores of the two raters.[1]

---

k [1]Two children (both CAH girls) who played with no toys during their sessions were excluded from all analyses. These girls are similar to the other subjects in disease characteristics. Analyses including these subjects do not change the interpretation of the results.

mental group. The Illness Characteristics section gives a further description of CAH and its features.

The dependent variable is operationally stated in **(h)**. In **(i)** we learn that the sessions were videotaped for later scoring. The videotapes also might provide important documentation of the actual play sessions should other investigators or the authors want to reexamine the data for other behavioral characteristics.

In **(j)** the authors tell us that two people who were blind as to which children were in which group independently scored the behavior of the children. Although reason would suggest that there is little ambiguity in scoring the behavior—time playing with a specific type of toy leaves little room for mistakes—the authors exhibit meticulous attention to potential experimenter bias that might creep into the observations.

In footnote 1 **(k)** the authors mention another issue: subject attrition. In experimental work in psychology, subjects are often "lost" for one reason or

RESULTS

Statistical tests are one-tailed when hypotheses are directional (sex differences and female CAH–control comparisons for time spent in play with boys' and girls' toys) and two-tailed when no difference is hypothesized (all comparisons for play with neutral toys) or when the direction of the difference is not specified (male CAH–control comparisons).

Sex Differences

As expected, control boys and girls differed in the amount of time they played with boys' toys and girls' toys, but not neutral toys (see Fig. 1). The magnitudes of the differences (in standard deviation units, or d; Cohen, 1977) are consistent with those reported by other investigators. Further, control boys preferred boys' toys to girls' toys, $t(17) = 4.58, p < .001$. Control girls had the opposite preference, but the difference was not significant, $t(14) = -1.17$.[2]

CAH Patient–Control Comparisons

Females.   As hypothesized, CAH girls spent significantly more time playing with boys' toys than did control girls $(d = .89)$, $t(37) = 2.66, p < .01$, and about as much time as the control boys (see Figure 1). **Further, like control boys, CAH girls played significantly more with boys' toys than with girls' toys,** $t(23) = 2.93, p < .01$. This effect is also seen in the subsample of patients with

[2]Because the distributions of play scores are skewed, we conducted all analyses on data transformed in various ways (e.g., arcsine, square root) and with nonparametric procedures. All analytic procedures produced similar results.

another. We mean lost in the sense that, for a variety of reasons, a subject's data may not be usable. Some reasons are (1) subjects drop out of the experiment; (2) subjects don't or can't follow instructions, and thus their data cannot be used; and (3) data are inadvertently lost, deleted, or destroyed. It is prudent to anticipate these losses and have a systematic way to deal with them *before* the experiment begins (insofar as such farsighted planning is possible). The researcher should have a plan for replacing or in some way compensating (e.g., statistically) for lost data. In this experiment, two little girls simply did not play with the toys; in effect, they did not produce any data on the dependent variable **(h)**. The data from these two subjects were excluded from all analyses. In this passage the word *analysis* is left undefined; it could mean statistical analysis (likely) or inspection of the data.

Results

In section **(l)** the main results of the two groups of girls are presented first. The probability (*p*) value is also presented. In **(m)** the authors statistically test the results, showing how much the CAH girls played with girls' toys and how much

(analysis continues on page 236)

a same-sex relative control ($N = 11$ pairs): The mean time in play with boys' toys was 327.23 s for CAH girls and 166.55 s for matched girls, $t(10) = 2.20$, $p < .05$.

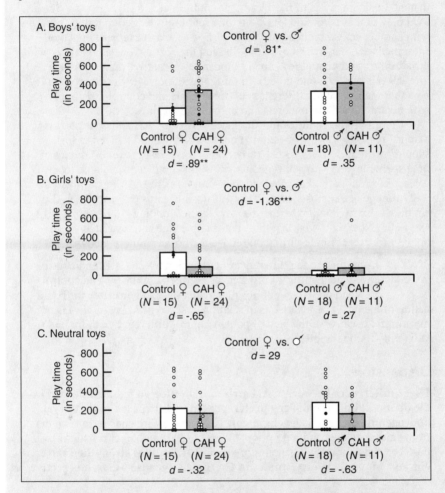

FIGURE 1 Time spent in play with sex-typed toys by female and male CAH patients and controls during 10 min of play. Scores are the sum of play with individual toys and therefore may exceed 600 s. Bars represent group means; lines represent standard errors; points represent individual subjects; d = difference between group means/average standard deviation. Group differences were evaluated by t test; $^{*}p < .05$, $^{**}p < .01$, $^{***}p < .001$, one-tailed.

CAH girls also played less with girls' toys than did the control girls, $t(37)$ = -2.02, $p < .05$, but this effect is smaller than that for boys' toys ($d = .65$). Perhaps because of low statistical power, the difference is not significant in matched-pairs analysis of the 11 patient-control pairs, $t(10) = -1.09$. Because total play time was limited, play with one set of toys tended to reduce play with another set, so reduced play with girls' toys may have partly resulted from increased play with boys' toys. In fact, the correlations among play with boys', girls', and neutral toys are all moderately negative, ranging from $-.30$ to $-.69$ (all $ps < .01$, one-tailed). In this context, however, it is important to note that there were no differences between CAH and control girls in play with neutral toys (both matched and unmatched t-values < 1.0).

There were no significant differences between CAH and control girls in parents' responses to the question "I encourage my child to act as a girl should," with 59.1% and 63.6% responding "yes," respectively. Amount of time spent playing with sex-typed toys was not significantly related to any disease characteristic. For play with boys' toys, rs are $-.10$ for virilization, $-.29$ for age at diagnosis, and .25 for salt-losing status (1 = salt-loser, 0 = simple virilizer). For play with girls' toys, corresponding rs are $-.09$, $-.14$, and $-.06$. Note, however, that the small sample size and restricted range (e.g., only 2 girls were simple virilizers) reduce the power of these analyses.

Males. In contrast to the differences observed between CAH and control girls, there were no significant differences between CAH boys and control boys on sex-typed play ($ps > .20$ for play with boys' and girls' toys). Examination of medical characteristics in relation to sex-typed play in boys is not meaningful because of the lack of patient-control differences and limited variability in the sample.

DISCUSSION

n **Large differences between CAH girls and unaffected female relatives indicate masculinization of toy preferences in girls exposed to high levels of androgen during early development.** These results are consistent with data from animal models and with prior studies of CAH and other females exposed to masculinizing hormones *in utero.* **Our findings strengthen the conclusions of previous play studies in CAH girls because we used objective,**

o

they played with boys' toys. Further tests are conducted on the data and these details are presented in the next two paragraphs.

Discussion

The discussion section begins with a restatement of the principal findings and conclusion **(n)**. The results are then related to previous findings **(o)**. The authors also state the rigor involved in the present studies, thus addressing some issues

quantifiable measures and behavioral ratings made without knowledge of patient or control status. The data also suggest a relative defeminization of toy preferences, although this result was less robust. Other studies of hormone-exposed samples have also been more likely to observe "masculinizing" than "defeminizing" effects of prenatal hormones, perhaps in part because the studies have concentrated on the former (Berenbaum, 1990; Ehrhardt & Meyer-Bahlburg, 1979; Hines, 1982). Although other hormones, such as 17-hydroxyprogesterone and corticosteroids, are also abnormal prenatally in CAH, it is unlikely that they account for the masculinized behavior in CAH girls, because these hormones have smaller and less consistent behavioral effects than androgen and may actually prevent masculinization (Erpino, 1975; Hull, Franz, Snyder, & Nishita, 1980).

It appears unlikely that the behavioral changes are due to social or illness factors. Our failure to find relationships between sex-typed play and physical virilization is consistent with other data in CAH patients indicating no relationship between degree of virilization and gender-role behavior (Slipjer, 1984). Although it is possible that any virilization results in different parental treatment, this argument is weakened by parents' retrospective reports that they did not treat CAH girls in a "masculine" fashion, here and in other studies (Ehrhardt & Baker, 1974; Resnick, 1982), and by data from rhesus macaques indicating that masculinization of juvenile play is unrelated to genital virilization or maternal behavior (Goy, Bercovitch, & McBrair, 1988). Nevertheless, given the disproportionate rate of return of questionnaires for our CAH and control girls and other problems inherent in questionnaire measures, direct observation of parental behavior would be valuable.

Our data indicate no changes in sex-typed toy preferences in CAH males, consistent with previous reports in nonhuman animals and people. CAH males have generally been reported not to differ from controls in sex-typed activities or abilities (Ehrhardt & Baker, 1974; Resnick et al., 1986).

Although the data are consistent with an androgen influence on sex-typed toy choices, it is not necessary that hormones have a direct influence on these choices. Hormones may affect toy choices indirectly, perhaps through an influence on activity level, motor skills, abilities, or temperament. For example, CAH girls may be more active than control girls, and boys' toys may facilitate active play (O'Brien & Huston, 1985).

Results from this study may also be relevant to understanding the development of sex-typed toy preferences in normal children. Normal males have higher testosterone levels than normal females from approximately week 8 to

---

raised in the statement of the problem **(e)**. Further findings are presented throughout the next several paragraphs. In section **(p)** the authors offer an expanded view of how their experimental results fit into the larger issue o hormones' influence on behavior. Of particular interest is that the researchers do not go beyond their data—

(analysis continues on page 241)

week 24 of gestation and from approximately the first to the fifth month of life (Smail, Reyes, Winter, & Faiman, 1981). These sex differences in hormones may contribute to subsequent sex differences in behavior, such as those in toy preferences. Further, natural variations in levels or availability of testosterone among normal males and females might contribute to individual differences in sex-typed behavior.

Our data may also be relevant to evidence that early sex-typed toy preferences predict later behavior, including sexual orientation (Green, 1987) and spatial ability (Newcombe, Bandura, & Taylor, 1983; Sherman, 1967), and to evidence that spatial ability (Resnick et al., 1986) and sexual orientation (Money, Schwartz, & Lewis, 1984) are masculinized in CAH females (for discussion, see Berenbaum, 1990). Specifically, it is possible that hormonal influences on adult behaviors are mediated by childhood sex-typed toy preferences, although it is also possible that various sex-typed behaviors are influenced separately by hormones (Arnold & Gorski, 1984; Goy & McEwen, 1980; Goy et al., 1988). Further studies of CAH and other endocrine syndromes should help us to understand not only whether gonadal hormones influence human behavior, but also how they do so.

REFERENCES

Allen, L. S., Hines, M., Shryne, J. E., & Gorski, R. A. (1989). Two sexually dimorphic cell groups in the human brain. *Journal of Neuroscience, 9,* 497–506.

Arnold, A. P., & Gorski, R. A. (1984). Gonadal steroid induction of structural sex differences in the central nervous system. *Annual Review of Neuroscience, 7,* 413–442.

Baum, M. J., & Schretlen, P. (1975). Neuroendocrine effects of perinatal androgenization in the male ferret. *Progress in Brain Research, 42,* 343–355.

Beatty, W. W. (1979). Gonadal hormones and sex differences in nonreproductive behaviors in rodents: Organizational and activational influences. *Hormones and Behavior, 12,* 112–163.

Berenbaum, S. A. (1990). Congenital adrenal hyperplasia: Intellectual and psychosexual functioning. In C. Holmes (Ed.), *Psychoneuroendocrinology: Brain, behavior, and hormonal interactions* (pp. 227–260). New York: Springer-Verlag.

Bussey, K., & Bandura, A. (1984). Influence of gender constancy and social power on sex-linked modeling. *Journal of Personality and Social Psychology, 47,* 1292–1302.

Cohen, J. (1977). *Statistical power analysis for the behavioral sciences* (rev. ed.). New York: Academic Press.

Connor, J. M., & Serbin, L. A. (1977). Behaviorally based masculine- and feminine-activity-preference scales for preschoolers: Correlates with other classroom behaviors and cognitive tests. *Child Development, 48,* 1411–1416.

Diamond, M., Llacuna, A., & Wong, C. L. (1973). Sex behavior after neonatal progesterone, testosterone, estrogen, or antiandrogens. *Hormones and Behavior, 4,* 73–88.

Ehrhardt, A. A., & Baker, S. W. (1974). Fetal androgens, human central nervous system differentiation and behavior sex differences. In R. C. Friedman, R. M. Richart, & R. L. Vande Wiele (Eds.), *Sex differences in behavior* (pp. 33–51). New York: Wiley.

Ehrhardt, A. A., Epstein, R., & Money, J. (1968). Fetal androgens and female gender identity in the early-treated adrenogenital syndrome. *Johns Hopkins Medical Journal, 122,* 160–167.

Ehrhardt, A. A., & Meyer-Bahlburg, H. F. L. (1979). Prenatal sex hormones and the developing brain: Effects on psychosexual differentiation and cognitive function. *Annual Review of Medicine, 30,* 417–430.

Erpino, M. J. (1975). Androgen-induced aggression in neonatally androgenized female mice, inhibition by progesterone. *Hormones and Behavior, 6,* 149–158.

Goy, R. W., Bercovitch, F. B., & McBrair, M. C. (1988). Behavioral masculinization is independent of genital masculinization in prenatally androgenized female rhesus macaques. *Hormones and Behavior, 22,* 552–571.

Goy, R. W., & McEwen, B. S. (1980). *Sexual differentiation of the brain.* Cambridge, MA: MIT Press.

Green, R. (1987). *The "sissy boy syndrome" and the development of homosexuality.* New Haven, CT: Yale University Press.

Hines, M. (1982). Prenatal gonadal hormones and sex differences in human behavior. *Psychological Bulletin, 92,* 56–80.

Hines, M., & Green, R. (1991). Human hormonal and neural correlates of sex-typed behaviors. *Review of Psychiatry, 10,* 536–555.

Hull, E. M., Franz, J. R., Snyder, A. M., & Nishita, J. K. (1980). Perinatal progesterone and learning, social and reproductive behavior in rats. *Physiology and Behavior, 24,* 251–256.

Huston, A. C. (1983). Sex-typing. In P. H. Mussen (Ed.), *Handbook of child psychology* (Vol. IV, 4th ed., pp. 387–467). New York: Wiley.

Liss, M. B. (1981). Patterns of toy play: An analysis of sex differences. *Sex Roles, 7,* 1143–1150.

MacLusky, N. J., & Naftolin, F. (1981). Sexual differentiation of the central nervous system. *Science, 211,* 1294–1303.

Money, J., Schwartz, M., & Lewis, V. G. (1984). Adult erotosexual status and fetal hormonal masculinization and demasculinization: 46, XX congenital virilizing adrenal hyperplasia and 46, XY androgen-insensitivity syndrome compared. *Psychoneuroendocrinology, 9,* 405–414.

Newcombe, N., Bandura, M. M., & Taylor, D. G. (1983). Sex differences in spatial ability and spatial activities. *Sex Roles, 9,* 377–386.

O'Brien, M., & Huston, A. C. (1985). Activity level and sex stereotyped toy choice in toddler boys and girls. *Journal of Genetic Psychology, 146,* 527–534.

Prader, A. (1954). Der genitalbefund beim Pseudohermaphroditismus femininus des kongenitalen adrenogenitalen Syndroms. *Helvetica Paediatrica Acta, 3,* 231–248.

Quadagno, D. M., Briscoe, R., & Quadagno, J. S. (1977). Effects of perinatal gonadal hormones on selected nonsexual behavior patterns: A critical assessment of the nonhuman and human literature. *Psychological Bulletin, 84,* 62–80.

Resnick, S. M. (1982). *Psychological functioning in individuals with congenital adrenal hyperplasia: Early hormonal influences on cognition and personality.* Unpublished doctoral dissertation, University of Minnesota, Minneapolis.

Resnick, S. M., Berenbaum, S. A., Gottesman, I. I., & Bouchard, T. J. (1986). Early hormonal influences on cognitive functioning in congenital adrenal hyperplasia. *Developmental Psychology, 22,* 191–198.

Sherman, J. (1967). Problem of sex differences in space perception and aspects of intellectual functioning. *Psychological Review, 74,* 290–299.

Slipjer, F. M. E. (1984). Androgens and gender role behavior in girls with congenital adrenal hyperplasia (CAH). In G. J. DeVries, J. P. C. DeBruin, H. B. M. Uylings, & M. A. Corner (Eds.), *Progress in brain research* (Vol. 61, pp. 417–422). Amsterdam: Elsevier.

Smail, P. J., Reyes, F. I., Winter, J. S. D., & Faiman, C. (1981). The fetal hormone environment and its effect on the morphogenesis of the genital system. In S. J. Kogan & E. S. E. Hafez (Eds.), *Pediatric andrology* (pp. 9–19). The Hague: Martinus Nijhoff.

Swaab, D. F., & Fliers, E. (1985). A sexually dimorphic nucleus in the human brain. *Science, 228,* 1112–1115.

White, P. C., New, M. I., & Dupont, B. (1987). Congenital adrenal hyperplasia. *New England Journal of Medicine, 316,* 1519–1524.

Note: This study was supported by National Institutes of Health Grants HD19644, HD24542, and NS20687. We thank the following people who contributed to this project: Drs. Stephen Duck, Orville Green, Ora Pescovitz, Julio Santiago, Jo Anne Brasel, Robert Clemons, Gertrude Costin, Richard Fefferman, Lynda Fisher, Francine Kaufman, and Thomas Roe generously provided access to their patients and answered medical questions; Brenda Henderson, Andrea Black, Ruth Estes, Erin Foy, Kim Kerns, Deena Krumdick, Jennifer Lawrence, Naomi Lester, Anne Maxwell, Kristie Nies, Ellen Rochman, Robyn Reed, Elizabeth Snyder, and Christopher Verbin helped with data collection, scoring, entry, and analysis; Kim Kerns established a superb data-entry and tracking system. We are particularly grateful to the subjects and their parents for their enthusiasm and cooperation. We also thank Michael Bailey, Susan Resnick, Michael Taylor, and Gary Oltmans for helpful comments on this paper. Portions of this paper were presented at the meeting of the Society for Research in Child Development, Kansas City, April 1989.

they confine their conclusions to the specific data reported in this study. The unseasoned researcher might be tempted to make sweeping generalizations regarding adult women who exhibit masculine tendencies or even social phenomena such as the women's movement. While such matters are of great interest, this research addresses a specific problem (which may ultimately be part of a larger matter) that yielded clear-cut results with direct implications for the authors' hypothesis. You should also note that this example is especially clear in exhibiting many of the features of precise experimental design mentioned throughout this book.

Questions

1. What other possible operational definitions are there for "toy preference," besides the one used in this study?
2. Why was it necessary to videotape the session?
3. Why was it important to have "blind" raters?
4. Are you satisfied with the type of control group that was used? Can you think of another?
5. What alternative explanations can you think of to explain the results of this study?

15 Maternal Behavior

Introduction

Maternal behavior (i.e., nest building, care of the young, nursing, etc.) has long been considered an instinct. However, in recent years it has become apparent that calling a behavior an instinct tells us little about its causes. Therefore, psychologists have begun to study the factors underlying such behavior. These factors include stimuli coming from the nest or the young, brain mechanisms, and past experience. Some suggest that hormones, too, may play a role in controlling such behavior. This idea derives from the fact that maternal behavior develops very gradually and fades away in the same manner; that is, nest building and the bodily changes accompanying maternity take place prior to birth and disappear gradually as the young grow older. This suggests that the behavior may be related to the gradual buildup and decline of some chemical substance in the blood. One way to demonstrate this is to inject the hormone and see whether it can induce the behavior. Previous studies of this type have failed to produce clear-cut results, and this study attempts to approach the problem in a somewhat different fashion.

This article illustrates several important issues in experimental design. Among these is the problem of control. Several types of control were considered. The experimental animals were divided into equal-sized groups (presumably in a random fashion). Some groups were defined as control groups, and other groups were designated the experimental groups. Also, all animals were treated identically except for the type of chemical injection they received. Another type of control involved the preparation of substances used in the injection.

This experiment has a distinctive independent variable and a control group. The experimenters measured the reaction of an experimental group against the reaction of a control group. You should note that something was done *to* the subjects—they were injected with various chemicals.

Special Issues

THE USE OF ANIMALS IN PSYCHOLOGICAL RESEARCH

Some of the earliest experiments in psychology were done with animals. Ivan Pavlov used dogs; E. L. Thorndike used cats; William James used chickens; Harry Harlow used monkeys; the Gardners used chimpanzees; and B. F. Skinner used rats. Other psychologists have used guinea pigs, seals, porpoises, monkeys, elephants, whales, planera, bees, pigeons, sheep, pigs, horses, rabbits, and so on. Given this, one might think psychologists were more interested in the behavior of nonhuman creatures than in the behavior of *Homo sapiens.* In most instances, however, experimental psychologists—even those who restrict their studies to animals—strongly assert that their experiments are designed to lead to a better understanding of humans.

The basic premise on which psychological experimentation is predicated is that conclusions reached through the study of nonhuman subjects are in some way applicable to an understanding of behavior in general. There are many reasons for using animals in psychological research. In general, animals are more available than human subjects. It is also possible to keep an animal under observation 24 hours a day, seven days a week, for months, if necessary. In addition, it is possible to perform procedures with animals that are impossible with humans. Such research could involve the use of noxious stimuli, prolonged periods of deprivation, psychosurgery, the use of experimental drugs, and so on. It would be almost impossible to get a college sophomore to volunteer for these experiments, and even if subjects were available, many of these experiments would constitute a serious breach of ethics. However, the maintenance of ethical restraints is also important for nonhuman subjects. The experimental psychologist who uses animals is honor bound to conduct his or her research within the guidelines described in Chapter 8.

This experiment by Joseph Terkel and Jay Rosenblatt on maternal behavior induced by injecting maternal blood plasma into virgin rats was selected for inclusion in Part Two (along with the article on the creative porpoise) because it illustrates an experiment in which animals serve as the experimental subjects. A similar experiment with humans would not be possible, and yet the conclusions reached may give us a clue as to the source of maternal behavior in humans.

MATERNAL BEHAVIOR INDUCED BY MATERNAL BLOOD PLASMA INJECTED INTO VIRGIN RATS

Joseph Terkel
Institute of Animal Behavior

Jay S. Rosenblatt
Rutgers University

Induction of maternal behavior (i.e., retrieving) in virgins by exposure to young pups was studied to investigate effects of blood plasma from a postparturient female. Control groups were injected with blood plasma from nonmaternal females in proestrus and diestrus phases of the vaginal estrous cycle and with saline solution. Virgins injected with maternal blood plasma had significantly shorter latencies of maternal behavior than other groups. Injections of saline and proestrus blood plasma had no effect on maternal behavior. Virgins injected with diestrus blood plasma were significantly delayed in displaying maternal behavior. The findings indicate that there is a humoral basis for the appearance of maternal behavior after parturition.

Several recent attempts to induce maternal behavior in the rat by means of various hormones (i.e., estrogen, progesterone, and prolactin) injected directly into virgin or experienced females have not yielded results that would increase our understanding of the hormonal basis of this behavior (Beach & Wilson, 1962; Lott, 1962; Lott & Fuchs, 1962). In this laboratory injected hormones (prolactin and oxytocin) have failed also to maintain maternal behavior in females that have become maternal after parturition or have been made maternal by Cesarean-section delivery of their fetuses several days before parturition. However, the conviction that maternal behavior in the rat is based upon hormones is supported by the success in inducing nest building in the mouse with progesterone (Koller, 1952, 1955) and in the hamster with estrogen and progesterone (Richards, 1965). Some success has been reported in inducing maternal nest building in rabbits using a combination of hormones (e.g., stilbestrol, progesterone, and prolactin were used by Zarrow, Sawin, Ross, & Denenberg, 1962).

In view of the difficulty of inducing maternal behavior in female rats with injected hormones, a difficulty no doubt based upon failure to introduce either the proper hormone or hormones in the proper order and dose level, we have attempted a different approach to the problem. Remaining close to the natural conditions under which maternal behavior normally appears at and

a

Source: Reprinted by permission from *Journal of Comparative and Physiological Psychology,* 1968, *65*(3), 479–482. Published by the American Psychological Association.

shortly after parturition, we have attempted to transfer blood plasma from postparturient females that have become maternal within the past 48 hr to virgins, hoping thereby to induce maternal behavior in the latter. **Establishing**

b   **that maternal blood plasma carries a substance or substances capable of inducing maternal behavior in virgins would be a first step in identifying the humoral basis of maternal behavior.**

We have shown recently that virgin females can be induced to show maternal behavior when they are exposed to young pups continuously for about 5 days (Rosenblatt, 1967). Cosnier (1963) reported a similar finding using shorter daily exposures. Both studies confirm an early suggestion by Wiesner and Shard (1933) which was only partially verified in their own studies. Maternal behavior induced under these conditions appears to be of nonhormonal origin since ovariectomizing or hypohysectomizing virgins before exposing them to pups did not prevent the appearance of maternal behavior or alter, significantly, latencies for the onset of a major item of maternal behavior, namely retrieving (Cosnier & Couterier, 1966; Rosenblatt, 1967). In this study, therefore, we observed whether the latency for the appearance of re-

c   trieving (and other items of maternal behavior) by virgins exposed to young pups was significantly reduced by prior injection of maternal blood plasma as compared to prior injection of blood plasma taken from virgins in the proestrus or diestrus phases of the vaginal estrous cycle, or prior injection of saline solution.

Analysis

Literature Review

In the literature review, Terkel and Rosenblatt (1968) carefully present two sides of a controversy surrounding the hormonal basis of maternal behavior: While some researchers have found strong evidence for the hormonal basis of maternal behavior, others have not. In **(a)** the authors speculate that the ambiguity of previous experimental results may be due to the fact that such studies have not employed the proper hormones in the proper order and at proper dose levels. They suggest that if the blood conditions in virgin rats (presumably behaviorally nonmaternal) were nearly identical to the blood conditions of rats who had recently delivered a litter of pups (presumably behaviorally maternal), then a reliable measure of the serological basis of maternal behavior would be possible. The authors suggest in **(b)** that we should identify a general hormonal basis of maternal behavior as a first step that would presumably lead to a more discrete analysis of specific chemicals that might be responsible for this behavior.

The last sentence of the review **(c)** contains the hypothesis to be tested and a brief version of the research plan. In effect, the researchers state the dependent variable (latency of retrieving pups) and the independent variable (injection of

METHOD

Subjects

Thirty-two virgin females, 60 days of age at the start of the experiment, were obtained from Charles River Breeding Farm, Dover, Mass. Twenty-four additional Ss of the same age provided blood plasma for the injections. Other rats provided the pups used in the maternal behavior tests. The Ss were housed individually in 45 × 50 × 40 cm. rectangular cages, each with transparent Plexiglas walls, grid floor, wall feeder, water bottle, and two bins containing hay and coarse wood shavings for nesting material. They were fed Purina chow and water ad lib supplemented twice weekly with vitamin-enriched bread, carrots, and lettuce.

The Ss were divided into four equal-sized groups. One group received plasma taken from maternal Ss; injections were given when Ss were in various unspecified phases of the vaginal estrous cycle. One control group consisted of Ss in proestrus that received plasma taken from females that were also in proestrus, and a second control group consisted of Ss in diestrus that received plasma taken from females that were also in diestrus. The fourth group of Ss received an injection of 0.9 percent saline solution at various unspecified phases of the vaginal estrous cycle.

Procedures

Blood was withdrawn from the donors within 48 hr after parturition, after it was clearly established that these Ss were performing maternal behavior normally. Blood taken from estrous-cycling donors was withdrawn within 1 hr

different groups with (1) maternal blood plasma, (2) blood from animals in the proestrus phase, (3) blood from animals in the diestrus phase, and (4) saline solution). One group was not injected and served as a control. The proestrus phase in rats is the period immediately prior to estrus ("heat"), and the diestrus period follows estrus. Presumably, these phases were selected to reduce the possibility that hormones present during the estrus phase would cause a general increase in the activity level, which could have been falsely interpreted as maternal behavior.

Method

Three parts are included in the method section: The subjects are identified, the procedures are described, and the tests of maternal behavior are specified. In this study, enough detail is present to allow its replication. For example, in describing the subjects the authors identify the breeding farm, age, sex, cage size and construction, feed, water schedule, and nesting material. There is a practical limit to the amount of methodological detail that can be presented, so some items, such as temperature, humidity, lighting, and so on, are omitted, but one could logically infer that these items were controlled.

after the vaginal smear indicated either proestrus or diestrus. Between 6 and 8 cc of blood was withdrawn from the heart. To withdraw the blood, the donors were anesthetized with ether, and the heart was surgically exposed by a chest incision to one side of the midline. The blood was withdrawn using a 40 mm 16-gauge needle with a 20-cc syringe containing 15–20 units of Heparin Sodium to prevent blood clotting.

About 4 min elapsed from the time the donor was judged to be completely anesthetized until the blood was first transferred from the syringe to a test tube and centrifuging was started. When a zone of clear plasma, free of blood cells, appeared 3–4 cc of plasma was drawn into a 5-cc syringe and injected into a subject with a 20 mm 27-gauge needle. Plasma injection was completed in 4 min. Each experimental S received all of its plasma from a single donor female.

The S was lightly anesthetized with ether, a small incision was made on the inner surface of the upper thigh, and the right femoral vein was exposed. The needle was inserted into the vein, a small amount of blood was withdrawn, and then the plasma (or saline solution) was injected slowly over a period of 2H min. The incision was closed with wound clips. In this inbred strain of rats, plasma transfer between any two strain mates does not result in anaphylactic shock.

Maternal Behavior Tests

Each animal was given a 15-min retrieving test 1 hr before blood was withdrawn from the proestrus and diestrus donors and plasma or saline was injected into the recipient Ss. Since no S retrieved during this test it was not necessary to eliminate any of them from the experiment.

Tests following the injection of either plasma or saline were begun after it was judged that Ss were fully recovered from the anesthetic used during the injection. Each S was judged to be recovered if it was able to walk around the edge of a bell jar maintaining its balance; if it fell from the edge it was retested at a later time. It was possible for the first postinjection test to begin in all Ss 1 hr after the injection since all Ss were fully recovered from the ether about 5 min after the injection.

Five pups, 5–10 days of age, were placed at the front of each Ss cage. Retrieving was observed for 15 min, following which observations for 1-min periods at 20-min intervals were made over the next 2 hr. During the 1-min period of observation the occurrence of retrieving, crouching over the young, licking the young, nest building, and other maternal and nonmaternal items of

In the procedure section, Terkel and Rosenblatt demonstrate their considerable talent for unambiguous writing. They explain in detail the method used for blood transfusion so that a researcher with some surgical skill could exactly replicate their procedure.

A critical aspect of this study is the definition of the dependent variable: maternal behavior. The validity of scientific inquiry rests to a large extent on the

behavior were recorded. Nesting material had previously been spread over the floor. At the end of the 2-hr test the pups were left with Ss until the next morning at which time they were removed and replaced by a fresh litter of five pups in the same age range. The test procedure was repeated daily until an S retrieved pups in two consecutive daily tests. Since retrieving is usually the last item of maternal behavior to appear when pups are used to induce it, all Ss had already shown the other main items of maternal behavior (i.e., crouching over young, licking young, nest building) by the termination of testing.

Several Ss that had been injected with maternal plasma were observed continually on the first day following the first test to see if times of maternal behavior would appear between the first and the second test, 22 hr later.

RESULTS

d

Mean latencies in days for the onset of retrieving for the various groups, shown in Table 1, indicate that plasma taken from a lactating mother within 48 hr after delivery is capable of inducing a more rapid maternal response to pups than saline and either proestrus or diestrus plasma ($F = 9.79$, $df = 3/28$, $p < .01$; data transformed to square roots). Under the combined influence of maternal plasma and stimulation from pups, retrieving appeared in an average of 2 days. This time was significantly shorter than when saline or proestrus plasma was injected or when diestrus plasma was injected (Duncan's New

operational definition of dependent variables and the testing of these variables. Terkel and Rosenblatt suggest several behavioral characteristics that typify maternal behavior, including latency in retrieval of pups, crouching over young, licking young, and nest building.

Results

The essence of this research paper is typified in the first sentence (**d**) of the results section. The main result of this experiment is plainly stated: Plasma of lactating rats is capable of inducing more rapid maternal behavior than other substances. Statistical evidence in the form of the F statistic is then presented. In addition, the authors employ Duncan's New Multiple Range test and the Mann–Whitney U statistic. Duncan's test ascertains whether significant differences exist between each of the means, while the Mann–Whitney statistic is a special type of analysis for ranking data with two classes of information.

In the second paragraph of the results section, the authors introduce an untreated control group used in a previous study. This is obviously not as desirable as it would be had the authors used their own control group. There may be differ-

TABLE 1   Mean Latencies in Days for the Onset of Retrieving

Group	N	Mean	SE
Maternal plasma	8	2.25	.97
Proestrus plasma	8	4.62	1.21
Diestrus plasma	8	7.00	2.96
Saline	8	4.00	1.41
Untreated[a]	14	5.79	2.69

[a]Taken from Rosenblatt (1967).

Multiple Range test at the .05 level). Proestrus plasma combined with the proestrus condition of the recipient virgin was similar in its effect on maternal behavior to saline but diestrus plasma given to females in diestrus produced a significant delay in the mean latency for the onset of retrieving (Duncan's New Multiple Range test at the .05 level).

In a previous study (Rosenblatt, 1967) it was established that maternal behavior (i.e., retrieving and other items) can be induced in virgins by exposure to pups, without any prior injection, with an average latency of 5.79 ± 2.69 days. The saline-injected proestrus plasma- and diestrus plasma-injected Ss of the present study had average latencies which did not differ significantly from Ss in the earlier study (Mann–Whitney $U = 40$–42, $p > .10$). The average latency of the maternal plasma-injected Ss was, however, significantly shorter than that of the Ss that were only exposed to pups (Mann–Whitney $U = 20$, $p = .02$).

The onset of retrieving was accompanied in all groups by the occurrence of the three other main items of maternal behavior (i.e., crouching over the young, licking, and nest building). With pups continuously present, the onset of an item of maternal behavior, and particularly the onset of retrieving, was followed by its appearance from then on in each of the subsequent daily tests. Observations of the Ss between the first and second tests led us to believe that the maternal plasma induced maternal behavior more rapidly than our formal test procedure was capable of detecting. Several Ss that were injected with maternal plasma began to show maternal behavior in attenuated fashion

ences between the two experiments in the sample of rats, the handling of the rats, or the experimental procedures. On the other hand, the procedure used in this series of studies is fairly standardized, which makes a cross-experiment comparison somewhat feasible (although not totally desirable). Data from one experiment should not be analyzed with data from a second experiment unless the experimenter is quite sure that the subjects and procedures of the two experiments are quite similar.

within 4–8 hr after the injection and the beginning of exposure to pups, although, several hours earlier, during the first scheduled test of maternal behavior, they were indifferent to the pups. Two of these were fully maternal, according to our criteria for the virgins, by the second test, which was begun 1 day after the injection. Others were not fully maternal until the third test was begun 2 days after the injection.

DISCUSSION

e Our study established for the first time that substances carried in the plasma of the newly maternal rat are capable of increasing the readiness of virgins to respond maternally to pups. We have, therefore, finally found a way of accomplishing what Stone (1925) set out to do when he joined in parabiosis a maternal and nonmaternal rat hoping that blood-borne substances responsible for maternal behavior in the former would induce maternal behavior in the latter. Were it not for the failure of these substances to cross from the maternal to the nonmaternal animal, because of selective transmission across the parabiotic union, Stone would have demonstrated what we have found and perhaps the effect would have been stronger with the continuous exchange of blood that he attempted.

f The present study does not enable us to identify the substance or substances that are responsible for increasing the maternal responsiveness of the virgins or to determine whether these substances act on the virgin via the endocrine system or directly upon the nervous system. Initially we thought that dividing our plasma control group into two groups, one receiving proestrus plasma and the other diestrus plasma, the virgins themselves being in the corresponding phases of the estrous cycle, would enable us to make a first step in

In the third paragraph of this section the authors introduce some observational data that their experimental procedures were not sensitive enough to detect. Observational data are often quite valuable in helping to clarify or further interpret results, but it should be noted that data of this type are usually not collected as systematically or precisely as the data we have just discussed. Therefore, these data should be treated as supplementary to the results found in the formal testing of the dependent variable, which is how the authors present them.

Discussion

The discussion section begins with a bold statement (**e**) that is a combination of empirically validated evidence and a logically inferred statement. Terkel and Rosenblatt quickly point out that their hypothesis is not a new one and suggest a reason for previous failures to validate the hypothesis. They also state a limitation (**f**) by noting that their study did not specifically identify the substance(s) within

identifying the active substances. To the extent that the diestrus blood plasma combined with the diestrus condition of the recipient virgin produced a delay in the onset of maternal behavior we have been partially successful. However, any identification of ovarian hormones or pituitary secretions as the active substances would be highly speculative and incapable of substantiation at this time. Our findings therefore await further analysis of hormonal secretions during the estrous cycle, pregnancy, and parturition.

An added finding of importance does emerge from this study which was surprising to us. Our previous work indicated that maternal responsiveness increases gradually during pregnancy (Lott & Rosenblatt, 1967), and we interpreted this as indicating that the hormonal conditions during pregnancy gradually sensitized the neural substrate of maternal behavior thereby preparing for the appearance of maternal behavior at parturition. The present study suggests that there need be no prolonged period (i.e., 22 days of pregnancy) of sensitization for substances contained in maternal plasma to have their effect on maternal behavior. It would appear that the gradual increase in maternal responsiveness which we found during pregnancy after Cesarean-section deliveries (Lott & Rosenblatt, 1967) need not be built up by a continual addition of "units" of maternal responsiveness. Rather the level of maternal responsiveness at each period of pregnancy reflects for that particular moment the current capability of the blood to stimulate maternal behavior and this capability presumably undergoes a continuous increase until it is fully established around parturition. In this respect then our findings agree with those of Moltz and Weiner (1966) and Denenberg, Grota, and Zarrow (1963) that hormonal secretions at parturition are likely to be important for the induction of maternal behavior.

References

Beach, F. A., & Wilson, J. R. (1962). Effects of prolactin, progesterone, and estrogen on reactions of nonpregnant rats to foster young. *Psychological Report, 13,* 231–239.

Cosnier, J. (1963). Quelques problèmes posés par le "comportement maternel provoqué" chez la ratte. *CR Soc. Biol.,* Paris, *157,* 1611–1613.

Cosnier, J., & Couterier, C. (1966). Comportement maternel provoqué chez les rattes adultes castrées. *CR Soc. Biol.,* Paris, *160,* 789–791.

Denenberg, V. H., Grota, L. J., & Zarrow, M. X. (1963). Maternal behavior in the rat: Analysis of cross-fostering. *Journal of Reproduction and Fertility, 5,* 133–141.

the blood responsible for increasing maternal behavior. Nonetheless, one can feel the excitement in this research, and even the newcomer to psychology can anticipate the next development.

Koller, G. (1952). Der Nestbau der Weiber Mause und seine hormonale Aus-
losung. *Verh. dtsch. zool. Ges.,* Freiburg, 160–168.

Koller, G. (1955). Hormonale und psychische Steuerung beim Nestbau
Weiber Mause. *Zool. Anz. (Suppl.), 19,* 125–132.

Lott, D. F. (1962). The role of progesterone in the maternal behavior of rodents. *Journal of Comparative and Physiological Psychology, 55,*
610–613.

Lott, D. F., & Fuchs, S. S. (1962). Failure to induce retrieving by sensitization
or the injection of prolactin. *Journal of Comparative and Physiological
Psychology, 55,* 1111–1113.

Lott, D. F., & Rosenblatt, J. S. (1967). Development of maternal responsiveness during pregnancy in the rat. In B. M. Foss (Ed.), *Determinants of infant behavior IV.* London: Methuen.

Moltz, H., & Weiner, E. (1966). Effects of ovariectomy on maternal behavior
of primiparous and multiparous rats. *Journal of Comparative and Physiological Psychology, 62,* 382–387.

Richards, M. P. M. (1965). *Aspects of maternal behaviour in the golden hamster.* Unpublished doctoral dissertation, Cambridge University, 1965.

Rosenblatt, J. S. (1967). Non-hormonal basis of maternal behavior in the rat.
Science, 156, 1512–1514.

Stone, C. P. (1925). Preliminary note on maternal behavior of rats living in
parabiosis. *Endocrinology, 9,* 505–512.

Wiesner, B. P., & Shard, N. M. (1933). *Maternal behaviour in the rat.* London: Oliver and Boyd.

Zarrow, M. X., Sawin, P. B., Ross, S., & Denenberg, V. H. (1962). Maternal
behavior and its endocrine bases in the rabbit. In E. L. Bliss (Ed.), *Roots
of behavior.* New York: Harper & Row.

Note: This research was supported by National Institute of Mental Health Research
Grant MH-08604 to J. S. R. and Biological Medicine Grant FR-7059 to J. T. We wish
to thank D. S. Lehrman and B. Sachs for reading the manuscript. Publication No. 50
from the Institute of Animal Behavior, Rutgers University, Newark.

Questions

1. Speculate about what might happen if greater quantities of blood had been
   transfused.
2. Based on the results of this experiment, would you make a generalization to
   human transfusion? Is this generalization warranted? Why or why not? Do
   you see any practical application of this study?
3. Why did the authors include a saline group? A proestrus group? A diestrus
   group? An untreated group?
4. What significance do you attribute to the results of the diestrus group?

5. What group(s) would you like to add?
6. In addition to the behavioral indices of maternal behavior, suggest several physiological measures of maternal tendencies. Could these be quantifiable? Would evaluation of these changes be important to this study? Why or why not?
7. This paper could just as easily have been published in a physiological journal. What is the relationship between psychology and physiology?
8. Why are rats used in psychological studies?

CHAPTER

16 Children's Reasoning

Introduction

This article by Giralt and Bloom (2000) concisely demonstrates how objects have a special status in cognitive development. You are to analyze this article.

How Special Are Objects? Children's Reasoning About Objects, Parts, and Holes

Nuria Giralt and Paul Bloom
University of Arizona

Discrete physical objects have a special status in cognitive and linguistic development. Infants track and enumerate objects, young children are biased to construe novel words as referring to objects, and, when asked to count an array of items, preschool children tend to count the discrete objects, even if explicitly asked to do otherwise. We address here the question of whether discrete physical objects are the only entities that have this special status, or whether other individuals are salient as well. In two experiments, we found that 3-year-olds are just as good at identifying, tracking, and counting certain nonobject entities (holes in Experiment 1; holes and parts in Experiment 2) as they are with objects. These results are discussed in light of different theories of the nature and development of children's object bias.

Discrete physical objects—entities such as dogs and cups—have a special status in cognitive and linguistic development. Even infants can parse the world into distinct physical objects, enumerate sets of such objects, and track them over time and space (Spelke, 1994; Wynn, 1995). Object names constitute a much larger proportion of young children's vocabularies than they do of the vocabularies of older children and adults (Brown, 1957; Macnamara, 1982). And when 2- and 3-year-olds are shown an object (such as a rabbit) and given a name for it, their default assumption is that the word refers to the entire object (the rabbit), and not to a part of the object (the tail), a property (white), or the stuff that the object is made of (rabbit meat; e.g., Golinkoff, Mervis, & Hirsh-Pasek, 1994; Macnamara, 1972; Markman & Wachtel, 1988; Waxman & Markow, 1995). It is often argued that this whole-object assumption plays a central role in word learning, allowing children to determine which of the infinity of logically possible meanings that a word could have is actually the correct one.

Shipley and Shepperson (1990) provided a particularly striking demonstration of the importance of objects. They showed children arrays of objects and gave them specific instructions as to what to count. For example, the children were shown the array depicted in Figure 1 and asked, "Can you count the forks?" Adults shown this display answer "five," but the 3- and 4-year-olds in Shipley and Shepperson's study tended to ignore the wording of the question and answer "six." Similarly, when shown different arrays and asked to count the kinds ("Here are some airplanes and some cars. How many different kinds of toys do I have here?") or colors ("Here are some red ducks, and some green ducks, and some yellow ducks. How many different colors do I have here?"), the dominant response was again to count the total number of

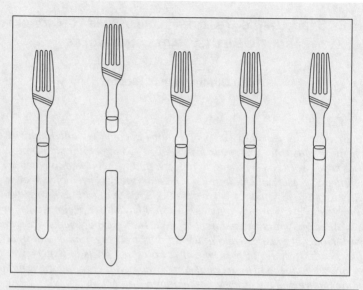

FIGURE 1   **Fork stimuli from Shipley and Shepperson (1990).**

objects. As Shipley and Shepperson concluded, "Young children are evidently predisposed to process discrete physical objects" (p. 109).

The experiments we report here explored the precise nature of this predisposition. One plausible theory is the one advanced by Shipley and Shepperson: Children are specifically biased to attend to objects—to bounded solids that are separately movable. This is also the proposal advanced by Spelke (1994) with regard to infants' individuation and tracking, by Markman and Wachtel (1988) with regard to the whole-object bias in word learning, and by Dehaene (1997) with regard to the origins of numerical cognition. There is an alternative, however. Perhaps it is not objects per se that have a special status in the mind of the child. Instead, there may exist certain features or properties that are particularly relevant to how children parse the world into distinct individuals—properties such as permanence; cohesive movement (the entire region moves as a whole); boundaries that are defined in terms of discontinuities of color, material, and contour; internal complexity; and nonrandom structure (e.g., Bloom, 1996, 2000; Hoffman & Richards, 1984; Imai & Gentner, 1997; Langacker, 1987; Prasada, 1999; Wynn, 1995). Discrete physical objects are special only because they tend to possess such properties; nonobject entities that also possess such properties should be salient as well.

To explore this hypothesis, we asked 3-year-olds questions about three types of entities: whole objects, parts, and holes. The objects were pieces of foam-core board shaped like either novel artifacts (Experiment 1) or novel animals (Experiment 2). The parts were designed to be as natural as possible (Tversky, 1989); they were segmented from the rest of the objects by abrupt changes in contour and (in Experiment 2) were familiar to children and had obvious functions. Young children will readily learn names for such salient parts (Kobayashi, 1998) and will categorize objects on the basis of their presence or absence (Smith, Jones, & Landau, 1996).

There is no developmental research thus far that has explored how children deal with holes. In certain regards, holes resemble parts, as both require a "host" object and do not typically undergo independent motion (Casati & Varzi, 1994). In fact, holes can be viewed as mirror images of objects: Objects are connected portions of matter surrounded by space, holes are connected portions of space surrounded by matter. It might be that these parallels make objects and holes equally salient as individuals. The holes in our experiments were constructed to be (by our own intuitions) salient: They were reasonably large and of a regular shape (round).

In the experiments, children were asked to perform three tasks: to identify the objects, parts, and holes; to count them; and to track them through space.

EXPERIMENT 1

Method

Subjects. Participants were twenty-two 3-year-old children from preschools in Tucson, Arizona. The data from 3 children was discarded because they were unable to complete the tasks, and the data from another child were discarded because of experimenter error. The remaining 18 children ranged in age from 3 years, 2 months to 3 years, 9 months, with a mean age of 3 years, 5 months. There were 13 girls and 5 boys.

Materials and Procedure. Figure 2 depicts the stimuli and the procedure. The objects used were made of foam-core board. Including the parts, the objects were between 15 and 17 cm wide, and from 10 to 19 cm high. The objects used in the identification task were green, those in the counting task were yellow, and those in the tracking task were blue.

Children were tested individually in their day-care centers while seated at a table with an experimenter. All subjects participated in three different tasks: identification, counting, and tracking, in that order. Each of the three tasks involved questions about whole objects (described to the children as "toys"), holes ("holes"), and parts ("handles"). Each subject was assigned to one of six possible orders of these questions (e.g., object, then part, then hole), and this order was maintained across the three tasks.

In the *identification* task, the children were presented simultaneously with three novel objects, each with one hole and one handle (see Fig. 2a). The experimenter gave each child a pile of several pieces of colored felt (about 7 × 5 cm each) and asked the child, in one part of this task, "Using these, can you cover the toys?" If the child did not respond, the question was repeated. If the child paused in the midst of putting down the pieces of felt, he or she was

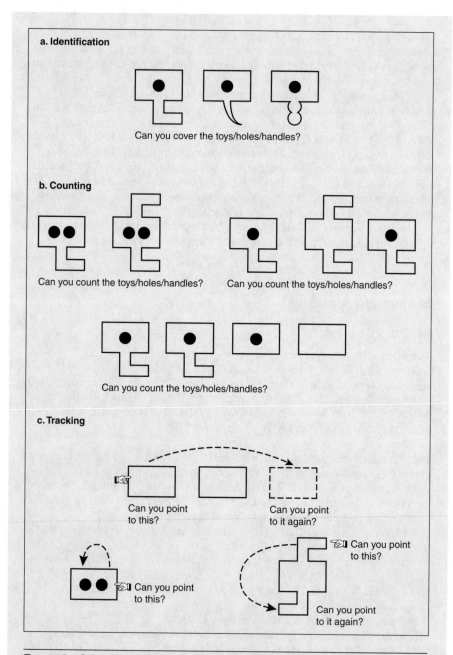

FIGURE 2　Stimuli and procedure for Experiment 1. See the text for details.

prompted with "Can you cover *all* the toys?" Once the child made it clear that he or she was finished (by refusing to put down any more felt pieces, or by saying that he or she was done), the trial was over. The identical procedure was carried out for parts ("Using these, can you cover the handles?") and holes ("Using these, can you cover the holes?")

In the *counting* task, the children were presented with three sets of novel objects (see Fig. 2b). For each set, the children were asked: "How many toys/handles/holes are here? Can you count the toys/handles/holes?" The sets were presented in a fixed order; the first set had two objects, three parts, and four holes; the second had two holes, three objects, and four parts; and the third had two parts, three holes, and four objects.

In the *tracking* task, the stimuli were different according to whether the children were being asked to track objects, holes, or parts (see Fig. 2c). For the object question, each child was shown two objects. The experimenter then pointed to one of the objects and asked the child, "Can you point to this?" After the child pointed, the experimenter said, "Look carefully at what I'm doing," and moved the object in a circular motion from the left of the second object to the right of the second object. The subject was then asked, "Can you point to it again?" For the handle and the hole, the procedure was identical except that subjects were presented with one object that had two handles or two holes. The object was rotated using the same sort of circular motion, so that the original hole was displaced from the right side to the left side, and the original handle was displaced from the top to the bottom.

Results and Discussion

We carried out a $6 \times 3 \times 3$ analysis of variance, with order as a between-subjects variable and with task (identification vs. counting vs. tracking) and entity (object vs. hole vs. part) as within-subjects variables. There was no effect of order, and no interactions involved order. There were significant main effects of both task, $F(2, 24) = 23.56, p < .001$, and entity, $F(2, 24) = 6.22$, $p < .005$; there was also a marginally significant task-by-entity interaction, $F(4, 48) = 2.53, p = .05$. The results are shown in Table 1.

TABLE 1   **Percentage Correct in the Identification Counting, and Tracking Tasks in Experiment 1**

	ENTITY		
Task	**Object**	**Hole**	**Part**
Identification	88.9 (32.3)	94.4 (23.6)	66.7 (48.5)
Counting	79.6 (23.3)	88.9 (28.0)	64.8 (37.0)
Tracking	61.1 (50.2)	38.9 (50.2)	11.1 (32.3)

Note. Standard deviations are in parentheses.

Subjects found identification to be the easiest task (83% correct), followed by counting (78%), and then tracking (37%). Post hoc tests revealed that the children did significantly worse on tracking than on both identification, $t(17) = 6.02$, and counting, $t(17) = 5.02$ (both $ps < .001$).

The main focus of this study was children's relative performances with objects, parts, and holes. Overall, children's performance with objects and holes was roughly identical (77% and 74%), but they did less well with parts (48%).

To explore the nature of the interaction between task and entity, we analyzed performance on each of the three tasks separately. For each task, there was a significant or marginally significant effect of entity: counting, $F(2, 34) = 3.50, p < .05$; identification, $F(2, 34) = 2.90, p = .07$; tracking, $F(2, 34) = 6.69, p < .005$. Post hoc tests revealed that for the counting task, performance was significantly worse with parts than holes, $t(17) = 2.40, p < .05$. For the identification task, performance was also significantly worse with parts than holes, though only marginally, $t(17) = 2.05, p = .06$; for the tracking task, performance was significantly worse with parts than objects, $t(17) = -4.42$, $p < .001$, and, again to a marginal extent, worse with parts than holes, $t(17) = 2.05, p = .06$.

In sum, there are three main findings. First, for all tasks, the children did just as well with holes as with objects. The counting result is particularly interesting, as it shows that children can count holes even if the correct count conflicts with the number of distinct physical objects. Second, the children tended to do worse with parts than with holes and objects. And third, the children found the tracking task particularly difficult.

It might be, however, that some of these findings were due to particular features of this experiment. One concern is that children's relatively poor performance with the parts might have been due to language problems. Although the words "toy" and "hole" are likely to be familiar to young children, perhaps the word "handle" was not. Another concern is that the tracking task might have been made unduly difficult by the fact that, in all cases, the resulting configuration of the display after movement was identical to the original configuration. This might have confused children; when they were asked, "Can you point to it again?" they may have interpreted the question as referring to the location, not the entity.

Experiment 2 addressed both of these concerns, and included a further modification to make the tasks simpler. In Experiment 1, the questions were ordered by tasks, so that all of the identification questions were done together, followed by the counting questions, followed by the tracking questions. One consequence of this ordering was that a question about an entity tended to be immediately followed by a question about a different type of entity; for instance, for a given child, every question about holes would usually be followed by a question about parts. (The exception to this was the counting questions, because there were three of these for any given entity.) Children might do better if the questions were instead ordered by entity, so that all of the questions about a given type of entity would be asked together.

EXPERIMENT 2

Method

Subjects.   Participants were eighteen 3-year-old children from preschools in Tucson, Arizona. They ranged in age from 3 years, 2 months to 3 years, 11 months, with an average age of 3 years, 9 months. There were 7 girls and 11 boys, none of whom participated in the first experiment.

Materials and Procedure.   The stimuli were two blue, elongated animals, each with two feet. One animal had two holes and the other had one hole. The animals were 35 cm wide and 15 cm tall.

There were three differences between this study and Experiment 1. First, the word used for the object was "animal," and the word for the part was "foot." Second, questions were grouped by entity and not by task. For instance, a given subject might complete the identification, counting, and tracking tasks with objects, then with holes, and then with parts. (As with Experiment 1, there were six possible orders in which the entities could be presented.) And third, in the tracking task, the animal was rotated 180° and slid to the right, so that the object, hole, and part all changed positions.

Results

We carried out a $6 \times 3 \times 3$ analysis of variance, with order as a between-subjects variable and with task (identification vs. counting vs. tracking) and entity (object vs. hole vs. part) as within-subjects variables. The only significant effect was that of task, $F(2, 24) = 16.26$, $p < .001$: Counting and identification were equally easy (93% and 91% correct), but tracking was much harder (48%). Post hoc tests revealed significant differences between tracking and identification, $t(17) = 4.11$, and tracking and counting, $t(17) = 4.97$, both ps $< .001$. The results are shown in Table 2.

TABLE 2   **Percentage Correct in the Identification, Counting, and Tracking Tasks in Experiment 2**

	ENTITY		
Task	**Object**	**Hole**	**Part**
Identification	83.3 (38.3)	94.4 (23.6)	94.4 (23.6)
Counting	94.4 (23.6)	88.9 (32.3)	94.4 (23.6)
Tracking	44.4 (51.1)	50.0 (51.4)	50.0 (51.4)

Note. Standard deviations are in parentheses.

Unlike in Experiment 1, children did just as well with parts as they did with objects and holes, presumably because the questions, instead of using "handle," used the more familiar word "foot." The modification to the tracking task and the different ordering of the questions did not lead to any improvement with regard to performance on the tracking task.

GENERAL DISCUSSION

The first experiment found that children were equally good at tasks involving objects and holes, but worse at tasks involving parts. The second experiment, in which the name of the part was changed from "handle" to "foot," found equal levels of performance with objects, holes, and parts.

How can we reconcile these findings with the research discussed earlier, especially with evidence that children are biased to count objects (Shipley & Shepperson, 1990)? It is clear that objects are salient to children, more so than certain other entities. What our findings suggest, however, is that objects are not the only salient individuals. Children had no special problems counting the holes and parts we used in the experiments reported here.

These studies do not prove that objects, parts, and holes are on an equal psychological footing. For one thing, even if this were the case for 3-year-olds, it might not be so for babies and younger children. We know that infants can identify, track, and enumerate objects, but there is no evidence that they can identify, track, and enumerate holes and parts. It might be that infants have innate object principles that govern how they make sense of the physical world (Spelke, 1994) and that an understanding of other sorts of entities emerges only later, sometime before the age of 3.

In fact, objects might have a special status even for 3-year-olds. Our experiments suggest that objects are not so salient that they preclude children from individuating parts and holes. But they might nonetheless be easier to process. In a situation that forces children to choose between these types of entities (such as deciding the interpretation of a name), objects might win out. There have been studies in which objects and parts were contrasted in this way (with somewhat ambiguous results; see Kobayashi, 1998; Markman & Wachtel, 1988), but none yet have dealt with holes.

Alternatively, perhaps objects are not easier to deal with than parts and holes, at least not always. The discussion thus far has treated objects, holes, and parts as homogeneous categories. But this is likely to be an oversimplification. Imagine, on the one hand, if we did the same studies reported here but with tiny pinpricks as holes, or with small bumps as parts. It is conceivable that 3-year-olds would have problems counting them, and would favor the objects. On the other hand, imagine that the holes were very large, taking up just about all of the objects, and were of interesting shapes (such as animal shapes). Or imagine that the parts were long, shiny dragon tails, affixed to small uninteresting bodies. In such cases, children might be more prone to focus on the holes and parts than on the objects. In general, a promising area of research would be to explore the conditions under which different entities are thought of as individuals by children and adults.

At the very least, the studies reported here show that the strongest version of the object-bias claim—that young children can cope only with whole objects—is mistaken. More tentatively, the results are consistent with the theory that objects have no special status in children's individuation. Instead, there are several factors that determine whether something is or is not a good individual. Objects are good individuals—for children and for adults—but so are some parts and some holes.

REFERENCES

Bloom, P. (1996). Possible individuals in language and cognition. *Current Directions in Psychological Science, 5,* 90–94.

Bloom, P. (2000). *How children learn the meanings of words.* Cambridge, MA: MIT Press.

Brown, R. (1957). Linguistic determinism and the part of speech. *Journal of Abnormal and Social Psychology, 55,* 1–5.

Casati, R., & Varzi, A. C. (1994). *Holes and other superficialities.* Cambridge, MA: MIT Press.

Dehaene, S. (1997). *The number sense: How the mind creates mathematics.* New York: Oxford University Press.

Golinkoff, R. M., Mervis, C. B., & Hirsh-Pasek, K. (1994). Early object labels: The case for a developmental lexical principles framework. *Journal of Child Language, 21,* 125–155.

Hoffman, D. D., & Richards, W. A. (1984). Parts of recognition. *Cognition, 18,* 65–96.

Imai, M., & Gentner, D. (1997). A cross-linguistic study of early word meaning: Universal ontology and linguistic influence. *Cognition, 62,* 169–200.

Kobayashi, H. (1998). How 2-year-old children learn novel part names of unfamiliar objects. *Cognition, 68,* B41–B51.

Langacker, R. W. (1987). Nouns and verbs. *Language, 63,* 53–94.

Macnamara, J. (1972). Cognitive basis of language learning in infants. *Psychological Review, 79,* 1–13.

Macnamara, J. (1982). *Names for things: A study of human learning.* Cambridge, MA: MIT Press.

Markman, E. M., & Wachtel, G. F. (1988). Children's use of mutual exclusivity to constrain the meanings of words. *Cognitive Psychology, 20,* 121–157.

Prasada, S. (1999). Names for things and stuff: An Aristotelian perspective. In R. Jackendoff, P. Bloom, & K. Wynn (Eds.), *Language, logic, and concepts: Essays in honor of John Macnamara* (pp. 119–146). Cambridge, MA: MIT Press.

Shipley, E. F., & Shepperson, B. (1990). Countable entities: Developmental changes. *Cognition, 34,* 109–136.

Smith, L. B., Jones, S. S., & Landau, B. (1996). Naming in young children: A dumb attentional mechanism? *Cognition, 60,* 143–171.

Spelke, E. S. (1994). Initial knowledge: Six suggestions. *Cognition, 50,* 443–447.

Tversky, B. (1989). Parts, partonomies and taxonomies. *Developmental Psychology, 25,* 983–995.

Waxman, S. R., & Markow, D. B. (1995). Words as invitations to form categories: Evidence from 12- to 13-month-old infants. *Cognitive Psychology, 29*, 257–302.

Wynn, K. (1995). Origins of numerical knowledge. *Mathematical Cognition, 1*, 35–60.

(Received 3/30/99; revision accepted 3/7/00)

Acknowledgments: The research reported here was completed as part of the first author's master's thesis at the University of Arizona, and was supported by a grant from the Spencer Foundation to the second author.

Questions

1. What is the theoretical motivation behind these experiments?
2. Who were the participants?
3. What is the independent variable?
4. How would you classify the design?
5. What was the dependent variable?
6. What controls were employed?
7. What would be a plausible third experiment?

17 Creative Porpoise

Introduction

Two models of learning dominated the research activities of learning psychologists during the early part of the 20th century. One model was developed by Ivan Pavlov and is commonly called *classical conditioning;* the other model was suggested by E. L. Thorndike and refined by B. F. Skinner and is referred to as *operant conditioning.* The initial experiments of both groups attempted to identify the conditions for learning using nonhuman subjects. Pavlov used his famous salivating dogs, while Thorndike studied the effects of reward on the behavior of cats. Skinner used rats in his early experiments, then pigeons, and finally, among other species, humans. The contemporary period has seen a great proliferation in the use of different species in the learning laboratory, all with the basic purpose of establishing laws of behavior. The use of porpoises in this study is a logical step to illustrate the effectiveness of operant conditioning in yet another species.

The authors of "The Creative Porpoise" have skillfully applied several basic components of the model developed by B. F. Skinner. An important principle of operant conditioning is that responses that are followed by a reward or positive reinforcement tend to increase, while responses that are not rewarded tend to decrease. Skinner demonstrated this principle in rats by measuring whether bar-pressing responses increased after a reward. The apparatus developed by Skinner has been described previously. The initial behavior of a rat placed in a "Skinner box" is normally exploratory in nature; it sniffs the corners, moves from one side to the other, examines the walls, and washes its face. Only a small number of these responses have anything to do with a bar-pressing response, but the skilled researcher can identify preparatory bar-pressing responses and reinforce them. The process of selectively reinforcing successive approximations of the principal response (bar pressing) is called *shaping.* Gradually the animal moves closer to the bar, then places its paw close to the bar, touches it, and eventually depresses it.

Much information has been collected regarding the specific conditions that facilitate operant conditioning. For example, if the reward is presented immediately after the appropriate response, then conditioning is more rapid than if the reward is delayed. In reading the article by Pryor, Haag, and O'Reilly (1969), notice how they try to present the reinforcement as soon after the appropriate response as is practical.

Other researchers have studied the role that secondary reinforcers (stimuli that have been associated with the primary reward) have on behavior. The general conclusion of these studies is that secondary reinforcers have strong rewarding properties. Consider the reward properties of the secondary reinforcement of money in many societies. In this study, Pryor et al. use a distinguishable signal (a whistle) as a conditioned reinforcer.

The results of operant conditioning experiments lend themselves to graphic representation in the form of a cumulative frequency record. On such a graph, the subject's responses are accumulated and scaled on the **ordinate,** while time is recorded on the **abscissa.** Since the responses are accumulative, the response curve never goes down; a nonresponse is depicted as a line parallel to the abscissa.

This article was selected not only to illustrate the principles of operant behavior, but to show you an experiment that is largely descriptive in nature. Note that only one subject was used, and the statistical portion of the paper is largely descriptive. The researchers show how data from psychological experiments can be effectively portrayed in graphic form. From the graphs we can quickly grasp their results.

Another feature of this experiment is that it combines a laboratory setting with a natural setting. The experiment was conducted in a large artificial pool, but the habitat is designed to simulate, as close as is practical, the natural environment of the subject. To do this research in the natural setting of the experimental animal (i.e., the ocean) is probably impractical (although not impossible, as the researchers cite research conducted in the open field), but to conduct the research in a confined and artificial environment may inhibit the responses of the porpoise.

Most research in psychology depends on large samples; however, to infer that psychological research must study large samples in order to be valid is an unwarranted conclusion. Pryor et al. describe the learning process with clarity by thoroughly examining the behavior of a single subject.

Special Issues

SMALL *n* DESIGNS

Research that is based on a single subject or small sample is called a small *n,* or small number of subjects, design. Most research in psychology is based on a large sample of subjects that generates a large amount of data. These designs are sometimes called large *n* designs.

Data gathered from these experiments are amenable to statistical analysis in which probabilistic conclusions and broad generalizations can be made. Because of the enormous popularity of large *n* experiments and their comparability with modern statistical techniques, it may seem that small *n* designs are methodologically inferior. However, three branches of psychology have resisted the trend toward large *n* experiments. The first of these groups is led by psychophysicists, another by clinical researchers (see Chapter 19, Special Issues: Single-Subject Design in Clinical Studies), and a third by operant learning psychologists.

PSYCHOPHYSICAL RESEARCH

Psychophysical experiments generally deal with the relationship between physical stimuli and a research participant's perception of those stimuli. In many psychophysical designs each subject may be exposed to dozens or even hundreds of different stimuli in a single experiment. Thus, the number of observations in psychophysical experiments, although based on only a few subjects (or even a single subject), may exceed the number of observations in a large *n* experiment. Further, many psychophysical experiments are not affected by the subject's knowledge of the potential outcome of the experiment. In fact, many researchers in this area act as subjects in their own experiments. The rationale is that the responses that the subject makes are physical ones, and are not affected by knowledge of theory or hypotheses. This argument is further strengthened when you consider how many trials each subject through.

OPERANT CONDITIONING

Studies of operant conditioning frequently use small *n* designs and, in some instances, a single subject. In these experiments a single subject (or only a few subjects) is intensely studied. As in psychophysical experiments and clinical studies, the design is frequently a within-subject design, where subjects serve in each condition. A chief proponent of small *n* designs has been B. F. Skinner, who has observed the development of behavior in a single subject. The research presented in this chapter is a clear example of a single-subject experiment. As you study the experiment, note that the authors do not use inferential statistics but instead use descriptive statistics. This is a general feature of small *n* experiments, but very sophisticated statistics are available to analyze the results obtained in single-subject experiments.

THE CREATIVE PORPOISE: TRAINING FOR NOVEL BEHAVIOR

Karen W. Pryor
Oceanic Institute

Richard Haag
Makapuu Oceanic Center

Joseph O'Reilly
University of Hawaii

Two rough-toothed porpoises (Steno bredanensis) were individuals trained to emit novel responses, which were not developed by shaping and which were not previously known to occur in the species, by reinforcing a different response to the same set of stimuli in each of a series of training sessions. A technique was developed for transcribing a complex series of behaviors onto a single cumulative record so that the training sessions of the second animal could be fully recorded. Cumulative records are presented for a session in which the criterion that only novel behaviors would be reinforced was abruptly met with four new types of responses, and for typical preceding and subsequent sessions. Some analogous techniques in the training of pigeons, horses, and humans are discussed.

a   The shaping of novel behavior, that is, behavior that does not occur, or perhaps cannot occur, in an animal's normal activity, has been a preoccupation of animal trainers for centuries. The fox terrier turning back somersaults,

Source: Reprinted by permission from *journal of the Experimental Analysis of Behavior,* 1969, *12,* 653–661. Copyright 1969 by the Society for the Experimental Analysis of Behavior, Inc. Some portions of the original article have been omitted.

Analysis

Other articles in this book began with a literature review, but Pryor, Haag, and O'Reilly introduce their paper with a general statement about the use of operant conditioning in a variety of species **(a)**. In two following paragraphs they describe

the elephant balancing on one front foot, or Ping-Pong playing pigeons (Skinner, 1962) are produced by techniques of successive approximation, or shaping. However, novel or original behavior that is not apparently produced by shaping or differential reinforcement is occasionally seen in animals. Originality is a fundamental aspect of behavior but one that is rather difficult to induce in the laboratory.

In the fall of 1965, at Sea Life Park at the Makapuu Oceanic Center in Hawaii, the senior author introduced into the five daily public performances at the Ocean Science Theater a demonstration of reinforcement of previously unconditioned behavior. The subject animal was a female roughtoothed porpoise, *Steno bredonensis,* named Malia.

Since behavior that had been reinforced previously could no longer be used to demonstrate this first step in conditioning, it was necessary to select a new behavior for reinforcement in each demonstration session. Within a few days, Malia began emitting an unprecedented range of behaviors, including aerial flips, gliding with the tail out of the water, and "skidding" on the tank floor, some of which were as complex as responses normally produced by shaping techniques, and many of which were quite unlike anything seen by Sea Life Park staff in Malia or any other porpoise.

b   **To see if the training situation used with Malia could again produce a "creative" animal,** the authors repeated Malia's training, as far as possible, with another animal, one that was not being used for public demonstrations or

c   any other work at the time. **A technique of record keeping was developed to pinpoint if possible the events leading up to repeated emissions of novel behaviors.**

some natural observations that led to the hypothesis **(b)** and they provide an abbreviated statement of their method **(c)**. It is important to note that the development of a hypothesis may emanate from many sources. Although the most frequent source of a hypothesis is previous research, another significant source is the observation of behavior in a natural setting.

METHOD

d

A porpoise named Hou, of the same species and sex as Malia, was chosen. Hou had been trained to wear harness and instruments and to participate in physiological experiments in the open sea (Norris, 1965). This individual had a large repertoire of shaped responses but its "spontaneous activity" had never been reinforced. Hou was considered by Sea Life Park trainers to be "a docile, timid individual with little initiative."

e

Training sessions were arranged to simulate as nearly as possible Malia's five brief daily sessions. Two to four sessions were held daily, lasting from 5 to 20 min each, with rest periods of about half an hour between sessions. Hou was given normal rations; it is not generally necessary to reduce food intake or body weight in cetaceans to make food effective as a reinforcer. Any food not earned in training sessions was given freely to the animal at the end of the day, and it was fed normal rations, without being required to work, on weekends. During the experimental period, no work was required of Hou other than that in the experiment itself. **A bell was rung at the beginning and end of sessions to serve as a context marker.** The appearance and positioning of the trainers served as an additional stimulus that the opportunity for reinforcement was now present.

f

To record the events of each session, the trainer and two observers, one above water and one watching the underwater area through the glass tank walls, wore microphones and made a verbal commentary; earphones allowed the experimenters to hear each other. The three commentaries and the sound of the conditioned reinforcer, the whistle, were recorded on a single tape. A typed transcript was made of each tape; then, by comparing transcript to tape,

Method

Paragraphs **(d)**, **(e)**, and **(f)** identify the subject, describe how conditioning was done, and explain the technique used to record the data. In paragraph **(e)** the authors describe the use of a bell that was rung at the beginning of the training session. The use of a signal at the outset of an experiment is called a *discriminative stimulus,* and it lets the conditioned operant know the experiment is beginning. In this experiment the bell signified to Hou, the porpoise, that it was time for her to "do her thing."

This paper may appear to be an observational study rather than an experiment. Upon closer examination, though, it is apparent that there are independent and dependent variables, operational definitions of terms, hypothesis testing, and controlled conditions, to name but a few of the characteristics of experimentation.

This experiment differs from many of the experiments reviewed in this book in that the dependent variable (novel behavior) is followed by the independent variable (reinforcement). Compare this sequence with Terkel and Rosenblatt's article, "Maternal Behavior Induced by Maternal Blood Plasma Injected into Virgin Rats" (Chapter 15), in which the dependent variable (maternal behavior) is

the transcript was marked at 15-sec intervals. Each response of the animal was then graphed on a cumulative record, with a separate curve to indicate each type of response in a given session (Figures 2 to 5).

It was necessary to make a relatively arbitrary decision about what constituted a reinforceable or recordable act. In general, a reinforceable act consisted of **any movement that was not part of the normal swimming action of the animal, and which was sufficiently extended through space and time to be reported by two or more observers.** Such behavior as eye-rolling, inaudible whistling, and gradual changes in direction may have occurred, but they could not be distinguished by the trainers and therefore could not be reinforced, except coincidentally. This unavoidable contingency probably had the effect of increasing the incidence of gross motor responses. Position and sequence of responses were not considered. An additional criterion, which had been a contingency in much of Hou's previous training, was that only one type of response would be reinforced per session.

The experimental plan of reinforcing a new type of response in each session was not fully met. Sometimes a previously reinforced response was again chosen for reinforcement, to strengthen the response, to increase the general level of responding, or to film a given behavior. Whether the "reviewing" of responses was helpful or detrimental to the animal's progress is open to speculation.

Interobserver reliability was judged from the transcripts of the taped sessions, in which a new behavior was generally recognized in concert by the observers. Furthermore, each new behavior chosen for reinforcement was later

preceded by the independent variable (maternal blood plasma). You may have observed, however, that in this article the porpoise's behavior and reinforcement were ongoing, so it could be argued that a chain of responses—reinforcement, response; reinforcement, response—would develop. The sequence of independent and dependent variable then becomes a matter of deciding which came first: the reinforcement or the behavior.

Several statements in paragraph **(f)** require comment. The researchers have the two observers tape-record their observations, which are then transcribed into a typed manuscript. They also keep a precise record of the time and frequency of the conditioned reinforcer (a whistle).

In **(g)** an operational definition of a reinforceable act is stated. They do this because in shaping behavior the act to be reinforced is sometimes ambiguous, and some researchers will "play it by ear"; that is, they will make a decision to reinforce or not reinforce on the basis of ongoing behavior. Since scientific procedure must be specified in sufficient detail to allow the experiment to be exactly replicated, Pryor et al. attempt to reduce the ambiguity of shaping by operationally defining reinforceable responses. In **(h)** they explain the measure of experimental reliability that they used.

(analysis continues on page 273)

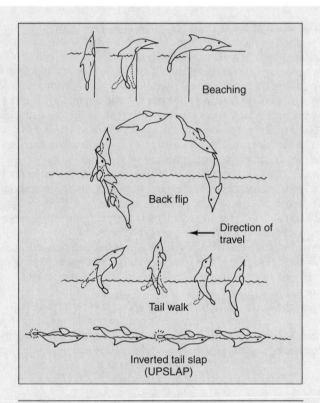

Beaching

Back flip

Direction of travel

Tail walk

Inverted tail slap
(UPSLAP)

FIGURE 1   Four reinforced novel behaviors, including one shaped behavior—the tail walk.

diagrammed in a series of position sketches. At no time did any of the three observers fail to agree that the drawings represented the behaviors witnessed. These behavior diagrams were matched, at the end of the experiment, with film of each behavior, and were found to represent adequately the topography of those behaviors that had been reinforced (see Figure 1).

After 32 training sessions, the topography of Hou's aerial behaviors became so complex that, while undoubtedly novel, the behaviors exceeded the powers of the observers to discriminate and describe them. This breakdown in observer reliability was one factor in the termination of the experiment.

To corroborate the experimenters' observation that certain of Hou's responses were not in the normal repertoire of the species, and constituted genuine novelties, the diagrams of each reinforced behavior were shown or sent to the past and present staff members who had had occasion to work with animals of this species. Each trainer was asked to rank the 16 behaviors in order of frequency of occurrence in a free-swimming untrained animal. The sketches were mounted on index cards and presented in random fashion to each rater separately. A coefficient of concordance (W) of 0.598 was found for agreement between trainers on the ranking of various behaviors; this value is significant at the 0.001 level, indicating a high degree of agreement (Siegl, 1956).

To test the possibility that the trainers were judging complexity rather than novelty in ranking, another questionnaire was prepared requesting ranking according to relative degree of complexity of action. Because some of the original group of 12 trainers were unavailable for retesting, the questionnaire was presented to a group of 49 naive students. The coefficient of concordance (W) for agreement between students was +0.295, significant at the 0.001 level. When the ranking for complexity and frequency were contrasted for each behavior, it was found that some agreement existed between the scores given by the two rating groups, Spearman Rank Correlation (RHO) +0.54, significant at the 0.05 level.

Thus, there seems to be some agreement between complexity and frequency, which should be expected, since complex behaviors require more muscle expenditure than simple ones. Furthermore, analysis was biased by the fact that the experienced group was asked to rate all behaviors serially, and had no way other than complexity to rate the several behaviors that many of them stated they had never seen. However, the agreement between complexity and frequency was not as large between groups as it was within groups; allowing for the fact that the use of two rating groups makes it

A final procedural question is raised in **(i)**, and some evidence is presented to answer the question. Complexity of responses rather than novelty of responses may have been conditioned, so to resolve the issue the experimenters used a form of validation, in which observations made by one experimenter are compared with observations made by another experimenter.

Results

The results reported in this article are generally self-explanatory, and we suggest that you thoroughly read the original transcript. Several general remarks may guide your reading.

First, you will notice the absence of F-tests or t-tests. Indeed, the paper is noticeably lacking in statistical analyses. In lieu of such analyses the writers present a well-documented protocol of the changing behavior of the porpoise. The authors also skillfully utilize cumulative frequency graphs. Pryor et al. provide a daily graph (Figures 2 to 5) in which the porpoise's behavior is charted using the coordinates of responses (vertical axis) and time (horizontal axis).

impossible to generalize the rating comparisons in a strict sense, the low frequency assigned to some noncomplex behaviors by the experienced group suggests that complexity and novelty are not necessarily positively correlated.

RESULTS

Sessions 1 to 14

In the first session, Hou was admitted into the experimental tank and, when given no commands, breached. Breaching, or lumping into the air and coming down sideways, is a normal action in a porpoise. This response was reinforced, and the animal began to repeat it on an average of four times a minute for 8 min. Toward the end of the 9-min session it porpoised, or leaped smoothly out of the water and in, once or twice.

Hou began the third session by porpoising: when this behavior was not reinforced, the animal rapidly developed a behavior pattern of porpoising in front of the trainer, entering the water in an inverted position, turning right side up, swimming in a large circle, and returning to porpoise in front of the trainer again. It did this 25 times without interruption over a period of 12.5 min. Finally, it stopped and laid its head against the pool edge at the trainer's feet. This behavior, nicknamed "beaching," was reinforced and repeated (Figure 1). Sessions 5, 6, and 7 followed the same pattern [Figure 2].

The trainers decided to shape specific responses in order to interrupt Hou's unvarying repetition of a limited repertoire. Session 8 was devoted to shaping a "tail walk," or the behavior of balancing vertically half out of the water. The tail walk was reinforced in Session 9, and Sessions 10 and 11 were devoted to shaping a "tail wave," the response of lifting the tail from the water. The tail wave was emitted and reinforced in Session 12.

At the end of Session 10, Hou slapped its tail twice, which was reinforced but not repeated. At the end of Session 12, Hou departed from the stereotyped pattern to the extent of inverting, turning right side up, and then inverting again while circling. The experimenters observed and reinforced this underwater revolution from a distance, while leaving the experimental area.

Although a weekend then intervened, Hou began Session 13 by swimming in the inverted position, then right side up, then inverted again. This be-

It is important for you to study these graphs, as they are used as the primary source of results. In Figure 2 there are three distinct components: (1) the number of actions, (2) the time in minutes, and (3) the behavior (inverted swim, porpoise, and corkscrew). Notice the relationship among the three behaviors and how the inverted swim rapidly increased. The same three components are in Figure 3, and numerous other behavior characteristics were observed. Trace the development of the flip in Figure 3.

(analysis continues on page 280)

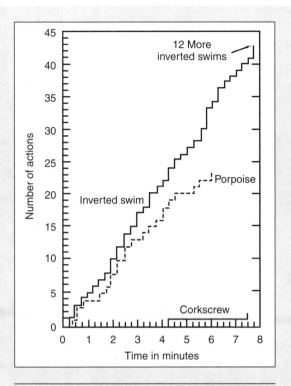

FIGURE 2   Cumulative record of Session 7, a typical early session, in which the porpoise began emitting the previously reinforced response. This response gradually extinguished when another response was formed.

havior, dubbed a "corkscrew," was reinforced, and by means of an increasing variable ratio, was extended to five complete revolutions per reinforcement. In Session 14, the experimenters rotated their positions, and reinforced any descent by the animal toward the bottom of the tank, in a further effort not only to expand Hou's repertoire but also to interrupt the persistent circling behavior.

Sessions 15 and 16
The next morning, as the experimenters set up their equipment, Hou was unusually active in the holding tank. It slapped its tail twice, and this was so unusual that the trainer reinforced the response in the holding tank. When Session 15 began, Hou emitted the response reinforced in the previous

session, of swimming near the bottom, and then the response previous to that of the corkscrew, and then fell into the habitual circling and porpoising, with, however, the addition of a tail slap on reentering the water. This slap was reinforced, and the animal then combined slapping with breaching, and then began slapping disassociated from jumping; for the first time it emitted responses in all parts of the tank, rather than right in front of the trainer. The 10-min session ended when 17 tail slaps had been reinforced, and other non-reinforced responses had dropped out.

Session 16 began after a 10-min break, Hou became extremely active when the trainer appeared and immediately offered twisting breaches, landing on its belly and its back. It also began somersaulting on its long axis in midair.

The flip occurred 44 times, intermingled with some of the previously reinforced responses and with three other responses that had not been seen before: an upside-down tail slap, a sideswipe with the tail, and an aerial spin on the short axis of the body (Figure 3).

This session also differed from previous ones in that once the flip had become established, the other behaviors did not tend to drop out. After 24 min, the varied activity—tail slaps, breaches, sideswipes with the tail, and the new behavior of spinning in the air—occurred more rather than less frequently, until the session was brought to a close by the trainer. The previous maximum number of responses in a given session was 110 (in Session 9, a 31-min session). In Session 16, Hou emitted 192 responses in a 23-min session, an average of 8.3 responses per min compared to a previous maximum average of 3.6 responses per min.

By Session 16, the experimenters had apparently been successful in establishing a class of responses characterized by the description "only new kinds of responses will be reinforced," and consequently the porpoise was emitting an extensive variety of new responses. The differences between Session 16 and previous sessions may be seen by comparing the cumulative record for Session 16 (Figure 3) with that of Session 7, a typical earlier session (Figure 2).

Sessions 17 to 27

In Sessions 17 to 27, the new types of responses emitted in Session 16 were selected, one by one, for reinforcement, and some old responses were reinforced again so that they could be photographed. Other new responses, such as unclassifiable twisting jumps, and sinking head downwards, occurred sporadically. The average rate of response and the numbers of types of responses per session remained more than twice as high as pre–Session 16 levels.

Hou's general activity changed in two other ways after Session 16. First, if no reinforcement occurred in a period of seven minutes, the rate and level of activity declined but the animal did not necessarily resume a stereotyped behavior pattern. Secondly, the animal's activity now included much behavior typically associated in cetaceans with situations producing frustration or

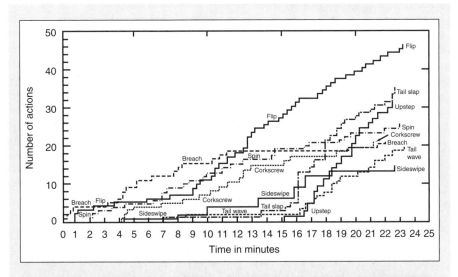

FIGURE 3 **Cumulative record of Session 16, in which the porpoise emitted eight different types of responses, four of which were novel (flip, spin, sideswipe, and upslap).**

aggressiveness, such as slapping the water with head, tail, pectoral fin, or whole body (Burgess, 1968).

Sessions 28 to 33

In all of the final sessions, the criterion that the behavior must be a new one was enforced. A new behavior that had been seen but not reinforced previously, the inverted tail slap, had been reinforced in Session 27. Session 28 began with a variety of responses, including another that had been seen but not reinforced before, a sideswipe at water surface with the tail, which was reinforced. In Session 29, Hou's activity included an inverted leap that fulfilled the criterion (Figure 4). In Session 30, Hou offered 60 responses over a period of 15 min, none of which were considered new and were not therefore reinforced.

In Sessions 31, 32, and 33, held the next day, Hou's behavior was more completely controlled by the criteria that only new types of responses were reinforced and that only one type of response was reinforced per session. In Session 31, Hou entered the tank and, after a preliminary jump, stood on its tail and clapped its jaws at the trainer, who, taken by surprise, failed to reinforce the maneuver. Hou then emitted a brief series of leaps and then executed a backwards aerial flip that was reinforced and immediately repeated 14 times without intervening responses of other types. In Session 32, after

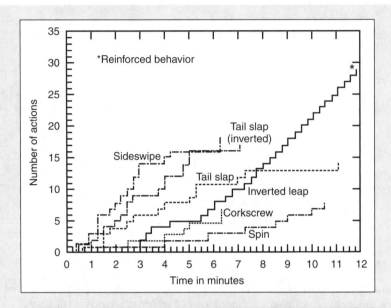

FIGURE 4   Cumulative record of Session 29, in which the porpoise emitted the three most recently reinforced responses initially, but soon emitted a novel response. When this response was reinforced, the others extinguished.

one porpoise and one flip, Hou executed an upside-down porpoise, and, after it was reinforced, repeated this new response 10 times, again without other responses (Figure 5).

In the third session of the day, Hou did not initially emit a response judged new by the observers. After 40 min and 72 responses of variable types, the rate of response declined to 1 per min and then gradually rose again to seven responses per minute after 19 min. No reinforcements occurred during this period. At the end of 19 min, Hou stood on its tail and clapped its jaws, spitting water towards the trainer; this time the action was reinforced, and was repeated five times.

Hou had now produced a new behavior in six out of seven consecutive sessions. In Sessions 31 and 32, Hou furthermore began each session with a new response and emitted no unreinforceable responses once reinforcement was presented. This establishment of a series of new types of responses was considered to be the conclusion of the experiment.

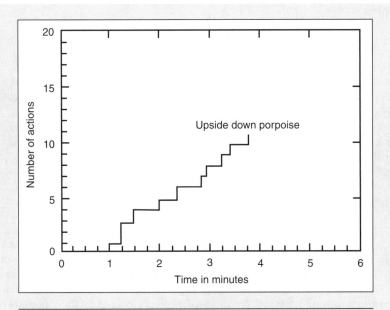

FIGURE 5   Cumulative record of Session 32. The porpoise emitted only a novel response in this session.

DISCUSSION

Over a period of 4 yr since Sea Life Park and the neighboring Oceanic Institute were opened, the training staff has observed and trained over 50 cetaceans of seven different species. Of the 16 behaviors reinforced in this experiment, five (breaching, porpoising, inverted swimming, tail slap, sideswipe) have been observed to occur spontaneously in every species; four (breaching, tail walk, inverted tail slap, spitting) have been developed by shaping in various animals but very rarely occur spontaneously in any; three (spinning, back porpoise, forward flip) occur spontaneously only in one species of *stenella* and have never been observed at Sea Life Park in other species; and four (corkscrew, back flip, tail wave, inverted leap) have never been observed to occur spontaneously. While this does not imply that these behaviors do not sometimes occur spontaneously, whatever the species, it does serve to indicate that a single animal, in emitting these 16 types of responses, would be engaging in behavior well outside the species norm.

A technique of reinforcing a series of different, normally occurring actions, in a series of training sessions, did therefore serve, in the case of Hou, as with Malia, to establish in the animal a highly increased probability that new types of behavior would be emitted.

j

This ability to emit an unusual response need not be regarded as an example of cleverness peculiar to the porpoise. It is possible that the same technique could be used to achieve a similar result with pigeons. If a different, normally occurring action in a pigeon is reinforced each day for a series of days, until the normal repertoire (turning, pecking, flapping wings, etc.) is exhausted, the pigeon may come to emit novel responses difficult to produce even by shaping.

k

A similar process may be involved in one traditional system of the training of five-gaited show horses, which perform at three natural gaits, the walk, trot, and canter, and two artificial gaits, the slow gait and the rack. The trainer first reinforces the performance of the natural gaits and brings this performance under stimulus control. The discriminative stimuli, which control not only the gait, but also speed, direction, and position of the horse while executing the gait, consist of pressure and release from the rider's legs, pressures on the reins and consequently the bit, shifting of weight in the saddle, and sometimes signals with whip and voice, To elicit the artificial gait, the trainer next presents the animal with a new group of stimuli, shaking the bit back and forth in the horse's mouth and vibrating the legs against the horse's sides, while preventing the animal from terminating the stimuli (negative reinforcement) by means of the previously reinforced responses of walking, trotting, or cantering. The animal will emit a variety of responses that eventually may include the pattern of stepping, novel to the horse though familiar to the trainer, called the rack (Hildebrand, 1965). The pattern, however brief, is reinforced, and once established is extended in duration and brought under stimulus control. (The slow gait is derived from the rack by shaping.)

l

Comparison may be made here between this work and that of Maltzman (1960). Working in the formidably rich matrix of human subjects and verbal behavior, Maltzman described a successful procedure for eliciting original responses, consisting of reinforcing different responses to the same stimuli, essentially the same procedure followed with Hou and Malia. It is interesting to note that behavior considered by the authors to indicate anger in the porpoise was observed under similar circumstances in human subjects by Maltzman: "An impression gained from observing Ss in the experimental situation is that repeated evocation of different responses to the same stimuli becomes quite frustrating; Ss are disturbed by what quickly becomes a surprisingly difficult

Discussion

The implication of training creative behavior in the porpoise is discussed in relation to achieving similar results with the pigeon (**j**) and the horse (**k**), and possible common features of the present study and previous work by Maltzman are suggested (**l**).

task. This disturbed behavior indicates that the procedure may not be trivial and does approximate a nonlaboratory situation involving originality or inventiveness, with its frequent concomitant frustrations.

Maltzman also found that eliciting and reinforcing original behavior in one set of circumstances increased the tendency for original responses in other kinds of situations, which seems likewise to be true for Hou and Malia. Hou continues to exhibit a marked increase in general level of activity. Hou has learned to leap tank partitions to gain access to other porpoises, a skill very seldom developed by a captive porpoise. When a trainer was occupied at an adjoining porpoise tank Malia jumped from the water, skidded across 6 ft of wet pavement, and tapped the trainer on the ankle with its rostrum, or snout, a truly bizarre act for an entirely aquatic animal.

Individual differences in the ability to create unorthodox responses no doubt exist; Malia's novel responses, judged *in toto,* are more spectacular and "imaginative" than Hou's. However, by using the technique of training for novelty described herein, it should be possible to induce a tendency toward spontaneity and creative or unorthodox response in most individuals of a broad range of species.

REFERENCES

Burgess, K. (1968). The behavior and training of a Killer Whale at San Diego Sea World. *International Zoo Yearbook, 8,* 202–205.

Hildebrand, M. (1965). Symmetrical gaits of horses. *Science, 150,* 701–708.

Maltzman, I. (1960). On the training of originality. *Psychological Review, 67,* 229–242.

Norris, K. S. (1965). Open ocean diving test with a trained porpoise (*Steno bredanensis). Deep Sea Research, 12,* 505–509.

Siegel, S. (1956). *Nonparametric statistics for the behavioral sciences.* New York: McGraw-Hill.

Skinner, B. F. (1962). Two synthetic social relations. *Journal of the Experimental Analysis of Behavior, 5,* 531–533.

Note: Contribution No. 35, the Oceanic Institute, Makapuu Oceanic Center, Waimanalo, Hawaii. Carried out under Naval Ordinance Testing Station Contract #N60530-12292, NOTS, China Lake, California. A detailed account of this experiment, including the cumulative records for each session, has been published as NOTS Technical Publication #4270 and may be obtained from the Clearing House for Federal Scientific and Technical Information. U.S. Department of Commerce, Washington, D.C. A 16-mm film, "Dolphin Learning Studies:" based on this experiment, has been prepared by the U.S. Navy. Persons wishing to view this film may inquire of the Motion Picture Production Branch, Naval Undersea Warfare Center, 201 Rosecrans Street, San Diego, California 92132. The authors wish to thank Gregory Bateson of the Oceanic Institute, Dr. William Wesit of Reed College, Portland, Oregon, and Dr. Leonard Diamond of the University of Hawaii for their extensive and valuable assistance; also Dr. William McLean, Technical Director, Naval Undersea Research and Development Center, San Diego, California, for his interest and support.

Questions

1. In this study identify and define the following:
   conditioned reinforcer
   discriminative stimulus
   cumulative frequency graph
   shaping
   creativity (operational definition)
   response-reinforcement latency
2. Can you suggest another technique for measuring the responses?
3. Why did the researchers avoid extensive statistical analysis in this paper?
4. From this research, have you changed your definition of "creativity"? If so, how?
5. List the control measures used in the creative porpoise experiment.
6. Take another species—for example, dog, goldfish, squirrel—and write a re-inforcement schedule for the training of novel behavior. Operationally define your terms.
7. Write a brief essay describing the usefulness of naturalistic observations. What are their strengths? Their weaknesses?
8. Write a lesson plan for 6-year-old children in which creative reactions are shaped and reinforced. What limitations to your lessons do you see?
9. Review the literature for a study on porpoises or dolphins that has been done more recently than this article. Are there differences in how the animals are treated or described?

18 Perspective Shifting

Introduction

Have you ever been to the movies with a friend where you each liked and identified with different characters? The hero was your favorite, the villain your friend's? Do you think your memory of the movie is different from your friend's memory? Do you think it's possible to have very different memories when you both saw the same movie at the same time? The perspective you take when you read a book or watch a movie might affect how you encode the information. If you take the perspective of the hero, you have certain expectancies about that person's behavior. How would your expectancies differ if you found out half way through the movie that your "hero" was really the "bad guy"? Anderson and Pichert (1978) set out to explore how people's perspectives (one could also call them schemas) affect information processing.

    This study's appeal lies in its simplicity. Important theoretical questions don't always require a complex method. These procedures were easy to administer and inexpensive. As always, though, the important question to ask yourself is whether the method captures the necessary factors to answer the research questions at hand.

RECALL OF PREVIOUSLY UNRECALLABLE INFORMATION FOLLOWING A SHIFT IN PERSPECTIVE

Richard C. Anderson and James W. Pichert
University of Illinois

College undergraduates read a story about two boys playing hooky from school from the perspective of either a burglar or a person interested in buying a home. After recalling the story once, subjects were directed to shift perspectives and then recall the story again. In two experiments, subjects produced on the second recall significantly more information important to the second perspective that had been unimportant to the first. They also recalled less information unimportant to the second perspective which had been important to the first. These data clearly show the operation of retrieval processes independent from encoding processes. An analysis of interview protocols suggested that the instruction to take a new perspective led subjects to invoke a schema that provided implicit cues for different categories of story information.

a_1

It has been known since the turn of the century that the important elements of a prose passage are more likely to be learned and remembered than the unimportant elements (Binet & Henri, 1894; Thieman & Brewer, in press). Recent years have seen increasingly precise formulations of the notion of importance in terms of story schemata (Mandler & Johnson, 1977; Rumelhart, 1975), propositional analysis schemes (Kintsch, 1974), and text grammars (Grimes, 1975; Meyer, 1975; Van Dijk, 1972). These systems yield structural descriptions of the content of a text, but they do not pinpoint the mechanisms by which importance has its effect. Possible explanations for the primacy of important text information abound in the literature. However, these explanations are notable for their informality and vagueness, and there has not yet been research that permits a confident choice among competing accounts.

a_2

In this paper we will enumerate possible explanations for the primacy of important text information. The explanations are of two classes: those that

Source: Reprinted in an abridged form by permission from the *Journal of Verbal Learning and Verbal Behavior*, 1978, *17*, 1–12.

Analysis

Literature Review

The authors provide a historical review of the literature pertinent to this study (a_1), as well as a more current one (a_2). This style of literature review conveys the scope of the topic area as well as delineates the current research questions. Next, the au-

suppose processes acting at the time of encoding are responsible and those that presume that the effect is due to processes acting later when information is retrieved and used. Next we shall summarize findings from previous research, paying special attention to evidence that would seem to support a distinction between encoding and retrieval. Finally we will report two experiments on possible retrieval mechanisms.

Our treatment will be couched in terms of schema theory. Schemata are abstract knowledge structures whose elements are other schemata, and *slots, placeholders,* or *variables* which can take on a restricted range of values (Minsky, 1975; Rumelhart & Ortony, 1977; Schank & Abelson, 1975). **A schema is structured in the sense that it indicates typical relationships among component elements.** In the simplest case the reader or listener will have a preformed schema adequate to *subsume* (Ausubel, 1963) a text. **The**

a_3 **encoded representation of such a text will consist of the subsuming schema in which the slots have been assigned specific values, that is, are** *instantiated* (Anderson, Pichert, Goetz, Schallert, Stevens, & Trollip, 1976) **with the particular information in the message.** A person will have the subjective sense that a passage has been comprehended when there is a good match between the information presented and the slots in the schema.

A schema at the level required to subsume a text will contain embedded subschemata (Rumelhart & Ortony, 1977). We shall assume that typically the subschemata form a hierarchy, or at least can be represented hierarchically without doing great violence to the interrelationships. The position of a subschemata in the hierarchy reflects its importance. The significant text elements are the ones that instantiate slots in high-order subschemata. In this fashion, schema theory provides an immediate gloss on the primacy in recall of important information. The explanation is saved from being circular because, at least for stereotyped genre such as folk tales, children's stories (Rumelhart, 1975), and detective novels (Cawalti, 1976; Mellard, 1972), it is possible to specify in advance the high-level schemata that normally will be brought to bear (Anderson, Spiro, & Anderson, 1977; Brown & Smiley, 1977; Mandler & Johnson, 1977).

Consider next the processes by which importance may influence encoding. Two alternative accounts seem compatible with schema conceptions. The first can be called the **"attention-directing" hypothesis.** The schema singles out important elements. More attention is devoted to these elements than to less important ones; therefore, they are more likely to be learned.

A second possibility on the encoding side has been termed the **"ideational scaffolding" hypothesis** (Ausubel, 1963). A schema is bound to contain a slot

thors provide a theoretical basis for their experiments and subsequent explanations **(a$_3$).** Their discussion of schema theory, especially as it relates to reading text, leads

(analysis continues on page 289)

for an important text element and it could be that the information gets stored precisely because there is a niche for it. Depending upon individual differences among readers, there may not be slots for less important elements. Or, there may be optional slots for unimportant elements, instantiated or not depending on the reader's motivation and on demand characteristics.

We turn now to the possibility that schemata facilitate information retrieval instead of, or in addition to, information storage. Again there is more than one plausible mechanism. Several investigators (Bower, 1977; Mandler & Johnson, 1977; Pichert & Anderson, 1977) have speculated that a schema might provide a retrieval plan. The idea is that memory search proceeds from the generic knowledge incorporated in the schema to the particular information stored when the text was read. A top-down schema-based search is very likely to give access to structurally important information but cannot turn up information unconnected to the schema. Thus, the latter categories of information are relatively inaccessible.

A second possibility is that schemata guide "output editing." This would require postulating that a schema contains within itself an index of importance which, in consort with the demand characteristics of the recall situation, causes the person to establish a response criterion. A person may terminate memory search when the criterion is reached. Or, when information occurs to a subject that falls below the criterion, he or she may not write it into the protocol.

A final possible retrieval process is "inferential reconstruction" (Spiro, 1977). Suppose that a subject was attempting to recall a story about a meal at a fine restaurant (Anderson et al., 1977; Schank & Abelson, 1975). He or she might fail to remember whether a drink was served with dinner, but since there is a slot in his or her schema for a beverage during the meal the subject is led to try to reconstruct this element. If the subject recalls that a beef dish was the entree, red wine becomes a candidate beverage. At this point red wine could be produced as a plausible guess; though after a long retention interval a subject may not be able to distinguish between an element that was in the text and an element produced by inference (Spiro, 1977). Alternatively, once a candidate, such as red wine, had been generated, it might be verified against an otherwise weak or inaccessible memory trace. In any event, the primacy of important text information in recall could be explained in terms of inferential reconstruction. The conceptual machinery of the schema will be biased toward reconstructing important elements.

At least three lines of evidence bear on a distinction between encoding and retrieval. First, there is the research of Dooling and Lachman (1971) and others demonstrating substantial facilitation when a schema-evoking context is furnished prior to difficult-to-understand passages. Bransford and Johnson (1973) went on to show that a context is not very helpful when presented after such a passage. The Bransford and Johnson materials were unlike normal text, deliberately written so that the referents of expressions were obscure.

Nevertheless, it is difficult to escape the conclusion that schemata play a role in encoding.

Two findings seem to implicate processes at work after a passage has been read. Several investigators (cf. Bartlett, 1932; Frederiksen, 1975) have found that the frequency of importations increases with the length of the retention interval. This finding can be taken as evidence for increasing reliance upon inferential reconstruction. If one additionally assumes that correct and incorrect elements are produced by the same process (Spiro, 1977), the finding also gives indirect support, along the lines argued above, to a reconstructive interpretation of the facts about the primacy of important text information. However, it is possible that importations reflect inferences made when a passage was read (Royer, 1977). Shortly after reading a subject may be able to discriminate between elements actually in the text and his own elaborations, so he suppresses the latter. As time passes, the discrimination becomes harder to make and, as a result, importations appear more often.

The best available evidence for an independent retrieval mechanism is the repeated finding that important elements continue to appear in recall protocols after a retention interval, whereas the appearance of unimportant elements declines sharply (cf. Bower, 1976; Newman, 1939). In research that was the immediate precursor of the present studies (Pichert & Anderson, 1977), college students read stories from either of two directed perspectives or from no directed perspective. One passage was about two boys playing hooky from school. They go to one of the boys' homes because his mother is never there on Thursdays. The family is well-to-do. They have a fine old home, set back from the road, with attractive grounds. Since it is old it has some defects—a leaky roof, a damp and musty basement. Because the family has considerable wealth, they have a lot of valuable possessions—ten-speed bikes, a color TV set, a rare coin collection. Different groups rated the importance of the elements in the story from one of three points of view: the viewpoint of a burglar, the viewpoint of a prospective homebuyer, or no directed perspective. Obviously a leaky roof is important to a homebuyer but unimportant to a burglar. The reverse is true of a color TV set or coin collection. The average intercorrelation of rated idea unit importance across three perspectives on each of two stories was .11.

Next, independent groups of subjects read the stories taking the various perspectives. The previously obtained ratings of idea unit importance were strongly related to immediate recall. This was true just of ratings obtained under the perspective the subject was directed to take, not other possible but nonoperative perspectives. Also significant was the effect of importance from the operative perspective on 1-week recall. The measure was recall of elements after 1 week given recall of the same elements shortly after reading.

Thus, importance was demonstrated to have independent effects on delayed recall.

The fact that importance has effects on delayed recall independent of those on immediate recall seems on its face to require a retrieval explanation, for any influence on what is encoded should show up immediately, or so the argument goes. Among the possible retrieval mechanisms discussed in the foregoing, the retrieval plan notion provides an especially appealing interpretation. All but the simplest stories contain secondary themes and incidental happenings. Normally these are perfectly comprehensible, so it is reasonable to suppose that they are encoded. However, if memory search starts with the generic knowledge in a schema there will be low probability of accessing information that does not connect with this schema. For instance, there presumably are no pointers in a burglary schema to defects in a house such as a musty basement; hence, even if it had been stored, this information could not be retrieved via a top-down search through a burglary schema.

The foregoing account is incomplete in that it still fails to explain why information unrelated to the dominant schema becomes less accessible as time passes. An auxiliary assumption is required, namely, that shortly after reading there are other routes, not mediated by the schema, to information unrelated to that schema; and further, that over time these alternative routes become increasingly problematical. This is not an unreasonable assumption. There could be some memory for surface aspects of the message immediately after reading, such as contiguously presented information. To illustrate, a subject mentally canvassing a house for loot under the aegis of a burglary schema might remember a valuable object asserted to be in the basement. This in turn could be a sufficient cue, just after reading but not later, that the next assertion was that the basement was damp and musty.

We have tried to construct a plausible retrieval explanation for the fact that more unimportant than important text elements drop out of recall protocols over a retention interval. However, there is a storage or encoding explanation that some will think equally plausible. A traditional interpretation would be that important elements tend to be overlearned and, therefore, have enough strength to appear at either immediate or delayed recall, whereas a larger proportion of the less well-learned unimportant elements is above threshold when recall is attempted shortly after reading but below threshold later.

To summarize, every established fact about prose recall can be given an encoding interpretation. While some findings can also be explained in retrieval terms, none in the previous literature demands such an explanation. On the other hand, the finding that a meaningful context facilitates recall when presented before, but not after, an ambiguous passage does seem to demand an encoding explanation.

The purpose of the experiments described in this paper was to attempt to provide incontestable grounds for the operation in prose recall of retrieval mechanisms distinct from storage mechanisms. Earlier, reasoning within a schema framework, we argued that people may store information when reading a text which they fail to produce when recalling that text. The theory also predicts that if people are caused to change schemata after reading a passage then they will recall additional information, specifically information important to the new schema but unimportant to the schema operative when the passage was read. There are three somewhat different formulations within schema theory of why this should happen. The first is the retrieval plan hypothesis, according to which the new schema will provide implicit cues for different categories of text information. The second is the output editing hypothesis: Under the aegis of a changed schema different categories of text information will fall above a response criterion. The third is the inferential reconstruction hypothesis: A new schema will furnish a different system of concepts for reconstructing important but unavailable information.

Subjects directed to take either a burglar or a homebuyer perspective read the story described earlier about two boys playing hooky from school. Everyone attempted to recall the story twice. Half of the subjects were directed to take a new perspective (from burglar to home buyer or vice versa) before the second attempt. **a₅ If these subjects were to recall additional information important to the new perspective this would be unequivocal evidence for a retrieval process.** We, at least, have been unable to think of an explanation for such a result solely in terms of encoding mechanisms.

EXPERIMENT I

Method

Subjects.   Thirty-nine introductory educational psychology students participated in this experiment in order to fulfill a course requirement.

Materials.   The experimental passage was a narrative about what two boys did at one of the boys' homes while they were skipping school. It contained a number of points of interest to a burglar or a real estate prospect. The story was 373 words long and contained 72 idea units which previously had been rated for their relative importance to a burglar and to a prospective homebuyer.

to the research questions at hand (a₄). Finally, they give an overview of the procedure and the desired result (a₅).

b₁

Design and Procedure.   Subjects were run in groups of three to eight. **b₁ Subjects were told that the study concerned "how people think about and remember stories . . . primarily in memory for the ideas in a story."** Subjects were randomly assigned envelopes, which contained instructions, the story, and a test booklet. They read instructions assigning them the burglar or homebuyer perspective and were then given 2 minutes to read the passage. Next, 12 minutes were allowed to do 84 items from the Wide Range Vocabulary Test (French, Ekstrom, & Price, 1963). Only the first 48 items were scored. The additional 36 items were employed to keep the retention interval uniform. All subjects finished the first 48 items and no subjects finished all 84 in the 12-minute period.

b₂

After the vocabulary test subjects turned to two blank pages and read instructions which emphasized, **b₂ "Please write down as much of the exact story as you can on these two sheets of paper. If you cannot remember the exact words of any sentence, but you do remember the meaning, write down a sentence or part of a sentence as close to the original as possible. It is extremely important that you write down every bit of the story which you can remember."**

When everyone had completed the first recall, 5 minutes were allowed to do six items from the Surface Development Test (French et al., 1963). This test requires subjects to mentally "fold" a two-dimensional figure to match a three-dimensional representation. The task is to match numbered edges on the two-dimensional figure with lettered edges on its three-dimensional representation.

Next, subjects turned to an instruction page which asked them to recall the story a second time. Half did so from the same perspective and half from the other. Subjects in the no-change condition were told the study was being done to determine whether or not people can remember things about a story they thought they had forgotten if they are given a second chance. Their original perspective instructions were then repeated. Subjects in the change-of-perspective condition were told, "This study is being done to determine whether or not people can remember things about a story they thought they

b₃

had forgotten if they are given a new perspective on that story . . . Please try to think of the story you read from this new perspective." The new perspective was then described exactly as it has been for those subjects given it originally. Recall instructions were repeated for both groups and the experimenter

b₄

stressed that "this study is attempting to determine differences in persons' recall from one time to the next so please write down every bit of the story which you can remember."

Following the second recall subjects completed a debriefing questionnaire and were thanked for their cooperation and dismissed.

Method

The instructions that the subjects were given are a very important aspect of this design. Pay close attention to them, as they are a critical factor in how the subjects will respond (b_1, b_2, b_3, b_4). A second experiment was conducted to replicate the first experiment and assess introspective reports on the encoding and retrieval

Scoring. Idea units were identified in the protocols which, according to gist criteria, matched any of the 72 idea units. In the earlier study (Pichert & Anderson, 1977), interrater reliability was .93. No reliability check was made this time.

Results

First Recall. Completed first was a **2 × 2 × 3** mixed analysis of variance involving all 72 of the idea units in the story. The between-subjects factors were perspective given prior to the story (Homebuyer, Burglar) and verbal ability (High, Low). Idea unit importance (High, Medium, Low) was a within-subjects factor. Table 1 summarizes performance on the dependent measure, proportion of idea units recalled. **A significant effect was found for idea unit importance, $F(2, 70) = 66.47, p < .01.$** More high than medium and more medium than low idea units were recalled under both perspectives, replicating our previous finding (Pichert & Anderson, 1977). The only other significant effect was the interaction between perspective and importance, $F(2, 70) = 19.50$, $p < .01$. This appeared because importance was more strongly related to recall under the burglar than under the homebuyer perspective, perhaps because college students are relatively less familiar with purchasing real estate.

c_1

c_2

c_3

TABLE 1   **Proportions of All Idea Units Recalled on the First Test at Each Importance Level**

Perspective	Idea Unit Importance		
	High	**Medium**	**Low**
Homebuyer	.55	.49	.41
Burglar	.66	.36	.23

Some information was important to both perspectives while a good deal was trivial from either point of view. A second analysis involved just those idea units whose rated importance was different from the two perspectives. The mean idea unit ratings obtained in the earlier study were converted to standard scores. Then two clusters of idea units were identified. Placed in the

processes. This experiment will not be presented or discussed here. See the original article if you are interested.

Results

This section starts off with a clear overview of the design (c_1) and the significant results (c_2). Further information is provided in the form of two tables and a graph (c_3, c_4, c_5).

(analysis continues on page 294)

first cluster were 15 units rated about 1.5 standard deviations higher under the burglar perspective than under the homebuyer perspective. This cluster will be called "burglar information." The complementary procedure was used to define a cluster of 13 idea units of homebuyer information.

Table 2 contains mean proportions of burglar and homebuyer information recalled. An analysis of the first recall data revealed an effect for cluster, $F(1, 35) = 26.31$, $p < .01$. The burglar information was better recalled than the homebuyer information. More interesting and important was the interaction between perspective and cluster, $F(1, 35) = 16.58$, $p < .01$, which is graphed in Figure 1. The group that had the burglar perspective recalled more burglar information whereas the group that had the homebuyer perspective recalled more homebuyer information. Again, this result confirms our earlier finding (Pichert & Anderson, 1977).

TABLE 2   **Proportions Recalled of Idea Units Whose Importance Varied as a Function of Perspective, Experiment I**

| | Information Cluster | | | |
| | Burglar | | Homebuyer | |
First/second perspective	First Recall	Second Recall	First Recall	Second Recall
Burglar/burglar	.68	.69	.39	.35
Homebuyer/homebuyer	.70	.68	.58	.58
Homebuyer/burglar	.54	.64	.58	.56
Burglar/homebuyer	.73	.61	.37	.42

c_4

Difference between First and Second Recall. Two predictions follow from the retrieval hypotheses developed in the introductory section. First, people who change perspectives should recall *more* information important to the second perspective but unimportant to the first. Subjects who changed perspective recalled an additional 7.1% of the now important information. In contrast, the comparison group which did not change perspective recalled 2.9% less of the still unimportant information on the second attempt. This difference was significant, $F(1, 35) = 9.57$, $p < .01$. Neither the particular perspective, $F < 1.00$, nor the interaction between perspective and whether or not there was a shift in perspective, $F = 1.12$, had an effect. Completed also was a subsidiary analysis, involving just the group that shifted perspective, evaluating the increment in recall observed in this group against the null hypothesis of zero change, which was also significant, $t(18) = 3.07$, $p < .01$.

It is also predicted that people who shift perspective will recall less information that is unimportant to the new perspective. In fact, subjects who changed perspective recalled a mean of 7.2% less on the second recall of what was now unimportant information whereas there was no change in the control group which maintained the same perspective. However, this differ-

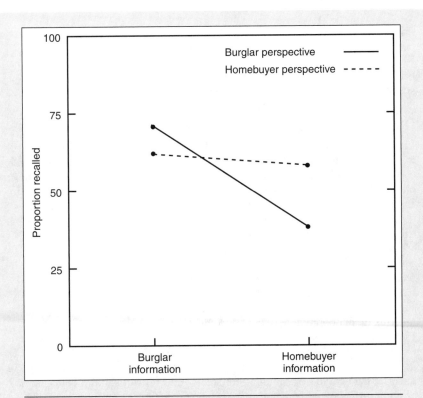

FIGURE 1   **Proportion of perspective-relevant and perspective-irrelevant information recalled on the first test.**

ence was not significant, $F(1, 35) = 2.22$, $p < .15$. Nor was the decrement in the group that changed perspective significantly different from zero, $t(18) = 2.06$, $.05 < p < .10$. The increment and decrement in the perspective shift group were the same size, but the latter result was not significant because of the relatively greater variability in the amount of information subjects lost.

Second Recall.   Considered alone, the data from the second recall are not very interesting. Tests for retrieval effects, much less sensitive than the ones involving first recall–second recall differences already reported, proved to be nonsignificant.

If perspective influences the likelihood that information will be stored, then on the second attempt subjects should have recalled more information important than unimportant to their original perspective. However, the present experiment was not optimally designed to assess encoding benefits, since subjects will have selectively rehearsed more of the information important to the original perspective on the first test. Balancing in the other direction, the experiment had too little power considering the magnitude of the error variance. For what it is worth, on the second attempt more information important to the original perspective was recalled than information unimportant to that perspective, an advantage that was not significant, $t(35) = 1.99$, $.05 < p < .10$.

DISCUSSION

d₁
In the present studies people recalled additional, previously unrecalled information following a shift in perspective. There was a significant increase in recall of information important to the new perspective but unimportant to the one operative when the passage was read. It would appear to be impossible to explain this phenomenon in terms of an encoding process, since the perspective shift occurred after the passage had been read and recalled once. A retrieval process seems to be implicated, therefore.

On the basis of previous research there is good reason to believe that schemata also affect encoding or storage processes but, as already noted, the recall data from the present studies did not permit a sensitive, unconfounded test of possible encoding benefits. The interview protocols, however, clearly suggest that readers selectively attend to elements of a story that are significant in terms of an operative perspective. Appropriately designed experiments would probably show evidence in recall of both encoding and retrieval effects.

d₂
One caveat about encoding seems well founded on the basis of the data in hand. Readers must have developed a richer representation for the story material than could be accounted for solely in terms of the dominant schema brought into play by the perspective instructions. Otherwise there would have been no information in the recesses of the mind which could be recovered when the perspective shifted. Evidently the principle of encoding specificity does not extend in a simple way to prose for, if it did, readers would fail to assimilate ideas irrelevant to the dominant schema. It appears, instead, that at least some "irrelevant" information is encoded, and that this information may become available later if a schema to which it connects is invoked.

Among the retrieval explanations for the increment in recall, subjects' self-reports supported the idea that a high-level schema provides the rememberer with a retrieval plan. Seven subjects described a process that fits this hypothesis. They said that they thought of particular information because the perspective led them to think of the general category subsuming this information. Six other subjects, who displayed less metamemorial awareness, made statements consistent with the retrieval plan hypothesis.

d₃
A plausible alternative explanation of the fact that subjects recalled previously unrecalled information is that they edited their output accord-

Discussion

First, the authors clearly state the overall results of their research **(d₁)**. Next, they offer a caution in interpretation **(d₂)**, an alternative explanation **(d₃)**, as well as

d_4

ing to shifting criteria of importance. d_4 Information remembered during the first recall might have been suppressed because it was unimportant to the perspective operative at that time. By and large, the protocol data were not consistent with this interpretation. Most subjects insisted that on the first recall they wrote down everything they could remember.

The recall data also showed decreased recall of information unimportant to the second perspective, again a fact consistent with either a retrieval plan, an output editing, or a reconstructive process. Regrettably, the interviewer did not systematically press subjects to explain why information included in the first protocol did not appear in the second. Nonetheless, it came out in a couple of cases that persons did not bother to write down information unimportant to the second perspective; in other words, they were editing their output.

d_5

Psychologists will have varying degrees of enthusiasm for the method of attempting to illuminate a process by the simple expedient of having subjects talk about it. We find compelling the argument that there is no good a priori reason to suppose that when a person tells you his mind worked in such and such a way that he is mistaken or lying. Many subjects told us that a perspective provided them with a plan for searching memory, specifically that considering the generic concerns of a burglar or homebuyer allowed them to access information relevant to these concerns. Naturally, converging evidence should be sought using other techniques. In the meantime, these self-reports make a prima facie case for the schema as retrieval plan. The self-reports weighed against the notion that the schema mediated editing of responses. However, this evidence should be interpreted conservatively. People are marvelously versatile information processors. If one believes the subjects' self-reports, most of them did not consciously edit their output when recalling the story for the first time. But they might under other circumstances. Indeed, some of them may have done so when recalling the story for the second time in the present studies.

Little has been said about the reconstructive interpretation of the increment in recall following a perspective shift, for the simple reason that the present data weigh neither for nor against this interpretation. We can only say that the variant of the reconstruction hypothesis which would attribute the increment to plausible fabrications seems unreasonable. Simple guessing is unlikely to have allowed subjects to produce the information that Mother was never home on Thursdays or that the roof leaked.

REFERENCES

Anderson, R. C., Pichert, J. W., Goetz, E. T., Schallert, D. L., Stevens, K. V., & Trollip, S. R. Instantiation of general terms. *Journal of Verbal Learning and Verbal Behavior,* 1976, *15,* 667–679.

evidence discounting this possible alternative explanation **(d_4)**. Finally, they address potential concerns regarding their method **(d_5)**.

Anderson, R. C., Spiro, R. J., & Anderson, M. C. *Schemata as scaffolding for the representation of information in connected discourse.* (Tech. Report No. 24). Urbana, Ill.: Center for the Study of Reading, University of Illinois, March 1977.

Ausubel, D. P. *The psychology of meaningful verbal learning.* New York: Grune and Stratton, 1963.

Bartlett, F. C. *Remembering.* Cambridge, England: The Cambridge University Press, 1932.

Binet, A., & Henri, V. La memoire des phrases. *L'année Psychologique.* 1894, *1,* 24–59.

Bower, G. H. *Comprehending and recalling stories.* Division 3 Presidential Address, Annual Meeting of the American Psychological Association, Washington, D.C., 1976.

Bower, G. H. Experiments on story understanding and recall. *Quarterly Journal of Experimental Psychology,* 1977, *28,* 511–534.

Bransford, J. D., & Johnson, M. K. Considerations of some problems of comprehension. In W. G. Chase (Ed.), *Visual information processing.* New York: Academic Press, 1973.

Brown, A. L., & Smiley, S. S. Rating the importance of structural units of prose passages: A problem of metacognitive development. *Child Development,* 1977, *48,* 1–8.

Cawalti, J. G. *Adventure, mystery, and romance.* Chicago: University of Chicago Press, 1976.

Dooling, D. J., & Lachman, R. Effects of comprehension on retention of prose. *Journal of Experimental Psychology,* 1971, *88,* 216–222.

Frederiksen, C. H. Effects of context induced processing operations on semantic information acquired from discourse. *Cognitive Psychology,* 1975, *7,* 139–166.

French, J. W., Ekstrom, R. B., & Price, L. A. *Kit of reference tests for cognitive factors.* Princeton, N.J.: Educational Testing Service, 1963.

Grimes, J. *The thread of discourse.* The Hague: Mouton, 1975.

Kintsch, W. *The representation of meaning in memory.* Hillsdale, N.J.: Erlbaum, 1974.

Mandler, J. M., & Johnson, N. S. Remembrance of things parsed: Story structure and recall. *Cognitive Psychology,* 1977, *9,* 111–151.

Mellard, J. Prolegomena to a study of the popular mode in narratives. *Journal of Popular Culture,* 1972, *6,* 1–19.

Meyer, B. J. F. *The organization of prose and its effects on memory.* Amsterdam: North-Holland, 1975.

Minsky, M. A framework for representing knowledge. In P. H. Winston (Ed.), *The psychology of computer vision.* New York: McGraw-Hill, 1975.

Newman, E. B. Forgetting of meaningful material during sleep and waking. *American Journal of Psychology,* 1939, *52,* 65–71.

Pichert, J. W., & Anderson, R. C. Taking different perspectives on a story. *Journal of Educational Psychology,* 1977, *69,* 309–315.

Royer, J. M. Comments on Professor Spiro's paper. In R. C. Anderson, R. J. Spiro, and W. E. Montague (Eds.), *Schooling and the acquisition of knowledge*. Hillsdale, N.J.: Erlbaum, 1977.

Rumelhart, D. E. Notes on a schema for stories. In D. Bobrow & A. Collins (Eds.), *Representation and understanding: Studies in cognitive science*. New York: Academic Press, 1975.

Rumelhart, D. E., & Ortony, A. The representation of knowledge in memory. In R. C. Anderson, R. J. Spiro, & W. E. Montague (Eds.), *Schooling and the acquisition of knowledge*. Hillsdale, N.J.: Erlbaum, 1977.

Schank, R., & Abelson, R. P. Scripts, plans, and knowledge. *Proceedings of the Fourth International Joint Conference on Artificial Intelligence*. Tblisi, Georgia: U.S.S.R., 1975.

Spiro, R. J. Remembering information from text: Theoretical and empirical issues concerning the 'State of Schema' reconstruction hypothesis. In R. C. Anderson, R. J. Spiro, & W. E. Montague (Eds.), *Schooling and the acquisition of knowledge*. Hillsdale, N.J.: Erlbaum, 1977.

Thieman, T. J., & Brewer, W. J. Alfred Binet on memory for ideas. *Genetic Psychology Monographs,* in press.

Van Dijk, T. *Some aspects of text grammars*. The Hague: Mouton, 1972.

Note: Address requests for reprints to Dr. Richard C. Anderson, Center for the Study of Reading, 51 Gerty Drive, Illinois 61820. The research reported herein was supported in part by the National Institute of Education under Contract No. MS-NIE-C-400-76-0116 and Grant No. HEW-NIE-G-74-0007. The authors wish to thank Larry Shirey for his assistance in interviewing subjects and scoring recall protocols and Andrew Ortony and Rand Spiro for their helpful comments on a draft of this paper.

Questions

1. The instructions were effective at inducing the role?
2. If you wanted to replicate this study, would you be able to given the information in the Method section? If you needed further information, what could you do?
3. Can you think of a way that the authors could have induced the schemas of burglar or homeowner, without assigning the subjects to those roles?
4. To what extent do you think this "role playing" affected the results? In what way?
5. Why did the authors think it important to have the subjects engage in the 5-minute task of mentally "folding" the two-dimensional figure?
6. Is there another theory that could explain these results differently or better than schema theory? Do your own literature review to find possible alternative explanations.

19 Therapy for Anger

Introduction

In our contemporary society, stress and anger are often apparent. The normal stressors that we encounter in daily living cause irritations, which frequently are manifested in anger. In this article, Raymond Novaco (1977) studies "anger disorders" and their treatment.

Several important problems encountered in research in clinical psychology are introduced in this article. Be aware of what those problems might be.

Special Issues

SINGLE-SUBJECT DESIGN IN CLINICAL STUDIES

In this study, only one subject was used. In other parts of this book we have discussed small *n* designs (see Chapter 17). Studies using a single subject present special problems. In these experiments, measurements are taken before and after the introduction of the independent variable, meaning the contrasts are made during different periods of time. During the initial period, careful measures are made to establish a base rate (or baseline) of the behavioral characteristics that exist before the introduction of the independent variable. These behavioral characteristics may be measured by multidimensional scales that measure several behavioral traits. If a researcher is interested in the emotional changes that occur after the introduction of an independent variable—say, the injection of a mood-altering drug—the baseline might include a description of several characteristics, such as expression of happiness, spontaneity, and sociability. After the introduction of the independent variable, in this case the mood-altering drug, subsequent evaluations on the same multidimensional characteristics are made.

These measures are contrasted with baseline data and constitute the main effect of the study.

Because individual differences play a critical role in single-subject designs, a thorough description of the subject is necessary. In research involving psychotherapy, this description includes a "case history," which we can see in this study by Novaco. The author reviews the clinical background of the subject, which includes a history of the subject's work situation, symptoms, hospitalization, reaction to stressful situations, and previous treatment. Identifying these characteristics is particularly important in clinical studies, as they provide the reader with a background upon which to base further generalization of the treatment.

STRESS INOCULATION: A COGNITIVE THERAPY FOR ANGER AND ITS APPLICATION TO A CASE OF DEPRESSION

Raymond W. Novaco
University of California, Irvine

Clinical interventions for anger disorders have been scarcely addressed in both theory and research in psychotherapy. The continued development of a cognitive behavior therapy approach to anger management is presented along with the results of its application to a hospitalized depressive with severe anger problems. The treatment approach follows a procedure called "stress inoculation," which consists of three basic stages: cognitive preparation, skill acquisition and rehearsal, and application practice. The relationship between anger and depression is discussed.

a

The treatment of anger-based disorders has escaped the attention of both psychotherapy theory and research. This is a puzzling state of affairs when one considers the abundance of laboratory research on aggression. An approach to the treatment of chronic anger and its experimental analysis has been presented by Novaco (1975). Although scattered reports of circumscribed interventions with anger exist (Herrell, 1971; Kaufmann & Wagner, 1972; Rimm, deGroot, Boord, Reiman, & Dillow, 1971), there is a distinct need for concerted work in this area. In an effort to promote a more detailed conception of anger problems and of therapeutic interventions for anger, the present article describes the further development of a cognitive behavior therapy and presents the results of its application to a hospitalized depressive with severe anger problems.

Persons having serious problems with anger control have been successfully treated by a cognitive behavior therapy approach (Novaco, 1975, 1976). In the present article, this treatment approach has been further developed to

Source: This article is abridged and reprinted by permission from *Journal of Consulting and Clinical Psychology,* 1977, *45,* 600–608, and from the author.

Analysis

Literature Review

The first paragraph **(a)** is an excellent example of an introductory statement. The author shows the need for the experiment, hints as to the treatment, and suggests how such results may be applied. Note that a formal hypothesis is not stated. This represents a departure from most of the previous studies analyzed in this book, but the practice is not erroneous. The author has provided sufficient detail for the reader to infer the hypothesis without formally stating it.

follow a procedure called *stress inoculation* that has been applied to problems of anxiety (Meichenbaum, 1975; Meichenbaum & Cameron, [Reference] Note 1) and pain (Turk, [Reference] Note 2). The stress inoculation therapy consists of developing the client's cognitive, affective, and behavioral-coping skills and then providing for the practice of these skills with exposure to regulated doses of stressors that arouse but do not overwhelm the client's defenses. The stress inoculation approach involves three basic steps or phases: (a) cognitive preparation, (b) skill acquisition and rehearsal, and (c) application practice. This approach to anger problems was first developed by me with regard to the training of police officers (Novaco, in press). The present article describes the further development of this approach as a clinical procedure and its application to the anger problems of a depressed patient in an acute psychiatric ward.

METHOD

Treatment Procedure

b ***Cognitive Preparation.*** The initial phase educates clients about the functions of anger and about their personal anger patterns, provides for a shared language system between client and therapist, and introduces the rationale of the treatment approach. This process is facilitated through an instructional manual for clients.[1] The text of the manual describes the nature and functions of anger, when anger becomes a problem, what causes anger, and how anger can be regulated.

The components of the cognitive preparation phase are (a) identifying the persons and situations that trigger anger; (b) fostering recognition of the difference between anger and aggression; (c) understanding the cognitive, somatic, and behavioral determinants of anger, with particular emphasis on anger-instigating self-statements; (d) discriminating justified from unnecessary anger; (e) recognizing the signs of tension and arousal early in a provocation sequence; and (f) introducing the anger management concepts as coping strategies.

c ***Skill Acquisition and Rehearsal.*** The process of skill acquisition involves a familiarization with the three sets of coping techniques, modeling of the techniques by the therapist, and then rehearsal by the client. At the cognitive

---

[1]The client instructional manual and the therapist treatment procedure manual may be obtained from the author.

Method

In the introduction, the author defines the "stress inoculation" approach, and in sections **(b)**, **(c)**, and **(d)** he describes the stages of this approach. Of special interest is his attempt operationally to define the concepts, thus allowing subsequent investigators to replicate the study. Notice the components of cognitive preparation

(analysis continues on page 303)

level, the client is taught how to alternatively view situations of provocation by changing personal constructs (Kelly, 1955) and by modifying the exaggerated importance often attached to events (Ellis, 1973).

Two central cognitive devices for anger regulation are a task orientation to provocation and coping self-statements. A task orientation involves attending to desired outcomes and implementing a behavioral strategy directed at producing these outcomes. Self-instructions are used to modify the appraisal of provocation and to guide coping behavior. Pragmatically, the self-instructions are designed to apply to various stages of a provocation sequence: (a) preparing for a provocation, (b) impact and confrontation, (c) coping with arousal, and (d) subsequent reflection in which the conflict is either unresolved or resolved. Stages (c) and (d) provide for the possible failure of self-regulation and for the prolongation or reinstigation of arousal by ruminations.

At the affective level, the client is taught relaxation skills and is also encouraged to maintain a sense of humor as a response that competes with anger.

Relaxation training was conducted via the Jacobsen method of tensing and relaxing sequential sets of muscle groups. Mental as well as physical relaxation is emphasized, as relaxation imagery is used to induce a light somnambulistic state. Deep breathing exercises supplement the muscle tension procedures. Previous research (Novaco, 1975) has found that the cognitive-coping component is comparatively more effective than the relaxation-training component. However, relaxation training enables the client to become aware of the tension and agitation that lead to anger and provides an important sense of mastery over troublesome internal states.

The behavioral goals of treatment are to promote the effective communication of feelings, assertive behavior, and the implementation of task-oriented, problem-solving action. Generally speaking, the client is induced to use anger in a way that maximizes its adaptive functions and minimizes its maladaptive functions (Novaco, 1976). Among the positive functions of anger are its energizing effects, the sense of control that it potentiates, and its value as a cue to cope with the problem situation.

The therapeutic procedure enables clients to recognize anger and its source in the environment and to then communicate that anger in a nonhostile form. This controls the accumulation of anger, prevents an aggressive overreaction, and provides a basis for changing the situation that caused the anger.

Inducing a task-oriented response set facilitates the occurrence of problem-solving behavior. It is emphasized that anger is an emotional reaction to stress or conflict that is due to external events being at variance with one's liking. Poor behavioral adjustment is linked to the inability to provide problem-solving responses that are effective in achieving desired goals (Platt & Spivack, 1972; Shure & Spivack, 1972). Anger management involves a strategic confrontation whereby the person learns to focus on issues and objectives. The execution of such behavior is explicitly prompted and progressively directed by the use of coping self-statements.

d   ***Application Practice.***   The value of application practice has been emphasized by a variety of skills-training approaches (D'Zurilla & Goldfried, 1971;

Meichenbaum, 1975; Richardson, 1973; Suinn & Richardson, 1971). The regulation of anger is a function of one's ability to manage a provocative situation, and in this treatment phase, clients are given an opportunity to test their proficiency. The client is exposed to manageable doses of anger stimuli by means of imaginal and role-playing inductions. The content of the simulations is constructed from a hierarchy of anger situations that the client is likely to encounter in real life. By progressively working on each hierarchy scene, first imaginally and then by role playing, the client is enabled to sharpen anger management skills that had been rehearsed with the therapist.

Case History

The client was a 38-year-old male who had been admitted to the psychiatric ward of a community hospital with the diagnosis of depressive neurosis. Upon admission he was judged to be grossly depressed, having suicidal ruminations and progressive beliefs of worthlessness and inadequacy. He was a credit manager for a national business firm and had been under considerable job pressure. Quite routinely, he developed headaches by midafternoon at work. He had recurrent left anterior chest pain that was diagnosed by a treadmill stress test procedure as due to muscle tension.

Their client had been hospitalized for 3 weeks when the attending psychiatrist referred him to me for the treatment of anger problems. At that time I had initiated a staff training program for the treatment of anger. The principal behavior setting in which problems with anger control emerged were at work, at home, and at church. The client was married and had six children, one of which was hyperactive.

Circumstances at work had progressively generated anger and hostility for this man's superiors, colleagues, and supervisees. His anger at work was typically overcontrolled. He would actively suppress his anger and would then periodically explode with a verbal barrage of epithets, curses, and castigations when a conflict arose. At home, he was more impulsively aggressive. The accumulated tensions and frustrations at work resulted in his being highly prone to provocation at home, particularly in response to the disruptive behavior of the children. Noise, disorders, and the frequent fights among the children were high anger elicitors. Unlike his behavior at work, he would quickly express his anger in verbal and physical outbursts. Although not an abusive parent, he

(a) through (f) in section **(b)** and the various stages of a provocation sequence in (a) through (d) in section **(c)**.

Case History.   Single-subject studies, especially those of a clinical nature, typically involve a comprehensive case history in which the salient psychological characteristics of the subject are documented **(e)**. The case history is designed to reveal the basic descriptive facts of the subject but not to interpret these facts. The writing style is clear, concise, and without embellishment.

would readily resort to physical means and threats of force (e.g., "I'll knock your goddamn head off") as a way to control the behavior of his children. The children's unruly behavior often became a problem during church services. The client's former training in a seminary disposed him to value family attendance at church, but serious conflict was often the result. In an incident just prior to hospitalization, the client abruptly removed two of his boys from church for creating a disturbance and threatened them to the extent that one ran away. At this point he had begun to realize that he was reacting "out of proportion," but he felt helpless about instituting the desired changes in behavior.

During hospitalization, treatment sessions were conducted three times per week for 3½ weeks. Following discharge, follow-up sessions were conducted biweekly for a 2-month period. During these sessions, anger diary incidents were discussed, and there was continued modeling, rehearsal, and practice of coping procedures.

Dependent Measures

f

Proneness to provocation was first assessed by means of an inventory of 80 situation descriptions for which the respondent rates anger on a 5-point scale. This is a revised version of the instrument reported in Novaco (1975). The current scale has been found to have a high degree of internal consistency across various subject populations.

g

Behavior ratings were obtained by a clinical psychologist with 9 years of postdoctoral experience. Dichotomous ratings were obtained on 14 behavior descriptions indexing the expression of anger (e.g., impatient with others, expresses resentment toward others, threatens to harm someone, quick to react with antagonism) and 8 behavioral descriptions indexing constructive coping and improvement (e.g., humorous and good natured, optimistic about future, tolerant and considerate of others, deals with conflict constructively, is positively assertive). Scaled ratings were obtained on three behavioral dimensions: (a) "The person is relaxed and at ease," (b) "the person demonstrates hostility or anger (expressed anger)," and (c) "the person is restraining anger and resentment (suppressed anger)." These items were rated on 8-point scales ranging from "not at all" to "exactly so" verbally anchored at each interval point.

h

The reliability of the behavior ratings for the dichotomous items was examined for behavior in group therapy, occupational therapy, and recreation for a total of nine observation periods with an average of eight patients observed in each setting. Four psychiatric nurses with an average of 6 years of experience served as the raters along with the clinical

Dependent Measures

Measurement of a person's response in a clinical study frequently poses a problem of objectivity. What indices of reduced anger could be used that would reflect a valid measure of emotional change and yet could be used by subsequent researchers in a replication of the study? The author is very specific in identifying the special tests (f) and behavioral ratings (g and i). Furthermore, in (h) the

psychologist. The mean percentage of agreement was 84.6% for each pair of raters on the 22 items. For the 3 scaled items, the ratings of the psychologist were correlated with those of three psychiatric nurses who, respectively, observed the patient in three group therapy sessions. The average correlations were .7581 for Item 1, .8593 for Item 2, and .6621 for Item 3. Thus, greatest consistency was obtained for ratings of "expressed anger" and least consistency for ratings of "suppressed anger." The psychologist's ratings were also correlated with the patient's ratings of himself for behavior in group therapy, which resulted in correlations of .9242, .6770, and .7521 for the respective items. The judgments of this observer were concluded to be sufficiently reliable for the present case analysis.

Self-monitoring of anger reactions by the patient is integral to the treatment procedure, as in other self-control therapies (Mahoney & Thoresen, 1974). The patient was asked to maintain a diary of anger experiences for which two ratings on a 7-point scale were obtained—(a) the degree of anger arousal experienced and (b) the degree of anger management achieved. Although the reduction in frequency and intensity of anger is a central goal of treatment, it is assumed that in certain instances, the arousal of anger is justified and appropriate. Therefore, it is also important to assess the degree to which anger regulation resulted in a constructive response to provocation. This patient's anger experiences were concentrated at home and at work. Only rarely was he provoked while in the hospital. Hence, the self-ratings were obtained for weekend home visits while on pass from the hospital and then on a daily basis following discharge and return to work.

RESULTS

Pretreatment assessment of the patient's proneness to provocation by means of the anger inventory resulted in a total inventory score of 301. At discharge, the inventory was readministered and a total score of 258 was obtained. This decrease of 43 points represents a decrease of greater than 1 standard deviation

reliability of the ratings is assessed. The patient also monitored his own anger response **(j)**.

One may argue that the dependent measures in this experiment lack the objectivity of measures made in some nonclinical experiments. For example, the dependent measure of a rat pressing a bar in a Skinner box leaves little room for ambiguity. Judgments about emotional states in clinical research can also achieve a high degree of objectivity; one just needs to specify, as completely as possible, the measurement instruments and their validity.

k | based on the recent random college sample and on the chronic anger clients of previous research. It also is comparable to the change obtained on this instrument for subjects in a controlled treatment design (Novaco, 1975).

l | Continuous measures of change were obtained from the behavior rating scales and from the client's self-ratings. Behavior ratings of anger were obtained during group therapy. Since the patient had already been in the hospital for 3 weeks prior to the referral for treatment, only a 1-week baseline could be obtained. **Results for the behavior description measures and for the scaled ratings of affect are contained in Figure 1.** It can be seen that over the course of treatment, the patient underwent improvement on each index. The number of positive behavior descriptions endorsed and the scaled judgments of relaxed appearance increased over time, whereas antagonistic behav-

m | ior and judgments of demonstrated and suppressed anger decreased. **After the third week of treatment, the attending psychiatrist, the staff, and the patient concurred in the decision for discharge.**

Convergent evidence of the patient's improvement was obtained from the self-monitored ratings of anger and anger management. Data were recorded on a weekend pass during the hospitalization period and on a continuous daily

n | basis after discharge. **Results for the 60 days of recorded self-monitoring for frequency, degree of anger, and degree of control are contained in Figure 2.** The first 15 days of observation represent 5 weekends during the hospitalization period. As previously indicated, little anger was experienced with regard to events in the hospital environment, and these data are not plotted.

In the absence of a more satisfactory baseline period (which could not be extended due to the patient's length of stay in an acute facility prior to referral for treatment), changes in behavior must be examined as treatment progresses. On the weekend prior to treatment, the mean frequency was 4.0 per day, and by the patient's report this was quite standard. It can be seen that the mean frequency of anger incidents decreased from 1.55 per day during the first 20-day period to 1.10 per day for the second 20-day interval, and to .40 per day for the third interval. The mean anger magnitude ratings for the intervals were 4.30, 4.62, and 4.25, whereas the mean ratings of anger management were 4.30, 4.97, and 4.50, respectively. This indicates that when he did

Results

In this section, a comparison is made between the inventory scale given during pretreatment and the scale given at discharge **(k)**. The results are also presented in Figure 1 **(l)**. In this figure the researcher has shown five different measures of the patient's behavior for anger and anger management. Study the relationship between "relaxed" behavior and "restrained anger" in this curve.

In section **(m)** we learn that the psychiatrist, the staff, and the patient decided the patient should be discharged.

The long-term effects of the treatment are shown in **(n)** and in Figure 2.

(analysis continues on page 308)

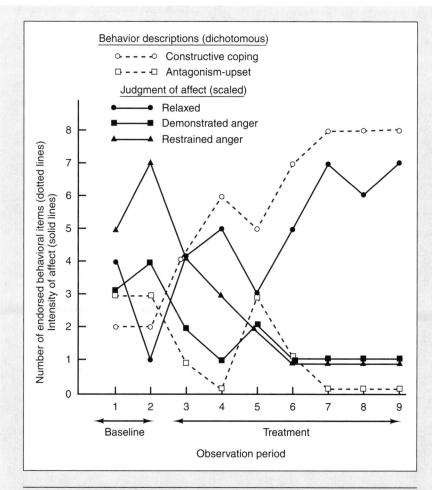

FIGURE 1   **Clinician's ratings of patient's behavior for anger and anger management during hospitalization.**

become angry, the degree of regulation was commensurate with or greater than the degree of arousal. It should also be noted that incidents of high achievement in self-control were occasionally not recorded by the client, who, like many depressives, was reluctant to "make too much" of his accomplishments. Hence, he periodically neglected to record an incident of high control and low anger. Although ratings were unfortunately not obtained from his wife, she consistently remarked that he was showing progressive improvement, in marked contrast to his previous behavior.

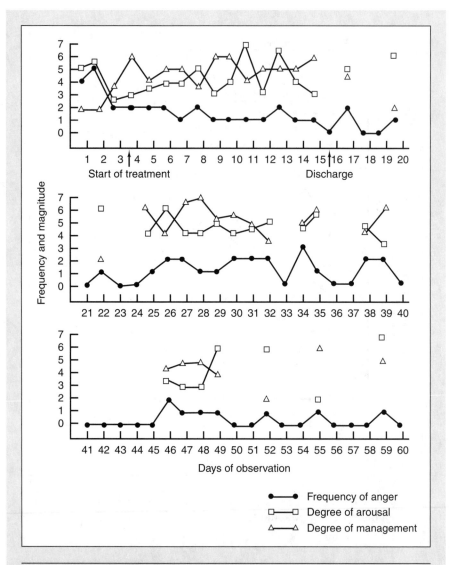

FIGURE 2   **Self-monitored ratings of frequency of anger, magnitude of anger, and degree of anger management.**

Among the most apparent and important behavioral changes achieved was the reduction of impulsive aggression as a punitive response to disruptive behavior by the children. During the treatment period numerous incidents of

o

In section (**o**) the author gives a very personal insight into the success of the treatment and the severity of the original problem.

physical fighting among the boys were recorded in the diary as having aroused anger. There were 10 recorded incidents in the home, 5 in the car, and 2 in church. Considering the latter two settings, one can appreciate the magnitude of the disturbance and its potential impact. The incidents described as having occurred in the car, for example, were indeed unnerving. Fist fights between the boys resulted in bleeding mouths, black eyes, and lumps on the head. In one instance, a weight-lifting bar was used as a weapon. Despite the magnitude of these disturbances, the client only struck his children three times during the 3-month treatment period. Prior to treatment it had been quite routine for him to hit the boys in response to fighting or prephysical quarrels.

DISCUSSION

The self-regulation of anger is an important facet of the ability to cope with stress. The present article has reported the continued development of a cognitive behavior therapy approach to the treatment of anger problems and the extension of these procedures to a hospitalized depressed patient. **The stress inoculation model, first developed by Meichenbaum (1975), has been extended to the domain of anger and has been shown to be effective with someone having a severe psychological disturbance.**

The severity of the clinical problem is a nontrivial factor. That this factor is not to be overlooked is demonstrated by comparing the length of treatment in the present case with that of previous controlled research. In the clinical sample investigated by Novaco (1975), extensive pretreatment assessment eliminated all but those subjects having serious anger problems. Novaco (1975), however, used an outpatient sample, and significant results were achieved in 6 treatment sessions. Yet in the present case, comparable results required 11 sessions in the hospital and 4 as an outpatient. In addition, the clinical procedures had improved, an instructional manual had been incorporated, and relaxation therapy was available on a daily basis by tape. In the present case the severity of the anger problem was interlocked and compounded with the psychological deficits associated with depression.

REFERENCE NOTES

1. Meichenbaum, D., & Cameron, R. (1973). *Stress inoculation: A skills training approach to anxiety management.* Unpublished manuscript, University of Waterloo, Ontario, Canada.
2. Turk, D. (1974). *Cognitive control of pain: A skills-training approach.* Unpublished manuscript, University of Waterloo, Ontario, Canada.

Discussion

In keeping with the format outlined in this book, the author discusses his research in the context of a theoretical issue raised in the introduction **(p)**.

REFERENCES

D'Zurilla, T., & Goldfried, M. (1971). Problem solving and behavior modification. *Journal of Abnormal Psychology, 78,* 107–126.

Ellis, A. (1973). *Humanistic psychology: The rational–emotive approach.* New York: Julian Press.

Feshbach, N. D. (1975). Empathy in children: Some theoretical and empirical considerations. *Counseling Psychologist, 5,* 25–30.

Herrell, J. M. (1971). Use of systematic desensitization to eliminate inappropriate anger. *Proceedings of the 79th Annual Convention of the American Psychological Association, 6,* 431–432. (Summary)

Kaufmann, L., & Wagner, B. (1972). Barb: A systematic treatment technology for temper control disorders. *Behavior Therapy, 3,* 84–90.

Kelly, G. A. (1955). *The psychology of personal constructs* (Vol. 2). New York: Norton.

Meichenbaum, D. A. (1975). Self-instructional approach to stress management: A proposal for stress inoculation training. In C. Spielberger & I. Sarason (Eds.), *Stress and anxiety* (Vol. 2). New York: Wiley.

Novaco, R. W. (1974). The treatment of anger through cognitive and relaxation controls. *Journal of Consulting and Clinical Psychology, 44,* 681.

Novaco, R. W. (1975). *Anger control: The development and evaluation of an experimental treatment.* Lexington, Mass.: Lexington Books.

Novaco, R. W. (1976). The functions and regulation of the arousal of anger. *American Journal of Psychiatry, 133,* 1124–1128.

Novaco, R. W. (In press). A stress inoculation approach to anger management in the training of law enforcement officers. *American Journal of Community Psychology.*

Platt, J. J., & Spivack, G. (1972). Problem-solving thinking of psychiatric patients. *Journal of Consulting and Clinical Psychology, 39,* 148–151.

Richardson, F. (1973). A self-study manual for students on coping with test-taking anxiety. (Tech. Rep. No. 25) Austin: University of Texas Press.

Rimm, D. C., deGroot, J. C., Boord, P., Reiman, J., & Dillow, P. V. (1971). Systemic desensitization of an anger response. *Behavior Research and Therapy, 9,* 273–280.

Shure, M. B., & Spivack, G. (1972). Means-ends thinking, adjustment, and social class among elementary-school-aged children. *Journal of Consulting and Clinical Psychology, 38,* 348–353.

Suinn, R., & Richardson, F. (1971). Anxiety management training: A nonspecific behavior therapy program for anxiety control. *Behavior Therapy, 2,* 498–510.

Weissman, M. M., Klerman, G. L., & Paykel, E. S. (1971). Clinical evaluation of hostility in depression. *American Journal of Psychiatry, 128,* 261–266.

Note: Requests for reprints should be sent to Raymond W. Novaco, Program in Social Ecology, University of California, Irvine, California 92717.

Questions

1. Discuss the special problems in developing objective dependent measures in clinical research.
2. The results are not discussed in terms of statistical probability. Why not?
3. Why were pretreatment measures made?
4. Why did the investigator choose to use multidimensional measures of behavior?
5. What precautions were undertaken to assure the objectivity of behavioral ratings?
6. Why is a detailed case history part of this study?
7. What special ethical issues are raised by this study?

20 Prosocial Behavior

Introduction

A topic that continues to be of interest to psychologists is the effect of television viewing on children's behavior. The average American child spends more hours per week watching television than attending school, and educators have suggested that television may have replaced school as the primary "socializing" influence outside of the family.

The effects of television on children's behavior has been the subject of numerous psychological experiments, governmental studies, and congressional investigations. Most of this effort has centered on whether television violence leads to violence in society. Less often studied is whether television can lead to *prosocial behaviors,* which are behaviors that are believed to benefit others, such as helping people in distress.

This article (Sprafkin, Liebert, & Poulos, 1975) presents an experimental study of the effect of television viewing on prosocial behavior. We have left this case for your analysis.

EFFECTS OF A PROSOCIAL TELEVISED EXAMPLE ON CHILDREN'S HELPING

Joyce N. Sprafkin, Robert M. Liebert, and Rita Wicks Poulos
State University of New York at Stony Brook

The possibility that regularly broadcast entertainment television programs can facilitate prosocial behavior in children was investigated. Thirty first-grade children, 15 boys and 15 girls, were individually exposed to one of three half-hour television programs: a program from the Lassie *series which included a dramatic example of a boy helping a dog, a program from the* Lassie *series devoid of such an example, or a program from the family situation comedy series* The Brady Bunch. *The effects of the programming were assessed by presenting each child with a situation that required him to choose between continuing to play a game for self-gain and helping puppies in distress. Children exposed to the* Lassie *program with the helping scene helped for significantly more time than those exposed to either of the other programs.*

Since its spectacular rise as an entertainment medium in the 1950s, television's possible effects on the behavior of the young has captured the interest of many investigators. Throughout the years the most compelling question has remained the possible detrimental effects of violent programming, resulting in considerable knowledge of the influence of televised aggression (e.g., Liebert, Neale, & Davidson, 1973). Remarkably little is known, on the other hand, about the degree to which the medium might also inculcate prosocial attitudes and behaviors. The present report is concerned with this latter issue.

That certain commercially broadcast programs may serve as positive socializers is suggested by numerous investigations employing specially prepared programming presented in a television format. Such studies have shown that modeling cues provided by a television set can increase the generosity of young observers (Bryan, 1970), foster adherence to rules (Stein & Bryan, 1972; Wolf & Cheyne, 1972), augment delay of gratification (Yates, 1974), and facilitate positive interpersonal behaviors (O'Connor, 1969). Only one study, so far as we know, endeavored to determine the potential of *broadcast* televised materials for instigating prosocial forms of behavior in children. Over the course of 4 weeks, Stein and Friedrich (1973) exposed 3- to 5-year-olds to one of three television diets: aggressive (Batman and Superman cartoons), prosocial (episodes taken from *Mister Rogers' Neighborhood*), or neutral (such scenes as children working on a farm). Generally confirming earlier work, certain types of prosocial behavior were found to increase after

Source: Reprinted by permission from *Journal of Experimental Child Psychology,* 1975, *20,* 119–126.

exposure to the "Mister Rogers" program, relative to the other two types of input. In this important demonstration, as the investigators themselves indicated (Friedrich & Stein, 1973), it was not feasible to control for factors such as the format of the programs, the characters displayed, and the relative balance of entertainment vs. instructional components in each diet. Equally important, "Mister Rogers" is not a commercially produced network program and its direct, exhortative format also might serve to limit the size of its child audience.

In the experiment reported, we wished to determine whether the presence of a specific act of helping that appeared in a highly successful commercial series would induce similar behavior in young viewers when they later found themselves in a comparable situation. To control for various broad characteristics of the program, children in the two principal groups viewed one of two programs from the series Lassie, complete with commercial messages. The Lassie programs both featured the same canine and human main characters, took place in the same setting, apparently were written for the same audience, and presumably were motivated by the same entertainment and commercial interests. Whereas the programs necessarily differed somewhat in story line, the critical difference was that one of them had woven into it the particular prosocial example while the other did not. This combination of similarities and differences, it was reasoned, would optimize detecting the potential effect of specific modeling cues from entertainment television upon youngsters' later behavior. As a further comparison, a third group was also included, in which a generally pleasant situation comedy program, *The Brady Bunch,* was viewed.

METHOD

Design and Participants
A 3×2 factorial design was used, employing the television experience (observation of prosocial *Lassie,* neutral *Lassie,* or *Brady Bunch* program) and the sex differentiation of the subjects. The participants were 30 children, 15 boys and 15 girls, from four first-grade classes in middle-class, predominantly white suburban neighborhood. All prospective subjects were given forms to be signed by their parents authorizing their participation. The letter described the nature of the project, but requested parents to withhold this information from their children. Subjects were selected randomly from the pool of youngsters whose parents returned the consent forms; approximately 80% did so. Within each class and sex, the children were assigned randomly to the treatment conditions.

One experimenter escorted the child from the classroom to the television viewing room, conducted the screening of the videotape, and then brought the child to the second experimenter in an adjacent room. The second experimenter, who was blind to the treatment condition, administered the dependent measure. The former role was assumed by four graduate students over the course of the study; the latter role was always filled by the same 24-yr-old white, female graduate student.

APPARATUS AND MATERIALS

The television viewing room contained a black and white television monitor with a 9-in. screen, programmed by a hidden Sony video recorder. The experimental room, in which assessment was conducted, contained two pieces of apparatus: a Point Game and a Help button, separated by a distance of 5 ft and each placed on a child-size desk.

The Point Game consisted of a response key and a display box. The response key was a 1½ by ¼ in. rectangular blue button mounted on a 4 by 6½ in. inclined platform which served as a handrest. The display box was a 6 by 8 in. gray metal box on which a blue 15-W light bulb and a Cramer digital timer were mounted. The 10's and 1's columns of the timer were covered with black tape. When the button was pressed, the bulb lit and the timer was activated.

The Help button was a small, green, circular button mounted on a 7 by 5 in. gray metal box with the word "Help" printed in black letters directly below it. The Help button activated a second Cramer digital timer which was located outside the experimental room.

Earphones were located next to the game on the desk. They were connected via an extension cable to a tape recorder located outside the experimental room. The tape contained 30 sec of silence followed by 120 sec of dogs barking.

Procedure

Introduction to the Treatment Condition. The first experimenter escorted the child from the classroom to the television viewing room, which was a small classroom containing desks, chairs, and the videotape monitor. She told the child that he was going to play a game shortly, but that Miss [*the second experimenter*] was not ready for him yet. She then turned on the video recorder surreptitiously, turned on the monitor openly, and suggested that the child watch while she did some work in the back of the classroom. All children appeared quite interested in the half-hour programs and the experimenter worked busily to discourage the child from initiating conversation.

Experimental and Control Conditions. Children in the experimental condition viewed the prosocial Lassie program. The episode dealt largely with Lassie's efforts to hide her runt puppy so that it would not be given away. The story's climax occurred when the puppy slipped into a mining shaft and fell onto the ledge below. Unable to help, Lassie brought her master, Jeff, and Jeff's grandfather to the scene. Jeff then risked his life by hanging over the edge of the shaft to save the puppy. The selection of the program was based on the inclusion of this dramatic helping scene.

In one control condition, the neutral Lassie program was shown. Featuring the same major characters as the prosocial program, it dramatized Jeff's attempts to avoid taking violin lessons. It was devoid of any example of a human helping a dog, but necessarily featured the animal in a positive light.

In the second control condition, the youngsters viewed *The Brady Bunch,* a nonaggressive, nonanimated children's program which did not feature a dog. The program depicted the youngest Brady children's efforts to be important by trying to set a record for time spent on a seesaw. It provided a measure of children's willingness to help after exposure to a popular program that showed positive interpersonal family encounters but no cues pertinent to either human or canine heroism.

Assessment of Willingness to Help Puppies in Distress. Assessment consisted of placing the child in a situation that required him to choose between continuing to play a game for self-gain and trying to get help for puppies in distress.

1. *Introduction of the game.* After the television program was viewed, the first experimenter told the child that Miss [*the second experimenter*] was ready for him, escorted the child to the experimental room, performed appropriate introductions, and departed. The child was invited to play the Point Game in which he could earn points by pressing a button that lit a bulb. The number of points obtained was displayed on a timer visible to him. The experimenter showed the child a display of prizes, situated on two desks, that varied in size and attractiveness—from small, unappealing erasers to large, colorful board games. It was noted that "some prizes are bigger and better than others," and that "the more points you get in the game, the better your prize will be." The experimenter then told the child that she was going to let him play the game alone so that she could finish some work down the hall.

2. *Introduction of distress situation.* The experimenter started to leave, then returned and exclaimed:

> Oh, there's something else I'd like you to do while I'm gone. You see, I'm in charge of a dog kennel a few miles from here—that's a place that we keep puppies until a home can be found for them. I had to leave the puppies alone so that I could come here today, but I know whether the dogs are safe or not by listening through these earphones [indicating] which are connected to the kennel by wires. When I don't hear any noises through the earphones, I know the dogs are OK—they're either playing quietly or sleeping. But if I hear them barking, I know something is wrong. I know that they are in trouble and need help. If I hear barking, I press this button [indicating Help button], which signals my helper who lives near the kennel, and when he hears the signal, he goes over to the kennel to make sure nothing bad happened to the dogs.
>
> While I'm gone, I'd like you to wear the earphones for me while you play your game. If you don't hear any barking, everything is OK at the kennel; but if you hear barking, you can help the puppies if you want by pressing the Help button. You might have to press the button for a long time before my helper hears the signal, and there's a better chance he'll hear it if you press it a lot. You can tell when he has heard the signal when you hear the dogs stop barking.
>
> Remember, this game is over as soon as I come back—you won't be able to get any points after that. Try to get as many points as you can because the more points you get, the better your prize will be. You know, if the puppies

start barking, you'll have to choose between helping the puppies by pressing the Help button and getting more points for yourself by pressing the blue button. It's up to you.

After being assured that the child understood the situation, the experimenter placed the earphones on the child and left the room. When outside the experimental room, she immediately turned on the tape recorder and a stopwatch. The child first heard 30 sec of silence followed by 120 sec of increasingly frantic barking. The experimenter recorded the latency of helping, reentered the experimental room 60 sec after the cessation of barking, and awarded a prize that was loosely based on the number of points earned. After the child was escorted to his classroom, the total seconds of helping was recorded from the timer located outside the experimental room.

RESULTS AND DISCUSSION

The primary dependent measure was the number of seconds the Help button was pressed. The mean helping scores for all cells of the design, and the standard deviations for each, are shown in Table 1. A 3 (Treatment) 2 (Sex) analysis of variance of these scores yielded only one significant effect, for treatment conditions ($F \times 4.97$, $p < .025$); the main effect for Sex was not significant ($F = 2.18$). Dunnett's t tests revealed that subjects who saw the prosocial *Lassie* program helped significantly more than those in the neutral *Lassie* ($t = 2.08$, $p < .05$) or the *Brady Bunch* condition ($t = 2.79$, p .01). The latter groups did not differ from one another ($t = .66$).[1]

There was also a marginal tendency for sex and treatment condition to interact ($F = 2.80$, $p < .10$). As is apparent descriptively in Table 1, the effect

TABLE 1   **Means [and SD] of Helping Scores in Seconds for All Groups**

	SEX OF SUBJECT		
	Female	**Male**	**Combined**
Prosocial Lassie	105.48	79.80	92.64
	[20.37]	[47.38]	[36.94]
Neutral Lassie	34.80	68.20	51.50
	[46.30]	[53.36]	[50.28]
Brady Bunch	8.50	66.50	37.50
	[14.18]	[45.55]	[44.13]

[1]A parallel 3 × 2 analysis of variance of latency to help scores revealed no significant differences, but the tendency was consistent with amount of helping; 24.6 for the prosocial *Lassie*, 36.1 for the neutral *Lassie*, and 55.4 for the family situation comedy.

appeared because the impact of the prosocial *Lassie* program, relative to the neutral one, tended to be greater for girls than for boys; moreover, the girls tended to respond differently to the neutral *Lassie* and *Brady Bunch* programs, whereas the boys did not. Both of these tendencies may be due, in part, to a possible ceiling effect for the boys; in the two control conditions they tended to help more than their female counterparts. Further, nine out of the ten boys in the two control conditions rendered some help, whereas only five out of ten girls in the control conditions did so. (Four of the five boys who saw the prosocial *Lassie* program, and all five of the girls, rendered some help to the distressed puppies.)

Despite these different tendencies, the overall results of this experiment disclose clearly the validity of the basic demonstration we sought to produce: At least under some circumstances, a televised example can increase a child's willingness to engage in helping behavior. This finding extends the earlier work with simulated television materials and the experimental field study reported by Stein and Friedrich (1973) by demonstrating the influence of commercial broadcast programming designed primarily as entertainment. The present design also permitted us to isolate the particular aspect of the program, a prosocial example by the protagonist, as the central ingredient necessary for such an effect to occur; the alternative *Lassie* show and the generally warm *Brady Bunch* program produce significantly less helping. Inasmuch as the former control program featured the same major characters, setting, and general dramatic style as the prosocial Lassie show, it is unlikely that factors other than the specific modeled example influenced helping. This conclusion is further bolstered by the comparison of helping responses between children who saw either the neutral *Lassie* or *Brady Bunch* shows; the mere presence of a canine hero in the former did not itself significantly facilitate helping of puppies in distress. Theoretically, then, the present results support the social learning view of Bandura (1969, 1971) and Liebert (1970, 1973; Liebert, Neale, & Davidson, 1973) that the effects of television on behavior are mediated by specific modeling cues and the interpretation of these cues by the child, rather than general format and other global considerations. What is more, the dependent measure involved helping the experimenter as well as helping the puppies; to the extent that the children responded to this aspect of the situation, the results represent even more generalization from the specific altruistic behavior modeled in the prosocial show.

The practical implications of the present demonstration are also clear: It is possible to produce television programming that features action and adventure, appeals to child and family audiences, and still has a salutary rather than negative social influence on observers. A detailed understanding of the modeling processes involved in such influences may contribute to the production of other socially desirable programs in the future.

REFERENCES

Bandura, A. (1969). *Principles of behavior modification.* New York: Holt, Rinehart & Winston.

Bandura, A. (1971). Analysis of modeling processes. In A. Bandura (Ed.), *Psychological modeling.* New York: Aldine-Atherton.

Bryan, J. H. (1970). Children's reactions to helpers: Their money isn't where their mouths are. In J. Macauley & L. Berkowitz (Eds.), *Altruism and helping behavior.* New York: Academic Press.

Friedrich, L. K., & Stein, A. H. (1973). Aggressive and prosocial television programs and the natural behavior of preschool children. Society for *Research in Child Development, 38* (whole Monogr.).

Liebert, R. M. (1970). Television and social learning: Some relationships between viewing violence and behaving aggressively (overview). In J. P. Murray, E. A. Rubinstein, & G. A. Comstock (Eds.), *Television and social behavior. Vol. II: Television and social learning.* Washington, D.C.: U.S. Government Printing Office.

Liebert, R. M. (1973). Observational learning: Some social applications. In P. J. Elich (Ed.), *Fourth Western symposium on learning.* Bellingham, Wash.: Western Washington State College.

Liebert, R. M., Neale, J. M., & Davidson, E. S. (1973). *The early window.* New York: Pergamon Press.

O'Connor, R. D. (1969). Modification of social withdrawal through symbolic modeling. *Journal of Applied Behavior Analysis, 2,* 15–22.

Stein, A. H., & Friedrich, L. K. (1970). Television content and young children's behavior. In J. P. Murray, E. A. Rubinstein, & G. A. Comstock (Eds.), *Television and social behavior. Vol. II: Television and social learning.* Washington, D.C.: U.S. Government Printing Office.

Stein, G. M., & Bryan, J. H. (1972). The effect of a television model upon rule adoption behavior of children. *Child Development, 43,* 268–273.

Wolf, T., & Cheyne, J. (1972). Persistence of effects of live behavioral, televised behavioral, and live verbal models on resistance to deviation. *Child Development, 43,* 1429–1436.

Yates, G. C. P. (1974). Influence of televised modeling and verbalisation on children's delay of gratification. *Journal of Experimental Child Psychology, 18,* 333–339.

Note: This study was supported, in part, by grants from General Foods Corporation and General Mills, Inc. to Eli A. Rubinstein, John M. Neale, and the second and third authors for the investigation of television's prosocial influence. Grateful acknowledgment is due the Wrather Corporation for providing the *Lassie* programs, and to the principal, Mrs. Ann Littlefield, and staff of Smithtown Elementary School, Smithtown, New York, for valuable collaboration in this work. Special thanks also are due Elaine Brimer, Ann Covitz, Francine Hay, David Morgenstern, and Steven Schuetz for their capable assistance as experimenters.

Questions

1. What is the research problem?
2. What are the authors testing that has not been done in previous research; that is, what is unique about this experiment?
3. What is the hypothesis?
4. Name the independent variable(s).
5. Name the dependent variable(s).
6. How were participants assigned to treatments?
7. What controls were used to prevent extraneous variables from confounding the results?
8. Summarize the results. Draw a bar graph illustrating the results.
9. What design principles are illustrated in this experiment? Is the sample potentially biased by this constraint? Explain.
10. Think of another experiment that would test some of the hypotheses or issues raised by this experiment.
11. Why did the experimenter get parental consent? When do you need the consent of parents or the subjects themselves before an experiment?
12. Do you think that the children believed that the situation was real or contrived? Explain.
13. The experiment involved deception in that the children were led to believe they were monitoring a dog kennel. Discuss the issue of deception in psychological research. Under what conditions is it permissible?
14. The experimenters apparently did not debrief the participants by telling them the true nature of the experiment after it was over. When is debriefing necessary or desirable, and when can it be ignored?
15. Compare your answers to questions 3, 5, and 6 with the ethical principles in Chapter 8.
16. Do you think the findings of this 1975 study hold true today? Are there any changes you would make if you were conducting this experiment today? What would those changes be?

CHAPTER

21 Alcohol and Condoms

Introduction

Social issues are often ripe for experimental research, not only because they are interesting but also because society might benefit from the results. Alcohol use and sexual activity are not uncommon pastimes for college students. The authors in this study explore the issue of how alcohol use potentially impairs the decision to use a condom during casual sex.

This study by MacDonald, Zanna, and Fong (1996) not only tackles a very important and timely social issue, but does it in a methodologically interesting way. These experiments also raise some very interesting ethical issues.

Special Issues

MULTIPLE EXPERIMENTS

In the past several years psychological research has become increasingly complex. Because of the expanded nature of the subject, researchers often undertake studies that examine several aspects of a problem. Some APA journals encourage multiple-experiment manuscripts, a fact that even a casual reading of the current literature in psychology will confirm.

Multiple-experiment articles have several strengths, but perhaps the most salient is that it is possible to approach a psychological issue from various experimental viewpoints, with each single experiment providing a portion of the answer. Several experiments may reveal a more complete picture of the issue. Another aspect of multiple-experiment studies is that "programmatic" research can be reported in a single article. Many contemporary researchers develop a long-range, progressive research scheme. This scheme may involve a series of experiments in which later experiments are predicated on the outcome of earlier experiments. This type of research is particularly amenable to multiple-experiment articles.

STUDYING COMPLEX SOCIAL BEHAVIOR IN THE LABORATORY

Studying social behavior is not always an easy task, especially if one is interested in the benefits of a laboratory setting (control over variables, etc.). There are ways to accomplish this task, but one must be careful to preserve the very "social" qualities that one is interested in analyzing. There are methodological ways of accomplishing this. One is finding a task with reasonable similarities. This is sometimes called **transposition.** Transposition to the laboratory is the process of carefully evaluating the behavior of interest to isolate the critical variables inherent in the behavior, and transposing or transfering those variables to the laboratory in the form of an accomplishable task. Another method is by creating **experimental realism,** or **verisimilitude.** Studies that employ this method run the gamut from having subjects act "as if" they are engaged in a given activity, all the way to deception studies, in which the subjects are truly behaving in response to the experimental situation. These methods are not mutually exclusive. Some studies employ varying degrees of both methods.

WHY COMMON SENSE GOES OUT THE WINDOW: EFFECTS OF ALCOHOL ON INTENTIONS TO USE CONDOMS

Tara K. MacDonald, Mark P. Zanna, and Geoffrey T. Fong
University of Waterloo

Four studies tested the hypothesis that alcohol decreases the likelihood of condom use during casual sex. First, in a correlational study, it was found that among men who reported that they usually use condoms, those who were intoxicated when they last had intercourse were less likely than sober men to have used one. Further, in two laboratory experiments and one field experiment, intoxicated people reported more positive intentions to have unprotected sex than sober people. These results are consistent with alcohol myopia as introduced by Steele and associates—the notion that alcohol decreases cognitive capacity, such that intoxicated people are more likely to attend to the most salient cues in a situation. Intoxicated people may focus on the perceived benefits of having intercourse rather than on the negative consequences of not using condoms. These studies provide strong evidence that alcohol causes a decrease in condom use and suggest a mechanism for that relationship.

a₁

In a recent poll of Canadian university students, one undergraduate noted that "just because you see people putting condoms in their pockets, it doesn't mean they are using them. If you meet someone at a bar and there is alcohol involved, then common sense can go out the window" (Wallace, 1991, p. 26). This observation provides one possible explanation for this puzzling social phenomenon: People generally hold negative attitudes about engaging in casual sex without a condom, and great efforts are made to educate people about the dangers of doing so. Yet the rate of casual sexual intercourse without the use of a condom is alarmingly high. Numerous studies with Canadian and American high school and college students have found that despite the attendant risks, such as contracting AIDS or other sexually transmitted diseases, or unwanted pregnancy, only 15% to 38% of sexually active young

Source: Reprinted by permission by *Personality and Social Psychology Bulletin,* 1996, 22(8), 763–775.

Analysis

Literature Review

The authors explore the apparent dichotomy between intentions to use condoms and actual behavior (a₁). They attempt to explain this discrepancy between attitudes and behavior with a review of the literature pertaining to alcohol and high-risk

people report using a condom every time they have intercourse (Anderson et al., 1990, as cited in Poppen & Reisen, 1994; Baldwin & Baldwin, 1988; Butcher, Manning, & O'Neal, 1991; Campbell, Peplau, & DeBro, 1992; Catania et al., 1992; Fong, Parent, & Poppe, 1994; Levin, 1993). In this article, we address the possibility that alcohol intoxication might be a factor that could lead one to engage in this type of risky sexual behavior.

a₂

A great deal of research has explored the relationship between alcohol and high-risk sexual behavior, and findings in this area are often inconsistent (for a review, see Leigh & Stall, 1993). In general, studies have shown that people who regularly consume alcohol or use drugs are more likely to engage in high-risk sexual behavior. Moreover, in young adults, alcohol use and sexual activity often coincide. Leigh and Morrison (1991) report that 50% of both male and female adolescents had been drinking at the time of their first sexual experience; they note that this may occur because young people tend to experiment with sex and alcohol at approximately the same age, and both activities are timed to occur when parents are not present. Even more important, alcohol intoxication at the time of first sexual intercourse is associated with a decrease in condom use (Robertson & Plant, 1988), particularly when intercourse is unplanned (Flanigan & Hitch, 1986).

a₃

However, virtually all research examining the relationship between alcohol intoxication and condom use has been correlational and is therefore constrained by the limitations inherent in this type of design (e.g., any correlation between alcohol and condom use cannot be interpreted as causal—it could arise from the fact that "risky" people are more likely to consume alcohol and are also more likely to have unprotected sex). The present article reports one correlational study using a control that decreases the possible effect of the "risky personality" third variable and three experimental studies of alcohol and condom use that both eliminate problems inherent in the correlational studies and lend support to the psychological processes that may explain how alcohol affects condom use. To our knowledge, these are the first experiments testing whether alcohol causes people to form less negative attitudes and intentions toward the behavior of unprotected sexual intercourse.[1]

---

[1]In the final stage of preparation of this article, we became aware of one other randomized experiment conducted by Gordon and Carey (in press) demonstrating that intoxicated men reported more negative attitudes toward condoms and lower confidence in their ability to initiate condom use than did sober men.

sexual behavior **(a₂)**, and then point to a serious methodological limitation with previous investigations **(a₃)**. Next, the authors provide results from their earlier research **(a₄)**, which leads them to the current hypothesis **(a₅)**.

(analysis continues on page 326)

In a recent series of correlational and experimental studies, we tested the theory of alcohol myopia in the domain of attitudes and intentions toward the behavior of drinking and driving (MacDonald, Zanna, & Fong, 1995). We tested the hypothesis that when an impelling cue to drink and drive was made salient, alcohol intoxication would cause intoxicated participants to report attitudes and intentions that were less negative toward drinking and driving than those reported by sober participants. When asked general, noncontingent questions about drinking and driving (e.g., "I will drink and drive the next time that I am out at a party or bar"), sober and intoxicated participants reported equally negative attitudes and intentions. However, when asked contingent questions that included an excuse, or impelling reason to drink and drive (e.g., "If I only had a short distance to go, I would drink and drive the next time that I am out at a party or bar"), intoxicated participants were significantly less negative about the behavior of drinking and driving than were sober participants. These results were consistent with alcohol myopia—when intoxicated, participants were more influenced by salient impelling cues than the less immediate inhibiting cues (i.e., the potential negative consequences of drinking and driving).

When a person is considering whether to engage in unprotected sexual intercourse, there are typically both impelling cues (e.g., being in a passionate situation where it is desirable to have sex) and inhibiting cues (e.g., the risks associated with this behavior). On the basis of our research in the domain of drinking and driving (MacDonald, Zanna, & Fong, 1993, 1995), we predicted that intoxicated people are more influenced by the more salient impelling cues than by inhibiting cues and would therefore be more likely to engage in risky sexual behavior. This is consistent with the notion of myopia in that people are not able to see the possible long-term costs of their actions, attending instead to the short-term benefits.

STUDY 1: CORRELATIONAL STUDY

Method

Participants.   At the beginning of eight academic terms, we distributed a survey to students enrolled in introductory psychology classes. Participants were assured that their responses were completely confidential, and they were instructed not to write their names anywhere on the questionnaire. We included in our analyses only those students who indicated that they were single (i.e., we excluded those who were married, engaged, or cohabiting) and had been sexually active in the previous 6 months. We also asked participants how often they used condoms when they had sexual intercourse, on a 9-point scale with points labeled 1 (never), 3 (seldom), 5 (sometimes), 7 (usually), and 9 (always). We selected only those people who scored above the midpoint on this measure—that is, those who reported that they often used condoms. Overall, 4,090 people completed the survey, of whom 1,069 (598 female, 471 male) met the criteria for inclusion in the analyses.

b_1

Procedure.   The survey asked participants to think back to the last time they had had sexual intercourse and whether they had in fact used a condom and whether they had consumed alcohol. If participants had consumed alcohol when they last had sexual intercourse, they were asked to indicate how intoxicated they were on a 9-point scale with endpoints labeled 1 (*not at all intoxicated*) and 9 (*extremely intoxicated*), with 5 (*moderately intoxicated*) at the midpoint. We classified participants as sober if they reported being below the midpoint of the scale, and compared their responses with those of participants who reported being moderately to heavily intoxicated.

b_2

Results.   When males were asked about their most recent experience of sexual intercourse, alcohol was associated with a decrease in condom use: 337 of 402 (84%) who reported consuming little or no alcohol also reported using a condom on that occasion, compared with 47 of 69 males (68%) who reported being moderately or heavily intoxicated, $\chi^2 = 9.66, p < .0001.$[2] These results are consistent with the notion that alcohol is a factor in risky sexual behavior,

---

[2]We analyzed the data separately for nondating males (i.e., those who were not in a dating relationship) and dating males. Alcohol was associated with a significant decrease in condom use for both nondating males ($n = 260$), $\chi^2 = 4.83, p < .05$, and dating males ($n = 211$), $\chi^2 = 5$–$44, p < .025$.

Study 1

The purpose of this initial study was to evaluate the possible relationship between alcohol use and the use of a condom during sexual intercourse. The authors used a survey to evaluate past behavior (b_1). They present clearly the survey results (b_2) and the questions and possible answers these results lead them to formulate (b_3).

(analysis continues on page 328)

even among males who claim to use condoms regularly. We analyzed the data using a more stringent criterion, including in the analyses only those males who scored 7 (*usually*) or above on the item asking how often they use condoms when they have sexual intercourse, and obtained a similar pattern of results: 335 of 396 (85%) who reported being sober also reported using a condom the last time they had sexual intercourse, compared with 46 of 66 males (70%) who reported being moderately or heavily intoxicated, $\chi^2 = 8.68$, $p < .005$. Interestingly, we did not find the same pattern of results for females: There was no association between alcohol and condom use at the last time they had intercourse. Among females who scored above 5 on the item about condom use, 411 of 526 (78%) who had consumed little or no alcohol had used a condom the last time they had sexual intercourse, compared with 54 of 72 (75%) who were moderately or heavily intoxicated, $\chi^2 = 0.36$, n.s.

Why would alcohol intoxication be associated with a lower likelihood of condom use for males but not for females, and how could this be explained by the alcohol myopia perspective? We speculate that the use of oral contraceptives may provide at least a partial solution to this puzzle. For females who are not on the pill, the fear of pregnancy is probably a very powerful, chronically accessible inhibiting cue that would be highly salient even when they were intoxicated. Thus, for these women, intoxication would not decrease (indeed, it might possibly increase) the rate of condom use. In contrast, for females who are on the pill, the fear of pregnancy is essentially absent, and the far less salient fear of sexually transmitted diseases is the relevant inhibiting cue. But because the fear of sexually transmitted diseases (STDs) is relatively weak and is probably not so chronically accessible as the fear of pregnancy, we would expect that for females on the pill, alcohol intoxication would lead to a lower frequency of condom use, similar to the pattern of results found for males. We are currently investigating this hypothesis.

b$_3$

EXPERIMENTAL STUDIES

In Study 1, our results supported the findings of other correlational studies demonstrating that alcohol intoxication decreases condom use. We made a new contribution to this research by including only people who use condoms regularly: By demonstrating that alcohol decreases condom use *among males who do use condoms,* we can make a stronger case for the hypothesis that alcohol intoxication increases the likelihood that a person will engage in risky sexual behaviors, such as sex without a condom. However, to establish whether alcohol *causes* a decrease in condom use, it is necessary to examine this relationship experimentally. In the laboratory and field studies reported below, we compared participants who had been randomly assigned to a sober or intoxicated condition. We hypothesized that intoxicated people would express more favorable intentions toward having unprotected sex than sober people.

c_1

Obvious challenges arise when attempting to examine the effects of alcohol on condom use in a laboratory environment. **Even the most ambitious of scientists would have to concede that it is impossible to observe the effects of intoxication on actual condom use in a controlled laboratory setting.** Instead of measuring actual condom use behavior, we chose to compare sober and intoxicated participants' intentions to engage in unprotected sexual intercourse. To do this, we created a video that depicted a realistic, engaging scenario in which a young couple find themselves in the predicament of having to decide whether to engage in intercourse without a condom. We tried to create a high-conflict situation: We made salient both impelling cues (e.g., both persons were very attractive and clearly interested in having sex, it was established that the female character was on the pill and would not get pregnant) and inhibiting cues (e.g., neither partner had a condom, and it would be difficult to obtain one). As in the correlational study, we used only participants who reported on a pretest that they usually use condoms when having intercourse—these were individuals who had positive attitudes toward condom use. We hypothesized that participants who consumed alcohol before they saw the video and completed the measures would be less negative about having unprotected sex than their sober counterparts when asked how they would respond in a situation similar to the one presented in the video.

Study 2: Laboratory Experiment

Method

Participants.   Over the course of two academic terms,[3] 54 male participants were recruited from the introductory psychology subject pool in return for course credit and payment. Participants were paid $5 in the sober condition (which took less than 1 hr) and $8 in the alcohol condition (which took 2.5 hr).[4] We recruited only males who reported on a pretest that they were at least 19 years old (the legal drinking age in Ontario) and frequently consumed alcohol when in social situations, were not in an exclusive romantic relationship of more than 2 years, and were sexually active people who usually used condoms (i.e., scored 7 or above on our survey question about condom use).

---

[3]The data collected in these two terms are reported together. We analyzed the data using term as a between-subjects factor. Except for the one instance reported in the text, there were no main effects for term, nor did it interact with condition on any of the dependent variables.

[4]Participants in the intoxicated condition were required to remain in the laboratory until they were sober, and we paid them for their time.

Study 2

The authors discuss the important methodological difficulty of studying some aspects of behavior in the laboratory (c_1). Sexual activity is clearly one of those be-

Because of the potential negative health consequences of consuming alcohol while pregnant, we did not administer alcohol to females in the laboratory study.

Materials. We commissioned the production of a video vignette that would simulate a realistic situation where University of Waterloo undergraduates would be faced with the dilemma of whether to engage in sexual intercourse without a condom.[5] In this 10-min video, two undergraduates, Mike and Rebecca, have a friendly conversation in a hallway after writing an exam, and Mike asks Rebecca out on a date at the campus bar. The next scene shows them at the campus bar, where they are having fun drinking and dancing with friends. At the end of this scene, they slow dance and then kiss. Mike then offers to walk Rebecca home to her apartment, where the final scene takes place. After talking briefly, Mike and Rebecca begin to kiss passionately and make out on the couch. Rebecca then suggests that they move to her bedroom, where they can listen to music and will be more comfortable on her bed. After some hesitation, Mike discloses that he does not have any condoms with him. The two, somewhat awkwardly, discuss how to resolve this dilemma. Rebecca points out that although she too does not have any condoms, she is on the pill, so there is no need to worry. Mike explores ways to obtain a condom by asking about the nearby convenience store (Rebecca tells him it closed 3 hrs ago) and whether there is a 24-hr store nearby (they realize that it is not within walking distance). Appearing a little embarrassed, Mike and Rebecca then discuss that they are "clean" and do not "sleep around." Mike then asks Rebecca what she wants to do. She kisses him and replies, "I don't know. What do *you* want to do?" The video then ends with a freeze frame.

Colleagues who have viewed the video have been consistently impressed with its high quality. **We are satisfied that the situation presented is very**

---

[5]The video was written, directed, and produced by, and is copyright of, Darlene Spencer, Department of Drama, University of Waterloo.

haviors that are difficult to capture in the laboratory! However, there are ways to study complex social behavior in a controlled manner (see Special Issues). Pay careful attention to the critical variables in these studies: the video (c_2) and its

c_3

credible and holds a great deal of conflict for the participants in our study. The female drama student who plays Rebecca is unanimously rated by participants as being very attractive. In the video, Rebecca makes it clear to Mike that she is interested in having sexual intercourse with him; if they were to have sex, it would be completely consensual. Additionally, it is made evident that she takes oral contraceptives, virtually eliminating the possibility of pregnancy. However, we created the situation so that the possibility of obtaining a condom is ruled out—if participants state that they would intend to have sexual intercourse with Rebecca, if they were in Mike's position, it would certainly be without a condom.

Procedure.   Participants were run in groups of two or three and were randomly assigned to one of two conditions by group. Participants in the *sober* condition ($n = 24$) completed the informed consent in the same room and were then separated into different rooms where they viewed the video. Before viewing the video, participants were told that the video would depict a male and a female student and that while viewing the video, they were to imagine themselves in the role of Mike, the lead male character. They were also instructed that a freeze frame would appear at the end of the video, at which time they were to turn a switch that would indicate to the experimenter that the video was finished. The experimenter then gave participants the measures described below, and they completed the questionnaire while the freeze frame was still in view. Participants completed the measures anonymously and were instructed not to put their names on the questionnaire.

c_4

This procedure was identical in the intoxicated condition ($n = 30$), except that participants were given a dose of alcohol before completing the experimental measures. To determine the amount of alcohol (40% alc/vol) that would be given, the weight of each subject was obtained at the outset of the session. Soda (Wink) was used to dilute the alcohol, with a ratio of 1 part alcohol to 2 parts soda. Each subject drank three drinks, spaced 20 min apart. Fifteen minutes after the third drink, participants viewed the video and completed the measures. Immediately after completion of the questionnaires, their blood alcohol level (BAL) was assessed using an AlcoSensor IV breathalyzer (manufactured by Intoximeters, Inc.). The BAL for participants in the intoxicated condition was 0.084% ($SD = 0.040$).

Measures

c_5

We created a questionnaire to assess participants' predicted intentions to engage in sexual intercourse with Rebecca if they were in the situation presented in the video. The instructions for the questionnaire reiterated the fact that in the video, Mike is faced with a dilemma, in that he is very interested in having sexual intercourse with Rebecca but does not have a condom available. Participants were then instructed to "answer the following questions,

validity (c_3); the procedures used in the intoxicated condition (c_4); and the questionnaire (c_5). The results of Study 2 are presented succinctly in (c_6).

(analysis continues on page 333)

and indicate what you would do if faced with a similar dilemma." All questions were answered on 9-point rating scales with endpoints labeled 1 (*strongly disagree*) and 9 (*strongly agree*).

General Intentions.   The first question assessed participants' general intention to have sex with Rebecca ("If I were in this situation, I would engage in sexual intercourse with Rebecca").[6] We hypothesized that intoxicated participants would be more likely to endorse this item than sober participants because of the many impelling cues contained in the video.

Justifications.   Each of the next five questions reminded participants of an impelling cue to engage in unprotected sex in the situation presented in the video ("Because Rebecca's on the pill and won't get pregnant, there's little for me to worry about if we have intercourse," "If she's not worried about using a condom, then there's no reason for me to be," "A situation like this occurs only once in a while, so it would be worth the risk involved for me to have intercourse," "She looks totally healthy, so it's unlikely that she has AIDS or other sexually transmitted diseases," and "I can tell that Rebecca is not the type who sleeps around, so it's unlikely that she has AIDS or other STDs."). We aggregated these five items containing an impelling cue to have sexual intercourse into an index of justifications (Cronbach's $\alpha = .86$). We expected that intoxicated participants would indicate more agreement with these justifications than sober participants.

Arousal.   Three items assessed the extent to which participants found Rebecca attractive and whether they found the video sexually arousing and realistic.

Risk Perception.   Two items assessed whether participants believed that using a condom would protect them from contracting AIDS or other STDs. In the first term, these questions read "Using a condom in this situation would protect me from getting AIDS (other STDs)" and were presented in the middle of the questionnaire. In the second term, we changed the wording to "I would not get AIDS (other STDs) if I used a condom in this situation" and presented these items at the end of the questionnaire. We made these changes to increase the clarity of the questions and to decrease the possibility that reminding participants of AIDS and STDs would influence their responses to the other items. Because of these changes, the results for these items are presented separately for each term.

---

[6]For the intentions item, we wanted to know whether participants would engage in vaginal sexual intercourse with Rebecca, immediately after the freeze frame. We decided on the present wording of the question to avoid having the question sound clinical in nature or emphasizing that subjects were indeed watching a video presentation. It is possible that some participants might have misinterpreted this item. However, we feel that this is unlikely, for past research in the area of sexual behavior using University of Waterloo undergraduates has shown that invariably the term *sexual intercourse* means "vaginal sexual intercourse" to this population. Moreover, any problems associated with participants' interpretation of this question cannot be offered as an alternative explanation for our findings: If a small number of participants were incorrectly interpreting the question, this should only weaken the results, because the reliability of the measure would be decreased.

Attitudes.   Two items assessed the extent to which participants thought that engaging in sexual intercourse without a condom in the situation presented in the video was (a) foolish and (b) irresponsible. We expected that sober participants would have more negative attitudes toward engaging in unprotected sexual intercourse with Rebecca than would intoxicated participants.

Results

General Intentions.   Alcohol had a very strong effect in enhancing participants' intentions to have sexual intercourse if in the situation presented in the video, $M = 6.78$ (on the 9-point rating scale) in the intoxicated condition and $M = 3.63$ in the sober condition, $t(52) = 4.72, p < .0001$.

Justifications.   Males in the sober condition did not endorse the justifications for having unprotected sexual intercourse in the situation presented in the video ($M = 1.89$). Although intoxicated subjects were still below the midpoint of the scale on these items, they expressed significantly more agreement with these items ($M = 2.87$), $t(52) = 2.75, p = .008$.

Arousal.   All participants reported that they found Rebecca attractive, and there was absolutely no difference between sober and intoxicated participants on this item (both $Ms = 7.67$). Clearly, the difference in intentions was not merely due to the possibility that participants in the intoxicated condition found her more appealing and the situation therefore more tempting.

Risk Perception.   When the questions pertaining to risk perception were phrased "Using a condom in this situation would protect me from getting AIDS (other STDs)," there were no differences between the two conditions: Both the sober participants ($n = 10$) and the intoxicated participants ($n = 11$) agreed that condoms would provide protection from AIDS (M sober $= 7.50$; M intoxicated $= 8.27$) and other STDs (M sober $= 7.50$; M intoxicated $= 8.18$), both $ts < 1$.

In response to the items "I would not get AIDS (other STDs) if I used a condom in this situation," sober participants ($n = 14$) were less likely than intoxicated participants ($n = 19$) to agree that they would be protected if they used a condom. This was true for both the AIDS item (M sober $= 4.21$; M intoxicated $= 6.00$), $t(31) = 2.02, p = .052$, and the other-STDs item (M sober $= 4.00$; M intoxicated $= 6.00$), $t(31) = 2.44, p = .021$. Although intoxicated participants were more likely than sober participants to express intentions to have sexual intercourse without a condom, they were more cognizant of the fact that a condom would help protect them against sexually transmitted diseases when this question was explicitly put to them.

Attitudes.   When asked whether they believed that engaging in intercourse without a condom in the situation presented in the video would be foolish and irresponsible, the two groups did not differ. Both sober and intoxicated participants responded that this behavior would be extremely foolish (M sober} = 8.08; M intoxicated = 7.67), $t(52) = 1.04$, n.s., and extremely irresponsible (M sober = 8.04; M intoxicated = 7.83), $t(52) = 0.62$, n.s. This is an intriguing finding, given the data from the intention subscale; intoxicated participants reported that they would have unprotected sex if in a situation similar to the one presented in the video. The relationship between attitudes and intentions was higher for sober participants, $r = .50$, $p = .014$, than for intoxicated participants, $r = .32$, $p = .081$, though not significantly so, $z = .75$, n.s.

c₆

Summary.   Intoxicated participants were more likely to express intentions to have sexual intercourse with Rebecca and more likely to agree with justifications for this behavior than sober participants.[7] Interestingly, all participants reported negative attitudes toward having unprotected sexual intercourse in this situation: They regarded this behavior as foolish and irresponsible.

STUDY 3: PLACEBO EXPERIMENT

d₁

We were concerned about expectancy effects, or the extent to which the significant results of the laboratory study could be explained in terms of how people think an intoxicated person would behave in a given situation. **To be certain that our results were caused by alcohol, not by alcohol expectancy effects, we ran a placebo laboratory experiment.**

Method

Participants.   Fifty-five participants were selected using the same criteria as in Study 2. Participants in the sober condition were paid $5 for their participation, and participants in the placebo and intoxicated conditions were paid $8.

Procedure.   The procedures for participants in the sober condition ($n = 20$) and intoxicated condition ($n = 16$) were identical to those described in Study 2. Participants in the placebo condition ($n = 19$) were led to believe that they were consuming alcohol and Wink through smell, sight, and taste cues, but they really received only a tiny amount of alcohol. From our reading of alcohol studies that included a placebo condition (e.g., Lyvers & Maltzman, 1991;

---

[7]Participants' dating status did not affect our findings. There was no difference in the proportion of nondating and dating males in the sober and intoxicated conditions, $\chi^2 = 0.63$, n.s. Moreover, there was no interaction between dating status and condition on the intentions, $F(1, 50) = 0.91$, and justification, $F(1, 50) = 0.002$, subscales. Finally, there was no difference in the reported frequency of condom use (from the pretest measure) of nondating ($M = 7.53$) and dating males ($M = 7.43$), t(52) = 0.17.

Study 3

The authors dispel potential criticism by conducting this experiment, which sets to rest the question of whether or not their results are due to effects other than alcohol **(d₁)**. This is a major benefit in conducting multiple experiment studies: You can address potential criticisms and extend findings all in the same article.

(analysis continues on page 335)

Rohsenow & Marlatt, 1981; Ross & Pihl, 1989), we took a number of steps to ensure that our manipulation was convincing to participants. While participants were completing a measure in another room, we sprayed the room where they would be consuming their drinks with a mixture of water and alcohol to provide smell cues. Participants also saw us pour their drinks: We had put flattened tonic water into an alcohol bottle, and so participants in the placebo condition could see us pouring a clear liquid from an alcohol bottle into their drinks. Finally, we put a very small amount of alcohol (1 tablespoon) disguised as lime juice on top of the drinks, so that the first taste of their drinks was mostly alcohol. Our manipulation did convince placebo participants that they had consumed alcohol: The average BAL estimate for the placebo group was 0.072% (their actual breathalyzer readings were .000 or .001 in all cases). In addition, none of our placebo participants expressed any suspicion during the debriefing: In fact, they usually expressed great surprise when told they had not consumed any alcohol.[8] Participants completed measures identical to those described in Study 2. For the risk perception subscale, participants were asked the second version of the questions, "I would not get AIDS (other STDs) if I used a condom in this situation."

Results

General Intentions.   There was a marginal main effect for the mean differences between the three groups, $F(2,52) = 2.43$, $p = .098$. We conducted planned orthogonal contrasts and found that there were no differences between the sober ($M = 3.20$) and the placebo ($M = 3.95$) conditions, $t(52) = 0.87$, n.s. As expected, we did find a significant difference between the mean of these two groups versus the intoxicated condition ($M = 5.19$), $t(52) = 2.01$, $p = .049$.

Summary.   By demonstrating that the placebo subjects do not differ from sober subjects but that there are differences between the mean of these two groups and the intoxicated condition, we can rule out alcohol expectancy effects as a plausible alternative explanation for our findings. Although placebo subjects believed that they had consumed alcohol and that they were intoxicated, they did not report intentions or justifications that differed from the sober participants'. In fact, the more intoxicated placebo participants believed themselves to be, the more cautious were their intentions.

---

[8]Using the same placebo protocol in another study (MacDonald, Zanna, & Fong, 1995), one participant in the placebo condition actually refused to believe that he was not intoxicated. After the experimenter showed him the breathalyzer reading of .000, he argued that the breathalyzer must be "rigged," and he insisted on remaining in the laboratory until he felt sober enough to leave.

STUDY 4: CAMPUS PUB FIELD EXPERIMENT

In the correlational study and the laboratory studies, we found support for our hypothesis that intoxicated males would be more likely than sober males to engage (or intend to engage) in casual sexual intercourse without a condom. In the laboratory, we were able to employ only males as participants. In light of the potential negative health consequences of consuming alcohol while pregnant, we could not administer alcohol to females in an experimental setting. However, in the field experiment reported below, we did not encourage people to consume alcohol; instead, we assessed males and females whose decision to consume alcohol was not related to their participation in the study. **In this way, it was possible to test for any gender differences in the alcohol myopia effect found in the laboratory experiments for males.**

In the laboratory experiments reported above, participants were being assessed in a situation far removed from the one where they would be facing the decision whether to have sex without a condom. In a laboratory situation, it is very apparent to participants that they are participating in a psychology study. Further, drinking alcohol in a lab setting is a very unusual experience (e.g., being drunk at school, in the presence of a sober experimenter), which may cause participants to feel self-conscious. Conducting a field experiment enabled us to assess sober and intoxicated participants in a context where it did not seem unusual to consume alcohol and where they were in a situation that was more similar to the one presented in the video (in fact, we ran the study at the same campus pub as the one shown in the video).

Method

Participants. An experimenter[9] approached patrons who entered a campus bar between 8:00 P.M. and 9:30 P.M. and asked them to complete a one-page survey for the Department of Psychology. Among other questions, the survey contained items pertaining to the patron's age and dating status, as well as questions asking whether the patron was sexually active and consumed alcohol. Patrons were instructed not to put their name anywhere on the questionnaire and to return it to the experimenter when they had finished. When they

---

[9]During any given evening, we recruited only males or females. Because of the sensitive nature of the study, we tried to minimize any embarrassment among the participants by ensuring that a same-sex experimenter handed out the surveys and scanned them, and a same-sex experimenter introduced the video, collected the dependent measures, and debriefed the participants.

Study 4

These researchers answer additional research questions **(e₁)** and address further potential criticism **(e₂)** in this clever field study **(e₃)**.

(analysis continues on page 339)

did, the experimenter quickly scanned the survey to establish whether the patron was at least 19, was sexually active, was not in an exclusive dating relationship of more than 2 years, and drank alcohol frequently. Patrons who met all the criteria were asked by the experimenter to go to a nearby table, where a second experimenter invited them to participate in an experiment about social attitudes. Patrons who agreed completed a consent form and then took an initial breathalyzer test to ensure that they were sober (BALs = 0.03% or below) at the outset of the study.

Procedure.   After informed consent was obtained, participants were randomly assigned to either the early (sober) or the late (intoxicated) condition. In groups of three to five, participants in the early condition ($n = 20$) were directed to a room where they completed the Marlowe–Crowne Social Desirability Scale (Crowne & Marlowe, 1964). An experimenter then introduced the video and instructed participants to put themselves in the male (or female) character's place as they were watching the video. After the video had finished, participants anonymously completed the dependent measures (identical to those in the laboratory study) while the freeze frame was still on the screen. Before they left, participants were told that they would be approached by the experimenter later in the evening and would be asked to complete a final short measure. Between 11:30 P.M. and 1:30 A.M., the experimenter found the participants who had participated in the study in the early condition and administered a breathalyzer test to them. Only those who were intoxicated at the end of the evening (i.e., had a breathalyzer reading of at least 0.06%) were included in the analyses.

Participants randomly assigned to the late condition ($n = 28$) completed the informed consent at the beginning of the evening but were told that they would be approached later in the evening to participate in the study. Between 11:30 P.M. and 1:30 A.M., these participants were run in groups of three to five, in exactly the same manner as those in the early condition. After completing the dependent measures, participants in the late condition were given a breathalyzer test. We included only those who had a breathalyzer reading of at least 0.06% in the analyses.

As in the previous two studies, we were interested in the effects of alcohol on condom use among *people who usually use condoms* (i.e., those who typically have positive attitudes and intentions about condom use). Approximately 2 months after their participation in the study, we called all participants and asked them about their frequency of condom use on a 0-to-100% scale. If participants reported using condoms at least 70% of the time, we included their data in the analyses.[10] Although 157 people agreed to participate, only 48 (25 female, 23 male) met all the criteria required: These participants were intoxicated at the end of the evening (both those who were randomly assigned to the early condition and those assigned to the late condition) and accordingly are reported in the analyses that follow.[11]

By giving participants a breathalyzer test at the beginning and at the end of the evening, we were able to examine whether the four conditions (females early, females late, males early, males late) were comparable: We compared the BALs of males and females who were sober when they completed the measures but intoxicated at the end of the evening with the BALs of those who were already intoxicated at the time of testing. Unexpectedly, we found a significant 2 (Gender) by 2 (Time of Testing) interaction, $F(1, 44) = 9.84$, $p = .003$. Females in the early condition ($n = 13$, $M = 0.10$) were less intoxicated at the end of the night than females in the late condition ($n = 12$, $M = 0.13$), though not significantly so, $t(23) = 0.77$, n.s. In contrast, males in the early condition ($n = 7$, $M = 0.20$) were more intoxicated at the end of the night than males in the late condition ($n = 16$, $M = 0.10$), and this difference is significant, $t(21) = 2.87$, $p = .026$. Although we randomly assigned participants to the early and late condition, the BALs differed for the two conditions, and the direction of this difference varied as a function of gender.

Measures.   In this field experiment, we used the same measures as those in the laboratory experiment described above, the only change being that we created a different version of the questionnaire for female participants. For example, the general intention item, "If I were in this situation, I would engage in sexual intercourse with Rebecca," became "If I were in this situation, I would engage in sexual intercourse with Mike." For the risk perception

---

[10]To reduce demands for consistency, we did not ask participants about their frequency of condom use on the same evening that they participated in the study. For example, if a participant reported on the survey that he or she always uses condoms when having sexual intercourse, that person might be inclined to say that he or she would not have unprotected sexual intercourse when responding to the video. Similarly, if we asked about the frequency of condom use just after participants viewed the video, participants who reported they would engage in sexual intercourse when responding to the video might be inclined to answer the survey differently than they would have without viewing the video. By asking about condom use frequency 2 months after participation in the study, we reduced the likelihood that participants' responses to the video would affect their self-reports of condom use. There were no differences in condom use behavior between the early ($M = 91.6\%$) and the late ($M = 92.4\%$) conditions, $t(46) = 0.15$.

[11]We also compared the responses of people who were tested in the early condition and were sober at the end of the evening ($n = 24$) with those of people who were tested in the late condition and were sober at the time of testing ($n = 40$). That is, we did the same analyses as those presented in the text, with participants who were sober, rather than intoxicated, at the end of the evening. In this way, we were able to ensure that alcohol intoxication, not time of testing, accounted for our findings. There were no significant differences between the early and late groups on any of the dependent measures. As one might expect, some gender differences did emerge, but gender did not interact with time of testing on any of the measures.

subscale, participants were asked the second version of the questions, "I would not get AIDS (other STDs) if I used a condom in this situation."

Results

General Intentions.   We examined all items in a 2 (Gender) × 2 (Condition: early or late) analysis of variance. For the intentions measure, the interaction between gender and condition was not reliable, $F(1, 44) = 1.04$, n.s. There was a main effect of condition: Participants in the early (i.e., sober) condition ($M = 2.45$) were less likely to report strong intentions to have sexual intercourse with Mike/Rebecca than participants in the late (i.e., intoxicated) condition ($M = 4.43$), $F(1, 44) = 5.98, p = .019$.

There was also a marginal main effect for gender, such that females were less positive about having intercourse with Mike ($M = 2.80$) than males were about having intercourse with Rebecca ($M = 4.48$), $F(1, 44) = 3.73, p = .06$.

Justifications.   As in the experiments reported above, we formed a composite scale of the five justification items (Cronbach's $\alpha = .87$). For this measure, neither the main effect of gender nor the interaction between gender and condition was reliable. As expected, there was a main effect for condition, $F(1, 44) = 7.48, p < .01$. Participants in the late condition, who were intoxicated when they viewed the video and completed the measures, were more likely to endorse the justification items ($M = 2.46$) than participants in the early condition, who were sober when they did so ($M = 1.28$). Justifications and intentions were highly correlated for participants in both the early, $r(18) = .79, p = .0001$, and the late, $r(26) = .53, p = .004$, conditions. The difference in the magnitude of these correlations is marginal, $z = 1.53, p = .12$.

Arousal.   As in the laboratory study, males found Rebecca to be very attractive ($M = 7.17$). Again, males in the late condition ($M = 7.06$) found her as attractive as males in the early condition ($M = 7.43$), $t(21) = 0.42$, n.s. However, the females in our study did not find Mike to be as attractive ($M = 3.24$), resulting in a large main effect for gender, $F(1, 44) = 50.81, p < .0001$. Moreover, females in the late condition ($M = 1.75$) reported finding Mike to be less attractive than females in the early condition ($M = 4.62$), $t(23) = 3.44$, $p < .005$. It is interesting to note that although females in the late condition found Mike less attractive than those in the early condition, they were more likely to report intentions to engage in sexual intercourse if they were in the situation presented in the video, presumably because they were less able to attend to the potential negative consequences of this behavior than those who were sober when they completed the measures.

When we asked participants in the early and late conditions whether they thought the video was realistic, there were no differences between the groups (overall $M = 6.40$). When we asked whether the video was sexually arousing, there was a main effect for gender, $F(1, 44) = 12.36, p = .001$. As one might expect given the attractiveness ratings, males ($M = 4.39$) reported that the video was more sexually arousing than females did ($M = 2.00$).

Risk Perception.   All participants mildly disagreed with the items "I would not get AIDS if I used a condom in this situation" (overall $M = 3.94$) and "I would not get other STDs if I used a condom in this situation" (overall $M = 4.42$). There were no differences between the groups for either item.

Attitudes.   Again, we asked participants whether they believed that having sexual intercourse without a condom in this situation would be foolish and irresponsible. There were no effects for condition for these items, nor did condition interact with gender. However, there was a main effect for gender on both items. Females thought that having sexual intercourse without a condom was more foolish ($M = 8.80$) and more irresponsible ($M = 8.52$) than males (respective $Ms = 7.22$ and 7.78), respective $Fs(1, 44) = 8.86, p = .005$, and $2.78, p < .10$.

Summary.   In this field study, our hypothesis that intoxicated participants would report more positive intentions toward engaging in sexual intercourse than sober participants when responding to a video vignette was supported. As in the laboratory experiments, people who were intoxicated when they viewed the video were also more likely to agree with justifications for having intercourse than those who were sober when they viewed it.

Females were generally less positive about unprotected casual sex than were males. They reported less positive attitudes and intentions about having sex when responding to the situation presented in the video. However, females also found the video less arousing than did males and found the lead male character less attractive than males found the female character. It could be that these gender differences would not be so apparent if the situation presented in the video were equally enticing for females and males.

SUMMARY OF RESULTS

f   **We conducted a meta-analysis, comparing the mean differences between the sober/placebo and intoxicated conditions on the intentions and justification subscales.** For the intentions subscale, we included Studies 2, 3, and 4, for a total of three studies. For the justifications subscale, we also included a preliminary laboratory study (Koch, 1994), for a total of four studies. Using the method of adding ts (Winer, 1971, as described in Rosenthal, 1984), we found that there was a highly significant difference between the sober/placebo and intoxicated conditions for the intentions subscale ($z = 5.43, p < .0001$) and the justifications subscale ($z = 4.89, p < .0001$), such that intoxicated participants reported more positive intentions, and were more likely to endorse

Summary of Results

Not only did the researchers analyze the data for each experiment or study, but they conducted a **meta-analysis** for the research as a whole **(f)**.

justifications to have sexual intercourse, than were participants in the sober/placebo conditions.

In response to reviewers' comments, we conducted mediational analyses to determine whether the data were consistent with the notion that the justifications subscale mediates the relationship between condition (sober/placebo vs. intoxicated) and intentions. It is important to note that we did not design our questionnaire to test this mediation hypothesis. Across the three experiments (Studies 2, 3, and 4), intentions to have intercourse were assessed first (before the justification items), because the intentions subscale was our primary dependent measure and we did not want to risk contamination by other variables. Therefore, it is questionable to use justifications as a mediating variable, because intentions had temporal precedence over justifications. For this reason, these mediational analyses should be interpreted with caution.

GENERAL DISCUSSION

g_1

The pattern of results lends support for the hypothesis that alcohol intoxication increases the likelihood that a person will engage in risky sexual behaviors, such as having casual sexual intercourse without a condom. In the correlational study, we found that single males who were intoxicated the last time they had sexual intercourse were less likely to have used a condom than males who were not intoxicated when they last had intercourse. In the experimental studies, we found that intoxicated participants reported more positive intentions to engage in casual sex when a condom was not available, and were more likely to agree with justifications for this behavior, than their sober counterparts. Across all studies, intentions and justifications were highly correlated for participants in both the sober and the intoxicated conditions. The correspondence between intentions and justifications tended to be higher for sober participants, but this difference was significant only in the placebo experiment.

g_2

Of course, there is one inconsistent finding in our data that we cannot overlook. When subjects reported past behavior (correlational study), there was no evidence for a relationship between intoxication and condom use in females, yet when they reported intentions to have sexual intercourse (field experiment), we did find such a relationship. As mentioned earlier, alcohol intoxication may cause a decrease in condom use primarily among women who are on the pill, for whom the fear of pregnancy is not a salient inhibiting cue. We intend to explore whether taking oral contraceptives moderates the relationship between alcohol and condom use in females.

Discussion

First, the authors clearly state all of the findings (g_1). Second, they point out an interesting finding that they intend to explore in future experiments (g_2). Finally,

Summary

h   **Using different methodologies (i.e., correlational and experimental, laboratory and field studies), we have found evidence that alcohol intoxication is associated with a decrease in condom use.** In all four studies reported, we included only people who report that they usually use condoms. Our findings are therefore quite powerful—alcohol intoxication causes people to report more positive intentions to engage in unsafe sex even among those who believe in the benefits of using condoms. Most important, we have suggested that a compelling psychological process, alcohol myopia, may underlie this relationship. It is a common belief that alcohol acts as a general disinhibitor, which may lead one to expect that in most cases alcohol intoxication would cause a person to throw caution to the winds and engage in risky behaviors such as having casual sex without a condom. What makes the alcohol myopia perspective so intriguing, and potentially important, is that this account predicts that alcohol intoxication may make a person more or less likely to engage in risky behaviors, depending on the types of cues that are salient in the environment: If enough cues promoting condom use are made salient, it is possible that alcohol may actually be associated with an increase in condom use.

References

Baldwin, J. D., & Baldwin, J. I. (1988). Factors affecting AIDS-related sexual risk-taking behavior among college students. *Journal of Sex Research, 25,* 181–196.

Butcher, A. H., Manning, D. T., & O'Neal, E. C. (1991). HIV-related sexual behaviors of college students. *Journal of American College Health, 40,* 115–118.

Campbell, S. M., Peplau, L. A., & DeBro, S. C. (1992). Women, men, and condoms: Attitudes and experiences of heterosexual college students. *Psychology of Women Quarterly, 16,* 273–288.

Catania, J. A., Coates, T. J., Stall, R., Turner, H., Peterson, J., Hearst, N., Dolcini, M. M., Hudes, E., Gagnon, J., Wiley, J., & Groves, R. (1992). Prevalence of AIDS-related risk factors and condom use in the United States. *Science, 258,* 1101–1106.

Crowne, D., & Marlowe, D. (1964). *The approval motive.* New York: John Wiley.

Flanigan, B. J., & Hitch, M. A. (1986). Alcohol use, sexual intercourse, and contraception: An exploratory study. *Journal of Alcohol and Drug Education, 31,* 6–40.

they provide an overall summary outlining the theoretical and practical importance of utilizing different methodologies **(h)**.

Fong, G. T., Parent, M., & Poppe, C. (1994, April). *Predicting and understanding condom intentions and condom use among university students: A test of the theory of planned behavior.* Paper presented at the annual meeting of the Society of Behavioral Medicine, Boston.

Koch, A. (1994). *The effects of alcohol intoxication on attitudes and intentions towards condom use among male university students.* Unpublished undergraduate thesis, University of Waterloo.

Leigh, B. C., & Morrison, D. M. (1991). Alcohol consumption and sexual risk-taking in adolescents. *Alcohol Health and Research World, 15,* 58–63.

Leigh, B. C., & Stall, R. (1993). Substance use and risky sexual behavior for exposure to HIV. *American Psychologist, 48,* 1035–1045.

Lyvers, M. F., & Maltzman, I. (1991). The balanced placebo design: Effects of alcohol and beverage instructions cannot be independently assessed. *International Journal of Addictions, 26,* 963–972.

MacDonald, T. K., Zanna, M. P., & Fong, G. T. (1993, August). *The effects of alcohol on intentions to drinking and driving.* Poster presented at the annual meeting of the American Psychological Association, Toronto.

MacDonald, T. K., Zanna, M. P., & Fong, G. T. (1995). Decision making in altered states: The effects of alcohol on attitudes toward drinking and driving. *Journal of Personality and Social Psychology, 68,* 973–985.

Poppen, P. J., & Reisen, C. A. (1994). Heterosexual behaviors and risk of exposure to HIV: Current status and prospects for change. *Applied and Preventive Psychology, 3,* 75–90.

Robertson, J. A., & Plant, M. A. (1988). Alcohol, sex, and risks of HIV infection. *Alcohol Dependence, 22,* 75–78.

Rohsenow, D. J., & Marlatt, G. A. (1981). The balanced placebo design: Methodological considerations. *Addictive Behaviors, 6,* 107–122.

Rosenthal, R. (1984). *Meta-analytic procedures for social research.* Beverly Hills, CA: Sage.

Ross, D. F., & Pihl, R. O. (1989). Modification of the balanced-placebo design for use at high blood alcohol levels. *Addictive Behaviors, 14,* 91–97.

Steele, C. M., & Josephs, R. A. (1990). Alcohol myopia: Its prized and dangerous effects. *American Psychologist, 45,* 921–933.

Steele, C. M., & Southwick, L. (1985). Alcohol and social behavior: I. The psychology of drunken excess. *Journal of Personality and Social Psychology, 48,* 18–34.

Wallace, B. (1991, October). The mood on campus. *Macleans,* pp. 24–26.

Authors' Note: Preparation of this article was supported in part by a Social Sciences and Humanities Research Council of Canada (SSHRC) Doctoral Fellowship to the first author and SSHRC research grants to the second and third authors. We gratefully acknowledge Andy Koch, an undergraduate thesis student, for the important role he played in the initial stages of this research and for helping to develop the video vignette and the dependent measures used in the preliminary laboratory study. We would also like to thank Andy Muller, Wendy Telford, and Adam Zanna for their assistance with data collection. We also extend our appreciation to Darlene Spencer, Mary Moore, and Jonathon Goad of the drama department for their excellent work on the video vignette, and we thank Peter Hopkins, the Federation of Students at the University of Waterloo, and the management of Federation Hall for allowing us to use the campus pub for the field study. Requests for reprints should be sent to Tara MacDonald, Department of Psychology, University of Waterloo, Waterloo, Ontario, Canada N2L 3G1.

Questions

1. Why was it important to have additional data from experimental studies, as opposed to relying just on the data that the correlational study provided?
2. What concerns are there with correlational studies?
3. Discuss in what ways each of these studies and experiments used *transposition* or *experimental realism,* or both.
4. Do you think paying the subjects had any effect on the results of this study?
5. Evaluate the placebo study. Is it a true placebo group? Why or why not?

22 Karate Techniques

Introduction

Good research ideas come not only from exploring, reading, and discussing the literature, but also from who we are. The following article by Bedon and Howard (1992) is a good example of how many research projects often derive from one's own experiences and interests. The first author incorporated his interest, knowledge, and expertise about karate into his academic interest of memory. This is a particularly accessible article, easy to read and understand.

Special Issues

SUBJECT VARIABLES

As discussed in Chapter 3, subject variables are an experimenter-selected independent variable. This type of variable is not actively manipulated by the experimenter; rather, it is selected for, as a characteristic inherent in the subject. Some common subject variables are, for example, gender, race, age, social status, personality types, or IQ. It is easy to see that these variables would not be able to be manipulated in the laboratory. (You couldn't assign some subjects to be age 25, and others to be 35. Instead, you need 25-year-olds and 35-year-olds.) One caution though is that the experimenter must try to ensure that the selected subject variable is not related in some systematic way to another subject variable. This is called subject variable confound and you can read more about it in Chapter 5.

MEMORY FOR THE FREQUENCY OF OCCURRENCE OF KARATE TECHNIQUES: A COMPARISON OF EXPERTS AND NOVICES

Bernard G. Bedon and Darlene V. Howard
Georgetown University

Karate techniques were presented in a pattern to a group of karate students, half experts and half novices. The frequency with which these techniques appeared varied from 0 through 11. The experts and novices did not differ in the accuracy with which they judged the frequency of the techniques, but the experts showed a significant advantage over the novices in recalling the techniques. The results indicate that memory for the frequency of observed actions is not affected by subject variables such as prior knowledge, a finding consistent with the conclusion that memory for frequency is based on automatic processes.

Research (e.g., Hasher & Zacks, 1979, 1984) has shown that people are good at judging the frequency with which events have occurred, even when they do not originally intend to remember that frequency. Most of the earlier research on memory for frequency was done with verbal materials (e.g., word lists); in recent research, however, the earlier findings have been extended through the use of nonverbal materials as diverse as photographs of faces and line drawings of objects (Ozekes & Gilleard, 1989) and Japanese Kanji characters presented to English speakers (Brooks & Watkins, 1989; Wiggs, 1991). In the present study, we extend this research still further by examining observers' memory for a series of karate moves.

a_1 Hasher and Zacks (1979, 1984) proposed that the encoding of frequency is automatic, but there is controversy on this point (see, e.g., Fisk, 1986; Sanders, Gonzalez, Murphy, Liddle, & Vitina, 1987; Zacks, Hasher, & Hock, 1986). One kind of evidence cited in favor of the automaticity of encoding

Source: Reprinted by permission. *Bulletin of the Psychonomic Society,* 1992, *30*(2), 117–119.

Analysis

Literature Review

The authors provide us with the necessary background information on the controversy surrounding automaticity of frequency encoding (a_1). Therefore, they have set the stage for further exploring this phenomenon to see on which side of the controversy their data fall. Because the authors are interested in evaluating

frequency is that people who differ from each other in intelligence or prior relevant knowledge usually show similar accuracy when asked to judge the frequency with which events have occurred (see, e.g., Hasher & Zacks, 1984). This contrasts with recall measures, which usually reveal large differences that are related to intelligence and prior knowledge. For example, experts recall more data in their domains of expertise than novices do (Ericsson, Chase, & Faloon, 1980).

a$_2$ In order to obtain further evidence regarding the automaticity of frequency encoding, in the present experiment we compared the memory for karate moves of karate experts and novices. The karate moves were presented in a kata—a logical sequence that consists of a list of prearranged martial arts techniques in a pattern. In karate, certain blocks and kicks have to occur in certain stances, depending on one's body motion, directional movement, and weight distribution. Karate techniques are used to make fighting more efficient and natural; particular stances provide a stable foundation for certain blocks and punches. Furthermore, the type of stance has to flow with the direction of body motion and weight distribution. For example, there are stances in which 70% of the weight is on the back leg and the stance is stable in all directions (fugal stance), and there are some stances in which the weight is evenly distributed but only stable in one direction (e.g., kima, chongul). Thus, there are some "illegal" moves that do not make sense in karate according to these principles. In the present experiment, no such illegal moves were used.

a$_3$ **Given the literature on the effects of expertise (e.g., Charness, 1976; Chase & Simon, 1973), we expected that the experts would recall more karate moves than the novices would, because the experts already possessed an existing knowledge structure of the sport. However, we also expected that if the encoding of the frequency was automatic, the two groups would be equally accurate at judging the frequency with which moves had occurred.**

METHOD

Design
The experiment had the between-subjects variable of expertise (experts vs. novices) and two within-subjects variables, the latter being the type of test (frequency judgment vs. recall) and actual presented frequency (0, 1, 2, 3, 4, 5, 6, 7, 9, 11).

this phenomenon in the context of karate techniques, it is necessary to provide the reader with some information about karate moves. They do this in section (a$_2$). Next, they state very clearly their hypotheses (a$_3$).

Method

In this section the authors provide sufficiently detailed information regarding the subjects, materials, and procedures, so that this study could be replicated. Since

Subjects

The subjects were 30 student volunteers from the Tompkins Karate Association (TKA) Summer Karate Clinic, drawn from classes of experts and novices so that there were 15 subjects in each group.

An expert was defined as a first-degree black belt or other karate practitioner with at least 3.5 years of experience in Tang Soo Do Moo Duk Kwan (taught at TKA). The most experienced expert had 8 years of training, and the least experienced had 3.5 years. The group was composed of 5 female and 10 male experts, with an age range of 15–45.

A novice was defined as a white belt or yellow belt, or any karateka with fewer than 1.5 years of training. The least experienced novice had 4.5 months of training; the most experienced had 1 year of karate training. There were 2 females and 13 males in this group, with an age range of 14–37 years.

Materials

A total of 20 karate techniques with variable frequencies were chosen from a kata created by the first author to ensure that the subjects had no prior exposure to it. The techniques and their frequencies were: upblock (4), downblock (2), reverse punch (11), front kick (2), sidekick (3), sudo block (6), round kick (1), U-punch (0), ridgehand (2), palmup tension (3), X-block (1), down tension (2), kima stance (6), chongul stance (9), fugal stance (7), cat stance (2), mountain block (2), spinkick (0), hook kick (0), and elbow smash (1). This was the order in the subsequent frequency test list, but not the order of presentation, for these techniques must be presented within the logical confines of karate kata (e.g., mountain blocks must occur in a kima stance).

Procedure

The experiment began with the presentation of the following spoken instructions: "Please pay close attention to the kata you are about to see, because later your memory for the techniques in the kata will be tested." Then a kata, performed by the first author (a second-degree black belt karate instructor with 13 years experience), was presented to all subjects simultaneously, although the experts were seated separately from the novices. Afterward, they were asked for their judgment of the frequency with which each technique occurred; for example, "How many times did a downblock occur?" As this was

the subject variable of expertise in karate techniques is the independent variable, it is, of course, important that the groups be defined unambiguously. The authors do this in section **(b)**. Simply defining the groups as "expert" and "novice" would not have been enough information to have an unequivocal understanding of who the subjects were.

Section **(c)** is a good example of a Procedure section: It is clear, in order of occurrence, and provides sufficient detail for replication.

asked, the isolated technique was executed, so there would be no ambiguity. The subjects recorded their responses on an answer sheet, which was collected immediately following this part of the experiment and was replaced with a blank sheet. There followed a 5-min retention interval, during which time subjects were asked to count aloud by threes as a group. At the end of this period, a free-recall test was conducted for 60 sec, during which the subjects wrote down any techniques they could remember.

RESULTS

Frequency Estimation

A mean frequency estimate for each actual frequency was obtained by calculating a mean across subjects for every technique that occurred with a certain frequency. Mean frequency estimates for the two groups are shown in Figure 1.

d_1

As the figure makes clear, the subjects' judgments about the frequency with which the technique occurred was close to the actual frequency. Furthermore, there was little difference between the experts' and the novices' judgments. In fact, the correlation between actual frequency and judged frequency was .907 ($n = 9$, $p < .0007$) for the experts and .909 ($n = 9$, $p < .0007$) for the novices.

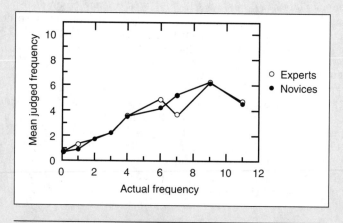

FIGURE 1   **Mean judged frequency of karate techniques, as a function of actual frequency, for experts and novices.**

Results

The authors clearly present the data for both dependent variables (frequency estimation and free recall) (**d_1**), and in the Recall section report their criteria for

Recall

d₂ | **Any item written down on the subjects' answer sheets that was recognizable as one of the presented techniques in the kata was counted as correct, even if it was misspelled.** No one recalled items that were not in the initial sequence. As expected, the experts recalled substantially more techniques than did the novices, with the experts recalling on the average nearly twice as many techniques as did the novices. The mean number recalled by the experts (of a possible maximum of 20) was 14.9 items ($SD = 2.0$; range, 13–16), and the mean number recalled by the novices was 8.3 items ($SD = 2.0$; range, 6–12). This difference is statistically significant [$t(28) = 11.2, p < .001$].

DISCUSSION

e₁ | **This study shows that experts and novices are equally accurate at judging the frequency of karate moves, although experts are notably better than novices at free recall of the moves. In subsequent conversation, the subjects expressed surprise at being able to judge the frequency of the tech-**

e₂ | **niques so accurately. In fact, most thought that they had had particularly poor memories for the frequency of the various moves. This surprise is consistent with the argument that frequency information is encoded without awareness or effort, and that frequency encoding is automatic for a wide variety of events, including actions such as karate techniques.**

For the most part, the pattern of accuracy in memory for the frequency of karate moves is quite similar to that obtained in studies done with other types of stimuli. Typically in such studies (e.g., Hasher & Zacks, 1984), mean judged frequency is almost identical to the actual frequency up to frequencies of approximately four, but for higher frequencies, people tend to underestimate. There was one technique that neither group judged very accurately—reverse punch—which was the only technique presented 11 times.

correcting the answer sheets **(d₂)**. This is very important, as another researcher might have counted misspelled karate moves as incorrect. These researchers presumably made this decision based on the idea that even if a subject spelled a technique incorrectly, this was not a reflection of the absence of the knowledge of whether or not the technique occurred.

Discussion

In section **(e₁)** the authors state the overall results of the study. They do not, however, expressly tell the reader whether or not these results supported their hypotheses. You may need to refer to their hypotheses to see if they were in fact supported. In **(e₂)** the authors provide some extra information about conversations

e_3 **When subjects were asked about this, their responses suggested a presentation error, in which the reverse punch was thrown too fast relative to other techniques in the kata to be noticed.** This discrepancy in speed probably affected the judgment of the subjects, for research has shown that the bias of understanding the frequency of an event can be traced to a number of possible sources, including disproportionate exposure duration (Lichtenstein, Slovic, Fischoff, Layman, & Combs, 1978).

e_4 **In the case of recall, the fact that the experts were better than the novices was not likely due to a difference in the ability to generate the names; both the experts and the novices were familiar with the names of all karate moves used.**

e_5 **When the subjects were questioned about their responses on the recall task, the novices indicated only that they tried to remember as many techniques as they could. The experts, on the other hand, reported that they used recall strategies.** For example, when trying to remember whether sudo blocks were used, they remembered that sudo blocks usually occur in fugal stances and that upblocks and downblocks usually occur in chongul stances. That is, instead of trying to recall individual bits of information, the experts gathered whole patterns of information into "chunks." It has been shown that the chunks recalled by experts are richer than those recalled by novices in the domains of digit span skill (Chase & Ericsson, 1982), basketball (Allard, Graham, & Paarsalu, 1980), computer programming (Soloway, Adelson, & Erlich, 1988), and medical practice (Norman, Brooks, & Allen, 1989).

The karate experts relied on a storehouse of prior relevant knowledge gained through years of experience in seeing these techniques paired together; the novices did not have the necessary martial arts background from which to draw inferences and chunk the material into meaningful packets of information. The recall strategies that the experts used were based on frequency-of-occurrence information that they encoded into long-term memory from exposure to the techniques over the years. This is consistent with the argument that frequency information is used in acquiring new knowledge and in organizing and retrieving existing knowledge (see, e.g., Hasher & Zacks, 1984; Wiggs, 1991).

with the subjects *after* the experiment. You might ask yourself why the authors included this information. In Discussion sections it is appropriate to bring in other information about the experimental situation. While not being a part of the procedures of the actual experiment, understanding the experimental context provides information with which one can further evaluate and consider the results. The authors then tie this more qualitative information into known research literature that supports its applicability. The authors note a possible weakness of the experiment (e_3), as well as provide evidence refuting a possible alternative explanation (e_4). In (e_5) we notice again that the experimenters utilized information garnered after the experiment to expand their understanding of the data.

REFERENCES

Allard, F., Graham, S., & Paarsalu, M. (1980). Perception in sport: Basketball. *Journal of Sport Psychology, 2,* 14–21.

Brooks, J. O., III, & Watkins, M. J. (1989). Recognition memory and the mere exposure effect. *Journal of Experimental Psychology: Learning, Memory, & Cognition, 15,* 968–976.

Charness, N. (1976). Memory for chess positions: Resistance to interference. *Journal of Experimental Psychology: Human Learning & Memory, 2,* 641–653.

Chase, W. G., & Ericsson, K. A. (1982). Skill and working memory. In G. Bower (Ed.), *The psychology of learning and motivation* (Vol. 16, pp. 1–58). New York: Academic Press.

Chase, W. G., & Simon, H. (1973). Perception in chess. *Cognitive Psychology, 4,* 55–81.

Ericsson, K. A., Chase, W. G., & Faloon, S. (1980). Acquisition of a memory skill. *Science, 208,* 1181–1182.

Fisk, A. D. (1986). Frequency encoding is not inevitable and is not automatic: A reply to Hasher & Zacks. *American Psychologist, 41,* 215–216.

Hasher, L., & Zacks, R. T. (1979). Automatic and effortful processes in memory. *Journal of Experimental Psychology: General, 108,* 356–388.

Hasher, L., & Zacks, R. T. (1984). Automatic processing of fundamental information. *American Psychologist, 39,* 1372–1388.

Lichtenstein, S., Slovic, P., Fischoff, B., Layman, M., & Combs, B. (1978). Judged frequency of lethal events. *Journal of Experimental Psychology: Human Learning & Memory, 4,* 551–578.

Norman, G. F., Brooks, L. R., & Allen, S. W. (1989). Recall by expert medical practitioners and novices as a record of processing attention. *Journal of Experimental Psychology: Learning, Memory, & Cognition, 15,* 1166–1174.

Ozekes, M., & Gilleard, C. (1989). Remembering faces and drawings: A test of Hasher & Zacks' model of automatic processing in a Turkish sample. *Journal of Gerontology, 44,* 122–123.

Sanders, R. E., Gonzalez, E. G., Murphy, M. D., Liddle, C. L., & Vitina, J. R. (1987). Frequency of occurrence and the criteria for automatic processing. *Journal of Experimental Psychology: Learning, Memory, & Cognition, 13,* 241–250.

Soloway, E., Adelson, B., & Erlich, K. (1988). Knowledge and processes in the comprehension of computer programs. In M. T. H. Chi, R. Glaser, & M. J. Farr (Eds.), *The nature of expertise* (pp. 129–152). Hillsdale, NJ: Erlbaum.

Wiggs, C. L. (1991). *Aging and memory for frequency of occurrence of novel visual stimuli: Direct and indirect measures.* Unpublished doctoral dissertation, Georgetown University, Washington, DC.

Zacks, R. T., Hasher, L., & Hock, H. S. (1986). Inevitability and automaticity: A response to Fisk. *American Psychologist, 41,* 216–218.

Note: This study was completed as part of an undergraduate research project by B. G. Bedon under the direction of D. V. Howard. We are grateful to Caitlin Brune for her help in completing the manuscript and to Jeffrey Howard for preparing the figure. Bernard G. Bedon is now a graduate student in the Department of Psychology, University of Maryland, College Park, MD 20742. Correspondence may also be sent to Darlene V. Howard at the Department of Psychology, Georgetown University, Washington, DC 20057 (E-mail: D_howard@guvax.bitnet).

Questions

1. What is your opinion of how the two groups (experts and novices) were defined? Do you think there are other ways for defining those groups that might have affected the outcome of the experiment?
2. The authors assume that the subjects had no prior experience with the kata that was created by the first author to be the independent variable. What kind of effect would there have been if they did have prior experience with it? Is there a way that the authors could have made sure that the subjects had no experience with that set of moves?
3. What effect do you think the instructions "Please pay close attention to the kata you are about to see, because later your memory for the techniques in the kata will be tested" had on the experiment? Could the instruction have been eliminated? Should it have been?
4. Why were the subjects asked to count aloud by threes for five minutes before they started the next phase of the experiment?
5. Given the information in the Results section pertaining to recall, sketch a meaningful histogram. Do you think a graph such as this should have been included in the article?
6. Is there a recreational activity in your life that you could base an experiment on?

23 Disputes in Japan

Introduction

Justice and psycholegal issues comprise a burgeoning area of research in psychology. Issues such as jury decision making, eyewitness identification, procedural justice, and the use of social science as evidence in the court are just some of the legal issues that interest social scientists today. These topics lend themselves to theoretical and experimental consideration.

A growing body of research in the area of dispute resolution has suggested that people are more concerned about the fairness of the procedures involved in resolving a dispute than in the actual outcome itself. In other words, as long as the procedures are perceived as fair, the outcome, regardless of whether or not it is favorable, will likely be acceptable.

Of particular interest to Sugawara and Huo (1994) is the question of what the impressions are of people from non-Western countries regarding the importance of fair procedures in dispute resolutions. In order to address this question, the researchers used standard procedural justice methodology and used students from Fukushima University in Japan as participants.

This article is reprinted from *Social Justice Research,* which is an international multidisciplinary journal that publishes papers regarding the origins, structures, and consequences of justice in human affairs, of interest to psychologists, sociologists, anthropologists, economists, and other social scientists. The style is very similar to APA style, but there are some minor changes. Since psychologists may read and publish their results in journals not published by the APA, it is important to be acquainted with these sources and their styles. Analyze this article carefully.

DISPUTES IN JAPAN: A CROSS-CULTURAL TEST
OF THE PROCEDURAL JUSTICE MODEL

Ikuo Sugawara
Fukushima University, Japan

Yuen J. Huo
University of California, Berkeley

Research on procedural justice has provided ample evidence that people are concerned not only with the outcome of disputes but also with the fairness of the procedures used to solve the disputes. The majority of the studies examining the importance of procedural justice have been conducted in the United States and Western European countries. This study tests the generality of the procedural justice model by examining the importance of fair procedures to people in a non-Western country, Japan. This study also examines the meaning of a fair procedure from a legal perspective. Past studies have drawn the procedural justice criteria considered from social psychology. We examine several additional criteria derived from the legal concept of due process of law. Results indicate that fair procedures are more important to subjects than fair outcomes in both a traffic accident dispute and a breach of contract case. Furthermore, across both types of disputes, fairness concerns are more important than nonfairness concerns. These results are consistent with findings from studies conducted in Western countries. A new finding that emerges from the study is that the clarity with which a procedure is formulated and presented is a strong determinant of procedural justice judgment.

In their research on disputes, Thibaut and Walker (1975, 1978) found considerable evidence in support of the importance of procedural justice as a determinant of preferences for and satisfaction with legal procedures. Procedural justice effects found in these early studies have been replicated in a variety of dispute situations in settings such as the courtroom, business organizations, the political arena, and educational institutions (see Lind and Tyler, 1988, for a review). Although most of these studies have examined the views of Americans subjects, evidence in support of the procedural justice model has also been found in several Western European countries (Lind et al., 1978) and in Hong Kong (Leung, 1987, 1988; Leung and Lind, 1986). Hong Kong can be considered a non-Western country, but it can also be argued that its history and culture have both been greatly influenced by its heritage as a British colony. For example, people in Hong Kong speak English, and they have adopted the British adversarial procedure for resolving disputes into

Source: Reprinted by permission in an edited version.

their legal system. To date there has been no attempt to directly examine the importance of procedural justice to people in a country that has not been greatly influenced by Western culture. This study tests the generality of the procedural justice model by examining its importance in a country with a distinctly East Asian culture, Japan.

According to Thibaut and Walker's (1975) original formulation, disputants care about procedural justice because when a procedure is fair, it will most likely lead to an equitable outcome for those involved. Furthermore, Thibaut and Walker's theory assumes that when there is a conflict of interest, each party to the dispute wants to ensure good outcomes for themselves. To achieve such an outcome, disputants need to exercise process control, which involves presenting arguments and evidence for their respective case. Process control has been found to be an important determinant of procedural justice judgments (e.g., Houlden et al., 1978; Thibaut and Walker, 1975, 1978). One consequence of procedures that invest process control in the disputants, such as the adversarial legal system found in U.S. courtrooms, is a high likelihood of argument and open conflict.

We predict that the procedural justice concerns described by Thibaut and Walker may be influenced by cultural differences in values. The cross-cultural distinction of individualism-collectivism (see Triandis, 1989, for a discussion) allows us to make specific predictions about the importance of procedural justice to different cultures. Past research (Hofstede, 1980, 1983) suggests that people in countries that fall on the individualism end of the dimension such as the United States and most Western European countries are primarily concerned about the consequences of their actions for their own needs, interests, and goals. People in these individualistic countries place importance on such values as autonomy, competitiveness, and achievement. In contrast, people in countries identified as highly collectivist, which include most Asian and Latin American countries, tend to emphasize the importance of interpersonal harmony and group solidarity. Such value differences are predicted to influence a variety of social interactions. In this study, we examine specifically how individualism–collectivism may affect the role that justice concerns play in dispute resolution.

In Study 1, we ask the subjects to respond to a dispute scenario in which two variables are manipulated, the significance of the dispute for the disputants and the level of conflict between them. We predict that for collectivists, procedural justice concerns may be sacrificed to preserve harmony within relationships. This prediction might be particularly applicable in a dispute about a significant problem, for example, when the victim of the accident has suffered a severe injury or in one that involves a high level of conflict between the disputants. Because of the importance of the dispute to both parties and the high degree of animosity between them, outcome concerns may be highly relevant while procedural justice concerns diminish in importance.

Study 1

Method

Subjects.   The subjects in Study 1 were 143 undergraduate students enrolled in a legal study course at Fukushima University in Japan. The majority of the subjects were students in the education department. The study was administered to the students during a class meeting.

Experimental Design.   The study was a 2 × 2 factorial design in which two situational variables were varied: the significance of the dispute for those involved (high vs. low) and the degree of conflict between the two parties (high vs. low). Subjects were randomly assigned to one of the four conditions.

Procedure.   Subjects were asked to read a scenario describing a traffic accident in which the driver of the car hit a pedestrian at a crossroad with a traffic signal. The driver of the car and the pedestrian did not know each other. Subjects were asked to imagine themselves as the pedestrian. In the high significance condition, the situation was described as one involving serious injury (the pedestrian broke a leg as a result of the accident). Alternatively, in the low significance condition, the scenario was described as a minor one involving only stains on the pedestrian's clothes. In the high conflict condition, each disputant insisted that the other was to blame for failing to observe the traffic signal. In the low conflict condition, the driver admitted his fault but did not agree with the amount of compensation based on contributive negligence on the part of the pedestrian. (In Japan, when the victim is responsible for contributive negligence, the amount of the compensation may be adjusted according to the degree of the negligence on the part of the victim.)

A series of questions followed the scenario. They included two manipulation checks and questions which asked the subject to rate the importance of several relevant factors including (i) opportunity to present the case, (ii) opportunity to reject the decision, (iii) a procedure that reflects your opinion, (iv) fair procedure, (v) clarity of the procedure, (vi) dispute resolved in short time, (vii) fair outcome, (viii) effectiveness of procedure in solving the problem. Each subject gave ratings on a 7-point scale that ranges from *not at all important* (0) to *extremely important* (6).

The dispute scenario and all other written and verbal directions were given in the subjects' native language, Japanese.

Results

Manipulation Check.   Analysis of variance (ANOVA) showed that both of the independent variables were successfully manipulated. Subjects in the low significance condition perceived the dispute to be relatively minor relative to subjects in the high significance condition, $F(1, 141) = 24.62, p < 0.01$. Subjects in the low conflict condition perceived there to be significantly less conflict between the two disputants than subjects in the high conflict condition, $F(1, 141) = 17.69, p < 0.01$.

Importance Ratings. Subjects rated the importance of both fairness and nonfairness issues. The mean important ratings for each of the relevant issues are presented in Table 1.

Fairness issues were rated as more important than nonfairness issues. A t-test indicated that the average fairness rating was significantly higher than the average nonfairness rating, $t(142) = 5.03, p < 0.01$ and between the two nonfairness issues $t(142) = 7.72, p < 0.01$, with procedural fairness rated as more important than distributive fairness and the effectiveness of the dispute rated as more important than the speedy resolution of the dispute.

Situational Effects. When collapsed across the four conditions, fairness emerged as important to the Japanese. It may, however, be the case that the importance of fairness varied according to the situation. We examined the effects that the situation may have on importance ratings of fairness and nonfairness concerns. Two situational variables were examined: the significance of the dispute and the level of conflict between the disputants.

Although the level of conflict of the dispute did not have a significant effect on the average fairness ratings, $F(1,139) = 0.08$, n.s., the significance of the dispute effect approached statistical significance with fairness issues being rated more important when the dispute was significant ($X = 5.69$) than when it was not ($X = 5.52$), $F(1, 139) = 3.58, p < 0.10$.

The significance of the dispute did not have an effect on the average nonfairness ratings, $F(1, 139) = 0.01$, n.s. The level of conflict, on the other hand, did have a significant effect on the average ratings of nonfairness issues. Nonfairness issues were rated as more important when the dispute involved a low level of conflict ($X = 4.11$) than when the level of conflict was high ($X = 3.67$), $F(1, 130) = 4.64, p < 0.05$. Neither of the manipulated variables had a significant effect on the individual issues of procedural fairness, distributive

TABLE 1   **Accident Dispute: Mean Ratings for Fairness and Nonfairness Issues**

Dispute Issues	RATINGS OF IMPORTANCE	
	Mean	**SD**
Fairness issues		
Fair procedure	5.79	0.50
Fair decision	5.45	0.80
Average fairness rating	5.62	0.53
Nonfairness issues		
Effective procedure	4.55	1.31
Dispute resolved in short time	3.30	1.76
Average nonfairness rating	3.93	1.22

fairness, or effectiveness of the procedure. A speedy resolution of the dispute, however, was rated as more important when the dispute involved a low level of conflict ($X = 3.60$) than when it involved high conflict ($X = 2.88$), $F(1, 139) = 5.91, p < 0.05$.

Meaning of Procedural Justice.   Table 2 displays the correlations between the importance ratings of procedural fairness and the importance ratings of each of the criteria of procedural justice.

The correlational analysis showed that the importance rating of the opportunity to present the case (process control) was significantly correlated with the importance rating of procedural fairness. Procedural fairness was also significantly correlated with subjects' ratings of the importance of having a procedure that reflected their opinion and with the clarity of the procedure. The only nonsignificant correlation was between procedural fairness and the opportunity to reject the decision (decision control). Regression analysis indicated that the most important predictor of procedural fairness was the clarity of the procedure.

Discussion

The findings of Study 1 indicate that fairness, in general, and the fairness of the procedure, in particular, are important to the Japanese. This set of results suggests that the typical findings of procedural justice research in the United States and Europe can be generalized to subjects in an East Asian culture within the context of a dispute involving a traffic accident between strangers. In general, the findings indicate that the procedural justice model can be generalized to an East Asian culture. Similar to their Western counterpart, Japanese subjects are concerned with procedural justice issues. The findings in this study are consistent with the findings of a study about the political process conducted in Japan (Takenishi and Takenishi, 1990) which also suggests that procedural justice concerns matter to the Japanese. Furthermore, evidence is provided that across a variety of situations the Japanese consider the fairness of the procedure relatively more important than the fairness of the outcome.

TABLE 2   Accident Dispute: Correlations and Beta Weights for Procedural Justice Criteria

Criteria of Procedural Justice	Correlation	β^a
Opportunity to present the case	.26[b]	.18[c]
Procedure reflects disputants' opinion	.22[b]	.16
Opportunity to reject the decision	.04	−.04
Procedure clear	.31[b]	.24[b]
R^2		16%[b]

[a] Values are standardized regression coefficients.

[b] $p < 0.01$.

[c] $p < 0.05$.

These findings are similar to findings of procedural justice studies conducted in Western countries.

Contrary to our predictions, the findings in the study suggest that procedural justice concerns, if not universal, can at least be generalized to a distinctly Asian culture. The prediction that procedural justice may not be as important to the Japanese as it is to Westerners stems from Thibaut and Walker's theory of procedural justice in conjunction with a cross-cultural theory of value differences. In contrast to Thibaut and Walker's formulation (1975, 1978), an alternative, relational-based theory of procedural justice provides contrasting predictions that procedural justice concerns may be universal. According to the relational model of procedural justice (Lind and Tyler, 1988; Tyler and Lind, 1992), people care about fair treatment because it informs them about their stature within a group. In other words, people care about procedural justice because it satisfies their basic human need to be accepted and highly regarded by important others. This desire to be a valued member of a group may transcend any existing minor variations in cultural values. If the relational model is correct, only minimal cross-cultural differences in procedural justice judgments would be observed. There has already been some theoretical discussion of cross-cultural consistencies in justice judgments which developed out of the relational model (Lind and Earley, 1993). The predictions generated from the relational model should be tested in future studies. Future research should also employ simultaneous data collection in multiple cultures to provide a more direct comparison of the relative importance of procedural justice concerns.

REFERENCES

Adler, J. W., Hensler, D. R. & Nelson, C. E. (1983). Simple justice: How litigants fare in the Pittsburgh Court Arbitration Program, Rand, Santa Monica, CA.

Delgado, R., Dunn, C., Brown, P., Lee, H., & Hubbert, D. (1985). Fairness and formality: Minimizing the risk of prejudice in alternative dispute resolution. *Wisconsin Law Rev.* 1359–1404.

Haley, J. (1978). The myth of the reluctant litigant. *J. of Japan. Stud. 4,* 359.

Hofstede, G. (1980). *Culture's Consequence: International Differences in Work-Related Values,* Sage, Beverly Hills, CA.

Hofstede, G. (1983). Dimensions of national cultures in fifty countries and three regions. In Deregowaki, J. B., Dziurawiec, S., & Annis, R. C. (Eds.), *Expiscations in Cross-Cultural Psychology,* Sets and Zeitlinger, Lisse, The Netherlands, pp. 335–355.

Houlden, P., LaTour, S., Walker, L., & Thibaut, J. (1978). Preferences for modes of dispute resolution as a function of process and decision control. *J. Exp. Soc. Psychol. 14,* 13–30.

Kawashima, T. (1963). Dispute resolution in contemporary Japan. In von Mehren, A. T. (Ed.), *Law in Japan: The Order of a Changing Society,* Harvard University Press, Cambridge, MA.

Kidder, R. L., & Hostetler, J. A. (1990). Managing ideologies: Harmony as ideology in Amish and Japanese societies. *Law Soc. Rev. 24,* 895–922.

La Tour, S., Houlden, P., Walker, L., & Thibaut, J. (1976). Procedure: Some determinants of preference for modes of conflict resolution. *J. Conflict Resolution 20,* 319–355.

Leung, K. (1987). Some determinants of reaction to procedural models for conflict resolution: A cross-national study. *J. Pers. Soc. Psychol. 53,* 898–908.

Leung, K. (1988). Some determinants of conflict avoidance. *J. Cross-Cultural Psychol. 19,* 125–136.

Leung, K., & Lind, E. A. (1986). Procedural justice and culture: Effects of culture, gender, and investigator status on procedural preferences. *J. Pers. Soc. Psychol. 50,* 1134–1150.

Leventhal, G. S. (1980). What should be done with equity theory? New approaches to the study of fairness in social relationships. In Gergen, K., Greenberg, M., and Willis, R. (Eds.), *Social Exchange: Advances in Theory and Research,* Plenum Press, New York.

Lind, E. A., & Earley, P. C. (1993). Procedural justice and culture. *Int. J. Psychol. 27,* 227–242.

Lind, E. A., Erickson, B. E., Friedland, N., & Dickenberger, M. (1978). Reactions to procedural models for adjudicative conflict resolution. *J. Conflict Resolution 22,* 318–341.

Lind, E. A., Lissak, R. I., & Conlon, D. E. (1983). Decision control and process control effects on procedural fairness judgments. *J. Appl. Soc. Psychol. 13,* 338–350.

Lind, E. A., MacCoun, R. J., Ebener, P. A., Felstiner, W. F., Hensler, D. R., Resnik, J., & Tyler, T. R. (1989). The perception of justice: Tort litigants' view of trial, court-annexed arbitration, and judicial settlement conferences, Rand, Santa Monica, CA.

Lind, E. A., & Tyler, T. R. (1988). *Social Psychology of Procedural Justice,* Plenum Press, New York.

Merry, S. E., & Silbey, S. S. (1984). What do plaintiffs want? Reexamining the concept of dispute. *Justice Syst. J. 9,* 151–178.

Resnik, J. (1987). Due process: A public dimension. *U. Flor. Law Rev. 39,* 405–431.

Takenishi, M., & Takenishi, A. (1990). Why Japanese citizens evaluate the new indirect tax as unfair: Fairness criteria and their relative importance. *Soc. Justice Res. 4,* 251–263.

Tanase, T. (1990). The management of dispute: Automobile accident compensation in Japan. *Law Soc. Rev. 24,* 651–691.

Thibaut, J., & Walker, L. (1975). *Procedural Justice: A Psychological Analysis,* Erlbaum, Hillsdale, NJ.

Thibaut, J., and Walker, L. (1978). A theory of procedure. *Calif. Law Rev. 66,* 541–566.

Triandis, H. C. (1989). The self and social behavior in differing cultural contexts. *Psychol. Rev. 54,* 323–338.

Trubeck, D. M. (1972). Max Weber on law and the rise of capitalism. *Wis. Law Rev.* 720–753.

Tyler, T. R., and Lind, E. A. (1992). A relational model of authority in groups. In M. Zanna (Ed.), *Advances in Experimental Social Psychology,* 25, Academic Press, New York.

Note: We gratefully acknowledge E. Allan Lind and Tom R. Tyler for their encouragement in pursuing this research and for their helpful comments on earlier drafts of this article. The Yamashita Taro Memorial Foundation for Education and Science in Akita, Japan provided support for this study. Yuen J. Huo was supported by an American Psychological Association Graduate Fellowship.

Questions

1. Notice how the researchers develop their argument in the literature review section. What differences do you see in this article compared to previous articles?
2. What is the general conclusion reached in this paper?
3. What measures were made?
4. How did the authors treat their data?
5. What is the problem?
6. What is the hypothesis?
7. What type of scale was used in the experiment?
8. What is a manipulation check? Why are they important?
9. Do you think the manipulation check used in this experiment was effective?
10. How would you classify this research?

CHAPTER

24 False Confessions

Introduction

This article by Kassin and Kiechel (1996) raises several interesting issues. One is the issue of studying real-life problems in the laboratory in an effort to provide information and guidelines to practitioners. Some topics that are studied in this way are education and teaching techniques, health-related behaviors, and legal issues. This is sometimes called "applied psychology." Another important issue present in this article is the use of deception. While you are reading, you should consider the ethical guidelines you learned in Chapter 8 and ask yourself (1) how you would feel as a subject in this study and (2) whether you are satisfied with the protections in place for the participants.

THE SOCIAL PSYCHOLOGY OF FALSE CONFESSIONS: COMPLIANCE, INTERNALIZATION, AND CONFABULATION

Saul M. Kassin and Katherine L. Kiechel
Williams College

An experiment demonstrated that false incriminating evidence can lead people to accept guilt for a crime they did not commit. Subjects in a fast- or slow-paced reaction time task were accused of damaging a computer by pressing the wrong key. All were truly innocent and initially denied the charge. A confederate then said she saw the subject hit the key or did not see the subject hit the key. Compared with subjects in the slow-pace/no-witness group, those in the fast-pace/witness group were more likely to sign a confession, internalize guilt for the event, and confabulate details in memory consistent with that belief. Both legal and conceptual implications are discussed.

In criminal law, confession evidence is a potent weapon for the prosecution and a recurring source of controversy. Whether a suspect's self-incriminating statement was voluntary or coerced and whether a suspect was of sound mind are just two of the issues that trial judges and juries consider on a routine basis. To guard citizens against violations of due process and to minimize the risk that the innocent would confess to crimes they did not commit, the courts have erected guidelines for the admissibility of confession evidence. Although there is no simple litmus test, confessions are typically excluded from trial if elicited by physical violence, a threat of harm or punishment, or a promise of immunity or leniency, or without the suspect being notified of his or her Miranda rights.

a₁

To understand the psychology of criminal confessions, three questions need to be addressed: First, how do police interrogators elicit self-incriminating statements (i.e., what means of social influence do they use)? Second, what effects do these methods have (i.e., do innocent suspects ever confess

Source: Reprinted by permission in its entirety. *Psychological Science,* 1996, 7(3), 125–128.

Analysis

Literature Review

In this section, the authors recognize the need not only to provide some background in the psychological literature pertinent to this study, but also to educate the reader on the relevant legal issues, procedures, case law, and definitions

to crimes they did not commit)? Third, when a coerced confession is retracted and later presented at trial, do juries sufficiently discount the evidence in accordance with the law? General reviews of relevant case law and research are available elsewhere (Gudjonsson, 1992; Wrightsman & Kassin, 1993). The present research addresses the first two questions.

Informed by developments in case law, the police use various methods of interrogation—including the presentation of false evidence (e.g., fake polygraph, fingerprints, or other forensic test results; staged eyewitness identifications), appeals to God and religion, feigned friendship, and the use of prison informants. A number of manuals are available to advise detectives on how to extract confessions from reluctant crime suspects (Aubry & Caputo, 1965; O'Hara & O'Hara, 1981). The most popular manual is Inbau, Reid, and Buckley's (1986) *Criminal Interrogation and Confessions,* originally published in 1962, and now in its third edition.

After advising interrogators to set aside a bare, soundproof room absent of social support and distraction, Inbau et al. (1986) describe in detail a ninestep procedure consisting of various specific ploys. In general, two types of approaches can be distinguished. One is *minimization,* a technique in which the detective lulls the suspect into a false sense of security by providing face-saving excuses, citing mitigating circumstances, blaming the victim, and underplaying the charges. The second approach is one of *maximization,* in which the interrogator uses scare tactics by exaggerating or falsifying the characterization of evidence, the seriousness of the offense, and the magnitude of the charges. In a recent study (Kassin & McNall, 1991), subjects read interrogation transcripts in which these ploys were used and estimated the severity of the sentence likely to be received. The results indicated that minimization communicated an implicit offer of leniency, comparable to that estimated in an explicit-promise condition, whereas maximization implied a threat of harsh punishment, comparable to that found in an explicit-threat condition. Yet although American courts routinely exclude confessions elicited by explicit threats and promises, they admit those produced by contingencies that are pragmatically implied.

Although police often use coercive methods of interrogation, research suggests that juries are prone to convict defendants who confess in these situations. In the case of *Arizona* v. *Fulminante* (1991), the U.S. Supreme Court ruled that under certain conditions, an improperly admitted coerced confession may be considered upon appeal to have been nonprejudicial, or "harmless error." Yet mock-jury research shows that people find it hard to believe that anyone would confess to a crime that he or she did not commit (Kassin & Wrightsman, 1980, 1981; Sukel & Kassin, 1994). Still, it happens. One cannot estimate the prevalence of the problem, which has never been systematically examined, but there are numerous documented instances on record

$\mathbf{a_1}$, $\mathbf{a_2}$, $\mathbf{a_3}$, $\mathbf{a_4}$). Next, they offer a brief review of memory research, and pose some questions for how it might be related to the legal issue of confessions (**b**).

(analysis continues on page 366)

a₄

(Bedau & Radelat, 1987; Borchard, 1932; Rattner, 1988). Indeed, one can distinguish three types of false confession (Kassin & Wrightsman, 1985): *voluntary* (in which a subject confesses in the absence of external pressure), *coerced–compliant* (in which a suspect confesses only to escape an aversive interrogation, secure a promised benefit, or avoid a threatened harm), and *coerced–internalized* (in which a suspect actually comes to believe that he or she is guilty of the crime).

This last type of false confession seems most unlikely, but a number of recent cases have come to light in which the police had seized a suspect who was vulnerable (by virtue of his or her youth, intelligence, personality, stress, or mental state) and used false evidence to convince the beleaguered suspect that he or she was guilty. In one case that received a great deal of attention, for example, Paul Ingram was charged with rape and a host of satanic cult crimes that included the slaughter of newborn babies. During 6 months of interrogation, he was hypnotized, exposed to graphic crime details, informed by a police psychologist that sex offenders often repress their offenses, and urged by the minister of his church to confess. Eventually, Ingram "recalled" crime scenes to specification, pleaded guilty, and was sentenced to prison. There was no physical evidence of these crimes, however, and an expert who reviewed the case for the state concluded that Ingram had been brainwashed. To demonstrate, this expert accused Ingram of a bogus crime and found that although he initially denied the charge, he later confessed—and embellished the story (Ofshe, 1992; Wright, 1994).

b

Other similar cases have been reported (e.g., Pratkanis & Aronson, 1991), but, to date, there is no empirical proof of this phenomenon. Memory researchers have found that misleading postevent information can alter actual or reported memories of observed events (Loftus, Donders, Hoffman, & Schooler, 1989; Loftus, Miller, & Burns, 1978; McCloskey & Zaragoza, 1985)—an effect that is particularly potent in young children (Ceci & Bruck, 1993; Ceci, Ross, & Toglia, 1987) and adults under hypnosis (Dinges et al., 1992; Dywan & Bowers, 1983; Sheehan, Statham, & Jamieson, 1991). Indeed, recent studies suggest it is even possible to implant false recollections of traumas supposedly buried in the unconscious (Loftus, 1993). As related to confessions, the question is, can memory of one's own actions similarly be altered? Can people be induced to accept guilt for crimes they did not commit? Is it, contrary to popular belief, possible?

Because of obvious ethical constraints, this important issue has not been addressed previously. This article thus reports on a new laboratory paradigm used to test the following specific hypothesis: The presentation of false evidence can lead individuals who are vulnerable (i.e., in a heightened state of uncertainty) to confess to an act they did not commit and, more important, to internalize the confession and perhaps confabulate details in memory consistent with that new belief.

METHOD

c   Participating for extra credit in what was supposed to be a reaction time experiment, 79 undergraduates (40 male, 39 female) were randomly assigned to one of four groups produced by a 2 (high vs. low vulnerability) $\times$ 2 (presence vs. absence of a false incriminating witness) factorial design.

Two subjects per session (actually, 1 subject and a female confederate) engaged in a reaction time task on an IBM PS2/Model 50 computer. To bolster the credibility of the experimental cover story, they were asked to fill out a brief questionnaire concerning their typing experience and ability, spatial awareness, and speed of reflexes. The subject and confederate were then taken

d   to another room, seated across a table from the experimenter, and instructed on the task. The confederate was to read aloud a list of letters, and the subject was to type these letters on the keyboard. After 3 min, the subject and confederate were to reverse roles. Before the session began, subjects were instructed on proper use of the computer—and were specifically warned not to press the "ALT" key positioned near the space bar because doing so would cause the program to crash and data to be lost. Lo and behold, after 60 s, the computer supposedly ceased to function, and a highly distressed experimenter accused the subject of having pressed the forbidden key. All subjects initially denied the charge, at which point the experimenter tinkered with the keyboard, confirmed that data had been lost, and asked, "Did you hit the 'ALT' key?"

Two forensically relevant factors were independently varied. First, we manipulated subjects' level of *vulnerability* (i.e., their subjective certainty concerning their own innocence) by varying the pace of the task. Using a mechanical metronome, the confederate read either at a slow and relaxed pace of 43 letters per minute or at a frenzied pace of 67 letters per minute (these settings were established through pretesting). Two-way analyses of variance revealed significant main effects on the number of letters typed correctly ($Ms = 33.01$ and 61.12, respectively; $F[1, 71] = 278.93, p < .001$) and the number of typing errors made ($Ms = 1.12$ and 10.90, respectively; $F[1, 71] = 38.81, p < .001$), thus confirming the effectiveness of this manipulation.

Second, we varied the use of *false incriminating evidence,* a common interrogation technique. After the subject initially denied the charge, the experimenter turned to the confederate and asked, "Did you see anything?" In the false-witness condition, the confederate "admitted" that she had seen the subject hit the "ALT" key that terminated the program. In the no-witness condition, the same confederate said she had not seen what happened.

Method

The authors clearly state the design (c) and procedure (d). The level of detail provided in explaining the procedures of the experiment is necessary due to the use of a confederate and a cover story. The believability of the experimental scenario

As dependent measures, three forms of social influence were assessed: compliance, internalization, and confabulation. To elicit *compliance,* the experimenter handwrote a standardized confession ("I hit the 'ALT' key and caused the program to crash. Data were lost.") and asked the subject to sign it—the consequence of which would be a phone call from the principal investigator. If the subject refused, the request was repeated a second time.

To assess *internalization,* we unobtrusively recorded the way subjects privately described what happened soon afterward. As the experimenter and subject left the laboratory, they were met in the reception area by a waiting subject (actually, a second confederate who was blind to the subject's condition and previous behavior) who had overheard the commotion. The experimenter explained that the session would have to be rescheduled, and then left the room to retrieve his appointment calendar. At that point, the second confederate turned privately to the subject and asked, "What happened?" The subject's reply was recorded verbatim and later coded for whether or not he or she had unambiguously internalized guilt for what happened (e.g., "I hit the wrong button and ruined the program"; "I hit a button I wasn't supposed to"). A conservative criterion was employed. Any reply that was prefaced by "he said" or "I may have" or "I think" was not taken as evidence of internalization. Two raters who were blind to the subject's condition independently coded these responses, and their agreement rate was 96%.

Finally, after the sessions seemed to be over, the experimenter reappeared, brought the subjects back into the lab, reread the list of letters they had typed, and asked if they could reconstruct how or when they hit the "ALT" key. This procedure was designed to probe for evidence of *confabulation,* to determine whether subjects would "recall" specific details to fit the allegation (e.g., "Yes, here, I hit it with the side of my hand right after you called out the 'A' "). The interrater agreement rate on the coding of these data was 100%.

At the end of each session, subjects were fully and carefully debriefed about the study—its purpose, the hypothesis, and the reason for the use of deception—by the experimenter and first confederate. Most subjects reacted with a combination of relief (that they had not ruined the experiment), amazement (that their perceptions of their own behavior had been so completely manipulated), and a sense of satisfaction (at having played a meaningful role in an important study). Subjects were also asked not to discuss the experience with other students until all the data were collected. Four subjects reported during debriefing that they were suspicious of the experimental manipulation. Their data were excluded from all analyses.

is essential for the success of this experiment, therefore a clear presentation of how the authors achieved this *experimental realism* is critical. Notice, also, the very important section on debriefing the subjects **(e)**.

RESULTS AND DISCUSSION

Overall, 69% of the 75 subjects signed the confession, 28% exhibited internalization, and 9% confabulated details to support their false beliefs. More important, between-group comparisons provided strong support for the main hypothesis. As seen in Table 1, subjects in the slow-pace/no-witness control group were the least likely to exhibit an effect, whereas those in the fast-pace/witness group were the most likely to exhibit the effect on the measures of compliance ($\chi^2[3] = 23.84$, $p < .001$), internalization ($\chi^2[3] = 37.61$, $p < .001$), and confabulation ($\chi^2[3] = 18.0$, $p < .005$).

Specifically, although 34.78% of the subjects in the slow-pace/no-witness group signed the confession, indicating compliance, not a single subject in this group exhibited internalization or confabulation. In contrast, the two independent variables had a powerful combined effect. Out of 17 subjects in the fast-pace/witness cell, 100% signed a confession, 65% came to believe they were guilty (in reality, they were not), and 35% confabulated details to support their false belief (via chi-square tests, the differences in these rates between the slow-pace/no-witness control group and fast-pace/witness group were significant at $ps < .001$, .001, and .005, respectively).

Additional pair-wise comparisons revealed that the presence of a witness alone was sufficient to significantly increase the rates of compliant and internalized confessions, even in the slow-pace condition ($\chi^2[1] = 12.18$, $p < .005$, and $\chi^2[1] = 16.39$, $p < .001$). There were no sex differences on any measures (i.e., male and female subjects exhibited comparable confession rates overall, and were similarly influenced by the independent variables).

The present study provides strong initial support for the provocative notion that the presentation of false incriminating evidence—an interrogation ploy that is common among the police and sanctioned by many courts—can induce people to internalize blame for outcomes they did not produce. These

TABLE 1   Percentage of Subjects in Each Cell Who Exhibited the Three Forms of Influence

	No Witness		Witness	
Form of Influence	Slow Pace	Fast Pace	Slow Pace	Fast Pace
Compliance	35_a	65_b	89_{bc}	100_c
Internalization	0_a	12_{ab}	44_{bc}	65_c
Confabulation	0_a	0_a	6_a	35_b

Note. Percentages not sharing a common subscript differ at $p < .05$ via a chi-square test of significance.

Results and Discussion

The overall results are presented statistically (**f**), graphically (**g**), and then verbally (**h**). In (**i**) the authors address a very important theoretical and empirical

results provide an initial basis for challenging the evidentiary validity of confessions produced by this technique. These findings also demonstrate, possibly for the first time, that memory can be altered not only for observed events and remote past experiences, but also for one's own recent actions.

An obvious and important empirical question remains concerning the external validity of the present results: To what extent do they generalize to the interrogation behavior of actual crime suspects? For ethical reasons, we developed a laboratory paradigm in which subjects were accused merely of an unconscious act of negligence, not of an act involving explicit criminal intent (e.g., stealing equipment from the lab or cheating on an important test). In this paradigm, there was only a minor consequence for liability. At this point, it is unclear whether people could similarly be induced to internalize false guilt for acts of omission (i.e., neglecting to do something they were told to do) or for acts that emanate from conscious intent.

It is important, however, not to overstate this limitation. The fact that our procedure focused on an act of negligence and low consequence may well explain why the compliance rate was high, with roughly two thirds of all subjects agreeing to sign a confession statement. Effects of this sort on overt judgments and behavior have been observed in studies of conformity to group norms, compliance with direct requests, and obedience to the commands of authority. But the more important and startling result—that many subjects privately internalized guilt for an outcome they did not produce, and that some even constructed memories to fit that false belief—is not seriously compromised by the laboratory paradigm that was used. Conceptually, these findings extend known effects of misinformation on memory for observed events (Loftus et al., 1978; McCloskey & Zaragoza, 1985) and for traumas assumed to be buried in the unconscious (Loftus, 1993). Indeed, our effects were exhibited by college students who are intelligent (drawn from a population in which the mean score on the Scholastic Aptitude Test is over 1300), self-assured, and under minimal stress compared with crime suspects held in custody, often in isolation.

At this point, additional research is needed to examine other common interrogation techniques (e.g., minimization), individual differences in suspect vulnerability (e.g., manifest anxiety, need for approval, hypnotic susceptibility), and other risk factors for false confessions (e.g., blood alcohol level, sleep deprivation). In light of recent judicial acceptance of a broad range of self-incriminatory statements, increasing use of videotaped confessions at the trial level (Geller, 1993), and the U.S. Supreme Court's ruling that an improperly admitted coerced confession may qualify as a mere "harmless error"

point: whether or not the results from this laboratory technique can really be generalized to interrogations and confessions. After addressing this concern, they defend their position **(j)**. Are you convinced? Lastly, they suggest some additional research to inform this area of inquiry **(k)**.

(*Arizona* v. *Fulminante,* 1991), further research is also needed to assess the lay jury's reaction to this type of evidence when presented in court.

REFERENCES

Arizona v. *Fulminante,* 59 U.S.L.W. 4235 (1991).

Aubry, A., & Caputo, R. (1965). *Criminal interrogation.* Springfield, IL: Charles C Thomas.

Bedau, H., & Radelet, M. (1987). Miscarriages of justice in potentially capital cases. *Stanford Law Review, 40,* 21–179.

Borchard, E. M., (1932). *Convicting the innocent: Errors of criminal justice.* New Haven, CT: Yale University Press.

Ceci, S. J., & Bruck, M. (1993). Suggestibility of the child witness: A historical review and synthesis. *Psychological Bulletin, 113,* 403–439.

Ceci, S. J., Ross, D. F., & Toglia, M. P. (1987). Suggestibility of children's memory: Psycholegal implications. *Journal of Experimental Psychology: General, 116,* 38–49.

Dinges, D. F., Whitehouse, W. G., Orne, E. C., Powell, J. W., Orne, M. T., & Erdelyi, M. H. (1992). Evaluating hypnotic memory enhancement (hypermnesia and reminiscence) using multitrial forced recall. *Journal of Experimental Psychology: Learning, Memory, and Cognition, 18,* 1139–1147.

Dywan, J., & Bowers, K. (1983). The use of hypnosis to enhance recall. *Science, 222,* 184–185.

Geller, W. A. (1993). *Videotaping interrogations and confessions* (National Institute of Justice: Research in Brief). Washington, DC: U.S. Department of Justice.

Gudjonsson, G. (1992). *The psychology of interrogations, confessions, and testimony.* London: Wiley.

Inbau, F. E., Reid, J. E., & Buckley, J. P. (1986). *Criminal interrogation and confessions* (3rd ed.). Baltimore, MD: Williams & Wilkins.

Kassin, S. M., & McNall, K. (1991). Police interrogations and confessions: Communicating promises and threats by pragmatic implication. *Law and Human Behavior, 15,* 233–251.

Kassin, S. M., & Wrightsman, L. S. (1980). Prior confessions and mock juror verdicts. *Journal of Applied Social Psychology, 10,* 133–146.

Kassin, S. M., & Wrightsman, L. S. (1981). Coerced confessions, judicial instruction, and mock juror verdicts. *Journal of Applied Social Psychology, 11,* 489–506.

Kassin, S. M., & Wrightsman, L. S. (1985). Confession evidence. In S. M. Kassin & L. S. Wrightsman (Eds.), *The psychology of evidence and trial procedure* (pp. 67–94). Beverly Hills, CA: Sage.

Loftus, E. F. (1993). The reality of repressed memories. *American Psychologist, 48,* 518–537.

Loftus, E. F., Donders, K., Hoffman, H. G., & Schooler, J. W. (1989). Creating new memories that are quickly accessed and confidently held. *Memory and Cognition, 17,* 607–616.

Loftus, E. F., Miller, D. G., & Burns, H. J. (1978). Semantic integration of verbal information into visual memory. *Journal of Experimental Psychology: Human Learning and Memory, 4,* 19–31.

McCloskey, M., & Zaragoza, M. (1985). Misleading postevent information and memory for events: Arguments and evidence against memory impairment hypotheses. *Journal of Experimental Psychology, 114,* 3–18.

Ofshe, R. (1992). Inadvertent hypnosis during interrogation: False confession due to dissociative state; misidentified multiple personality and the satanic cult hypothesis. *International Journal of Clinical and Experimental Hypnosis, 40,* 125–156.

O'Hara, C. E., & O'Hara, G. L. (1981). *Fundamentals of criminal investigation.* Springfield, IL: Charles C Thomas.

Pratkanis, A., & Aronson, E. (1991). *Age of propaganda: The everyday use and abuse of persuasion.* New York: W. H. Freeman.

Rattner, A. (1988). Convicted but innocent: Wrongful conviction and the criminal justice system. *Law and Human Behavior, 12,* 283–293.

Sheehan, P. W., Statham, D., & Jameson, G. A. (1991). Pseudomemory effects and their relationship to level of susceptibility to hypnosis and state instruction. *Journal of Personality and Social Psychology, 60,* 130–137.

Sukel, H. L., & Kassin, S. M. (1994, March). *Coerced confessions and the jury: An experimental test of the "harmless error" rule.* Paper presented at the biennial meeting of the American Psychology Law Society, Santa Fe, NM.

Wright, L. (1994). *Remembering Satan.* New York: Alfred A. Knopf.

Wrightsman, L. S., & Kassin, S. M. (1993). *Confessions in the courtroom.* Newbury Park, CA: Sage.

Note: This research was submitted as part of a senior honor's thesis by the second author and was funded by the Bronfman Science Center of Williams College.

Questions

1. What is your perception of the deception that was used in this experiment? Was it warranted?
2. Can you think of a way that this research could have been done without deceiving the participants?
3. Do you think a laboratory experiment can accurately capture these processes? Why or why not?
4. What are the benefits of laboratory experimentation of legal issues? What are the drawbacks?
5. Design a follow-up study.
6. What other aspects of the legal system do you think could be subjected to experimental inquiry?

Computational Procedures for Basic Statistics

Otto MacLin
University of Northern Iowa

Levels of Measurement

Determining the proper level of data measurement will help you decide which statistical analysis to use. The four levels of measurement that are commonly accepted and used are **nominal, ordinal, interval,** and **ratio** (Stevens, 1946). Both nominal and ordinal are qualitative, while interval and ratio are quantitative. The more elaborate analyses (parametric) such as the F-test and t-test require quantitative data, while other generally less powerful nonparametric data analyses, like chi-square (χ^2) and Spearman's rank correlation, use categorical data.

Nominal

Data classified as *nominal* have the least amount of restrictions, are generally used as labels to denote categorical data or class members, and have no mathematical properties. An example of nominal data as a categorical label would be numbers assigned to a variable such as GENDER, where 1 = male and 2 = female. Since these numbers only represent labels and not values, assigning the numbers 17 to male and 4 to female would have no effect on the categories. Rather than assigning a number to a category, alphanumeric characters may suffice, as in the case of a variable for LEVEL OF STUDY, where L = low and H = high. Nominal data are also used to identify individual class members. Often numbers are assigned to participants in a research study. These numbers can be interchanged as long as each participant has a unique number (e.g., the variable ID NUMBER). Analysis on nominal level values is limited to procedures such as *chi-square* (χ^2) and to descriptive statistics such as *frequencies* and *mode*. We can only determine how many members fall under each class. Nominal data are often used as the independent variable to separate class members when comparing performance on tests or other dependent (outcome) variables.

Understanding what test to run on your data first requires that you understand what type of data you have. Data can be classified in several ways, but in general data are continuous or categorical. The numbers that represent continuous data are inherently meaningful (e.g., someone can be 11 years old, 66 years old or 33.5 years old). With categorical data, the numbers act as a placeholder and aren't inherently meaningful (e.g., we might code male as 1 and female as 2 when entering data from a survey). Those numbers could easily be 11 and 22 because it is an arbitrary decision about what number to assign to that particular category, in this case gender. Just knowing this allows you to make some preliminary decisions about data analysis.

Ordinal

When data are categorical but are ranked within the categories, they are considered to be *ordinal*. Consider a variable that assigns numbers to BIRTH ORDER of siblings. The oldest child receives a value of 1, the next oldest 2, and so on. By looking at these values, a sense of order is obtained, yet nothing can be said of how much older one sibling is than another. If there are three children in a family, the oldest cannot be said to be twice as old as the youngest. The same descriptive statistics used for nominal data can be used for ordinal data; however, rank order statistics like Spearman's correlation and the Mann-Whitney test can also be applied.

Interval

When data are ranked and the intervals between each successive value are equal, the level of measurement is said to be an *interval* scale. A notable characteristic of interval data is that it lacks a value of "true" zero. Fahrenheit temperature and age are examples of interval data because at zero degrees there is still temperature and when we are born we are not of zero age. Interval data are quantitative and almost all statistical analyses and descriptive statistics are applicable unless the technique requires a "true" zero point, which, to reiterate, is not a property of interval data.

Ratio

Ratio data have a "true" zero plus all of the qualities of the other levels of measurement and, if desired, can be transformed into interval, ordinal, or nominal data. Distance, height, and elapsed time are examples of the ratio level. At zero feet there is no distance or height, and at zero time nothing has happened. Ratio data allow for ratio comparisons. Four inches is half the length of eight inches and 300 milliseconds is twice the elapsed time of 150 milliseconds. Ratio numbers satisfy all the properties of real numbers; therefore, all descriptive statistics and statistical analyses are applicable for ratio data.

Using Appendix A

Appendix A addresses the mathematical procedures for a few of the statistical tests mentioned in this book. There are many statistics available for data analysis, and there are assumptions which must be adhered to for each statistic. In the following discussion only the basics are described, and it is advised that you consult a textbook on statistics for more detailed discussion.

Assume we were interested in creativity in men and women. Our research questions might be: Are women more creative than men? Is GPA related to creativity? Are their any racial or ethnic differences related to creativity? We might further hypothesize that women who have over a 3.0 are more creative than women with lower than a 3.0 GPA, and more creative than men in general. Next, we need to operationalize creativity. We could decide to operationalize creativity as the ability to solve a creativity puzzle, the time to solve the puzzle, and the score on a creativity questionnaire. We would justify these decisions in the introduction section of our manuscript. We would then recruit men and women to participate in our study and have them fill out a questionnaire where we collect their age, race/ethnicity, gender and their GPA. We will also have them fill out a 10-item questionnaire with the items being answered on a 1–7 scale, then time them in a puzzle task, as well as record whether or not they were able to finish the puzzle task. So what type of data do we have?

Variable	Type of Data
Age	Continuous (e.g., 23)
Race/ethnicity	Categorical (e.g., 1 = White, 2 = Black, 3 = Asian, 4 = Native American, 5 = Biracial, 6 = other, etc.)
Gender	Categorical (e.g., 1 = male, 2 = female)
GPA	Continuous (e.g., 3.2)
Individual Items of questionnaire	Continuous (e.g., 1, 2, 3, 4, 5, 6, 7)
Total Score on questionnaire	Continuous (e.g., 63 out of a possible of 70)
Time to Solve puzzle	Continuous (e.g., 134 sec)
Completion of puzzle	Categorical (e.g., 1 = yes, 2 = no)

There are many statistical tests, but the following will give you a good start on choosing an appropriate test for our study.

Statistical Test	Rationale
Frequencies	Counts of variables in the study
Mean, median, mode, etc.	Calculated on continuous variables to describe the factor of interest

Statistical Test	Rationale
Chi-square	When the two or more variables under evaluation are categorical
Correlation	Determines the relationship between two continuous variables
t-test	The dependent (or grouping) variable has two levels and their differences are being tested against a continuous variable
One-way ANOVA	The dependent (or grouping) variable has three or more levels and their differences are being tested against a continuous variable
ANOVA	There are two or more dependent variables (categorical and/or continuous) and their differences are being tested against a continuous variable
Linear regression	Predicting a continuous dependent variable from continuous or categorical independent variables

So on to our research questions.

Question	Independent Variable (number of levels, if appropriate)	Dependent Variable	Statistical Test
How many women were in the study?	Gender		Frequency count
What was the average age of the participants?	Age		Mean
Are women more creative than men?	Gender (2)	Total score on questionnaire	t-test
	Gender (2)	Time to complete puzzle	t-test
	Gender (2)	Completion of puzzle	Chi-square
Is GPA related to creativity?	GPA	Total score on questionnaire	Correlation
	GPA	Time to complete puzzle	Correlation
	GPA	Completion of puzzle	t-Test
Are there any racial or ethnic differences related to creativity?	Race (6)	Total score on questionnaire	One-way ANOVA
	Race (6)	Time to complete puzzle	One-way ANOVA
	Race (6)	Completion of puzzle	Chi-square

(*continued*)

Question	Independent Variable (number of levels, if appropriate)	Dependent Variable	Statistical Test
GPA and gender are related to creativity.	GPA, gender (2)	Total score on questionnaire; time to complete puzzle; completion of puzzle	ANOVA
Can creativity be predicted from GPA?	GPA	Total score on questionnaire; time to complete puzzle; completion of puzzle	Linear regression

As you can see, the answers to our research questions are only as good as the data we've collected, which arose from the operationalization decisions we made, and goes back to the research questions and hypotheses we developed.

Data Set

Typical data sets are arranged in grids (like spreadsheets) with the variables represented in the columns and the individual participant's data represented in the rows (commonly called "records"). The data set in Table A.1 will be used in this section to calculate the statistics in the examples. You can use a hand calculator or analyze the data with a computer program such as SPSS, SAS, or SYSTAT. The data set has been "dry-labbed," or fabricated, for your analyses as though it were data from a small survey for an experimental class project. The survey was designed to collect data so we could pose questions to determine factors that may influence a student's grade point average (GPA).

There are nine variables in the data set: Five are qualitative and four are quantitative. As discussed earlier, the level of measurement dictates which type of test can be used to analyze any given variable; therefore, it is worthwhile to examine the level of measurement for each variable used in our survey. ID NUMBER is nominal data; each number is a "name" that represents an individual person. ID NUMBER is used to identify records and should never be used in any analysis aside from calculating the number of records (n). The variable GENDER is also nominal; each category of gender is mutually exclusive in that a participant can belong to only one category. For GENDER the numbers are labels for categories: 1 = male and 2 = female. BIRTH RANK is an ordinal scale: 1 represents the first born, 2 equals second born, and so on. AGE is interval data, as is GPA (measured on a 4-point scale). There are two variables for GPA, fall and

TABLE A.1

ID Number	Gender	Birth Rank	Age	Fall GPA	Spring GPA	Hours Worked	School Satisfaction	Study Level
1	1	3	60	2.9	2.9	38	1	L
2	1	3	22	3.6	3.0	15	2	H
3	2	2	17	3.7	4.0	10	2	H
4	1	2	19	3.2	3.0	30	2	H
5	2	1	23	4.0	3.9	12	3	H
6	1	3	27	2.7	2.9	35	3	H
7	2	4	18	2.7	3.5	30	1	L
8	2	2	32	3.4	3.9	30	2	L
9	2	2	22	3.6	3.7	20	3	L
10	2	1	20	3.9	4.0	10	1	H
11	1	2	29	4.0	4.0	20	3	H
12	2	2	18	3.0	3.0	35	3	L
13	1	2	18	3.6	2.7	30	1	H
14	1	2	20	3.2	3.5	30	1	L
15	2	3	19	3.0	3.1	35	2	L
16	1	1	19	3.9	3.8	10	1	H
17	2	3	37	3.7	3.5	10	3	L

spring. HOURS WORKED is per week; thus it is ratio level. The variables SCHOOL SATISFACTION (1 = high satisfaction and 3 = low satisfaction) and STUDY LEVEL (alphanumeric; L = low, H = high) are both ordinal.

Central Tendency

A value representative of all scores in a distribution is called *central tendency*. Three measures of central tendency are the *mean, median,* and *mode*. The mean ($\overline{X}$) is the mathematical average, and is calculated by summing all scores (ΣX) and dividing by the number of scores (n). The median is the score located in the center of the distribution so that the scores are divided, with half on each side. The mode is the value or category that occurs most often. The formula for calculating the mean is:

$$\overline{X} = \frac{\Sigma X}{n}$$

Research Question. What is the mean age of the females who participated in the study? Since we are excluding males from this analysis, we have to calculate AGE scores only for records with a value of 2 for GENDER. (ID NUMBERs are not needed in the analysis; they are included for reference.)

ID Number	Age (X)
3	17
5	23
7	18
8	32
9	22
10	20
12	18
15	19
17	37
$n = 9$	$\Sigma X = 206$

$$\overline{X} = \frac{\Sigma X}{n} = \frac{206}{9} = 22.88$$

Measure of Variability

The *standard deviation* (*SD*) is the most frequently used index of how much scores vary around the mean. The formula for calculating a standard deviation is:

$$SD = \sqrt{\frac{\Sigma(X - \overline{X})^2}{n - 1}}$$

Research Question.   What is the standard deviation of the number of hours worked per week by the males? Select from the data set HOURS WORKED for the males (male has a value of 1 for the variable GENDER). Calculate the group mean $(\overline{X})$. Subtract the mean from the numbers of hours worked for each individual $(X - \overline{X})$, then square each of these values $(X - \overline{X})^2$ and sum them up, $\Sigma(X - \overline{X})^2$. Substitute these values back into the formula.

ID Number	Hours Worked (X)	$(X - \overline{X})$	$(X - \overline{X})^2$
1	38	12	144
2	15	−11	121
4	30	4	16
6	35	9	81
11	20	−6	36
13	30	4	16
14	30	4	16
16	10	−16	256
$n = 8$	$\Sigma X = 208$		$\Sigma(X - \overline{X})^2 = 686$

$$\bar{X} = \frac{\sum X}{n} = \frac{208}{8} = 26$$

$$SD = \sqrt{\frac{\sum(X - \bar{X})^2}{n - 1}} = \sqrt{\frac{686}{7}} = 9.89$$

Measure of Association

The strength of the association between two variables can be determined by measuring the *correlation coefficient.* There are several different formulas for calculating correlation, depending on the levels of measurement for the variables used. The most common method for calculating correlation is the *Pearson product– moment correlation,* which requires interval- or ratio-level data for each variable. However, if at least one of the variables is ordinal, the Spearman rank-order correlation, a nonparametric statistic, must be used to calculate the measure of association (r_s or rho).

Spearman Rank-Order Correlation

The formula for calculating r_s is:

$$r_s = 1 - \frac{6\sum(R_X - R_Y)^2}{n(n^2 - 1)}$$

Research Question. What is the correlation between BIRTH RANK and fall GPA for the individuals working 20 hours or less? Since BIRTH RANK is an ordinal variable, the formula for Spearman's must be used to find the correlation coefficient r_s. Select the records with values of 20 or less from the variable HOURS WORKED. Enter the ID NUMBERs in the first column, and fall GPA (X) in the second column. Rank GPA from low to high, and enter in the GPA RANK (R_X) and BIRTH RANK (R_Y) in columns 3 and 4. Find the difference between GPA RANK and BIRTH RANK ($R_X - R_Y$); square each difference ($R_X - R_Y)^2$; and then sum them up, $\sum(R_X - R_Y)^2$. Substitute the values back into the formula.

ID Number	Fall GPA (X)	GPA Rank (R_X)	Birth Rank (R_Y)	($R_X - R_Y$)	($R_X - R_Y)^2$
2	3.6	1	3	−2	4
3	3.7	2	2	0	0
5	4.0	4	1	3	9
9	3.6	1	2	−1	1
10	3.9	3	1	2	4

(continued)

ID Number	Fall GPA (X)	GPA Rank (R_X)	Birth Rank (R_Y)	$(R_X - R_Y)$	$(R_X - R_Y)^2$
11	4.0	4	2	2	4
16	3.9	3	1	2	4
17	3.7	2	3	-1	1
$n = 8$					$\Sigma(R_X - R_Y)^2 = 27$

$$r_s = 1 - \frac{6\sum(R_X - R_Y)^2}{n(n^2 - 1)} = 1 - \frac{6(27)}{8(64 - 1)} = 1 - \frac{162}{504} = .678$$

The significance of ρ can be determined by finding the critical value (the probability level set by the experimenter that reaches statistical significance) in Table B.1 in Appendix B. In our example, $r_s = 0.678$ and $n = 8$. By using the level of significance $p = 0.05$, we can see that our value of r_s does not fall beyond the critical value of 0.738 and therefore is not statistically significant, which is not surprising given the limited number of observations.

Pearson Product-Moment Correlation

Another commonly used correlation coefficient, called the *Pearson product–moment correlation coefficient* (r), is used to measure the relationship between two variables on interval scales. The raw score formula (Kirk, 1978) for r is

$$r = \frac{\sum XY - \dfrac{(\sum X)(\sum Y)}{n}}{\sqrt{\left[\sum X^2 - \dfrac{(\sum X)^2}{n}\right]\left[\sum Y^2 - \dfrac{(\sum Y)^2}{n}\right]}}$$

Research Question. What is the correlation between the number of hours worked and the individual's fall GPA? Begin the analysis by creating columns for ID NUMBER, GPA (X), and HOURS WORKED (Y). Next find the *cross product* by multiplying GPA by HOURS WORKED (XY), and then square X (X^2) and Y (Y^2)Sum up all the columns, and substitute these values back into the formula.

ID Number	GPA (X)	Hours Worked (Y)	(XY)	(X^2)	(Y^2)
1	2.9	38	110.2	8.41	1444
2	3.6	15	54	12.96	225
3	3.7	10	37	13.69	100

ID Number	GPA (X)	Hours Worked (Y)	(XY)	(X²)	(Y²)
4	3.2	30	96	10.24	900
5	4.0	12	48	16.00	144
6	2.7	35	94.5	7.29	1225
7	2.7	30	81	7.29	900
8	3.4	30	102	11.56	900
9	3.6	20	72	12.96	400
10	3.9	10	39	15.21	100
11	4.0	20	80	16.00	400
12	3.0	35	105	9.00	1225
13	3.6	30	108	12.96	900
14	3.2	30	96	10.24	900
15	3.0	35	105	9.00	1225
16	3.9	10	39	15.21	100
17	3.7	10	37	13.69	100
$n = 17$	$\Sigma X = 58.1$	$\Sigma Y = 400$	$\Sigma XY = 1303.7$	$\Sigma X^2 = 201.71$	$\Sigma Y^2 = 11{,}188$

$$r = \frac{\sum XY - \dfrac{\left(\sum X\right)\left(\sum Y\right)}{n}}{\sqrt{\left[\sum X^2 - \dfrac{\left(\sum X\right)^2}{n}\right]\left[\sum Y^2 - \dfrac{\left(\sum Y\right)^2}{n}\right]}}$$

$$= \frac{1303.7 - \dfrac{(58.1)(400)}{17}}{\sqrt{\left[201.71 - \dfrac{(58.1)^2}{17}\right]\left[11{,}188 - \dfrac{(400)^2}{17}\right]}}$$

$$= \frac{1303.7 - \dfrac{23{,}240}{17}}{\sqrt{\left[201.71 - \dfrac{3375.6}{17}\right]\left[11{,}188 - \dfrac{160{,}000}{17}\right]}}$$

$$= \frac{1303.7 - 1367.05}{\sqrt{[201.71 - 198.56][11{,}188 - 9411.76]}}$$

$$= \frac{-63.35}{\sqrt{[3.15][1776.24]}} = \frac{-63.35}{\sqrt{5595.15}} = \frac{-63.35}{74.8} = -0.846$$

To find the level of significance for *r,* we need to calculate the degrees of free-dom, or $df(n - 2)$, and then consult Table B.2. With $df = 15$ and using a 0.05 level of significance, we can determine if our obtained value $r = 0.846$ falls be-yond the critical value given in the table. (*Note:* Since the minus sign of the cor-relation coefficient represents the direction of the relationship and not the magnitude, all look-up values are positive.) The critical value is 0.456 and falls before our value of 0.846; thus there is a significant *negative* correlation between the number of HOURS WORKED and fall GPA. The more one works, the lower the fall GPA.

Chi-Square

Chi-square (χ^2) is a nonparametric statistic used to determine if the observed fre-quency of scores differs from the expected frequency of scores. Since frequencies are needed to calculate χ^2, both qualitative and quantitative level variables can be used. The formula for χ^2, where O represents the observed frequency and E rep-resents the expected frequency, is

$$\chi^2 = \Sigma \frac{(O - E)^2}{E}$$

The degrees of freedom (*df*) for χ^2, where R is the number of rows and C is the number of columns in the contingency table, is found using the formula

$$df = (R - 1)(C - 1)$$

Research Question. Is there a difference in frequency between females and males and their level of study? When calculating χ^2 it is a good idea to use con-tingency tables to organize the observed and the expected frequencies. In the *ob-served* contingency table, column totals, row totals and the grand total (*n*) are calculated. To calculate the value for each cell in the *expected* contingency table, multiply the row total by the column total and divide by the grand total (*n*). These observed and expected values are then used in the chi-square formula.

Observed Frequencies Contingency Table

	Low	High	Row Total
Female	6	3	9
Male	2	6	8
Column total	8	9	$n = 17$

Expected Frequencies Contingency Table

	Low	High	Row Total
Female	$(9 \cdot 8)/17 = 4.23$	$(9 \cdot 9)/17 = 4.76$	9
Male	$(8 \cdot 8)/17 = 3.76$	$(8 \cdot 9)/17 = 4.23$	8
Column total	8	9	$n = 17$

Category	Study Level	O	E	$(O - E)$	$(O - E)^2$	$(O - E)^2/E$
Female	Low	6	4.23	1.77	3.13	.739
	High	3	4.76	−1.76	3.09	.649
Male	Low	2	3.76	−1.76	3.09	.821
	High	6	4.23	1.77	3.13	.739

$$\sum \frac{(O - E)^2}{E} = 2.94$$

$$\chi^2 = \sum \frac{(O - E)^2}{E} = 2.94$$

In our example, $R = 2$ and $C = 2$; thus $df = 1$. To determine if our χ^2 value of 2.94 falls beyond the desired critical value, we consult Table B.3. The critical value with 1 df at the 0.05 level of significance is 3.84. Our value of 2.94 falls short of the specified critical value; therefore there is no significant difference in the amount of studying between males and females (possibly due to a small n in some of the table cells).

t-Test

The t-test is used to determine if a difference in the distribution of scores for an interval or ratio level variable across two groups (categorical variables) occurs by chance or is statistically significant. There are two types of t-test you should be familiar with, the independent t-test and the dependent t-test. Of the two, the independent t-test is used more often. The formula for what is often called the independent groups t-test is

$$t = \frac{(\overline{X}_1 - \overline{X}_2)}{\sqrt{\left[\frac{SS_1 + SS_2}{(n_1 - 1) + (n_2 - 1)}\right]\left[\frac{1}{n_1} + \frac{1}{n_2}\right]}}$$

To calculate a value for t, you will need formulas to calculate SS, the sum of squares, and df, the degrees of freedom:

$$SS = \sum X^2 - \frac{(\sum X)^2}{n} \quad \text{and} \quad df = n_1 + n_2 - 2$$

Research Question: Do students reporting a high level of study have higher fall GPAs than the students who study less? Begin by creating two columns of fall GPA scores, one for the low study group (X_1) and one for the high study group (X_2). For both groups compute n, $\sum X, \overline{X}, X^2, \sum X^2$, and $(\sum X)^2$; then substitute these values into the formulas above to calculate df, SS, and then t.

Low Study ID Number	Fall GPA (X_1)	$(X_1{}^2)$	High Study ID Number	Fall GPA (X_2)	$(X_2{}^2)$
1	2.9	8.41	2	3.6	12.96
7	2.7	7.29	3	3.7	13.69
8	3.4	11.56	4	3.2	10.24
9	3.6	12.96	5	4.0	16.00
12	3.0	9.00	6	2.7	7.29
14	3.2	10.24	10	3.9	15.21
15	3.0	9.00	11	4.0	16.00
17	3.7	13.69	13	3.6	12.96
			16	3.9	15.21
$n_1 = 8$	$\sum X_1 = 25.5$	$\sum X_1{}^2 = 82.15$	$n_2 = 9$	$\sum X_2 = 32.6$	$\sum X_2{}^2 = 119.56$
	$(\sum X_1)^2 = 650.25$			$(\sum X_2)^2 = 1062.76$	
	$\overline{X}_1 = 3.187$			$\overline{X}_2 = 3.622$	

$$df = n_1 + n_2 - 2 = 8 + 9 - 2 = 15$$

$$SS_1 = \sum X_1{}^2 - \frac{(\sum X_1)^2}{n_1} = 82.15 - \frac{650.25}{8} = 82.15 - 81.281 = 0.868$$

$$SS_2 = \sum X_2{}^2 - \frac{(\sum X_2)^2}{n_2} = 119.56 - \frac{1062.76}{9} = 119.56 - 118.084 = 1.475$$

$$t = \frac{(\overline{X}_1 - \overline{X}_2)}{\sqrt{\left[\dfrac{SS_1 + SS_2}{(n_1 - 1) + (n_2 - 1)}\right]\left[\dfrac{1}{n_1} + \dfrac{1}{n_2}\right]}}$$

$$= \frac{(3.187 - 3.622)}{\sqrt{\left[\dfrac{0.868 + 1.475}{(8 - 1) + (9 - 1)}\right]\left[\dfrac{1}{8} + \dfrac{1}{9}\right]}}$$

$$= \frac{-0.435}{\sqrt{\left[\frac{2.343}{15}\right][0.125 + 0.111]}} = \frac{-0.435}{\sqrt{[0.156][0.236]}}$$

$$= \frac{-0.435}{\sqrt{0.0368}} = \frac{-0.435}{0.191} = -2.27$$

When we consult Table B.4 for the t-value where $df = 15$ and the level of significance $= 0.05$, we obtain a critical value of 2.13. Ignoring the minus sign of the t-value we calculated, we can see that 2.27 falls beyond 2.13 and is considered significant at the 0.05 level. Therefore, we can conclude that the GPAs for those who study more are significantly different than for those who study less, but the question remains: Who has the higher GPAs? Notice in the formula that we subtracted group means from each other ($\overline{X}_1 - \overline{X}_2$). The mean for group 2, the high group, was subtracted from the mean for group 1, the low group, and the result was negative. Therefore, the high study group has a significantly higher GPA.

Matched or Paired-Samples *t*-Test (Dependent *t*-Test)

Dependent t-tests are generally used (1) for pretest and posttest situations in which pairs of scores from each individual are being analyzed, or (2) for cases where individuals have been carefully matched to control for variables such as age, gender, intelligence, or task performance. Unlike the data for the independent t-test which consisted of values from a quantitative variable (GPA) separated by two levels of a categorical variable (STUDY), the dependent t-test examines the differences between two qualitative variables. The formula for the dependent t-test is:

$$t = \frac{\overline{D}}{\frac{SD}{\sqrt{n}}}$$

To calculate a t-value, you will also need to calculate the standard deviation (SD) of the difference between the two variables in the analysis and degrees of freedom. The formula for SD and df is:

$$SD = \sqrt{\frac{\Sigma D^2}{(n - 1)}} \qquad df = (n - 1)$$

Research Question. Is there a difference between spring GPA and fall GPA for the students with a high level of study? For this analysis, we need to create columns for both fall and spring GPAs (X, Y). Calculate the difference between the two GPAs ($X - Y$) for each individual (D). Next, compute n, ΣD, $\overline{D}$, D^2, ΣD^2, and SD.

ID Number	Fall GPA (X)	Spring GPA (Y)	$GPA_F - GPA_S$ (D)	(D^2)
2	3.6	3.0	0.6	0.36
3	3.7	4.0	−0.3	0.09
4	3.2	3.0	0.2	0.04
5	4.0	3.9	0.1	0.01
6	2.7	2.9	−0.2	0.04
10	3.9	4.0	−0.1	0.01
11	4.0	4.0	0.0	0.00
13	3.6	2.7	0.9	0.81
16	3.9	3.8	0.1	0.01
			$\Sigma D = 1.3$	$\Sigma D^2 = 1.37$
$n = 9$			$\overline{D} = 0.1444$	

$$SD = \sqrt{\frac{\Sigma D^2}{n-1}} = \sqrt{\frac{1.37}{9-1}} = \sqrt{\frac{1.37}{8}} = \sqrt{0.171} = 0.413$$

$$t = \frac{\overline{D}}{\dfrac{SD}{\sqrt{n}}} = \frac{0.1444}{\dfrac{0.413}{\sqrt{9}}} = \frac{0.1444}{\dfrac{0.413}{3}} = \frac{0.1444}{0.137} = 1.05$$

$$df = (n-1) = 9 - 1 = 8$$

When we consult Table B.4 for the t-value where $df = 8$ and the level of significance $= 0.05$, we obtain a critical value of 2.3. We can see that 1.05 does not fall beyond 2.3 and would not be considered significant at the 0.05 level, and thus conclude that there is no significant difference between fall and spring GPAs.

Analysis of Variance

The *analysis of variance* (ANOVA) is one of the most useful and versatile of all statistics used in psychology today. It can be used with between-subject or within-subject designs and with experiments that have several levels of a categorical independent variable, but only one quantitative dependent variable. Analysis of variance is based on an F distribution. The main formula for F is:

$$F = \frac{MS_{bg}}{MS_{wg}}$$

$$MS_{bg} = \frac{SS_{bg}}{df_{bg}} \quad \text{with} \quad df_{bg} = k - 1$$

$$MS_{wg} = \frac{SS_{wg}}{df_{wg}} \quad \text{with} \quad df_{wg} = N - k$$

$$SS_{bg} = \frac{(\sum X_1)^2}{n_1} + \frac{(\sum X_2)^2}{n_2} + \cdots + \frac{(\sum X_i)^2}{n_i} - \frac{(\sum X_t)^2}{n_t}$$

$$SS_{wg} = SS_{tot} - SS_{bg}$$

$$SS_{tot} = \sum X_t^2 - \frac{(\sum X_1 + \sum X_2 + \cdots + \sum X_i)^2}{N_t}$$

Research Question. Is there a difference in the number of hours worked across the three levels of school satisfaction? For this analysis we need to create three columns of data, one for each level of SCHOOL SATISFACTION $(k)(X_1, X_2, X_3)$. Next we square all values of $X(X_1^2, X_2^2, X_3^2)$ and sum them $(\sum X_1^2, \sum X_2^2, \sum X_3^2,$ and $\sum X_t^2)$. Finally, we need values for N_t, n_1, n_2, and n_3.

Hours Worked, Satisfaction Low (X_1)	(X_1^2)	Hours Worked, Satisfaction Medium (X_2)	(X_2^2)	Hours Worked, Satisfaction High (X_3)	(X_3^2)	
38	1444	15	225	12	144	
30	900	10	100	35	1225	
10	100	30	900	20	400	
30	900	30	900	20	400	
30	900	35	1225	35	1225	
10	100			10	100	
$\sum X_1 =$ 148	$\sum X_1^2 =$ 4344	$\sum X_2 =$ 120	$\sum X_2^2 =$ 3350	$\sum X_3 =$ 132	$\sum X_3^2 =$ 3494	$\sum X_t^2 =$ 11,188
$n_1 = 6$		$n_2 = 5$		$n_3 = 6$	$N_t = 17$	

$$SS_{bg} = \frac{(\sum X_1)^2}{n_1} + \frac{(\sum X_2)^2}{n_2} + \frac{(\sum X_3)^2}{n_3} - \frac{(\sum X_t)^2}{n_t}$$

$$= \frac{(148)^2}{6} + \frac{(120)^2}{5} + \frac{(132)^2}{6} - \frac{(400)^2}{17}$$

$$= 3650.66 + 2880 + 2904 - 9411.76 = 22.9$$

$$SS_{tot} = \sum X_t^2 - \frac{(\sum X_1 + \sum X_2 + \sum X_3)^2}{N_t}$$

$$= 11{,}188 - \frac{(148 + 120 + 132)^2}{17}$$

$$= 11{,}188 - \frac{160{,}000}{17} = 11{,}188 - 9411.76 = 1776.24$$

$$SS_{wg} = SS_{tot} - SS_{bg} = 1776.24 - 22.9 = 1753.34$$

$$df_{wg} = N - k = 17 - 3 = 14$$

$$df_{bg} = k - 1 = 3 - 1 = 2$$

$$MS_{wg} = \frac{SS_{wg}}{df_{wg}} = \frac{1753.34}{14} = 125.23$$

$$MS_{bg} = \frac{SS_{bg}}{df_{bg}} = \frac{22.9}{2} = 11.45$$

$$F = \frac{MS_{bg}}{MS_{wg}} = \frac{11.45}{125.23} = 0.091$$

Now that we have calculated an F-value, we need to consult Table B.5. Unlike the tables for the other distributions that have columns representing different levels of significance, the values in Table B.5 are given in pairs for 0.05 and 0.01 levels of significance. Columns are ordered by degrees of freedom between groups (df_{bg}) and rows by degrees of freedom within groups (df_{wg}). To obtain a critical value for our analysis, move down the column for 2 df_{bg} until you reach the row representing 14 df_{wg}. There are two values, 3.74 and 6.51, with the top number representing a critical value at the 0.05 level and the bottom number at the 0.01 level of significance. Since our F-value 0.091 does not fall beyond the value 3.74, we find our results are not significant; thus there is no difference between the number of hours worked and the level of school satisfaction.

Appendix B consists of tables to help you determine whether the statistical values (sometimes called look-ups or look-up values) you calculate are significant. There are three steps in using Appendix B. Step 1 is to determine the shape of the distribution. Basically, all the possible values for each statistic we calculate (χ^2, ρ, r, F, and t) have a unique distribution. For many of the distributions, the shape will change as the number of observations varies. You will need to know the size of your sample and how to calculate *degrees of freedom* (df) because they determine the distribution. Step 2 is to determine the level of significance. Next you will have to decide on the *level of significance* (α, or *alpha*) to use. The .05 level of significance is commonly used in social sciences, but will vary depending on the application. Step 3 is to find the critical value. Knowing the df and α, we can turn to the statistical reference tables and obtain a *critical value.* The critical value is the cutoff point in a distribution beyond which any statistical value is significant.

Linear Regression

Linear regression is similar to the Pearson Product-Moment Correlation we calculated earlier in this section. Both indicate whether a significant relationship between two variables exists and both indicate whether the relationship is positive or negative. An additional benefit of linear regression is that more than one independent variable can be used and the linear regression procedure will yield a formula that can be used to predict values of the dependent measure when values of the independent measure (or measures) is known.

In our Pearson's correlation example we found that a significant negative correlation exists for GPA and the number of hours worked. Knowing that a relationship exists, we might want to predict a student's GPA knowing that he or she works 30 hours per week. One might reason that GPA values already exist for students working 30 hours per week in the data set. The problem is that there are 5 students in the data set working 30 hours per week, and each have a different GPA. This is why it is beneficial to have a regression equation that takes into account all values in the data set and predicts a single value.

The regression equation is basically the equation for a line and it looks like this

$$Y = a + b*X$$

where Y is the dependent variable and X is the independent variable. The other variables in the equation: a represents the Y intercept and is a constant, while b represents the slope of the line. If b is positive, the slope will move upward to the right when graphed. If b is negative, the slope will move downward to the right when graphed. For a regression, both a and b must be calculated. Given that we are interested in predicting GPA from hours worked, GPA is the dependent variable and will be represented by Y. Hours worked is the independent variable and will be represented by X.

Begin the analysis using the computational formula (Kirk, 1978) by creating columns for the subject number, hours worked (X_i), and GPA (Y_i). Calculate means for X and Y by summing the values and dividing by n. Next, we need to calculate the cross-product. Do so by creating a column for the difference between the actual values and means for both X and Y. Calculate the cross product by multiplying the differences of $X (X_i - \bar{X})$ and the differences of $Y (Y_i - \bar{Y})$. Finally create two new columns by squaring the differences of $X (X_i - \bar{X})^2$ and $Y (Y_i - \bar{Y})^2$

Next calculate the sum of the cross-product and the differences in $(X_i - \bar{X})^2$ and $(Y_i - \bar{Y})^2$.

Subject	HoursWorked X_i	GPA Y_i	$(X_i - \bar{X})$	$(Y_i - \bar{Y})$	Cross Products $(X_i-\bar{X})(Y_i-\bar{Y})$	$(X_i - \bar{X})^2$	$(Y_i - \bar{Y})^2$
1	38	2.9	14.47	-0.52	-7.52	209.38	0.27
2	15	3.6	-8.53	0.18	-1.54	72.76	0.03
3	10	3.7	-13.53	0.28	-3.79	183.06	0.08
4	30	3.2	6.47	-0.22	-1.42	41.86	0.05
5	12	4.0	-11.53	0.58	-6.69	132.94	0.34
6	35	2.7	11.47	-0.72	-8.26	131.56	0.52
7	30	2.7	6.47	-0.72	-4.66	41.86	0.52
8	30	3.4	6.47	-0.02	-0.13	41.86	0.00
9	20	3.6	-3.53	0.18	-0.64	12.46	0.03
10	10	3.9	-13.53	0.48	-6.49	183.06	0.23
11	20	4.0	-3.53	0.58	-2.05	12.46	0.34
12	35	3.0	11.47	-0.42	-4.82	131.56	0.18
13	30	3.6	6.47	0.18	1.16	41.86	0.03
14	30	3.2	6.47	-0.22	-1.42	41.86	0.05
15	35	3.0	11.47	-0.42	-4.82	131.56	0.18
16	10	3.9	-13.53	0.48	-6.49	183.06	0.23
17	10	3.7	-13.53	0.28	-3.79	183.06	0.08
Sum	17.00	400.00	58.10			-63.36	1776.24	3.14
Mean		23.53	3.42					

$$N = 17$$
$$\Sigma X = 400$$
$$\bar{X} = 400/17 = 23.53$$
$$\Sigma Y = 58$$
$$\bar{Y} = 58/17 = 3.42$$
$$\Sigma (X_i - \bar{X})(Y_i - \bar{Y}) = -63.36$$
$$\Sigma (X_i - \bar{X})^2 = 1776.24$$
$$\Sigma (Y_i - \bar{Y})^2 = 3.14$$

There is now enough information to calculate b and a using the following formulas.

$$b = \frac{\Sigma(X_i - \bar{X})(Y_i - \bar{Y})}{\Sigma(X_i - \bar{X})} = \frac{-63.36}{1776.24} = -.0357$$

$$a = \bar{Y} - b*\bar{X} = 3.42 - (-.0357*23.53) = 4.26$$

Based on these calculations the regression formula is $Y = 4.26 + (-.0357*X)$

We can now predict GPA for a student working 30 hours. Based on the calculation below, the student is predicted to have a 3.19 GPA. We can look at the original data and see that this value approximates the GPA for other students working 30 hours per week.

$$Y = 4.26 + (-.0357*30)$$
$$= 4.26 - 1.07$$
$$= 3.19$$

APPENDIX

B Statistical Tables

TABLE B.1 Critical Values of p (Spearman Rank-Order Correlation Coefficient)

N	$p = 0.0500$	$p = 0.0100$
5	1.000	—
6	0.886	1.000
7	.786	0.929
8	.738	.881
9	.683	.833
10	.648	.794
12	.591	.777
14	.544	.715
16	.506	.665
18	.475	.625
20	.450	.591
22	.428	.562
24	.409	.537
26	.392	.515
28	.377	.496
30	.364	.478

Computed from Olds, E.G., Distribution of the sum of squares of rank differences for small numbers of individuals. *Annals of Mathematical Statistics,* 1938, IX, 133–148, and the 5% significance levels for sums of squares of rank differences and a correction, *Annals of Mathematical Statistics,* 1949, XX, 117–118, by permission of the Institute of Mathematical Statistics.

TABLE B.2 Critical Values of r (Pearson Product—Moment Correlation Coefficient)

	Level of Significance for Two-Tailed Test		
df	0.10	0.05	0.01
1	0.988	0.997	0.9999
2	.900	.950	.990
3	.805	.878	.959
4	.729	.811	.917
5	.669	.754	.874
6	.622	.707	.834
7	.582	.666	.798
8	.549	.632	.765
9	.521	.602	.735
10	.497	.576	.708
11	.476	.553	.684
12	.458	.532	.661
13	.441	.514	.641
14	.426	.497	.623
15	.412	.482	.606
16	.400	.468	.590
17	.389	.456	.575
18	.378	.444	.561
19	.369	.433	.549
20	.360	.423	.537
25	.323	.381	.487
30	.296	.349	.449
35	.275	.325	.418
40	.257	.304	.393
45	.243	.288	.372
50	.231	.273	.354
60	.211	.250	.325
70	.195	.232	.303
80	.183	.217	.283
90	.173	.205	.267
100	.164	.195	.254

Adapted from R. A. Fisher, *Statistical Methods for Research Workers,* 14th edition. Copyright 1973, Hafner Press.

TABLE B.3   **Critical Values of x^2**

df	$p = 0.05$	$p = 0.01$
1	3.84	6.64
2	5.99	9.21
3	7.82	11.34
4	9.49	13.28
5	11.07	15.09
6	12.59	16.81
7	14.07	18.48
8	15.51	20.09
9	16.92	21.67
10	18.31	23.21
11	19.68	24.72
12	21.03	26.22
13	22.36	27.69
14	23.68	29.14
15	25.00	30.58
16	26.30	32.00
17	27.59	33.41
18	28.87	34.80
19	30.14	36.19
20	31.41	37.57
21	32.67	38.93
22	33.92	40.29
23	35.17	41.64
24	36.42	42.98
25	37.65	44.31
26	38.88	45.64
27	40.11	46.96
28	41.34	48.28
29	42.56	49.59
30	43.77	50.89

Table B.3 is taken from Table 4 of Fisher & Yates, *Statistical Tables for Biological, Agricultural and Medical Research,* published by Longman Group Ltd., London (previously published by Oliver and Boyd Ltd., Edinburgh). By permission of the authors and publishers.

TABLE B.4   **Critical Values of t**

df	$p = 0.10$	$p = 0.05$	$p = 0.02$	$p = 0.01$
1	6.314	12.706	31.821	63.657
2	2.920	4.303	6.965	9.925
3	2.353	3.182	4.541	5.841
4	2.132	2.776	3.747	4.604
5	2.015	2.571	3.365	4.032
6	1.943	2.447	3.143	3.707
7	1.895	2.365	2.998	3.499
8	1.860	2.306	2.896	3.355
9	1.833	2.262	2.821	3.250
10	1.812	2.228	2.764	3.169
11	1.796	2.201	2.718	3.106
12	1.782	2.179	2.681	3.055
13	1.771	2.160	2.650	3.012
14	1.761	2.145	2.624	2.977
15	1.753	2.131	2.602	2.947
16	1.746	2.120	2.583	2.921
17	1.740	2.110	2.567	2.898
18	1.734	2.101	2.552	2.878
19	1.729	2.093	2.539	2.861
20	1.725	2.086	2.528	2.845
21	1.721	2.080	2.518	2.831
22	1.717	2.074	2.508	2.819
23	1.714	2.069	2.500	2.807
24	1.711	2.064	2.492	2.797
25	1.708	2.060	2.485	2.787
26	1.706	2.056	2.479	2.779
27	1.703	2.052	2.473	2.771
28	1.701	2.048	2.467	2.763
29	1.699	2.045	2.462	2.756
30	1.697	2.042	2.457	2.750
60	1.671	2.000	2.390	2.660
∞	1.645	1.960	2.326	2.576

Table B.4 is taken from Table 3 of Fisher & Yates, *Statistical Tables for Biological, Agricultural and Medical Research,* published by Longman Group Ltd., London (previously published by Oliver & Boyd Ltd., Edinburgh). By permission of the authors and publishers.

TABLE B.5   Critical Values of F

Note: Top number in each cell is for testing at 0.05 level; bottom number for testing at 0.01 level.

Degrees of Freedom for Numerator (df_{bg})

	1	2	3	4	5	6	8	12	24	∞
1	161.45	199.50	215.72	224.57	230.17	233.97	238.89	243.91	249.04	254.32
	4032.10	4999.03	5403.49	5625.14	5764.08	5859.39	5981.34	6105.83	6234.16	6366.48
2	18.51	19.00	19.16	19.25	19.30	19.33	19.37	19.41	19.45	19.50
	98.49	99.01	99.17	99.25	99.30	99.33	99.36	99.42	99.46	99.50
3	10.13	9.55	9.28	9.12	9.01	8.94	8.84	8.74	8.64	8.53
	34.12	30.81	29.46	28.71	28.24	27.91	27.49	27.05	26.60	26.12
4	7.71	6.94	6.59	6.39	6.26	6.16	6.04	5.91	5.77	5.63
	21.20	18.00	16.69	15.98	15.52	15.21	14.80	14.37	13.93	13.46
5	6.61	5.79	5.41	5.19	5.05	4.95	4.82	4.68	4.53	4.36
	16.26	13.27	12.06	11.39	10.97	10.67	10.27	9.89	9.47	9.02
6	5.99	5.14	4.76	4.53	4.39	4.28	4.15	4.00	3.84	3.67
	13.74	10.92	9.78	9.15	8.75	8.47	8.10	7.72	7.31	6.88
7	5.59	4.74	4.35	4.12	3.97	3.87	3.73	3.57	3.41	3.23
	12.25	9.55	8.45	7.85	7.46	7.19	6.84	6.47	6.07	5.65
8	5.32	4.46	4.07	3.84	3.69	3.58	3.44	3.28	3.12	2.93
	11.26	8.65	7.59	7.01	6.63	6.37	6.03	5.67	5.28	4.86
9	5.12	4.26	3.86	3.63	3.48	3.37	3.23	3.07	2.90	2.71
	10.56	8.02	6.99	6.42	6.06	5.80	5.47	5.11	4.73	4.31
10	4.96	4.10	3.71	3.48	3.33	3.22	3.07	2.91	2.74	2.54
	10.04	7.56	6.55	5.99	5.64	5.39	5.06	4.71	4.33	3.91
11	4.84	3.98	3.59	3.36	3.20	3.09	2.95	2.79	2.61	2.40
	9.65	7.20	6.22	5.67	5.32	5.07	4.74	4.40	4.02	3.60
12	4.75	3.88	3.49	3.26	3.11	3.00	2.85	2.69	2.50	2.30
	9.33	6.93	5.93	5.41	5.06	4.82	4.50	4.16	3.78	3.36
14	4.60	3.74	3.34	3.11	2.96	2.85	2.70	2.53	2.35	2.13
	8.86	6.51	5.56	5.03	4.69	4.46	4.14	3.80	3.43	3.00
16	4.49	3.63	3.24	3.01	2.85	2.74	2.59	2.42	2.24	2.01

18	8.53	6.23	5.29	4.77	4.44	4.20	3.89	3.55	3.18	2.75
	4.41	3.55	3.16	2.93	2.77	2.66	2.51	2.34	2.15	1.92
20	8.28	6.01	5.09	4.58	4.25	4.01	3.71	3.37	3.01	2.57
	4.35	3.49	3.10	2.87	2.71	2.60	2.45	2.28	2.08	1.84
25	8.10	5.85	4.94	4.43	4.10	3.87	3.56	3.23	2.86	2.42
	4.24	3.38	2.99	2.76	2.60	2.49	2.34	2.16	1.96	1.71
30	7.77	5.57	4.68	4.18	3.86	3.63	3.32	2.99	2.62	2.17
	4.17	3.32	2.92	2.69	2.53	2.42	2.27	2.09	1.89	1.62
40	7.56	5.39	4.51	4.02	3.70	3.47	3.17	2.84	2.47	2.01
	4.08	3.23	2.84	2.61	2.45	2.34	2.18	2.00	1.79	1.52
50	7.31	5.18	4.31	3.83	3.51	3.29	2.99	2.66	2.29	1.82
	4.03	3.18	2.79	2.56	2.40	2.29	2.13	1.95	1.74	1.44
60	7.17	5.06	4.20	3.72	3.41	3.19	2.89	2.56	2.18	1.68
	4.00	3.15	2.76	2.52	2.37	2.25	2.10	1.92	1.70	1.39
70	7.08	4.98	4.13	3.65	3.34	3.12	2.82	2.50	2.12	1.60
	3.98	3.13	2.74	2.50	2.35	2.23	2.07	1.89	1.67	1.35
80	7.01	4.92	4.07	3.60	3.29	3.07	2.78	2.45	2.07	1.53
	3.96	3.11	2.72	2.49	2.33	2.21	2.06	1.88	1.65	1.32
90	6.98	4.88	4.04	3.56	3.26	3.04	2.74	2.42	2.03	1.49
	3.95	3.10	2.71	2.47	2.32	2.20	2.04	1.86	1.64	1.30
100	6.92	4.85	4.01	3.53	3.23	3.01	2.72	2.39	2.00	1.46
	3.94	3.09	2.70	2.46	2.30	2.19	2.03	1.85	1.63	1.28
200	6.90	4.82	3.98	3.51	3.21	2.99	2.69	2.37	1.98	1.43
	3.89	3.04	2.65	2.42	2.26	2.14	1.98	1.80	1.57	1.19
∞	6.97	4.71	3.88	3.41	3.11	2.89	2.60	2.28	1.88	1.28
	3.84	2.99	2.60	2.37	2.21	2.09	1.94	1.75	1.52	1.00
	6.64	4.60	3.78	3.32	3.02	2.80	2.51	2.18	1.79	1.00

Adapted from Table F of H. E. Garrett, *Statistics in Psychology and Education*, 5th edition. Copyright 1958, David McKay Co., Inc.

GLOSSARY

AAA design   An AAA design is one where you observe untreated behavior (A), no treatment is introduced and you measure behavior again (A), and then, you measure behavior a third time (A).

ABA design   An ABA design is one where you observe untreated behavior (A), followed by an introduction of the experimental variable (B), and then removal of the experimental variable, and behavior is measured again (A). This way you can measure behavior before treatment, during treatment, and once treatment is removed.

Abscissa   The coordinate representing the position of a point along a line perpendicular to the *y*-axis in a plane Cartesian coordinate system.

Abstract   A summary of a journal article. In APA style, this summary should be fewer than 120 words.

Ad lib matching   Refers to matching subjects (e.g., rats) at their free feeding weight.

Alpha level   (α, or significance level)   The odds that the observed result is due to chance.

Alternative hypothesis   (see also Null hypothesis)   Says "there is no phenomenon." It is a hypothesis that is presumed true, that there is no difference, until statistical evidence in the form of a hypothesis test indicates otherwise.

Analysis of variance   (ANOVA)   An analysis of the variation in the outcomes of an experiment to assess the contribution of each variable to the variation. Each variable is analyzed separately, then the interactions between the variables are analyzed.

Apparatus   Equipment or device used in an experiment.

Applied research   Applied research is done to solve specific, practical questions. It is almost always done on the basis of basic research.

Archival research   Research that is being conducted using existing documents or data.

Attrition   Loss of subjects over the course of an experiment.

Balanced sequence   The situation where a single experimental subject receives a number of treatments during a period of time.

Bar graph   A chart with bars whose lengths are proportional to quantities of categorical data.

Baseline data   Baseline data is basic information gathered before an intervention begins. It is used later to provide a comparison for assessing the impact of that intervention.

Basic research   Research directed toward the increase of knowledge.

Between groups design   A design that uses a separate sample of subjects for each treatment condition.

Between-subject design   An experimental design in which each subject is tested under only one level of each independent variable.

Block randomization   A counterbalancing technique in which the treatment orders are randomized in blocks such that all of the conditions are present within the block.

Case study   A detailed, nonexperimental analysis of a person (or, sometimes, group).

Ceiling effect An effect where data cannot take on a value higher than some "ceiling."

Central tendency A value representative of all scores in a distribution (e.g., mean, median, and mode).

Chance An accidental or unpredictable event.

Closed system A highly controlled environment (e.g., a laboratory).

Confederate One who assists in an experiment under the pretense of being a subject, experimenter, or other person in the study.

Confounding variable A variable which is the common cause of two things that may falsely appear to be in a causal relationship.

Construct validity Whether or not your instrument reflects the content you are trying to measure.

Content validity Whether or not your instrument reflects the content you are trying to measure.

Contrasts To set in opposition in order to show or emphasize differences.

Control group The group in the between-subject experiment that does not receive the independent variable.

Convenience sample A sample where the subjects are selected, in part or in whole, at the convenience of the researcher. There is no explicit attempt for the sample to be representative of a population.

Correlated *t*-tests Parametric tests for testing differences between groups.

Correlation A statistical measure referring to the relationship between two or more variables (events, occurrences, etc.).

Correlation coefficient A number that can vary from -1.00 to $+1.00$ and indicates the degree of relation between two quantitative variables.

Correlational studies Research that shows both the degree and the direction of the relationship between two variables.

Counterbalancing A technique used in within-subject designs where subjects do not receive the different levels of the independent variable in the same order.

Data Measurements or observations of a variable.

Debriefing When subjects are told the details of an experiment after they have participated; an ethical obligation of the researcher.

Deception A research technique in which the subjects are misled about some aspect of the experiment.

Deduction The process of reasoning from general principles to particular examples.

Delayed information feedback A situation where a time delay occurs between when the subject takes a test and when the subject learns that he or she has made mistakes.

Demand characteristics Those cues available to the participants in the experiment that may enable them to determine the purpose of the experiment or what is expected by the experimenter.

Dependent *t*-test (also, Matched-samples or Paired-samples *t*-test)-A statistical test used for pretest and posttest situations in which pairs of scores from each individual are being analyzed, or for cases where individuals have been matched to control for variables such as age, gender, etc.

Dependent variable   The variable measured and recorded by the experimenter.

Descriptive statistics   Mathematical techniques used to characterize the subjects who are observed.

Determinism   The philosophical doctrine that every human event, act, and decision is the inevitable consequence of antecedent states of affairs.

Double blind   An experimental technique in which neither the participant nor the experimenter knows which type of experimental treatment is being used (or which condition the participant is in), or what type of effect might be expected.

Duration method   Requires that you record the length of time that elapses during each episode of a behavior.

Effect size   The strength or magnitude of the difference between two sets of data or, in outcome studies, between two time points for the same population. (The degree to which the null hypothesis is false).

Empiricism   The practice of relying on observation and experimentation to measure various factors of interest.

Experiment   Investigations in which at least one variable is manipulated in order to study cause and effect relationships.

Experimental design   The design of controlled conditions under which one might make empirical observations of actions, thoughts, or behaviors of humans or animals.

Experimental group   The group in an experiment that receives the independent variable.

Experimental realism   The believability of the experimental scenario, to the extent that the subjects are fully engaged in the task(s).

Experimenter bias   The phenomenon in experimental science by which the outcome of an experiment tends to be biased towards a result expected by the human experimenter.

External validity   The extent to which a finding applies (or can be generalized) to persons, objects, settings, or times other than those that were the subject of study.

Extraneous variable   (see also Confounding variable)   Other possible and plausible causes affecting the outcome of an experiment.

Face validity   The extent to which an instrument appears to be valid to those who are completing it.

Facts   Things we know are true because we can see, smell, hear, taste or touch them. Facts are measurable.

Factorial design   An experimental design in which each level of every independent variable occurs with all levels of the other independent variable.

Factors   Anything that contributes causally to a result; sometimes known as variables.

Falsifiability   The assertion that negative results are more informative than positive results.

Fatigue effect   When subjects become tired or bored and their performance decreases. Opposite of Practice effect.

Field-based study   Research conducted in a natural setting in which subjects typically do not know they are in an experiment

Floor effect   The lower limits of scores on tests.

Frequency distribution   A set of scores arranged in order along a distribution indicating the number of times each score occurs.

Frequency method   Requires that you record the frequency of a specific behavior within a certain period.

Function   (as in mathematical)   A relation such that one thing is dependent on another.

Functional design   An analysis of the antecedents and consequences of a particular behavior; usually undertaken before the implementation of a behavioral treatment.

Generalization of results   (see also External validity)   The extent to which a finding applies (or can be generalized) to persons, objects, settings, or times other than those that were the subject of study.

Hawthorne effect   Conditions under which performance in an experiment is affected by the knowledge of participants that they are in an experiment.

Histogram   Constructed from a frequency table. Thus the data are quantitative and continuous; as such, the bars touch.

Holding conditions constant   A method used to control for factors that have not been accounted for in the experiment by ensuring that treatment and control groups are treated exactly alike except for the introduction of the independent variable.

Hypothesis   A very specific testable statement derived from a theory that can be evaluated from observable data.

Illusory correlation   Believing there is some relationship between events, variables, etc., even though none really exists.

Independent variable   The variable manipulated by the experimenter.

Induction   Inferring general principles from specific examples.

Inferences   The act or process of deriving logical conclusions from premises known or assumed to be true.

Inferential statistics   Mathematical techniques in which a sample of information is gathered and generalizations about a population are made based on that sample.

Informed consent   A process by which a subject voluntarily confirms his or her willingness to participate in an experiment, after having been informed of all aspects of the experiment that are relevant to the subject's decision to participate. Informed consent is documented by means of a written, signed, and dated informed consent form.

Institutional review board (IRB)   A university campus committee that oversees the protection of human and animal subjects in research.

Interaction (as in statistics)   When the effect of one variable (or factor) is not the same at each level of the other variable (or factor).

Internal validity   The degree to which a study is logically sound and free of confounding variables.

Interrater reliability   The consistency with which the same information is rated or coded by different raters.

Interval method   Requires that observations occur at discrete intervals.

Interval scale   A scale with equal intervals but without a true zero point (e.g., temperature).

Intuition   The act of knowing or sensing without the use of rational processes.

Latin-square design   A counterbalancing procedure in which each condition occurs equally often during each time period of the experiment.

Law   A generalization that describes recurring facts or events in nature.

Law of parsimony   A good theory should explain many events with few statements or explanatory concepts.

Level of significance   Probability that an experimental finding is due to chance.

Likert scale   (pr. "lick-ert")   A type of scale often used in questionnaires; it asks respondents to specify their level of agreement to each of a list of statements.

Line graph   A way to summarize how two pieces of information are related and how they vary, depending on one another.

Literature review   Text designed to review the critical points of current knowledge on a particular topic. The literature review usually precedes a research proposal, methodology and results section.

Literature search   A review of the existing literature important for research projects.

Logic   The principles that guide reasoning within a given field or situation.

Longitudinal design   Testing one group of people repeatedly as they age.

Main effect   When the effect of one independent variable is the same at all levels of another independent variable.

Manipulation check   A measurement that is taken in an experiment to make sure that subjects accurately perceived the actual changes in the independent variable.

Matched pair design   Participants can be matched on variables that are considered to be relevant to the experiment in question. For example, pairs of participants might be matched for age, gender or their scores from intelligence or personality tests.

Matched subjects design   Each participant is exposed to only one level of independent variable and each participant has a match in another group.

Maturation   Changes in people over time because of growth and other historical factors.

Mean   A measure of central tendency; the average value of a set of numbers.

Median   A measure of central tendency; the middle value when observations are ordered from least to most.

Median split   dichotomizing a continuous subject variable to compare the resulting two groups on a second continuous variable.

Mental chronometry   Measuring the speed of mental events; drawing upon diverse methods such as neuroimaging, electrical recording, and Stroop tasks.

Meta analysis   A statistical technique for summarizing findings across many studies.

Mixed-model design   Occurs when there are two types of variables in an experiment: a between-subjects variable and a within-subject variable.

Mode   The number in a set that occurs most frequently.

Models   A conceptual or theoretical representation of a phenomenon.

Naturalistic observation   A method where the researcher very carefully observes and records some behavior or phenomenon, sometimes over a prolonged period, in its natural setting.

Nominal scale   A measurement scale that assigns numbers for the purpose of categorizing events, attributes, or characteristics. The nominal scale does not express any values or relationships between variables.

Nonexperimental research   Nonexperimental methods describe behavior, but do not identify the causes of the behavior.

Nonresponse bias   The difference in demographics or actual answers between respondents and nonrespondents.

Normal distribution   A theoretical frequency distribution for a set of variable data, usually represented by a bell-shaped curve symmetrical about the mean.

Null hypothesis   Means "there is no phenomenon." A hypothesis that is presumed true until statistical evidence in the form of a hypothesis test indicates otherwise.

Observation   The act of making and recording a measurement.

One-trial learning   Learning that occurs on the very first trial.

Open system   An environment where there is little or no control (e.g., the real world).

Operational definition   A definition of a concept in terms of the operations that must be performed to demonstrate the concept; defining a concept in terms of how it is measured or presented in a research study.

Order effects   Performance on a series of tasks often depends on the order in which the tasks are completed. Can confound experiment results when different orders are systematically associated with treatment and control conditions.

Ordinal scale   The categories have a logical or ordered relationship to each other. These types of scale permit the measurement of degrees of difference, but not the specific amount of difference.

Ordinate   The vertical axis *(or y axis)* in a graph.

Paradigm   A model or pattern used to organize research.

Participants   A subsection of the method section indicating the number and manner of selecting the human participants.

Perceptual defense   A term used to refer to the fact that the perception of some stimuli requires a longer exposure than perception of other stimuli.

Philosophy   The study of truths about reality; the search for wisdom.

Physiology   The biological study of the functions of living organisms and their parts.

Pilot study   A preliminary study to assess errors or problems in hypothesis, method, or design.

Placebo   A pill or injection that is inert.

Placebo control group   The group of subjects that receives the placebo.

Placebo effect   Improvement often shown in drug effectiveness studies in which patients believe they have received a drug when they actually received an inert substance.

Plagiarism   The uncredited use of another person's words or ideas.

Population   The entire set of individuals about which generalizations from survey or experimental data will be made.

Poster presentation   A presentation of current research methods and findings, presented at a conference.

Power   The probability that the statistical test will reject a false null hypothesis, that it will not make a Type II error. The higher the power, the greater the chance of obtaining a statistically significant result when the null hypothesis is false.

Practice effect   Effects that occur when a subject has been tested and retested on the same or similar material. These effects often mimic and might be mistaken for improvement in the area tested.

Probability   A number expressing the likelihood that a specific event will occur, expressed as the ratio of the number of actual occurrences to the number of possible occurrences.

Problem   A question to be considered, solved, or answered.

PsycINFO   A computerized database containing abstracts from many psychological journals.

Qualitative research   Research that relies on personal narratives. Qualitative data are subjective and narrative.

Quantitative research   Research that relies on the measurement of variables. Quantitative data are objective and numerical.

Quasi-experimental design   An experiment in which the independent variable occurs naturally and is not under direct control of the experimenter.

Random   By chance, like the flip of a coin.

Random assignment   A study in which participants are assigned by chance to one of two or more conditions. Randomization minimizes the differences among groups by equally distributing people with particular characteristics among all conditions.

Random blocks technique   Using matching techniques to try to equate groups on important characteristics.

Random sample   A sample from a population that has been selected in an unbiased way.

Random selection   A process or procedure that assures that the different units in your population have equal probabilities of being chosen.

Randomized subject design   When groups are randomly assigned to conditions in a between-subject design.

Ratio scales   The highest form of scale in which there is a true zero and in which it is meaningful to consider multiplicative differences among attributes.

Reliability   Refers to the repeatability of an experimental result or score on a test or instrument.

Repeated measures design   (see also within-in subject design)   Several measures are taken on the same participant.

Representative sample   A sample that closely matches the overall characteristics of the population.

Sample   A subset of the population selected as subjects.

Sampling error   The potential variation due to measuring a sample rather than the entire population.

Schedule of reinforcement   A schedule of reinforcement is a plan for presenting a reinforcer for a given response.

Scientific method   Principles and procedures for the systematic pursuit of knowledge involving the recognition and formulation of a problem, the collection of data through observation and experiment, and the formulation and testing of hypotheses.

Selection bias   Occurs when subjects are not selected randomly.

Single blind   A study in which one party, either the investigator or participant, is unaware of what condition the participant is in.

Small *n* design   Research design using a small number of subjects.

Speculation   A guess about something that is unknown. Speculations do not have enough data to support them or cannot be tested scientifically.

Spontaneous remission   The disappearance of symptoms that takes place spontaneously without any apparent treatment of the problem.

Standard deviation   How much scores vary around the mean.

Statistical testing   Separates significant effects from random chance.

Statistically significant   Rejecting the null hypothesis on the basis of a statistical test that yields an alpha level of less than .05 in the social sciences and .01 in the medical sciences.

Subject variable   Some characteristics of people that can be measured or described but cannot be varied experimentally (e.g., height, weight, sex, IQ)

Superstitions causes   In an attempt to make meaning out of the world, people will often latch on to causes for behavior that may appear to be legitimate but in fact are not supported by scientific data.

Survey research   The technique of obtaining a limited amount of information from a large number of people, usually through random sampling.

Synergistic effect   The interaction of two or more variables so that their combined effect is greater than the sum of their individual effects.

Test-retest reliability   Used to assess the consistency of a measure from one time to another.

Theories   Possible explanations for why things are the way they are. Theories are testable.

Theory   A set of statements or principles devised to explain a group of facts or phenomena, especially one that has been repeatedly tested or is widely accepted and can be used to make predictions about natural phenomena.

Third variable problem   The difficulty in correlational research whereby the relationship between two variables may be attributable to a third factor.

Transposition   Transposing relevant factors of a real world situation into the controlled environment of the laboratory.

Type 1 error   An error in a statistical test which occurs when a true hypothesis is rejected. The Type I risk is the chance of deciding that a significant effect is present when it isn't.

Type 2 error   An error in a statistical test which occurs when a false hypothesis is accepted. The Type II risk is the chance of not detecting a significant effect when one exists.

Tyranny of the senses   Given that our sensory capabilities are limited, signals outside our range of sensitivity remain unnoticed, meaning that those things that are detected take on disproportionately greater significance.

Unbiased language   Language free from bias in judgment, without prejudice and impartial.

Validity   Getting results that accurately reflect the concept being measured.

Verisimilitude   Experiments that retain the nature of the topic under study as it occurs in the real world.

Within-subject design   Each subject undergoes two or more experimental conditions.

REFERENCES

American Psychological Association. (1992). Ethical principles of psychologists and code of conduct. *American Psychologist, 47,* 1597–1611.

American Psychological Association 2001. *APA Publication Manual* (5th ed.). Washington DC: Author.

Anderson, R. C., & Pichert, J. W. (1978). Recall of previously unrecallable information following a shift in perspective. *Journal of Verbal Learning and Verbal Behavior, 17,* 13–28.

Asch, S. (1952). *Social psychology.* Englewood Cliffs, NJ: Prentice Hall.

Ayllon, T. (1963). Intensive treatment of psychotic behavior by stimulus satiation and food reinforcement. *Behavior Research and Therapy, 1,* 53–61.

Baumrind, D. (1985). Research using intentional deception: Ethical issues revisited. *American Psychologist, 40*(2), 165–174.

Bedon, B. G., & Howard, D. V. (1992). Memory for the frequency of occurrence of karate techniques: A comparison of experts and novices. *Bulletin of the Psychonomic Society, 30*(2), 117–119.

Benbow, C., & Stanley, J. C. (1980). Sex differences in mathematical ability: Fact or artifact? *Science, 210*(4475), 1262–1264.

Berenbaum, S. A. & Hines, M. (1992). Early androgens are related to childhood sex-typed toy preferences. *Psychological Science, 3,* 203–206.

Bitterman, M. E. (1969). Thorndike and the problem of animal intelligence. *American Psychologist, 24,* 444–453.

Boston, B. O. (1992, November). Portraying people with disabilities: toward a new vocabulary. *The Editorial Eye, 15,* 1–3, 6–7.

Bower, G. H., Karlin, M. B., & Dueck, A. (1975). Comprehension and memory for pictures. *Memory and Cognition, 3,* 216–220.

Brown, W. A. (1998). The placebo effect. *Scientific American,* 90–95. Vol 278 issue 1.

Bryson, J. B., & Hamblin, K. (1988). *Reporting infidelity: The MUM effect and the double standard.* Paper presented at the meeting of the Western Psychological Association, Burlingame, CA.

Campbell, D. T. (1969). Reforms as experiments. *American Psychologist, 24,* 409–429.

Campbell, D. T., & Stanley, J. C. (1966). *Experimental and quasi-experimental designs for research.* Chicago: Rand McNally.

Chi, M. T. (1978). Knowledge structures and memory development. In R. S. Siegler (Ed.), *Children's thinking: What develops?* Hillsdale, NJ: Erlbaum.

Conant, J. B. (1951). *Science and common sense.* New Haven, CT: Yale University Press.

Cook, T. D., & Campbell, D. T. (1979). *Quasi-experimentation: Design & analysis issues for field settings.* Chicago: Rand McNally.

Cunningham, M. (1988). Does happiness mean friendliness? Induced mood and heterosexual self-disclosure. *Personality and Social Psychology Bulletin, 14*(2), 283–297.

Dean, L. M., Willis, F. N., & Hewitt, J. (1975). Initial interaction distance among individuals equal and unequal in military rank. *Journal of Personality and Social Psychological, 32,* 294–299.

Dempster, F. N. (1981). Memory span: Sources of individual and developmental differences. *Psychological Bulletin, 89,* 66.

Diamond, R., & Carey, S. (1986). Why faces are and are not special: An effect of expertise. *Journal of Experimental Psychology: General, 115*(2), 107–117.

Dubowski, K. M. (1985). Absorption, distribution and elimination of alcohol: Highway safety aspects. *Journal of Studies on Alcohol,* (10), 98–108.

Ehrenfreund, D., & Badia, P. (1962). Response strength as a function of drive level and pre- and postshift incentive magnitude. *Journal of Experimental Psychology, 63,* 468–471.

Evans, M. A. & Saint-Aubin, J. (2005). What children are looking at during shared storybook reading. *Psychological Science, 16*(11), 913–920.

Ferster, C. B., & Perrott, M. C. (1968). *Behavior principles.* Englewood Cliffs, NJ: Prentice Hall.

Festinger, I. (1957). *A theory of cognitive dissonance.* New York: Harper & Row.

Gardner, R.A., & Garner, B.T. (1969). Teaching sign language to a chimpanzee. *Science.* 165, 664–672.

Gardner, B.T., & Garner, R.A. (1989). *A test of communication.* In R.A. Gardner, B.T. Gardner, & T.E. Van Cantfort's Teaching sign language to chimpanzees (pp. 181–197), Albany NY: Statue University of New York Press.

Giralt, N., & Bloom, P. (2000). How special are objects? children's reasoning about objects, parts, and wholes. *Psychological Science, 11*(6), 497–501.

Gold, D. B., & Wegner, D. M. (1991). *Fanning old flames: Arousing romantic obsession through thought suppression.* Paper presented at the meeting of the American Psychological Association, San Francisco, CA.

Homans, G. C. (1967). *The nature of social science.* New York: Harcourt, Brace, & World, Inc.

Howes, D. H., & Solomon, R. L. (1950). A note on McGuinnes's "Emotionality and perceptual defense." *Psychological Review, 57,* 229–234.

Howes, D. H., & Solomon, R. L. (1951). Visual duration threshold as a function of word-probability. *Journal of Experimental Psychology, 41,* 401–410.

Johnson, H. H., & Scileppi, J. A. (1969). Effects of ego-involvement conditions on attitude change to high and low credibility communicators. *Journal of Personality and Social Psychology, 13,* 31–36.

Kantowitz, B. H., Roediger, H. L., III, & Elmes, D. G. (1988). *Experimental Psychology: Understanding psychological research.* St. Paul: West.

Kaplan, A. (1963). *The conduct of inquiry: Methodology for behavioral science.* New York: Harper & Row.

Kassin, S. M., & Kiechel, K. L. (1996). The social psychology of false confession: Compliance, internalization and confabulation. *Psychological Science, 7*(3), 125–128.

Kirk, R. E. (1978). *Introductory statistics.* Monterey, CA: Brooks/Cole.

Klatzky, R. L., Loomis, J. M., Lederman, S. J., Wake, H., & Fujita, N. (1993). Haptic identification of objects and their depictions. *Perception and Psychophysics, 54*(2), 170–178.

Kleinke, C. L., Meeker, F. B., & Staneski, R. A. (1986). Preference for opening lines: Comparing ratings by men and women. *Sex Roles, 15,* 585–600.

Kuhn, T. S. (1970). *The structure of scientific revolutions* (2nd ed.). Chicago: The University of Chicago Press.

Lambert, W. W., & Solomon, R. L. (1952). Extinction of a running response as a function of block point from the goal. *Journal of Comparative and Physiological Psychology, 45,* 269–279.

Larson, C. C. (1982). Animal research: Striking a balance. *APA Monitor, 13* (Jan.), 1 ff.

Linder, D. E., Cooper, J., & Jones, E. E. (1967). Decision freedom as a determinant of the role of incentive magnitude in attitude change. *Journal of Personality and Social Psychology, 6,* 245–254.

Lorge, I. (1930). Influence of regularly interpolated time intervals upon subsequent learning. *Teachers College, Columbia University Contributions to Education* (Whole No. 438).

MacDonald, T. K., Zanna, M. P., & Fong, G. T. (1996). Why common sense goes out the window: Effects of alcohol on intentions to use condoms. *Personality and Social Psychology Bulletin, 22*(8), 763–775.

Maggio, R. (1991). *The bias-free word finder: A dictionary of nondiscriminatory language.* Boston: Beacon Press.

Martin, D. A. (2004). *Doing psychology experiments,* 6th edition. Belmont, CA: Wadsworth.

Mazur, A. (1986). U.S. trends in feminine beauty and overadaptation. *The Journal of Sex Research, 22,* 281–303.

More, A. J. (1969). Delay of feedback and the acquisition and retention of verbal materials in the classroom. *Journal of Educational Psychology, 60,* 339–342.

Novaco, R. W. (1977). Stress inoculation: A cognitive therapy for anger and its application to a case of depression. *Journal of Consulting and Clinical Psychology, 45,* 600–608.

Paul, G. L. (1966). *Insight versus desensitization in psychotherapy.* Stanford, CA: Stanford University Press.

Plant, E. A. & Peruche, B. M. (2005). The consequences of race for police officers' responses to criminal suspects. *Psychological Science, 16*(3), 180–183.

Platt, J. R. (1964). Strong inference. *Science, 146* (3642), 347–353.

Posner, M. I. (1969). Abstraction and the process of recognition. In J. T. Spence & G. H. Bower (Eds.), *The psychology of learning and motivation: Advances in learning and motivation* (Vol. 3). New York: Academic Press.

Posner, M. I., Boies, S. J., Eichelman, W., & Taylor, R. L. (1969). Retention of visual and name codes of single letters. *Journal of Experimental Psychology, 73,* 28–38.

Posner, M. I., & Keele, S. W. (1968). On the genesis of abstract ideas. *Journal of Experimental Psychology, 77,* 353–363.

Postman, L., Bronson, W. C., & Gropper, G. L. (1952). Is there a mechanism of perceptual defense? *Abnormal and Social Psychology, 48,* 215–224.

Principe, G. F., Kanaya, T., Ceci, S. J., & Singh, M. (2006). Believing is seeing: How rumors can engender false memories in preschoolers. *Psychological Science, 17*(3), 243–248.

Prokasy, W.F., & Harsanyi, M.A. (1968). Two-phase model for human classical conditioning. *Journal of Experimental Psychology, 78*(3, pt 1), 359–368.

Pryor, K. W., Haag, R., & O'Reilly, J. (1969). The creative porpoise: Training for novel behavior. *Experimental Analysis of Behavior, 12,* 653–661.

Raspberry, W. (1989, January 4). When "Black" becomes "African American." *The Washington Post,* p. A19.

Rayner, K., White, S. J., Johnson, R. L., & Liversedge, S. P. (2006). Raeding Wrods with jubmled letters. *Psychological Science, 17*(3), 192–193.

Roediger, H. (2004). What should they be called? *The APS Observer, 17*(4).

Rosenthal, R., & Fode, K. (1963). The effects of experimenter bias on the performance of the albino rat. *Behavioral Science, 8,* 183–189.

Rushton, J. P. & Bons, T. A. (2005). Mate choice and friendship in twins. *Psychological Science, 16*(7), 555–559.

Sands, S. F., Lincoln, C. E., & Wright, A. A. (1982). Pictorial similarity judgments and the organization of visual memory in the rhesus monkey. *Journal of Experimental Psychology: General, 3,* 369.

Simon, C. W., & Emmons, W. H. (1956). Responses to material presented during various levels of sleep. *Journal of Experimental Psychology, 51,* 89–97.

Smith, A. P., Tyrrell, D. A. J., Coyle, K., & Willman, J. S. (1987). Selective effects of minor illnesses on human performance. *British Journal of Psychology, 78,* 183–188.

Smith, M., Franz, E. A., Joy, S. M., & Whitehead, K. (2005). Superior performance of blind compared with sighted individuals on bimanual estimations of object size. *Psychological Science, 16*(1), 11–14.

Snodgrass, J. G., Levy-Berger, G., & Haydon, M. (1985). *Human experimental psychology.* New York: Oxford.

Solso, R. L. (1987a). The social-political consequences of the organization and dissemination of knowledge. *American Psychologist, 42,* 824–825.

Solso, R. L. (1987b). Recommended readings in psychology over the past 33 years. *American Psychologist, 42,* 1130–1132.

Solso, R. L. (2001). Brain activities in a skilled versus novice artist: An fMRI study. *Leonardo, 34*(1), 31–34.

Solso, R. L., & McCarthy, J. E. (1981). Prototype formation of faces: A case of pseudomemory. *British Journal of Psychology, 72,* 499–503.

Solso, R. L., & Short, B. A. (1979). Color recognition. *Bulletin of the Psychonomic Society, 14,* 275–277.

Schaie, K. W. (1993). Ageist language in psychological research. *American Psychologist, 48,* 49–51.

Sprafkin, J. N., Liebert, R. M., & Poulos, R. W. (1975). Effects of a prosocial televised example on children's helping. *Journal of Experimental Child Psychology, 20,* 119–126.

Sternberg, R. J. (2003). *The psychologist's companion: A guide to scientific writing for students and researchers* (4th ed.). New York: Cambridge University Press.

Stevenson, H. W., & Odom, R. D. (1962). The effectiveness of social reinforcement following two conditions of social deprivation. *Abnormal and Social Psychology, 65,* 429–431.

Sugawara, I., & Huo, Y. J. (1994). Disputes in Japan: A cross-cultural test of the procedural justice model. *Social Justice Research, 7*(2), 129–144.

Supa, M., Cotzin, M., & Dallenbach, K. M. (1944). "Facial vision": The perception of obstacles by the blind. *American Journal of Psychology, 57,* 133–183.

Terkel, J., & Rosenblatt, J. S. (1968). Maternal behavior induced by maternal blood plasma injected into virgin rats. *Journal of Comparative and Physiological Psychology, 65,* 479–482.

Thumin, F. J. (1962). Identification of cola beverages. *Journal of Applied Psychology, 46,* 358–360.

Underwood, B. J., Rehula, R., & Keppel, G. (1962). Item selection in paired-associate learning. *American Journal of Psychology, 75,* 353–371.

Walter, R. H., & Parke, R. D. (1964). Emotional arousal, isolation, and discrimination learning in children. *Journal of Experimental Child Psychology, 1,* 163–173.

Webb, E. J., Campbell, D. T., Schwartz, R. D., & Sechrest, L. (1966). *Unobtrusive measures: Nonreactive research in the social sciences.* Chicago: Rand McNally.

Wheeler, M. E. & Fiske, S. T. (2005). Controlling racial prejudice: Social-cognitive goals affect amygdale and stereotype activation. *Psychological Science, 16*(1), 56–63.

Witt, J. K. & Proffitt, D. R. (2005). See the ball, hit the ball: Apparent ball size is correlated with batting average. *Psychological Science, 16*(12), 937–938.

CREDITS

Photo Credits

p. 161 all: Copyright © 1982. Photographs courtesy of Anthony A. Wright, Ph.D./University of Texas Medical School; **p. 171:** Courtesy of M. Kimberly MacLin.

Text Credits

p. 24: From Bryson, J. B., & Hamblin, K. (1988). Reporting infidelity: The MUM effect and the double standard. Paper presented at the meeting of the Western Psychological Association, Burlingame, CA.

p. 27: Mazur (1986), "U.S. trends in feminine beauty and overadaptations" in *The Journal of Sex Research, 22,* 281–303. Reprinted with permission of *The Journal of Sex Research.*

p. 40: Reprinted by permission of Robert L. Solso.

p. 42: Dubowski, K. M. "Absorption, distribution and elimination of alcohol: highway safety aspects." *Journal of Studies on Alcohol—Supplement,* 10, 1985. Jul.: 98–108.

p. 60: From Chi, M. T. Knowledge structures and memory development. Copyright (c) 1978. In R. S. Siegler (ed.), *Children's thinking: What develops.* Reprinted by permission of Lawrence Erlbaum Associates, Inc.

p. 63: From Solso, R. L., & Short, B. A. Color recognition. *Bulletin of the Psychonomic Society,* 14, 275–277. Copyright © 1979. Reprinted with permission of the Psychonomic Society.

p. 64: From Solso, R. L., & Short, B. A. Color recognition. *Bulletin of the Psychonomic Society,* 14, 275–277. Copyright © 1979. Reprinted with permission of the Psychonomic Society.

p. 66: From Campbell (1969). Copyright © 1969 by the American Psychological Association. Reprinted by permission.

p. 67: From Campbell (1969). Copyright © 1969 by the American Psychological Association. Reprinted by permission.

p. 111: The Far Side® by Gary Larson (c) 1985 FarWorks, Inc. All Rights Reserved/Dist. by Creators Syndicate. The Far Side® and the Larson® signature are registered trademarks of FarWorks, Inc. Used with permission.

p. 122–126: Preamble, General Principles, and Ethical Standards 8.01 through 8.15 from "Ethical Principles of Psychologists and Code of Conduct." Copyright © 2002 by the American Psychological Association. Reprinted with permission. The official citation that should be used in referencing this material is http://www.apa.org/ethics/code2002.html and American Psychologist, 2002, 57, 1060–1073.

p. 127–128: APA Ethical Principle 9 ("research with Human Participants") from Ethical Principles in the Conduct of Research with Human Participants, 1973, 1982. Copyright © 1973, 1982 by the American Psychological Association. Reprinted with permission. The official citation that should be used in referencing this material is Ethical Principles in the Conduct of Research with Human Participants, 1973, 1982. APA cautions that the guidelines and information provided in the 1973 and 1982 Ethical Principles in the Conduct of Research with Human Participants are no longer current but may be of educative value to psychologists, courts, and professional bodies.

p. 147: Reprinted by permission of Robert L. Solso.